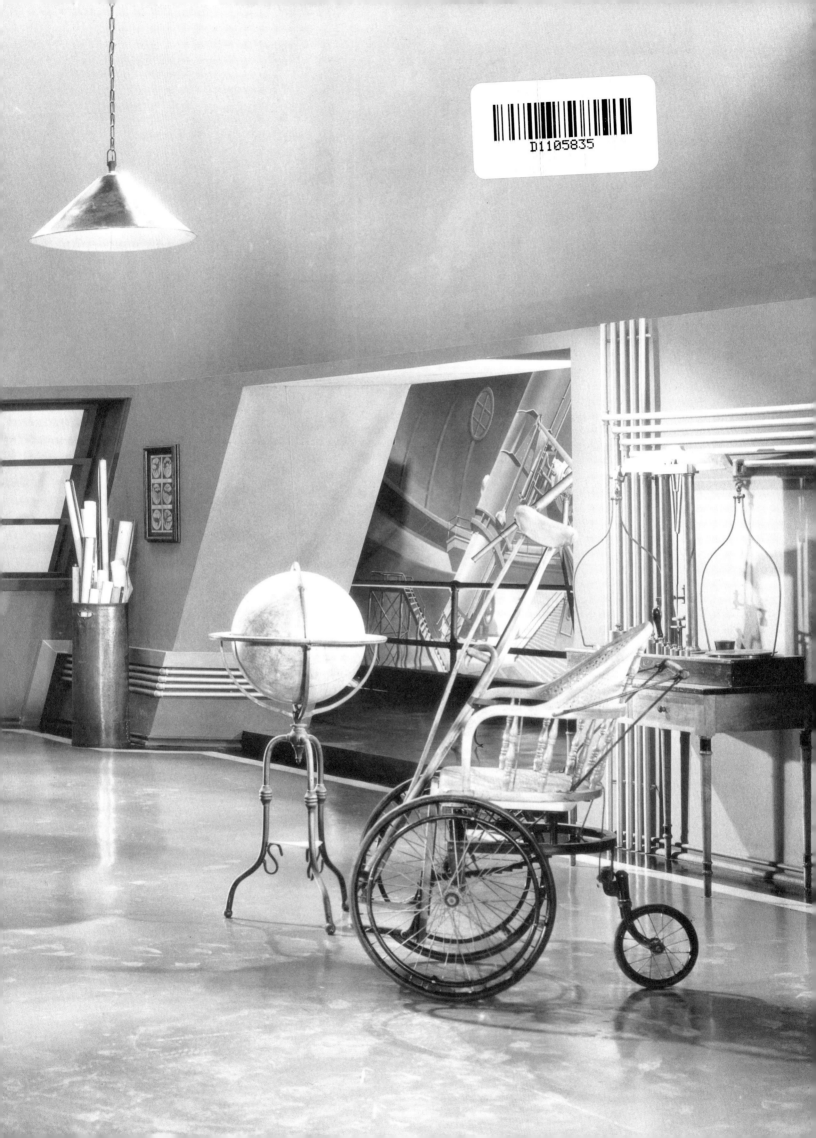

HOLLYWOOD HORROR

HOLLYWOOD HORROR *from Gothic to Cosmic*

MARK A. VIEIRA

Harry N. Abrams, Inc., Publishers

To my father and to the memory of my mother
— Mark Alan Vieira

519425l8

Editor: Elisa Urbanelli
Designer: Miko McGinty
Production Manager: Justine Keefe

LIBRARY OF CONGRESS CATALOGING-IN-PUBLICATION DATA
Vieira, Mark A.
  Hollywood horror : from gothic to cosmic / Mark A.
Vieira.
     p. cm.
Includes bibliographical references and index.
  ISBN 0–8109–4535–5 (hardcover)
  1. Horror films—United States—History and criti-
cism. I. Title.

PN1995.9.H6V58 2003
791.43'6164—dc21

2003006976

Published in 2003 by Harry N. Abrams, Incorporated,
New York.

Printed and bound in the United States of America

10 9 8 7 6 5 4 3 2 1

Harry N. Abrams, Inc.
100 Fifth Avenue
New York, N.Y. 10011
www.abramsbooks.com

Abrams is a subsidiary of
LA MARTINIÈRE
G R O U P E

front endpapers
A set reference still made on
March 28, 1932 of Anton Grot's
laboratory setting for the
Warner Bros. film, **DOCTOR X**.

back endpapers
A set reference still of a Charles
D. Hall setting for the Universal
Pictures film, **DRACULA**.

page 2
Boris Karloff poses for the unit
still photographer Sherman
Clark on the set of the 1931
Universal Pictures film
FRANKENSTEIN.

Illustrations on the following pages are from the
Ronald V. Borst Collection:
Pages 8, 16, 17, 21 (top), 30 (left), 33, 34, 39, 42, 46, 47,
50, 53, 57, 58, 60 (top), 61, 62, 64 (top), 67 (both), 68, 69,
70, 75 (right), 80, 83, 85 (all), 86 (bottom), 94 (both), 95,
101, 102 (top left), 110, 112 (bottom), 114 (top), 137, 141,
148, 167, 168, 190, 193 (top), 214, 231, 239

CONTENTS

PREFACE

The motion-picture camera was invented to record reality. This camera can preserve, in two moving dimensions, whatever passes in front of it. Its impartial lens evinces no emotion at what it sees. A coil of celluloid snakes through it at exactly the same rate, no matter what tickles its halides. Yet motion pictures are not objective. The feature film has achieved its vast popularity because it is subjective. More than an intellectual medium or a medium of ideas, film is a medium of fantasy, of dreams, of emotions. More graphically than prose, more intensely than poetry, and more permanently than music, film conveys emotion, be it love, lust, or horror.

In truth, film does not merely convey emotion. It makes it stick. The viewer sits in the dark, mesmerized by the movement on a lambent rectangle, as a potent mix of picture and sound is indelibly burned into his or her memory. The horror film, more than any other genre, employs this powerful property. Thirty years after viewing a horror film, one vividly remembers a scene, a moment, or a single image of horror. Here are three examples:

> An eighty-three-year-old man remembers: "When I saw *King Kong* with my schoolmates, we thought all those prehistoric animals were real."
>
> A forty-eight-year-old woman recalls: "I saw *The Mummy's Ghost* when I was seven or eight. For years, I clearly remembered the scene of the mummy carrying the girl into the swamp."
>
> A thirty-nine-year-old man says: "I saw this movie *The Beast with Five Fingers* on TV with my brother when I was little. That hand crawling up Peter Lorre's chest scared the hell out of me! I used to have dreams about that hand crawling up my chest."

In each case, the viewer remembered an image, not a synopsis. Horror films leave impressions that are not only long lasting but also are able to assert themselves at unexpected moments, when the viewer is stuck in traffic or adrift in the peaceful interlude between waking and sleep.

From the Gothic horror of Dracula, Frankenstein, and King Kong to the psychic terror of the Cat People and the atomic terror of the Thing, and finally to the cosmic horror of HAL the Computer, monster movies have sprung from prolific typewriters to crawl, jump, and fly across Hollywood soundstages and finally take residence in our consciousness. Horror films do not merely impose these frightful images on us. They tap the things that lurk in our imaginations—devils, bogeymen, space aliens, freaks of nature, apes, cats, wolves, bats, insects, closets, attics, graveyards, coffins, death—anything over which we have no control or that represents the evil that we fear in ourselves.

If the horror film is the most enduring of all American film genres, it is because it quickly mastered the techniques needed to make objective these very subjective fears. The story of Frankenstein was published in 1818 and that of Dracula in 1897, yet not until 1931 did they find a medium that could bring them to all levels of American society and make them part of the national lexicon. Seventy years later, Frankenstein and Dracula are so much a part of our national folklore that they have become TV sitcom characters, sold breakfast cereal, and graced postage stamps. Why do these characters still have currency?

One reason is that the horror genre did not simply appear, make an impression, and then vanish. It occasioned an amazing series of return engagements. In 1938 a second-run theater made exhibitor history by presenting *Frankenstein* and *Dracula* on the same bill. Universal Pictures decided to bolster a weak box-office year by doing the same thing on a large scale. This first reissue did unexpectedly well and paved the way for ten years of sequels. In the early 1950s, a small company called Realart leased the Universal horror films for another successful reissue. The classic horror film's most significant return engagement was on 1950s television. Local stations went wild, using zany characters to introduce the films on programs such as Shock! Theater and Creature Features. In San Francisco and New York, *King Kong* was welcomed with a wall-to-wall presentation—every night for a week in 1957. This splashy comeback was followed by college-campus screenings in the early 1970s, and eventually by cable TV, video, laser-disc, and DVD marketing. True, the continuing reexposure of Hollywood classics was not limited to horror films. It made icons of the Marx Brothers, W. C. Fields, Marlene Dietrich, and Humphrey Bogart. Yet, more than any other genre, the horror film has endured. Perhaps it is because no other genre recycles itself more than horror, with all its remakes and reinterpretations. More likely it is because of the unforgettable moments of horror in these films, those fright moments that we carry around in our subconscious.

Hollywood Horror: From Gothic to Cosmic is the first book to trace the evolution of this genre in narrative form, using the voices of producers, directors, writers, cinematographers, art directors, special-effects artists, and, of course, the actors who collaborated on these singular works of art. I have tried to include what I consider to be the most important horror, fantasy, and science-fiction films. Cinematic excellence is not my criterion for including one film and excluding another. *Plan 9 from Outer Space* displays no discernible technique, cinematic or otherwise, but it is nonetheless an important entry. Its horror moments, while possibly unintended, are unique. Likewise, any number of low-budget science-fiction films have a patina of weirdness that appears nowhere in the shooting script. This is perhaps the result of some alchemy in the production process or simply the dust of passing years. In the case of a textbook classic such as *Psycho*, I happily defer to critical and popular taste, but I am just as likely to single out a medium-budget unknown such as *The Mad Doctor*. It is not my intention to critique or analyze these films. I prefer to do what has not been done before, to combine a chronological account of their creation with a visual survey of their evolution.

This is the first book to organize the chronology of the American horror film into four periods. "The Gothic" treats films whose horror springs from the folklore of Central Europe. "The Psychic" deals with films whose terror floats on ghostly curtains or bubbles up from the subconscious.

Vincent Price, star of the 1959 Allied Artists production **THE BAT**, poses for a photo that contains most of the photographic conventions of the horror genre: lighting from below, a silhouette of a bat, and the subject looking behind himself, as if expecting something dreadful. A reviewer wrote: "As in every other film he has made over the past two years, Vincent Price casts enough furtive glances to register as the ghoul when, indeed, he isn't."

"The Atomic" features films whose fantasies were spawned by out-of-control science. "The Cosmic" covers films that import fear from the cold darkness of outer space.

This is also the first book to showcase images of horror captured by unit still men, the studio photographers responsible for selling each film to the public. To do justice to their work, I have endeavored to find pristine vintage prints, and, in some cases, I have made prints in my own darkroom from original camera negatives. Some of these images are familiar, but they have rarely been reproduced with such clarity, and they have never been presented in the context of fine-art photography.

The kind of research I accomplished in previous books was not possible this time. Unlike the pre-Code canon, the majority of horror films survives and is currently available, but equivalent files and archives do not exist. In the 1980s, a Los Angeles River flood destroyed the production files of many Universal horror films. Fortunately, a number of researchers had already gotten to them. Diligent writers such as Tom Weaver, David Skal, and Stephen Rebello were poring over studio files long before the untimely destruction of many of them and just before the rest were acquired by corporations that sometimes make them unavailable to film scholars. I have had to rely on the work of these conscientious individuals, just as I have had to rely on the interviews they conducted with the now-deceased artists who made these films.

Drawing on the body of information that they and others have amassed, I have tried to create a chronological catalogue of the American horror film, both textual and visual. I have sought to tell the story of the genre, how it evolved, and what these artists gave of their imagination and talent. As familiar as I am with their work, I have found many surprises, both historical and aesthetic. I hope to share this sense of discovery as we journey from 1923 to 1968, from the Gothic to the cosmic.

The American horror film is inextricably linked with one motion-picture studio: Universal. If one deems that a horror film must include a monster in its cast, then Universal City was indeed the spawning place of the horror film. According to the 1937 *Thorndike-Century Senior Dictionary*, a monster is "1. any animal or plant that is out of the usual course of nature. 2. huge creature or thing. 3. huge. 4. person too wicked to be human." Most of the classic monsters—the Phantom of the Opera, Dracula, the Frankenstein Monster, the Mummy, the Wolf Man, and the Creature from the Black Lagoon—match these definitions and were created at Universal City. The horror film, however, did not originate there. Documentation of early silent films is far from complete, so it is impossible to be certain, but the first feature-length American horror film was most likely David Wark Griffith's 1914 *The Avenging Conscience*. The first horror feature made by a major Hollywood studio was Paramount's 1920 *Dr. Jekyll and Mr. Hyde*, directed by John S. Robertson and starring John Barrymore. These were isolated productions. Only Universal Pictures accomplished what Paramount and the others had not: the creation of a horror template. This was the achievement of

three Universal employees: Irving Thalberg, Lon Chaney, and Tod Browning. Working separately, they found the elements that define the true horror film; once in collaboration, they fused them. Each man was uncommonly gifted, had an unusual childhood, and made a unique contribution to the genre.

Born in 1883, Lon Chaney grew up with parents who were deaf. When his mother was stricken with inflammatory rheumatism, the nine-year-old boy learned to use sign language and pantomime to bring the outside world to the bedridden woman. After a few years he took his skills on the road, first with musical comedy troupes and then in 1913 to the Universal Film Manufacturing Company, which was located at the corner of Sunset Boulevard and Gower Street in Hollywood. In 1915, when Carl Laemmle's company became Universal Pictures and moved to a 230-acre ranch in the foothills of the Santa Monica Mountains, Chaney went too. By 1922 his uncanny skill with makeup had earned him the title, "The Man of a Thousand Faces." In that year Chaney appeared in another film that vies for the distinction of the first horror feature. *A Blind Bargain* had Chaney portray both a mad scientist and his hunchbacked ape-man assistant. This film, like *Dr. Jekyll and Mr. Hyde*, had some, but not all, of the elements of future horror films. While looking for those elements, Chaney created characters that enthralled a growing legion of fans. Director Marshall Neilan expressed popular sentiment when a fellow partygoer was about to squish a spider: "Don't step on it! It might be Lon Chaney!"

Chaney's fame was due in part to the prescience of Universal's head of production, Irving Thalberg. Born in 1899, Thalberg joined Universal in 1918 after a vacation at Edgemere, Long Island, where he saw his neighbor projecting movies onto a bedsheet outside his house. The neighbor was "Uncle" Carl Laemmle, head of Universal Pictures. Thalberg's discerning critiques of the latest Universal product impressed Laemmle, who learned that the young man had spent much of his youth fighting heart disease and reading the classics. Only a mogul as expansive, eccentric, and nepotistic as Laemmle could make a self-educated nineteen-year-old "general manager in charge of

So young to be a father, twenty-three-year-old Irving Grant Thalberg was nonetheless responsible for the birth of the horror film. Portrait by Jack Freulich

Lon Chaney was a brilliant, reclusive enigma whose tortured characters popularized the new horror genre. Portrait by Clarence Sinclair Bull

production" at Universal City, paying him ninety dollars a week to manage what amounted to a film factory. Universal was concerned with quantity, not quality, sometimes releasing more than two hundred films a year. They were designated as low-budget Red Feather programmers, medium-budget Bluebird productions, the occasional big-budget Jewel, and the rare Super Jewel. Thalberg's sense of dramatic construction improved Universal's output and increased profits, which then allowed him the luxury of prestige productions such as Erich von Stroheim's *Foolish Wives*. It also gave him the power to fire Stroheim from another film when the extravagant director became intractable. When Thalberg introduced Lon Chaney to director Tod Browning, he laid the foundation of the American horror film.

Born in 1880, Tod Browning was an erratic talent who could not stay out of trouble. His childhood was marked by a desire to escape a dull middle-class life in Louisville, Kentucky. His inevitable flight led him to the world of the traveling show, where, among other things, he played the Hypnotic Living Corpse, a grisly act in which he was reportedly buried for days at a time. His theatrical aspirations brought him to New York, the Biograph studios, and D. W. Griffith, whom he followed to Los Angeles in 1914 when the director decided that East Hollywood would give him more artistic freedom. Browning acted for Griffith and others, but soon found himself wielding a megaphone for the Reliance-Majestic Company. He also found himself steeped in the Bohemian lifestyle of the early picture players. Having abandoned and then divorced one woman in the Midwest, he was now living "in sin" with another. In June 1915, a drinking party at a roadhouse put him on a collision course with a railway car. One man was killed and Browning was injured so seriously that he did not direct for two years.

When a series of profitable crime films brought Browning to Universal, the intuitive Thalberg matched him with Chaney. Their second film, *Outside the Law* (1920), was so

Tod Browning had knocked around—and been knocked around—Hollywood for years before he found his niche. Portrait by Jack Freulich

successful that Thalberg began preparing a Super Jewel for his new team, a project for which Chaney had been campaigning—Victor Hugo's *Notre Dame de Paris.* The trade papers announced that Browning would direct the epic, but a series of alcoholic episodes and an affair with Anna May Wong, an actress who was both underage and Chinese American, rendered him unacceptable. While Browning was doing his best to hit bottom, Thalberg worked with Chaney and a contract director, Wallace Worsley, to make *The Hunchback of Notre Dame* worthy of its source.

To do this, Thalberg had to convince Laemmle to approve a number of cinematic firsts: a six-month shooting schedule; nineteen acres of sets, including streets with real cobblestones and a cathedral facade built to last; the hiring of a thousand technicians and the rental of every arc light in Hollywood for the filming of hundreds of extras in the biggest night-for-night scenes yet staged; a weekly salary of $2,500 for Lon Chaney; and the unheard-of budget of $1,250,000. Laemmle said yes to Thalberg and departed for Europe. While he was away, Worsley and Chaney fashioned a film of such power that Thalberg authorized an additional $150,000 for crowd scenes. When Laemmle returned to Universal City, his shock at the film's final cost turned to satisfaction when *The Hunchback of Notre Dame*, presented in a special "road show" engagement, became the surprise success of 1923. It was not called a "horror" film—that designation was years away—but a monster was its star. Other elements of the newly pressed template included a famous book (with a Beauty-and-Beast fable at its center), an epic production, and an exotic setting. The first true horror film was reviled by *Variety*: "It's murderous, hideous, and repulsive." The reviewer predicted box-office failure for *The Hunchback* after its roadshow engagements. By the time of its very profitable general release, Thalberg had left Universal for a better-paying position at Metro-Goldwyn-Mayer, Chaney was a star, and Browning was pulling himself together.

The Gothic

CHAPTER 1

Silent Prototypes

The Monster Born and Bred

The cultural icon known as the Monster was born at Universal in 1923 but it was reared in 1924 at the newly merged Metro-Goldwyn-Mayer Studios. Its father was Irving Thalberg, vice president in charge of production. Thalberg was an unlikely father for the genre. He was not a theatrical impresario conversant with the demimonde or a worldly author steeped in the occult. He was a boyish, clean-cut twenty-three-year-old, a "soft-eyed, skimpy-limbed genius," according to writer Ben Hecht. The classics Thalberg had read while recovering from rheumatic fever had given him a taste for the offbeat, and when he became a producer, he exchanged the seclusion of one dark room for that of another. Said Hecht: "He lived two-thirds of the time in the projection room. He saw only movies. He never saw life. But he knew what shadows could do." *The Hunchback of Notre Dame* convinced him that the public was ready for darker shadows.

The 1922 Broadway season had seen an array of spooky plays, among them *The Bat, The Cat and the Canary, Trilby,* and *The Monster.* Hollywood looked askance at them, but Thalberg saw their appeal. He persuaded Louis B. Mayer, the new company's president, that their first film should be an excursion into the bizarre. Thalberg knew that the Theatre Guild's production of Leonid Andreyev's *He Who Gets Slapped* had been only mildly successful, but he saw in it a star-making vehicle not only for contract players Norma Shearer and John Gilbert but also for Lon Chaney. Chaney was still freelancing, and Thalberg promised him that if the film did well, he could have a long-term contract. To direct M-G-M's first vehicle, Thalberg engaged the renowned Swedish director Victor Seastrom, who was so impressed with the Russian play that he immediately wrote a scenario—in Swedish. It was duly translated and, typical of Thalberg's operation, assigned to another writer for minor revisions.

The tragic story was an odd choice for a new company's debut. According to *Vanity Fair* writer Jim Tully, "When Thalberg saw *He Who Gets Slapped* in the projection room, he walked out in despair." How would the public respond to this grim tale of a man so disappointed in life that he hides behind a clown's greasepaint? In typical fashion Thalberg took his own counsel and gave the film a major premiere, complete with a lavish stage show, at New York's Capitol Theatre.

In the film, Chaney portrayed HE, a circus clown famous for a masochistic act in which a hundred lesser clowns repeatedly slap him in the face. The slaps are an echo of the humbling betrayal he has experienced at the hands of his patron, Baron Regnard (Marc McDermott), who has stolen both his scientific formula and his wife. When HE falls in love with Consuelo (Norma Shearer), a bareback rider, the Baron once again threatens his happiness, this time by paying Consuelo's father for her hand. HE plots to avenge himself against the Baron and save Consuelo by releasing an angry circus lion. The lion kills the Baron, but Consuelo's father mortally wounds HE, and he dies in Consuelo's arms. Instead of rejecting the film's gloomy theme, audiences responded to it. With a profit of $349,000, *He Who Gets Slapped* was just the hit that the young studio needed. Significantly, the film included most of the elements that Chaney's fans had come to expect, elements unique to the actor's onscreen personality.

First, Chaney usually played a physically deformed man who endures a martyrdom that reveals a beautiful soul. His poignant Quasimodo in *The Hunchback of Notre Dame* made this element a Chaney hallmark. Second, he often played a good-bad character who lives outside the law but is forced by some conflict to choose a higher good, sometimes at the sacrifice of his own life. For instance, *The Miracle Man* (1919) had a scene in which "The Frog," a crippled beggar, reveals that he is a fraud by unwinding his hideously contorted body; he is eventually redeemed by a faith

overleaf

D. W. Griffith, the "Father of the American Film," starred Ricardo Cortez in his 1926 **THE SORROWS OF SATAN**. A reviewer complained that "some of the 'stills' in the souvenir pamphlet aren't viewed in the picture." There was also the problem that the stills were scarier than the film.

opposite

"In **THE PHANTOM OF THE OPERA**, people exclaimed at my weird makeup," said Lon Chaney. "It's all a matter of combining paints and lights to form the right illusion."

John Gilbert and Norma Shearer supported Lon Chaney (literally) in **HE WHO GETS SLAPPED**, the first film produced by the merger of Metro Pictures with Louis B. Mayer Productions and Samuel Goldwyn's former company. In this film, Chaney perfected the template of his horror characters.

healer. Third, Chaney repeatedly transformed his physical appearance, sometimes his entire body, creating a completely original character. *The Penalty* (1920) made Chaney a vengeful double amputee. In *Outside the Law* (1921), he was both a gang leader and his Chinese henchman. Thanks to vigorous press agentry, Chaney's public was aware that he achieved these transformations with his own makeup. For *A Blind Bargain* (1922), he became an ape-man by using rubber cigar holders to widen his nostrils, and cotton wool molded with collodion to create bags under his eyes.

The fourth element of Chaney's characterizations was physical discomfort, if not actual pain. To impersonate the double amputee of *The Penalty*, he wore a self-designed harness that doubled up his legs behind him. The device caused lower back pain and loss of circulation in his legs. The hump in *The Hunchback of Notre Dame* was made of plaster and weighed twenty pounds. Facial makeup for the same film—adhesive tape and putty to simulate a large wart over a dead eye—permanently impaired his eyesight. Chaney justified these torments philosophically: "When a makeup is as painful as that which I wore as Blizzard in *The Penalty*, when I had my legs strapped up and couldn't bear it more than twenty minutes at a time . . . it sometimes takes a good deal of imagination to forget your physical sufferings. Yet at that, the subconscious mind has a marvelous way of making you keep the right attitudes and make the right gestures when you actually are acting." For *The Phantom of the Opera*, Chaney planned a makeup that would be as awful to behold as it was to wear.

Still riding the success of *The Hunchback*, Universal found a vehicle that honored the template. Gaston Leroux's 1911 novel, *The Phantom of the Opera*, featured a famous Paris landmark, a full-blooded romance, and a monstrous central character. What troubled the studio's story department was the possibility of too much grimness. For all its vaunted sensationalism, the American cinema of 1924 was rather genteel. Even the spookiest of Broadway plays inevitably revealed its "monster" to be a deranged uncle or a greedy nephew trying to cheat the heroine out of her inheritance. Other than John Barrymore's *Dr. Jekyll and Mr. Hyde*, there had never been an out-and-out Hollywood horror film. No studio wanted to alienate a public satisfied with adventure, melodrama, and romance. Even mysteries did not ensure box-office success. "The mystery angle is no asset," cautioned studio reader Mel Brown. Some Universal executives mistakenly believed that the love scenes between Patsy Ruth Miller and Norman Kerry had made *The Hunchback* a success, so Edward T. Lowe, *Hunchback* scenarist, wrote: "The romance needs to be emphasized." Yet *The Hunchback* had made a star of Chaney, and M-G-M was angling for him; James Spearing, coauthor of the first treatment of *The Phantom*, wrote that it had "a perfect role for Lon Chaney," but added, "If we do it, for God's sake, let's not botch it." Universal very nearly did, with an irresolute script and a pompous director.

Rupert Julian, with whom Thalberg had replaced Stroheim on the over-budget *Merry-Go-Round,* was a former actor excelling in a new role, the self-important director. Actress Ruth Clifford described him: "He was extremely dignified, and that little waxed moustache—it wasn't caricature, it was really a stunning moustache. He was always beautifully groomed, a little flower in his buttonhole, and he was very, very strict." Included in his entourage were his opinionated wife, one-time director and actress Elsie Jane Wilson, and his stagestruck dog, for whom Julian would usually add a cameo scene. Julian had also used the same scenarist, Elliot J. Clawson, for nine years, so he gave him *The Phantom*.

Clawson adhered to Leroux's story except for one vital element. In the novel, Erik the Phantom was born hideous.

Removing the element that would make *The Phantom of the Opera* a true horror film, he attributed the Phantom's ugliness to a botched execution by the Sultan of Persia—he was rescued before his face was totally devoured by ants. Studio executives, however, began to feel uneasy about the disfigurement. They made Clawson remove the anthill scene and return to Leroux's concept of a born misfit. In the novel's rather anticlimactic ending, Christine, the opera singer Erik has furtively coached and then kidnapped, allows him to kiss her. Touched, he releases the friends who have been trying to rescue her. A few weeks later, he dies of undisclosed causes. Clawson tried two different endings, each of which had the Phantom dying of a broken heart. If Erik was indeed a monster, he could not be motivated by higher feelings. The studio told Clawson to write a more dramatic climax, in which the Phantom was an utterly evil creature whose misdeeds would be punished by an angry mob. This interpretation (and Chaney's makeup experiments) pushed the film into an untested realm: horror.

As Clawson wrote and rewrote, studio publicists trumpeted what was, next to Lon Chaney, the most significant aspect of this Super Jewel, Carl Laemmle's expensive re-creation of the Paris Opera House. On Hollywood's first concrete-and-steel stage, studio craftsmen labored through the summer of 1924 to manifest every detail, real or invented, of the Paris landmark—a magnificent stage, a 3,000-seat auditorium, a grand staircase, and a 16,000-pound chandelier. The August 1 start date was rolled, like another truckload of fabric, to October 1.

Worlds away from these mounting production costs, Chaney worked with his usual monklike concentration. Leroux's book described a visage so horrific that it resembled a living skull. How would Chaney accomplish this? He made a chalky cranium by means of a skullcap that had a wig sewn onto it. He glued his ears back, used his cotton-and-collodion technique to raise false cheekbones, and hollowed his eye sockets with dark makeup. He molded snaggle teeth with a hard dental rubber called *gutta-percha*. Creating a nose that was not there was his greatest challenge. Leroux had written: "His nose is so little worth talking about that you can't see it side-face; the absence of that nose is a horrible thing to look at." Working with a combination of fish skin, spirit gum, and wires, Chaney pulled his nose so high that it looked as if it had rotted away. "It's an art, not magic," Chaney said later. "I achieved the death's head of that role without wearing a mask. It was the use of paints in the right shades and the right places—not the obvious parts of the face—which gave the complete illusion of horror." Whether for art or magic, Chaney paid a price. "He suffered, you know," said cameraman Charles Van Enger. "He had two wires on his nose that pulled it up, and sometimes it would bleed like hell. We never stopped shooting. He would suffer with it."

Although the unit still man shot scores of plates showing Chaney in this makeup, the studio refrained from using them in publicity. No one but the cast and crew of the film knew what Chaney's newest face looked like. Carla Laemmle, who played the prima ballerina, watched Chaney work with Mary Philbin, the actress playing Christine. Laemmle said: "I remember seeing Lon in his makeup and it was pretty scary. I'd say ghastly. I don't know how Mary was able to work next to that face every day." It was this response that would isolate the most frightening image yet seen in a Chaney film.

As the scene played before an unsuspecting audience, the Phantom has been coaching Christine to opera stardom, but she has not yet seen his face. A mask covers it. As he plays the organ in his subterranean lair, she is overcome

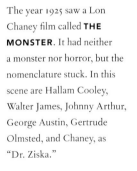

The year 1925 saw a Lon Chaney film called **THE MONSTER**. It had neither a monster nor horror, but the nomenclature stuck. In this scene are Hallam Cooley, Walter James, Johnny Arthur, George Austin, Gertrude Olmsted, and Chaney, as "Dr. Ziska."

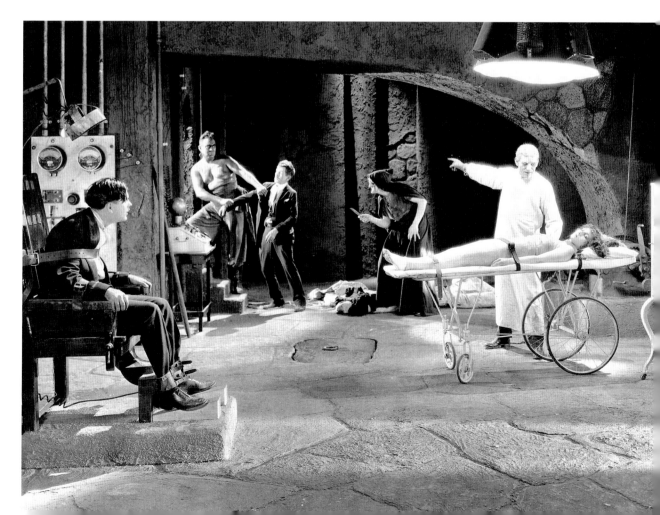

by curiosity. Ignoring his warning not to touch the mask, she creeps up behind him and impulsively pulls it from his face. Enraged, he rises, revealing a countenance that looks as if it has emerged from a crypt. It is a waxen skull, with black sockets instead of eyes, and a gaping mouth ringed with rotting feral teeth. Now—in a subjective closeup—the face moves toward the camera, and as it does, it goes out of focus, engulfing the viewer.

According to historian Michael Blake, at the typical screening of the film in the fall of 1925, "The entire audience uttered a synchronized and very audible gasp." There were reports of women fainting. *Variety* said: "The kick of the picture is the unmasking of the Phantom by the girl. . . . Between Chaney's horrible facial make-up and the expression thereon, it's a wallop that can't miss its objective." Yet even this box-office arbiter was ambivalent about the horror element. "It's impossible to believe that there are a majority of picture goers who prefer this revolting sort of tale on the screen." Universal had anticipated this reaction from two previews in January, when most of the cards had said: "There's too much spook melodrama. Put in some gags to relieve the tension." In response, Universal had an unpretentious director, Edward Sedgwick, shoot new comedy scenes. By the time of the San Francisco premiere in April the *Phantom* had become a muddle, and Universal decided to shelve it for six months. When the film officially premiered at New York's Astor Theatre in September, it had been recut by director Lois Weber. Fortunately, Lon Chaney's innovative performance escaped intact.

The Phantom of the Opera was but one of three Chaney successes in 1925. In late 1924, after completing work at Universal, Chaney went to Tec-Art Productions to portray the slick Dr. Ziska in *The Monster*. The title of this Roland West film was misleading. There is no real monster in it, only a madman who uses a mirror to wreck cars on a country road. His unwitting accident victims become subjects for the soul-transfer experiments he conducts in the asylum where he was once a patient. In spite of its spook-

house formula and wearisome comedy sequences, the film did well, and it firmly linked two words in the mind of the public: Chaney and Monster.

In January 1925, Thalberg cemented his relationship with Chaney in the most practical way: a one-year contract with a weekly salary of $2,500 and two yearly option renewals. He also got the jump on Universal by teaming Chaney with his old collaborator. Tod Browning had pulled out of his tailspin by trying to sell a studio—any studio—a strange C. A. Robbins novel, *The Unholy Three*. Thalberg took one look at it and put the film into production, even before contracting with Chaney, and released it a few weeks before the ballyhooed *Phantom*. *The Unholy Three* featured a very different Lon Chaney, a charismatic con man who disguises himself as a gentle old woman, the better to marshal his two henchmen, a dimwitted muscleman (Victor MacLaglen) and a vicious midget (Harry Earles). Audiences were delighted by further proof of Chaney's versatility and by his uncanny portrayal of the two-faced felon. His own face was as arresting and expressive as any of the bizarre guises he engineered. For *Variety*, it was a revelation: "Lon Chaney stands out like a million dollars. He's done that before, but always with a more or less grotesque make-up. No make-up this time. He isn't all hunched up, he isn't legless, he isn't this, that or the other in deformities. He's just Lon Chaney and that's great." *The Unholy Three* earned $706,000 in worldwide rentals, making it one of M-G-M's biggest hits of 1925 and restoring Tod Browning to his earlier prominence. For Chaney, it was one of three showcases playing side by side. The offbeat material that had brought him stardom would soon bring him competition, from both Hollywood and Europe.

The German Influence

In 1919 Germany was a humbled country. Its defeat in World War I had left it bereft of leadership, beset with inflation, and trembling with unrest. From the founding of the Weimar Republic in 1919 to its democratic stabilization in 1923, there were more than 500 assassinations, mostly reprisals for the signing of the Armistice. In this desperate climate, art and decadence flourished side by side. At a nightclub called the White Mouse, the seminude dancer (and cocaine addict) Anita Berber performed Dances of Horror, Lust, and Ecstasy. Between performances, clients were offered black-and-white "domino" masks so they could watch pornographic films without being named in the press. At the Kabaret der Komiker, satirist Kurt Tucholsky's iconoclastic cry was "We say no to everything!" Theatrical talents such as playwright Bertolt Brecht, director Max Reinhardt, and designer Erwin Piscator agreed, dispensing with conventional stagecraft and using mixed media to shove the stage into the laps of their audience. Actress Lotte Lenya remembered: "There was a tremendous zest. All of a sudden a nation was pouring out its creative possibilities." These included the movement known as Expressionism.

A group of German poets and artists defined Expressionism as an aesthetic style of expressing their subjective responses to the objective world. Rather than paint a picture of a flower, Expressionists would paint a picture of the

Robert Wiene's 1920 **THE CABINET OF DR. CALIGARI** was the first of four German feature films to profoundly influence the American film industry. This scene shows Cesare the Somnambulist (Conrad Veidt) and the heroine, Jane (Lil Dagover), in the inspired Expressionist settings of Hermann Warm. As Dagover recalled, Veidt threw himself into the character: "The scenes in the steep, dark, crooked alleyways belonged to him. Even when he was not in front of the camera, he would prowl around the studio and startle us."

feeling that the flower evoked. This intensely subjective philosophy pushed the Berlin theater far from its naturalistic traditions. On the stage, Expressionism dictated that actors perform in a mimetic shorthand called "dynamic synthesis," in which all unnecessary gestures were eliminated. Traversing sets that looked like the inside of a kaleidoscope, actors clad in formfitting black costumes recited "ideologues" rather than conventional speeches. This new acting style was almost like the pantomime seen on the silent screen. As the stage had been influenced by the screen, it began to return the influence; backed by financiers such as Gustav Krupp, the German film industry embraced Expressionism. The artistic ferment of postwar Berlin produced four films that would have as profound an influence on Hollywood horror as Thalberg, Browning, and Chaney.

Two poets living in Berlin, Austrian Carl Mayer and Czech Hans Janowitz, shared a hatred of authority. Mayer had been mistreated by an army psychiatrist and Janowitz had become obsessed with the failure of the police to capture a murderous rapist. Their anger at the authoritarians who caused the Great War became a scenario, *The Cabinet of Dr. Caligari*. An odd figure in a dark hat, flowing cape, and thick eyeglasses, Caligari is a carnival hypnotist whose act consists of making the sinuous somnambulist Cesare tell fortunes.

"How long will I live?" asks a student.

"Until dawn," answers Cesare. When the student is found murdered, Francis, his friend, conducts a campaign against Caligari until the hypnotist is caught sending Cesare on murderous errands. Mayer and Janowitz felt that their scenario clearly equated Caligari's exploitation of Cesare with the wartime slaughter of young men. They put their script on the market, and, in short order, film magnate Erich Pommer snapped it up for the Deutsches Éclair (Decla) Film Company of Berlin.

The much sought-after Fritz Lang prepared to direct the project, casting Werner Krauss as Caligari and Conrad Veidt as Cesare. When Lang became unavailable at the last minute, Pommer assigned the film to Robert Wiene, who stepped back and let his friends from the avant-garde group Der Sturm take over. Rudolph Meinert, Decla's production supervisor, thought that a film about insanity should have an "insane" style. Set designer Hermann Warm agreed: "The film image must become graphic art." He accomplished this goal with Expressionist effects such as distorted perspective and painted shadows. For the first time, a film was not aping reality; it was conveying madness, as if showing a shattered world through a warped window. By the time *The Cabinet of Dr. Caligari* reached the screen, Wiene and his collaborators had created a new type of film, but they had also subverted its anti-authoritarian message with a framing device written by Lang; Caligari's misdeeds are shown to be the delusions of Francis—an inmate in an asylum run by none other than the benevolent "Dr." Caligari.

The Cabinet of Dr. Caligari enjoyed lavish premieres in Berlin in February 1920 and in New York in March 1921. The orchestral accompaniment came from themes by Mussorgsky, Debussy, and Schoenberg. Audiences were thrilled and bewildered. In a season of comedies, melodramas, and

In **THE GOLEM: HOW HE CAME INTO THE WORLD**, Paul Wegener was a clay giant safeguarding the ghetto from anti-Semitism. The image of a lumbering "body without a soul" offered an archetype to Hollywood.

Westerns, this film stood alone. One critic called the film "a revelation of what the motion picture is capable of as a form of artistic expression." When *Caligari* reached Los Angeles it was met by an anti-German riot, and a theater owner placated the crowd by substituting another film. The incident made its point to Hollywood: the German film industry was alive and well, exporting Expressionism.

Its next appearance was in *The Golem: How He Came into the World*, a 1920 film cowritten and codirected by former Reinhardt Theatre student Paul Wegener, who also starred. Working with cinematographer Karl Freund and architect Hans Poelzig, Wegener told the story of the Golem, a clay giant created by a rabbi to protect the Prague ghetto from a pogrom. *The Golem* was produced by the Universum-Film AG Studios (Ufa), whose resources allowed Poelzig and Freund to create a fantastical vision of sixteenth-century Prague. Wegener's intuitive performance made the Golem more than a lurching creature. The legendary "body without a soul" assumed archetypal proportions, especially in the scene where a little girl offers the giant an apple and then snatches the Star of David from his chest, turning him back into clay. Like *Caligari*, *The Golem* was ballyhooed in Berlin and studied in Hollywood.

The third German film to send shock waves across the Atlantic was the 1922 *Nosferatu—A Symphony of Horror*. Its creator was Friedrich Wilhelm Murnau, another former Reinhardt student. Murnau was also a student of Eastern philosophy and the occult, and had already made two films dealing with horror, so Bram Stoker's novel *Dracula* was a natural choice. In an act of flagrant copyright violation, he had scenarist Albin Grau change a few characters and locales while retaining a character that was unmistakably Dracula. The film was a thematic breakthrough but, due to budgetary limitations, not a stylistic one; harsh, poorly matched lighting distracted from the unearthly mood Murnau sought to impose. Still, it was worthy of its uncredited source. When the vampire (Max Schreck) occupies the screen, Murnau creates moments of genuine horror. The

Another archetype that challenged the imagination—and copyright laws—was the vampire (Max Schreck) created by Friedrich Wilhelm Murnau in his 1922 German film, **NOSFERATU**.

tall, bald actor looks like an emaciated rodent, complete with pointed ears and protruding incisors. When Schreck enters a scene and raises his arms, he conveys the unearthly power of Stoker's character—perhaps a little too well. Stoker's widow, Florence, recognized plagiarism in *Nosferatu* and tried to suppress it; although few American theaters could play it, every Hollywood studio managed to grab a print. Murnau escaped any legal consequences and went on to direct *The Last Laugh, Tartuffe,* and *Faust* at Ufa.

A conspicuous presence at Ufa was Fritz Lang, directing that studio's most expensive film ever, a "horror tale of the future" called *Metropolis.* To afford its 5.3 million-mark budget, the German studio entered into a distribution arrangement with Paramount and M-G-M. It was under the banner of "Parufamet" that Lang and his wife, Thea von Harbou, dreamed up the world of 2026, where a city of cubist ziggurats is supported by the sweating labor of underground workers. With a cast of 750, and 31,000 extras, Lang spent a year filming his fabulous city, level by level, detail by painstaking detail. His four-hour film boasted many ingenious set pieces, but none captured the imagination of Hollywood as permanently as the laboratory scene in which the mad scientist Rotwang (Rudolph Klein-Rogge) uses the unconscious heroine, Maria (Brigitte Helm), to create a seductive robot who looks exactly like her. The scene is a pyrotechnic montage of flashing lights, bubbling beakers, and arcing electricity, building to the birth of a new, evil being. When the film reached America in February 1927 it had been trimmed of two hours by a nervous Ufa, but most of its innovations remained. "Nothing of the sort has ever been filmed before," wrote *Variety.* "Its effect is positively overwhelming. From a photographic and directorial standpoint, it is something entirely original." *Metropolis* became the fourth German film to influence the nascent Hollywood horror genre. Before long, Hollywood directors were aping German Expressionist techniques: distorted sets, stylized performances, sexy dream sequences, relentlessly mobile cameras, dramatic spotlights, and staccato editing.

Metropolis was still in production when D. W. Griffith, the "Father of American Film," embarked on a small-scale excursion into the outré. Griffith had pioneered the American feature-length horror film in 1914 with *The Avenging*

Conscience, and in 1922 unsuccessfully tried to produce *The Cat and the Canary.* Later that same year he did make the first "old dark-house" film, the disappointing *One Exciting Night;* it was not. By 1926 he was an anachronism, his antebellum sentimentality losing money for United Artists, the company he had founded with Mary Pickford, Douglas Fairbanks, and Charles Chaplin. In an effort to regain his stature, Griffith signed a three-picture deal with Paramount, which promptly assigned him a property that Cecil B. DeMille had turned down, Marie Corelli's best-selling novel, *The Sorrows of Satan.*

Griffith's penchant for the sentimental was ill served by this lugubrious tale of a starving author (Ricardo Cortez) who is ambivalent about selling his soul to the devil (Adolphe Menjou) while enjoying the pleasures served up by this mysterious man of the world. When the time comes for the author to pay up, his wronged girlfriend (Carole Dempster) prays for him. The story lets him off the hook, but not before scaring him with the devil's true appearance. Griffith's attempt at a German Expressionist effect backfired. The satanic wings projected on the wall behind Cortez were less frightening in the film than they appeared to be in the still photos; instead of flapping slowly, they wiggled, defusing any impact they might have had. One reviewer sniffed: "But it's Griffith, and he's symbolizing the whims of mankind." *The Sorrows of Satan* failed at the box office, but other American approaches to the fantastic were more profitable.

Some companies ignored the increasingly popular German imports. In 1925, First National Pictures had a gigantic hit with *The Lost World.* The small studio on Sunset Boulevard had taken a chance on a new photographic process and purchased the rights to Arthur Conan Doyle's very British adventure story. The magical process, patented by a young Californian named Willis O'Brien, was practiced behind closed doors for more than a year. Its result was a surprisingly realistic portrayal of prehistoric animals sharing the screen with live actors. With scenes of dinosaurs fleeing a volcanic eruption and a brontosaurus rampaging through London, *The Lost World* was a groundbreaking epic.

An earlier epic, Rex Ingram's 1921 *The Four Horsemen of the Apocalypse* had, besides making a star of Rudolph Valentino, demonstrated Ingram's ability to create terrifying images. His visions of plague and death far outstripped his grim battle scenes. Ingram was a handsome Irish eccentric who left Hollywood to set up his own studio in Nice, where he could direct his wife, Alice Terry, in such semimystical super-productions as *Mare Nostrum.* When M-G-M suggested that he direct a project in the German Expressionist mode, he chose *The Magician,* a Somerset Maugham novel loosely based on Aleister Crowley, the sometime novelist whose love commune in Sicily hosted satanic rites and sexual hijinks. Ingram then hired *The Golem's* Wegener and fashioned a weird tale of a scientist bent on creating a "homunculus," a miniature man.

The design of the mad scientist's laboratory, in which the curving lines of tubes and bottles mimicked the human body, helped refine the archetype. Equally stimulating was Ingram's depiction of a Bacchanalian rite, where the god Pan, portrayed as a naked satyr by the celebrated American artist-dancer Hubert Stowitts, thrusts his burnished torso at the ubiquitous Alice Terry before a fade-out tells us that he has raped her. Released in 1926, *The Magician* was more Ingram than Expressionism, but its scientist and laboratory were first-rate horror. The film was a success, proving that the public craved unearthly thrills, even when served with esoteric trimmings.

Sensing this new interest in weird stories, Roland West, the independent producer of *The Monster*, refined the old dark-house formula that had been introduced in numerous mystery-farces on Broadway. His 1926 UA production, *The Bat*, came from the stage hit by Avery Hopwood and Mary Roberts Rinehart. Its transition from proscenium arch to frameline was accomplished by two peerless collaborators: William Cameron Menzies, then making his name as Hollywood's greatest production designer; and Arthur Edeson, perhaps the most versatile of the major cinematographers. Together they gave West an eerie three-dimensional setting for a mixture of chills and laughs. The German Expressionist influence was discernible in Menzies's imposing sets, which featured bold contrasts of tone and texture, outsized accents, and vast expanses of wall for Edeson's projected shadows. The Bat is a master criminal who can scale walls and elude the most diligent detectives, but he is foiled by a stuffy matron and her maid in an eerie mansion. The trade paper *Harrison's Reports* said: "Few pictures have been released lately that hold the spectator as breathless as does *The Bat*, and not only does it hold him breathless but it thrills him and at the same time makes him laugh to his heart's content."

Now that an American director had made a hit of an old dark-house play, Carl Laemmle imported German directors Ewald André Dupont, Dmitri Buchowetski, and Paul Leni, hoping that one of them could bring Expressionist magic to another Broadway blockbuster, *The Cat and the Canary*. The honors went to Leni, whose claim to fame was the 1924 Conrad Veidt film *Waxworks*. In it, Leni had emptied his bag of Expressionist tricks to create a feeling of all-pervading dread. Perhaps his virtuosity would be too much for *The*

Cat and the Canary, an airtight all-American puzzle with no room for Germanic flair. Leni attacked the project as if he were both of the animals in the title. From the very first shot on the screen, in which a hand wipes away cobwebs to reveal the main title, Leni made the story his own. Cameraman Gilbert Warrenton described working on Leni's first American film. "If one can squeeze through knot holes, hang by his feet from the ceiling, stand on his head on a moving platform, and fly," said Warrenton, "one can follow Leni with ease and grace." The *New York Times* film critic Mordaunt Hall reviewed the Expressionistic result: "Mr. Leni has not lost a single chance in this new film to show what can be done with the camera. He creates excitement by pitching his camera high and low, or rolling it along. He makes you feel that you are one of the characters in the haunted house of the story."

The Cat and the Canary opened in September 1927. A month later, the first part-talking feature film, Warner Bros.' *The Jazz Singer*, premiered in New York. In another month, every Hollywood studio was scrambling to make part-talking pictures, adding one talking reel or merely musical scores and synchronized sound effects to already-completed silents. In mid-1928, sound pioneer Warner Bros. released its first all-talking picture, *Lights of New York*.

For its second all-talking venture, Warners chose a horror film. *The Terror* was directed by Roy Del Ruth, who tried to disguise the intractability of his newfangled recording equipment with German Expressionist touches, filming sequences from extreme angles and with bold camera movements. Since the camera that filmed the sound sequences was confined to a large booth, these purely cinematic shots had to be made with a silent camera. Mixing of multiple sound tracks was not yet possible, so these sequences, instead of being dramatic punctuation marks, looked like scenes from a different film. The rest of *The Terror* was not much better, a series of poorly recorded dialogues. Critic Mordaunt Hall wrote: "May McAvoy's voice is shy and shrinking, a lisping peep contrasted with

Jewel Carmen shrinks from the eponymous menace in Roland West's 1926 thriller, **THE BAT**. West made his cast work at night. "Given the quiet of the studio at midnight, when no other companies are working, and plenty of spooky music from an orchestra, the players really are in a mood to simulate dark deeds."

the bellowing of Mr. [Joseph] Girard." More effectively recorded were the sounds of howling winds, a whining pipe organ, and, as a portent of things to come, ear-piercing screams. Otherwise, as British critic James Agate wrote, *The Terror* was "interminable twaddle without either illusion or enchantment."

While the "talkers" tried to sate a voracious audience, studios had continued to make silent films, hoping that horror could compete with sound. In late 1927, William Fox filmed the 1912 Gaston Leroux novel *Balaoo* as *The Wizard*, which featured a monster that combined a gorilla's body and a half-human head. *The Gorilla, Seven Footprints to Satan,* and *Stark Mad* also had hairy menaces, some of which were simian and some of whom were costumed. But genuine horror could only be found in Lon Chaney's films at M-G-M, which were still silent because Irving Thalberg believed that silents and talkies would coexist. Silent horror was also alive at Universal, where producer Paul Kohner reunited *Waxworks* star Conrad Veidt with Paul Leni for the expensive production of the Victor Hugo novel *The Man Who Laughs,* one of many films released in late 1927 only to be withdrawn and then rereleased with a music-and-effects track.

The Man Who Laughs is the story of an orphan, Gwynplaine (Julius Molnar Jr.), who falls into the hands of the Comprachicos, "gypsy traders in stolen children and

practicing certain unlawful surgical acts whereby they carve the living flesh of these children and transform them into monstrous clowns and jesters." The scenes that follow his kidnapping show the tiny, winsome Gwynplaine, his lower face covered by a shawl, shoved into a brutal snowstorm by the escaping Comprachicos. He staggers through the bitterly cold night, passing decayed corpses hanging from a row of gallows. Struggling to find shelter, he stumbles on a mother and child huddled in a snowdrift. He rescues the infant from her dead mother's grip. Gwynplaine comes upon a lone wagon. The eccentric mountebank within, Ursus (Cesare Gravina), grudgingly admits the little boy, whose bulging coat hides the sleeping infant. In the dim light of the wagon, Ursus watches Gwynplaine sharing his soup with the infant. As Gwynplaine glances up, Ursus sees that his mouth has been surgically carved into a permanent smile.

That Paul Leni could film such material without crossing the line into the nauseating was proof of his skill. Further proof was the touching performance he elicited from Veidt as the adult Gwynplaine, especially in a scene in which the nymphomaniac Duchess Josiana (Olga Baclanova) attempts to seduce him. *The Man Who Laughs* was another example of the silent film in its last glorious bloom.

The team of Kohner, Leni, and Veidt appeared to be a sure thing for Universal's first supernatural sound film.

Hubert Stowitts, Paul Wegener, and Alice Terry appeared in Rex Ingram's **THE MAGICIAN**, a 1926 fantasy filmed in Paris and Nice, where M-G-M could not interfere with Ingram's creative process.

above
The Warner Bros.' second all-talking picture was a squawky attempt at horror called **THE TERROR**. Cameraman Barney McGill lit this scene of May McAvoy being menaced by Matthew Betz.

left
Universal Pictures photographer Jack Freulich made this portrait of Conrad Veidt in character as Gwynplaine for Paul Leni's 1928 silent film **THE MAN WHO LAUGHS**, the touching tale of a man whose face has been surgically altered into a permanent smile.

Martha Mattox prowls the corridors of Paul Leni's 1927 Universal film **THE CAT AND THE CANARY**. Leni said: "I have tried to create sets so stylized that they evince no reality. It is not extreme reality that the camera perceives, but the reality of the inner event, which is more profound, effective, and moving than what we see through everyday eyes."

Having heard of the Broadway hit *Dracula*, Kohner pitched it to Carl Laemmle. He did not get very far. *The Man Who Laughs* was faltering at the box office. Kohner was demoted. In the summer of 1929 Universal began corresponding with M-G-M about the possibility of borrowing Lon Chaney for *Dracula*. Veidt, still unknown to the American public, returned to Germany. Worst of all, in September 1929 the talented Leni suddenly fell ill with blood poisoning and died. The artist who was about to bring his creativity to sound films was now, like his film legacy, a memory. Who would carry the horror film from the eloquent silents into the still-awkward talkies?

Lon Chaney and Tod Browning

In 1925, Metro-Goldwyn-Mayer boasted that it had "More Stars than There Are in Heaven." Stardom for Lon Chaney was the foremost achievement of *He Who Gets Slapped*. Two years later, a survey by *Film Spectator* estimated that "The Man of a Thousand Faces," now making four films a year and $3,250 a week, was pulling ninety-two percent of America's movie audience into its theaters.

Since the success of *The Unholy Three,* Chaney had found a variety of colorful roles: a Scandinavian farmer in *The Tower of Lies* (1925); a petty criminal disguised as a bishop in *The Black Bird* (1926); and a South Seas saloon-keeper in *The Road to Mandalay* (1926). In George Hill's 1927 *Tell It to the Marines*, Chaney created a non-horror

archetype, the gruff but kindhearted sergeant. The film also benefited from William Haines's comic foil, and it made a profit of $664,000. This was twice the amount of Chaney's most popular Browning films. Even so, Thalberg encouraged Browning to continue dreaming up weird projects to make with Chaney.

"I like to make program films and give enough of myself to them so that they are not just ordinary program films," said Browning. "And in writing my own stories, I believe I am better able to do this than if I were to depend on somebody else's scenario." Browning developed most of his stories by acting them out for former reporter Waldemar Young. "Never having been a newspaperman," explained Browning, "I can express myself more easily in words than on paper." When a new M-G-M writer named Frederica Sagor met Young, she saw a man "about fifty pounds overweight. He was prematurely gray and looked physically worn out." This was the result, Young admitted, of working for Thalberg, Browning, and Chaney for two years without a break. Like them, he had little time for life outside the "glamorous" studio.

When Young was unavailable, Browning worked with Herman Mankiewicz, an émigré from the Algonquin Hotel's literary Round Table. They had appropriated the title and setting of Rudyard Kipling's *The Road to Mandalay*, but dumped his verse in favor of a squalid tale in which Chaney was "Singapore Joe," the proprietor of a waterfront saloon replete with the slimiest refuse that the casting department could suck from the gutters of downtown Los Angeles. To make himself more repulsive than this human detritus, Chaney visited a prominent Los Angeles optician, Dr. Hugo Keifer, who presented him with a white glass shield to wear over his cornea. Singapore Joe's dive has paid for the convent education of his daughter (Lois Moran), who knows him only as a menacing presence at her Mandalay gift shop. A reformed drunk (Owen Moore) catches her fancy, but the jealous Singapore Joe abducts him, thereby endangering his daughter, who must defend herself from a reptilian criminal (Sojin) and finally from her own father, whom she stabs to death without ever learning his true identity.

While not literally a horror film, *The Road to Mandalay*, with its twisted anti-hero and self-sacrificial climax, honored the Thalberg-Browning-Chaney formula. Its reviews were guarded (*Motion Picture Magazine* called it "sordid and morbid"), but it turned a $267,000 profit as audiences once more responded to a grim but honest portrayal. Chaney said: "I've tried to show that the lowliest people frequently have the highest ideals. In the lower depths, when life hasn't been too pleasant for me, I've always had that gentleness of feeling, that compassion of an underdog for a fellow sufferer."

When the corporate firmament at M-G-M needed replenishing, Louis B. Mayer and his executives sought new talent. A European trip resulted in a contract for the Swedish actress Greta Garbo. A New York chorus line yielded an eager dancer named Lucille LeSueur; before she became Joan Crawford, her first role was to double a star, Norma Shearer. In February 1927 it was Crawford's good fortune to be cast in a Chaney vehicle, *The Unknown*. This would be Chaney's ninth M-G-M film and his fourth collaboration there with Irving Thalberg and Tod Browning. The actor made a lasting impression on his twenty-two-year-old leading lady. Crawford later wrote: "He was armless in this picture—his arms strapped to his sides—and he learned to eat, even to hold a cigarette, by using his feet and toes. Mr. Chaney could have unstrapped his arms between scenes. He did not." Every day the same exchange took place between director and star.

"Lon, don't you want me to untie your arms?" asked Browning.

"No," answered Chaney. "The pain I am enduring now will help the scene."

The Unknown was Browning's most perverse tale yet. Alonzo the Armless is a circus performer who hides his arms in a punishing harness because his double thumbs will give him away as a murderer. Being armless is also an advantage when he falls in love with Nanon (Crawford), who has a phobia of men's arms. To prevent her from discovering his criminal identity—and in the hope that she will marry him— Alonzo blackmails a doctor (John Sainpolis) into amputating his arms.

The film's payoff could have come when Alonzo awakens armless in the hospital, but Browning saved it for the moment when Alonzo returns to Nanon, where a shock awaits him: she has overcome her phobia and is engaged to the circus strong man, Malabar (Norman Kerry). As Malabar proudly embraces the laughing Nanon and runs his hands over her body, Alonzo realizes that he has sacrificed his arms for nothing. The scene cuts back and forth between the lusty couple and a medium closeup of Alonzo. The smile on his face turns to a mad grimace and he fights the urge to scream. He laughs and laughs, his eyes stuck open, his head jerking back. Nanon innocently says: "Alonzo is laughing at the way things have turned out."

As Crawford remembered: "He kept [his arms] strapped one day for five hours, enduring such numbness, such torture, that when we got to this scene, he was able to convey not just realism, but such emotional agony that it was shocking . . . and fascinating." Most critics, however, felt that Thalberg, Browning, and Chaney had gone too far. *Variety* wrote: "Every time Browning thinks of Chaney he probably looks around for a typewriter and says, 'Let's get gruesome.'" The *New York Herald-Tribune* was diagnostic: "The case of Mr. Tod Browning is rapidly approaching the pathological." *Harrison's Reports* was censorious:

> One can imagine a moral pervert of the present day, or professional torturers of the times of the Spanish Inquisition that gloated over the miseries of their victims on the rack and over their roasting on hot iron bars enjoying screen details of the kind set forth in "The Unknown," but it is difficult to fancy average men and women of a modern audience in this enlightened age being entertained by such a thoroughly fiendish mingling of bloodlust, cruelty and horrors.

Either Chaney's fans did not read these reviews or did not believe them. *The Unknown* made a profit of $362,000. After making *Mockery* (1927), a Russian Revolution melodrama in which he played a half-witted servant, Chaney took the Hollywood film in a new direction.

In the 1927 *London After Midnight*, Browning presented Chaney as the Man in the Beaver Hat, whose nocturnal habits characterize him as a vampire, the same type of creature then being portrayed by Bela Lugosi in the Broadway play *Dracula*. Chaney's vampire makeup was simple but not painless. He stretched his eye sockets by putting two monoclelike wires in them; he could not close his eyes or even blink while wearing these devices. He also used wires to widen his mouth into a ravenous leer and to make room for two rows of fangs. His scraggly gray wig, beaver hat, and Inverness cape served as both a high-contrast setting for these hideous features and a nod to Dr. Caligari. To complete the characterization, he devised a bent, scuttling gait, and, to emphasize his vampiric nature, he would suddenly stop and raise his arms, revealing that his black cape had organdy bat wings.

Once made up, he customarily stayed in character. "Lon Chaney's concentration, the complete absorption he gave to his character," said Crawford, "filled all of us with such awe we never even considered addressing him with the usual pleasantries until he became aware of and addressed us." One day as a friend, Clarence Locan, watched him walking in his vampire getup from the set to his dressing room, "a commotion on the lawn stopped him. Several tiny birds had fallen out of a nest. Chaney

On the set of the 1927 M-G-M film **THE UNKNOWN**, Tod Browning fondles the empty sleeve of Lon Chaney's velvet bolero. Browning said: "When we're getting ready to discuss a new story, he'll amble into my office and say, 'Well, what'll it be this time, boss?' I'll say, 'This time a leg comes off, or an arm, or a nose'—whatever it may be."

retrieved the birds, climbed to the nest, and restored them to safety." Then he asked Locan not to mention the incident to the press. Chaney avoided interviews and advised newcomer Garbo to do the same: "If you let them know too much about you, they will lose interest."

Chaney was not only reticent but also reclusive. He rarely attended premieres, and he sidestepped the socializing essential to Hollywood politics. "I have never had an actor or an actress in my home," he said. "I want to keep my work and my personal life entirely apart. I have discovered that most of us have very false values." What little

THE ROAD TO MANDALAY
had nothing to do with Rudyard Kipling and everything to do with Chaney's fetish for self-mutilation. *Variety* wrote: "This time his deformity is a sightless white eye. It is remarkable how this particular detail contributes a sort of mood and tempo to the whole production."

time off he allowed himself was spent with his wife, Hazel, and his son, Creighton. Chaney was adamantly opposed to his son's acting ambitions, saying: "He's six feet two. That's too tall. He would always have had to have parts built around him. He couldn't build himself for the part. Besides, he's happy in business." Creighton, who was working in his father-in-law's plumbing company, ultimately rebelled, and pursued an acting career that only succeeded after he had (reluctantly) changed his name to Lon Jr.

Chaney's inner circle also included John Jeske, a garage mechanic whom he had befriended and hired as his chauffeur, and who became his constant companion. The unseemly friendship between M-G-M's most popular star and a working-class man annoyed some family members and titillated the caste-conscious, but Chaney's obsession with privacy precluded any comment. His hobbies included camping, trout fishing, and a 16mm movie camera. He wrote articles for diverse publications such as *American Cinematographer*, *The Encyclopedia Britannica*, and *The Island Lantern,* an in-house prison magazine. Besides Jeske, he had a small circle of friends, mostly conservative professionals with no ties to the film industry. To prefer their company to the M-G-M social circle made Chaney a mystery, and the few fan magazine writers to whom he granted interviews tried in vain to unravel it. *Photoplay*'s Ruth Waterbury observed him on the set of *London After Midnight*: "From his slobbering mouth pointed teeth gleamed and tears of agony flowed from his awful distended eyes. For nearly an hour it seemed impossible for a human body to suffer severer torture than that to which Lon subjected himself in order to gain that effect with his eyes . . . . Yet in this visible suffering, Lon was plainly an artist in the exquisite travail of creation."

The element of pain was now a sine qua non of the Chaney-Browning oeuvre. Before the cameras, the actor both caused and suffered pain; but whether playing a sadist or a masochist Chaney entranced his fans. *London After Midnight* was arguably Hollywood's first vampire film, and its $542,000 profit was the largest of any of the Chaney-Browning films. However, some fans complained when the vampire was unmasked as a disguised detective. After reading about (or seeing) *Dracula*, they were ready for an honestly supernatural character. So were Chaney and Browning, according to the *New York Times*: "Chaney wanted to act Dracula and often discussed the part with Tod Browning . . . both men believed the American public to be 90 percent superstitious and ripe for horror films. Chaney had a full scenario and a secret makeup worked out even at that early date, but Browning held out for a talkie." Was *London After Midnight* an audition for *Dracula*?

By the time that tantalizing property had become available, Chaney and Browning had parted—so they thought—temporarily. Their collaborations following *London After Midnight* had been slightly less profitable, with the exception of *West of Zanzibar* (1928), which had Chaney portraying a vengeance-crazed cripple who, like his character in *The Unknown,* falls into his own trap. The girl he has dragged through the swamps and brothels of the African coast is not his enemy's daughter, but his own. Added to this was the scene in which Chaney, as Dead Legs Flint, drops out of his wheelchair, drags himself across the filthy floor of a plantation hut, puts on a bug-eyed ritual mask, and crawls away to preside over the ceremonial burning of a live native woman.

Chaney's work with studio contract directors in less quirky films had each averaged $30,000 more profit than those made with Browning, whose solo projects (*The Mystic*, *The Show*, and *The Thirteenth Chair*) had been fairly profitable but not particularly memorable. Browning had also begun drinking again. As his contract lapsed, the director came to a fork in the road, just as talking pictures were bringing Chaney to the same fork. In mid-1929, Thalberg declined to renew Browning's contract.

Chaney, meanwhile, refused to do a talking picture or a silent picture with a talking sequence. He maintained that he was waiting for technical improvements. In truth, he was recovering from what appeared to be pneumonia. When he could not report for work in July 1929, M-G-M suspended his contract—while at the same time negotiating his loan-out to Universal for *Dracula*. In August, M-G-M warned Chaney not to consider working with any other company during his contract suspension. Universal put *Dracula* aside while waiting to see if Chaney would re-sign with M-G-M. In the fall of 1929, while the two studios watched and waited, Chaney's condition was diagnosed as bronchial cancer. He told no one.

The actor regained enough strength to enter into negotiations, and, on January 23, 1930, Chaney signed a new contract. Thalberg helped him choose his first talking vehicle, a remake of one of his greatest silent successes. *The Unholy Three* began filming on April 1, his forty-seventh birthday. Browning had decamped to Universal, so contract director Jack Conway coached Chaney. The Man of a Thousand Faces would now use his stage training to create five different voices: Professor Echo, his dummy, an old lady, a girl, and a parrot. When studio photographer George Hurrell wanted to photograph Chaney out of character, he was brought up short by Chaney's response: "I don't feel comfortable being photographed as myself." Chaney still reserved one face for himself. That face constituted the enigma.

The pain he endured on the set of *The Unholy Three* was, for once, not of his own making. The cancer was advancing, sapping his strength, and reducing the hours he could work. He missed two days of work because of hemorrhaging but managed to complete the film. M-G-M rushed it into theaters on July 3, and word quickly spread that Chaney's use of his voice was as clever as his makeup. Other than Charles Chaplin, Chaney was the last major star to make the transition to sound, and he had triumphed. If Universal could untangle the legal web surrounding the rights to *Dracula*, Chaney would be the obvious choice. However, he never reached his dream role.

On August 26, 1930, Lon Chaney succumbed to lung cancer. Delivering his eulogy, Irving Thalberg used the word "great" to describe the first Hollywood horror star. "Great not only because of his God-given talent, but also because he used that talent to illuminate certain dark corners of the human spirit. He showed the world the souls of those people who were born different than us."

above
"Such a picture is enough to turn the ordinary person's stomach inside out," said the review of **THE UNKNOWN** in *Harrison's Reports*. "The sight of an armless freak doing everything with his toes that the average person does with his hands may pass for amusement for a few idle moments. . . . Similar praise might well be given the work of a skilled surgeon engaged in ripping open the abdomen of a patient. But who wants to see him do it?"

left
"An Outpouring of the Cesspools of Hollywood!" was the title of the *Harrison's Reports* review of Tod Browning's 1928 **WEST OF ZANZIBAR**, which was based on the sensational play *Kongo*. It asked: "How any normal person thought that this horrible syphilitic play could have made an entertaining picture, even with Lon Chaney, who appears in gruesome and repulsive stories, is beyond comprehension."

In 1927, Browning and Chaney collaborated on Hollywood's first vampire film, **LONDON AFTER MIDNIGHT**. As this scene with Chaney and Edna Tichenor shows, it had all the trappings of *Dracula*.

left

Lon Chaney waited for two years before he made his first talking picture. "I don't want to talk and spoil any illusion," he said. Irving Thalberg countered: "You've done all kinds of dialect and character stuff on the stage. Just use a couple of voices and let 'em guess." In **THE UNHOLY THREE**, Chaney used five voices; it appeared that the talkies had a new star.

opposite

LONDON AFTER MIDNIGHT was the most successful of the Browning-Chaney films. Cameraman Virgil Miller recalled: "I'd worked with Lon for years experimenting with one makeup after another. He'd say, 'Virg, make me look frightening and repulsive, but at the same time make the audience love me.' He always wanted to be loved."

CHAPTER 2

The Horror Film

Tod Browning's Dracula

When Tod Browning arrived at Universal Pictures in early 1930, intent on making the first supernatural horror film, the studio was essentially the same nepotistic factory he and Irving Thalberg had left in 1923. The biggest difference was in Carl Laemmle's product. His twenty-two-year-old son, Carl Jr., was now head of production. Emulating M-G-M's Thalberg, "Junior" was shepherding prestige properties such as *All Quiet on the Western Front* to critical and popular success. At five-foot-three, Junior was three inches taller than his father, who nonetheless bossed him and told him whom he could and could not date—no *shiksas*.

In matters artistic, Junior prevailed. He wanted to film Bram Stoker's *Dracula*, which John L. Balderston had adapted for Hamilton Deane's 1927 London production. Senior had heard about the play from his studio readers. All but one had reviled it. A "Miss Hall" had written:

> Beautiful women with voluptuous mouths dripping with blood—huge bats with flapping wings—wolves with hungry mouths—vaults, dark and ominous—dusty chapels hung with cobwebs—graves—ships steered by dead men—a man with sharp white teeth and eyes as red as fire—a vampire feeding on the blood of innocent girls and children in order to perpetuate himself and his kind. . . . For mystery and blood-curdling horror, I have never read its equal. . . . It is daring, but if done, there can be no doubt as to its making money.

Senior decided *Dracula* was not for the Big U. On October 5 of the same year, Broadway impresario (and publisher) Horace Liveright opened *Dracula* on Broadway. Stoker's widow, Florence, had already spent five years pursuing the producers of *Nosferatu*, so it was only with great difficulty—and diplomacy—that Balderston, the charming, good-looking coauthor of the metaphysical romance *Berkeley Square*, had persuaded the grand old lady to allow an American production. *Dracula* became a sensation when it opened in New York, making a star of its leading man, the Hungarian-born actor Bela Lugosi. With raven-black hair, blue eyes, and long fingers, he had the appeal of a matinee idol. In a *Motion Picture Classic* magazine interview, Lugosi explained that appeal.

> When I was playing Dracula on the stage, my audiences were women. Women. There were men, too. Escorts the women had brought with them. For reasons only their dark subconscious knew. In order to establish a subtle sex intimacy. Contact. In order to cling to and feel the sensuous thrill of protection. Men did not come of their own volition. Women did. Came—and knew an ecstasy dragged from the depths of unspeakable things. Came—and then came back again. And again.
>
> Women wrote me letters. Ah, what letters women wrote me. Young girls. Women from seventeen to thirty. Letters of a horrible hunger. Asking me if I cared only for maidens' blood. Asking me if I had done the play because I was in reality that sort of Thing. And through these letters, couched in terms of shuddering, transparent fear, there ran the hideous note of—hope. They hoped that I was Dracula. They hoped that my love was the love of—*Dracula*.

The play ran for 261 performances and then went on tour, making a total of $2 million. In 1929 Lugosi returned to Hollywood, where the Fox Film Corporation cast him as a series of foreign heavies. Meanwhile, Junior Laemmle continued his *Dracula* campaign. Senior relented—but only if

In its first run, **DRACULA** ended with a "curtain speech" by Edward Van Sloan. He faced the camera and said: "Just a moment, ladies and gentlemen! Just a word before you go. We hope the memories of Dracula and Renfield won't give you bad dreams, so just a word of reassurance. When you get home tonight and the lights have been turned out and you are afraid to look behind the curtains—and you dread to see a face appear at the window—why, just pull yourself together and remember that after all, there *are* such things." The Production Code Administration made Universal cut this speech from the film's negative in March 1938. This publicity still shows Helen Chandler and Bela Lugosi. Photograph by Jack Freulich

Tod Browning would direct and Lon Chaney would star. As a result, Junior spent the summer waiting out Chaney's M-G-M suspension.

Perhaps Browning would lure Chaney, so Universal gave Browning a three-picture contract. He had directed only one talkie at M-G-M, *The Thirteenth Chair,* and had yet to reconcile himself to the new technique. "I think sound and dialogue should be used sparingly," Browning said, "perhaps 25 percent sound and 75 percent silence. This means that the bits and touches we used to put in our silent pictures and have since dropped—the speed, the pantomime, the subtlety of earlier days—need to be reinstated on the screen." Browning was not the only one looking wistfully to the silent screen. Actress Helen Chandler expressed the feelings of many when she said: "I used to love the silent movies—their beauty, the enchanting lighting, the slow gestures."

Browning was learning that sound-editing techniques were fairly inflexible. He could no longer shoot footage of players reacting and then make them coherent with intertitles in the editing room. He believed: "the director does the real writing of his story in the cutting and projection rooms." In the cutting rooms of the early sound era, a director who only spoke the language of silents was in trouble. Browning's first film for Universal, *Outside the Law,* was slammed by *Variety.* "It's one of the worst examples of

above

In the fall of 1930 director Tod Browning, actor Bela Lugosi, Broadway producer Horace Liveright, and scenarist Dudley Murphy posed on the set of **DRACULA,** a film that would be a regret to some, a curse to others, and a boon to a studio.

Looking at Bela Lugosi in attitudes taken from the film are David Manners, Helen Chandler, Dwight Frye, and Edward Van Sloan.

clap-trap since sound came in. Not a thread of continuity ... yards of film deal repetitiously with stupid conversation."

While Browning struggled to learn talkie technique, the *Dracula* project began to look uncertain. Battered by the stock market crash, Liveright had lost the screen rights. In February 1930 Harold Freedman, acting as agent for Balderston and Stoker, approached M-G-M, Pathé, Columbia, and Universal. They were all aware of Chaney's failing health, and without Chaney, no one wanted *Dracula*; it was too risky. "At your request, some months ago, I felt out all our supervisors on *Dracula*," wrote Paramount supervisor E. J. Montagne to production head B. P. Schulberg. "We did not receive one favorable reaction. The very things which made people gasp and talk about it, such as the blood-sucking scenes, would be prohibited by the Code and also by censors because of the effect of these scenes on children." Junior Laemmle, however, knew from his experiences with *All Quiet on the Western Front* that the new Production Code, which prohibited scenes of brutality and sex, could be circumnavigated.

Besides Freedman and Laemmle, there was another individual vitally interested in the project: Lugosi. Working behind the scenes, he and his manager (and translator), Harry Weber, looked for a studio to deal with the Stoker estate. Only Universal listened, surmising that if Lugosi were desperate enough to be an unpaid emissary, he could probably be gotten more cheaply than an established actor. Freedman visited Universal in May, at which time the economic depression was already cutting into box-office receipts. Senior was still opposed to *Dracula*, especially in view of the Code. Nonetheless, Junior assigned writer Frederick "Fritz" Stephani to prepare a treatment so that a budget could be drawn up. Lugosi continued his campaign,

even writing to Florence Stoker from a tour of *Dracula* in Oakland, California. Freedman continued negotiations "in [the] face of Mr. Laemmle Sr.'s definite written objection to the purchase of the picture." Meanwhile, a resolute Junior assigned Browning to the project, budgeted at $355,000.

Junior then brought the author Louis Bromfield from New York to write the screenplay. Just as it appeared that the deal could be made for $40,000, out of the woodwork came two monsters who almost scared away the widow Stoker: the elusive *Nosferatu*, being shown illegally in Greenwich Village, and the bankrupt Liveright, making the absurd claim that a film of *Dracula* would unfairly compete with his future stage productions. When Universal finally secured the rights to Dracula on August 22, it was only after: (1) paying Liveright a nuisance fee of $4,500; (2) suppressing *Nosferatu* by buying the print (for Browning et al. to study); and (3) dividing a payment of $40,000 between {a} Florence Stoker (for screen rights to her husband's novel) and {b} Hamilton Deane and John Balderston (for screen rights to their play). Everyone was happy except Lugosi. Years later, he complained to a *New York Post* interviewer, who faithfully (if unkindly) transcribed his speech patterns:

> De Bram Stoker heirs asked $200,000 for de film reidts, but Uniwersal didn't like to pay dat much. Zo dey asked me would I correspond wid Mrs. Stoker, de widow, and get it maybe a liddle cheaper. I wreidt and wreidt until I get cramps, and after about two months, Mrs. Stoker says O.K., we can haff it for $60,000 [sic]. Zo what does Uniwersal do from graddidude? From graddidude dey start to test two dozen fellows

Cinematographer Karl Freund was responsible for the eerie power of **DRACULA**. He made the film's opening scenes vignettes of horror. Here in the basement of Dracula's castle are his wives, played by Geraldine Dvorak, Dorothy Tree, and Cornelia Thaw.

for *Dracula*—but not me! And who was tested? De cousins and brodder-in-laws of de Laemmles—all deir pets and the pets of DEIR pets!

Among the actors seriously considered were stage actors Paul Muni, Ian Keith, and Joseph Schildkraut, and movie star Chester Morris. Four days after Universal secured the rights to *Dracula*, Lon Chaney died. Browning interrupted his preproduction duties to act as an honorary pallbearer.

Meanwhile, Bromfield grew tired of having his script undercut by Junior's new management policy. Box-office losses had gotten so bad that Junior was allowing no film but *Dracula* a budget higher that $225,000. After deleting a number of expensive Bromfield scenes, Universal decided to cut costs where it would not show: Bela Lugosi. According to his publicity agent, Evan Hoskins: "As he told me, it was a take-it-or-leave-it contract offering him $500 a week for a seven-week shooting schedule. Of course there was no such thing as royalties in those days, so if you didn't get it up front, you didn't get it at all. He knew there were five hungry actors waiting to get the part, so what could he do but accept the terms?" A wounded Lugosi accepted, and a grieving Browning finished the script with playwright

Garrett Fort after Bromfield walked out. Shooting began on September 29.

Browning had seen to it that Universal's economy drive did not affect *Dracula*'s art direction. Charles D. Hall provided a superb group of sets, including a ruined abbey, cozy London bedrooms, and a misty Carpathian castle hung with medieval tapestries and eighteen-foot cobwebs. Browning had instructed the art department to copy numerous elements from *London After Midnight*, even down to the armadillos roaming the castle. To photograph *Dracula*, Junior hired Karl Freund, whose portfolio included Paul Leni's *Waxworks*, F. W. Murnau's *The Last Laugh*, and Fritz Lang's *Metropolis*. The German cameraman was learning English, so a white-gloved translator accompanied him when he enthusiastically presented the art department with his sketch of Dracula's castle. Although it did not match the interiors already under construction, it was so atmospheric that a miniature was built from it and used for the establishing shot of the castle.

The first person to speak in *Dracula* was a Laemmle relative (one of seventy on the payroll), dancer-actress Carla Laemmle. The scene took place in a rocking coach traveling a bumpy mountain road in Transylvania. "I didn't even have to memorize the dialogue," Laemmle said, "because they handed me a booklet, and the dialogue was written there. I was told, 'Just read it from there: *Among the rugged peaks that frown down upon the Borgo Pass are found crumbling castles of a bygone age.*' "

Browning was shooting the film in sequence, an impractical way to work. Two weeks into shooting, he cast Edward Van Sloan (who after thirty-three weeks on Broadway had never read Stoker's book) as vampire fighter Professor Van Helsing. He also cast light comedy actor Dwight Frye as Dracula's slave Renfield, and the tremulous-voiced Helen Chandler as leading lady, Mina. He had to borrow leading man David Manners from Warner Bros. to play Mina's fiancé, John. Warners charged Universal $2,000 a week for Manners, an inequity that no doubt found its way to Lugosi's ears. Manners remembered the *Dracula* company as an unusual one, beginning with Lugosi. "He was mysterious and never really said anything to the other members of the cast except good morning when he arrived and good night when he left. He was polite, but always distant . . . I never thought he was acting, but being the odd man he was." Lugosi had an excuse for his aloofness:

> After I had been in the play for a month, I began to "take stock of myself," and I realized that for my own well-being I should make some attempt to conserve my mental and physical strength— to throw myself with less fervor into the depiction of the role. . . . But I could not do it. The role seemed to demand that I keep myself worked

After ten years of old darkhouse mysteries, audiences were unprepared for supernatural horror. A Los Angeles critic wrote: "The cat has crept, the bat has whispered, and the ghost has walked, but **DRACULA** would make the hair rise on a brass monkey. However, I wasn't really scared until some lady in the audience let out a piercing scream."

up to a fever pitch, and so I sat in my dressing room and took on, as nearly as possible, the actual attributes of the horrible vampire, Dracula.

And during all those two years I did not speak a word to any person behind the scenes during the progress of the play . . . I was under a veritable spell which I dared not break. If I stepped out of my character for even a moment, the seething menace of the terrible Count Dracula was gone from the characterization and my hold on the audience lost its force.

When Lugosi visited the home of script clerk Aileen Webster because he needed help with his English, her son, Nicholas, took a good look at him and decided that "this man was somehow slightly mad, as if he actually thought he *was* Dracula."

Browning treated Lugosi as he did the script, paring away whatever he did not have the interest or energy to improve. Lugosi thought that Browning was doing him a favor: "Tod Browning has continually had to hold me down. In my other screen roles I did not seem to have this difficulty, but I have played 'Dracula' a thousand times on the stage, and in this one role I find that I have become thoroughly settled in the technique of the stage and not of the screen." But Browning spent as much time directing armadillos as he did actors. After three weeks on the film, Junior's office told him to speed things up. As Lugosi recalled, "The studios were hell-bent on saving money—they even cut rubber erasers in half—everything that Tod Browning wanted to do was queried. Couldn't it be done cheaper? Wouldn't it be just as effective if . . .? That sort of thing. It was most dispiriting."

Browning, already distracted and losing interest, had marked the script up to the point where there was nothing left to cut. He began to delegate more and more authority. Manners recalled: "Tod Browning was always off to the side somewhere. I remember being directed by Karl Freund." Indeed, many of the film's most effective visuals (especially in the first half of the film) bespoke Freund's German Expressionist background—deliberate tracking shots, dramatic use of spotlights, innovative use of the latest in lighting technology, and deep-focus compositions that lead the viewer's eye exactly where it should go. Browning's fame as a director rested with his ability to imagine grotesque characters in weird settings, not with any ability to put the camera in the right place shot after shot. It was Freund, not Browning, who choreographed one of *Dracula*'s most celebrated sequences.

As the sun sets on the cobwebbed Transylvanian castle, the camera roams its debris-strewn basement. Dusty vermin scamper and squeak. A wolf bays in the distance. Mist crawls along the floor, directing the eye to several caskets. A male hand raises a coffin lid, and then with its fingertips senses the dank air around it. Another lid rises, and a hollow-cheeked woman with slicked-back blonde hair sits up and stares blankly around her. The camera glides past a stone staircase glistening with some foul putrescence, and reveals the black-caped figure of Count Dracula. A closeup shows his emotionless, masklike, thoroughly evil face. His eye sockets glow with an unnatural light. He is "undead."

Shooting ended on November 15, six days over schedule. An eighty-four-minute rough cut was quickly assembled for Senior. It upset him, as much for its sloppiness as for its creepiness. Browning had made too many master shots and too few cutaways. It was too slow and there were not enough closeups of Lugosi. Retakes were made on December 13 and January 2, and again they bore the stamp of Freund's German Expressionism. Haunting shots of Lugosi looking into the camera with the then still-unperfected "pin spots" shining into his eye sockets were touches that Browning could not have conceived, let alone executed. He was elbowed out of the editing room, where *Dracula* was trimmed to seventy-five minutes. Lugosi went back to the Fox Film Corporation, but not before he had fired a parting shot: "I hope never to hear of Dracula again," said the actor. "I do not intend that it shall possess me. No one knows what I suffer from this role."

Dracula premiered at the huge Roxy Theatre in New York on February 12, 1931. Universal's apprehension quickly turned to amazement. The film sold 50,000 tickets in two days, building a momentum that culminated in a $700,000 profit, the largest of the studio's 1931 releases. With the Great Depression pushing people onto the street, why would anyone pay to watch a forty-eight-year-old man come out of a casket? Browning said, "Ninety per cent of people are morbid-minded! . . . O. Henry once remarked that more people would gather to look at a dead horse in the street than would assemble to watch the finest coach pass by." Most reviewers were impressed with Lugosi's performance in this film, which they insisted on calling a "mystery."

Harold Weight, editor of *Hollywood Filmograph* magazine, summed up the country's response to *Dracula*. "Lugosi outdoes any of the performances of the undead count which we have seen him give on the stage. There are times when the force of the evil vampire seems to sweep from him beyond the confines of the screen and into the minds of the audience. His cruel smile—hypnotic glance—slow, stately tread, they make 'Dracula.'" He had less kind things to say about Browning. "Had the rest of the picture lived up to the first sequence in the ruined castle in Transylvania, *Dracula* would be acclaimed by public and critics . . . we cannot believe that the same man was responsible for both the first and latter parts of the picture."

Lugosi soon realized that he was part of a hit. He wrote a speech for a March 27 radio broadcast, in which he said that he had first read *Dracula* eighteen years earlier. "I always dreamed to create and to play the part of Dracula," he said. "I was born and reared in almost the exact location of the story, and I came to know that what is looked upon merely as a superstition of ignorant people, is really based upon facts which are literally hair-raising in their strangeness—but which are true." *Variety* did not care if vampires were true or not; it looked at the bottom line: "With *Dracula* making money at the box office for Universal, other studios are looking for horror roles." In 1930, Universal had lost $2.2 million in revenues. It could not afford to be lost in the shuffle. So Carl Laemmle Jr. announced: "As a result of the reception given *Dracula*, we're pushing plans for *Frankenstein* and *Murders in the Rue Morgue*. The stories are well under way." Lugosi assumed he would star in both of them.

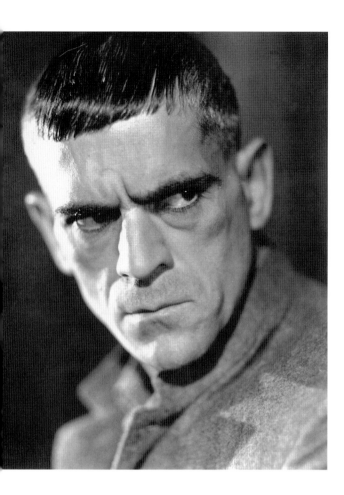

James Whale's Frankenstein

Also working at Universal Pictures in the spring of 1931 was a forty-two-year-old bit player named Boris Karloff. The thin, swarthy Englishman had endured twelve lean years in movies, waiting for a role that would lift him from the ranks of the occasionally employed. In 1926, one of his worst years, Karloff had almost given up, except for a chance meeting with a star whom he knew only from the few boxing matches that he could afford to attend.

> One day after work, as I walked through the studio gates and set off home, I heard a big car honking behind me. I thought the driver wanted me to get out of the way. I had only fifteen cents in my pocket, but I had plenty of pride and I resented the honking. I slowed down and walked calmly ahead. . . .
>
> The car slowed down, too, and a voice said: "Don't you recognize old friends, Boris?"
>
> I looked inside the car and saw Lon Chaney smiling at me. He invited me to ride with him and for more than an hour he talked to me of the motion picture industry and asked me about my ambitions. . . . One of the things Lon said was: "If you're going to act, you're going to act. Even if you have to starve, never give up. It's the only way."

Five years later, during another slow period, a casual visit to a casting office brought Karloff the role of a murderous inmate in a Los Angeles stage production of the Martin Flavin play *The Criminal Code*. Karloff at first thought that

no one had noticed him, but he was soon hired for the Columbia film version. This widely seen Howard Hawks production led to a flurry of work at Warners and Fox Film, as well as at Universal, where he reported in June for work as yet another gangster, in Christy Cabanne's *Graft*. Lunching daily in the studio commissary, Karloff may have heard talk of Universal's next horror show.

Frankenstein was born at Switzerland's Lake Geneva in the stormy summer of 1816. It was there that literary titans Lord Byron and Percy Shelley whiled away the hours with Byron's assistant, Dr. John Polidori, and with Shelley's mistress, Mary Wollstonecraft. Polidori's preoccupation with a German book called *Phantasmagoriana* led to a contest. Who could concoct the scariest ghost story? Byron, Shelley, and Polidori soon lost interest in the contest. Only nineteen-year-old Mary persevered, urged on by a vision. She later wrote: "I saw—with shut eyes, but acute mental vision—I saw the pale student of unhallowed arts kneeling beside the thing he had put together. I saw the hideous phantasm of a man stretched out, and then, on the working of some powerful engine, show signs of life, and stir with an uneasy, half vital motion." Within two years, the woman later known as Mary Shelley published a three-volume work titled *Frankenstein, or, the Modern Prometheus.*

In February 1930, Hamilton Deane made a hit of *Frankenstein* at The Little Theatre in London's West End, acting in an adaptation written by former theatrical prodigy Peggy Webling. Before long, Horace Liveright and John Balderston had gotten their hands on the property. Liveright fell by the wayside, but when *Dracula* became a successful film, Balderston had *Frankenstein* primed for purchase. Junior Laemmle asked his father. "I don't believe in horror pictures," answered Carl Laemmle Sr. "It's morbid. None of our officers are for it. People don't want that sort of thing."

"Yes, they do, Pop," retorted Junior. "They *do* want that sort of thing. Just give me a chance and I'll show you."

While *Dracula* continued to play to packed houses, the Depression worsened. The film's profits were not enough to put Universal in the black. In March, the Laemmles had to lay off 1,500 employees. In April, Junior purchased the rights to *Frankenstein* from Balderston, Deane, and Webling for $20,000 (and one percentage point of the gross), half of what *Dracula*'s rights had cost.

Junior had already assigned story editor Richard Schayer to write a *Frankenstein* scenario featuring Bela Lugosi as the monster. When French director Robert Florey importuned Schayer for work, Schayer dropped the project in his lap, and then brought Florey to read his treatment to Junior. As Florey recounted it:

> Junior listened impatiently, playing with the carnation in his lapel, to my first two lines, before talking to some girl for fifteen minutes on the phone, then going out for half an hour, returning to say, "Well, go on."
>
> As I was saying, "The monster—" he interrupted me with "What monster?" and then proceeded to place a bet on a race.

Nonetheless, Florey nabbed a contract to write and direct one film. He assumed that it would be *Frankenstein*.

In 1931 Boris Karloff barely had a film career. "At forty-two," he recalled, "I was an obscure actor playing obscure parts." A Los Angeles stage play changed that. **THE CRIMINAL CODE** gave Karloff a showy part as a vengeful convict. Hollywood took a second look at this unique face and cast him in the film version. It was not long before something bigger beckoned.

Schayer assigned *Dracula* scenarist Garrett Fort, who knew the Webling-Balderston play, to write dialogue for Florey, whose English was not good. Fort and Florey agreed that the monster should be strong, stupid, mute, and evil. Art director Charles D. Hall prepared a series of drawings to illustrate the screenplay, which Fort completed in June. Universal was about to go broke, so the Laemmles closed the studio for a month and went to New York to seek help.

Florey, meanwhile, got permission to shoot a test reel of *Frankenstein* sequences, including the creation of Frankenstein's Monster. On a set left over from *Dracula*, the director spent seventeen hours with cameraman Paul Ivano, three *Dracula* alumni (Lugosi, Edward Van Sloan, and Dwight Frye), and two minor contract players, trying to make a *Frankenstein* sampler. Lugosi was uncooperative, insisting on his own makeup. According to Van Sloan, "His head was about four times normal size, with a broad wig on it. He had a polished, claylike skin and looked more like something out of *Babes in Toyland*!" Lugosi expressed disdain for this speechless role, exclaiming to Florey that he "was not going to be a grunting, babbling idiot for anybody and that any tall extra could be the Monster." Florey and Ivano ignored him, concentrating on angles and lighting. Ivano recalled the first screening: "These trials were so successful, so beautiful from the artistic and photographic point of view, that all the directors of the studio wanted to make the film."

Junior Laemmle liked Florey's test, but he liked a new director's work even better. James Whale was just completing work on a film of Robert Sherwood's play *Waterloo Bridge*. The forty-two-year-old British director had come to Universal from tiny Tiffany Studios, where he had turned his stage success, *Journey's End*, into a hit film. The tall, sleek Whale had also been an actor on the London stage and had a knack for flavoring grim drama with mordant humor. What also appealed to Junior Laemmle was that Whale was bringing *Waterloo Bridge* to an early, under-budget completion. In gratitude, Laemmle offered Whale his pick of thirty projects. Having seen the Florey test, Whale did not take *Frankenstein* seriously. "At first I thought it was a gag," said Whale, "but *Frankenstein*, after all, is a great classic of literature, and I soon became absorbed in its possibilities. I decided I'd try to do something with it to top all thrillers." Laemmle promptly assigned Whale to direct *Frankenstein*. Florey, still assuming that it was his, got a surprise. "I was offered a contract to direct a feature based on Poe's 'Murders in the Rue Morgue,'" remembered Florey. "Then I heard about *Frankenstein* being prepared by Whale, but I couldn't do a thing about it." When he looked at his contract again, he realized that he had not read it carefully. It did not say that he would direct the film he had written—just *a* film.

As Whale worked with Fort, he watched *The Golem*, *The Cabinet of Dr. Caligari*, and *Metropolis* "to get some ideas" from German Expressionism. He also asked his housemate, Paramount associate producer David Lewis, to read the novel. Lewis said he felt "sorry for the goddamn monster." To make the character sympathetic had not occurred to Whale. This was a wholly new interpretation. He did not think that Lugosi would engender sympathy, so Laemmle shunted the actor to Florey's project while Whale

continued to refine the Monster. On August 12, Junior Laemmle approved the new script. Whale was now working with production designer Herman Rosse, who changed Hall's chrome Art Deco laboratory to the airy wood-and-stone interior of an abandoned watchtower. Its imposing electrical fittings and devices, designed by studio electrician Kenneth Strickfaden, looked like the inside of a radio set. Said Whale: "I want the picture to be a very modern, materialistic treatment of this medieval story—something of 'Doctor Caligari,' something of Edgar Allan Poe, and, of course a good deal of us."

Junior Laemmle wanted Leslie Howard to portray Henry Frankenstein, the "pale student of unhallowed arts," but Whale preferred the English actor Colin Clive, whom he had directed in both the stage and screen versions of *Journey's End*. Clive's portrayal of Captain Stanhope, a highly principled officer on the verge of a breakdown, made him an ideal choice for the highly strung scientist. Whale wrote to Clive: "Frankenstein's nerves are all to pieces. He is a very strong, extremely dominant personality, sometimes quite strange and queer, sometimes very soft, sympathetic, and decidedly romantic." All that remained was to cast the centerpiece of this thriller. The starting date, twice postponed, could not be delayed much longer. "Jimmy was absolutely bewildered," said Lewis, "although I didn't realize they needed a monster as badly as they did until he told me one day. I had seen Boris Karloff in *The Criminal Code* and he was *so* good." Lewis suggested Karloff to Whale, who made a point of locating this minor player. He found him in the commissary.

"I was having lunch," said Karloff, "and James Whale sent either the first assistant or maybe it was his secretary over to me, and asked me to join him in a cup of coffee after lunch." Whale made small talk about the problems of

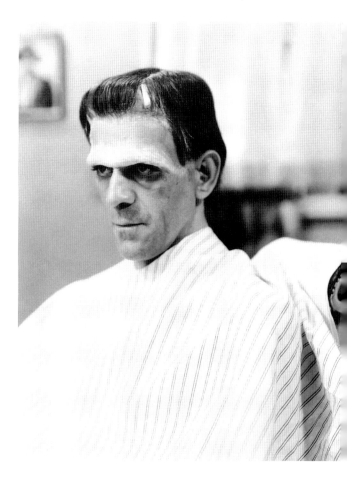

Karloff caught the attention of Universal Pictures, and he soon found himself in Lon Chaney's old dressing room, submitting to makeup tests for a strange new role.

British actors in the film capital. Then he came to the point. "Your face has startling possibilities." Karloff was taken aback when Whale asked him to make a test.

"What for?" Karloff asked.

"For a damned awful monster!" Whale said.

Karloff was happy at the prospect of more work. "Of course I was delighted, because it meant another job, if I was able to land it. Actually that's all it meant to me. At the same time I felt rather hurt, because at the time I had on very good straight makeup and my best suit—and he wanted to test me for a monster!"

Six studio artists had already submitted concept sketches of the monster, ranging from Neanderthal to robotic. To prepare Karloff's test, Whale now tried his own hand. "I made drawings of his head," the director said, "and added sharp, bony ridges where I imagined his skull might have been joined. His physique was weaker than I could wish, but that queer, penetrating personality of his I felt was more important than his shape, which could easily be altered." The artist charged with this alteration was a Greek immigrant and former Chicago semi-pro shortstop named Jack Pierce, head of Universal's makeup department. Behind the door of a bungalow designated Dressing Room Number Five, Lon Chaney's former makeup room, Pierce labored to create something extraordinary. All he said to Karloff was, "This is going to be a big thing."

Karloff immediately began research. "Of course I rushed out and bought the book," said Karloff. "But Mary Shelley's description of the Monster ['yellow skin barely covered the work of muscles and arteries beneath'] would have been impossible to duplicate, so we had to devise our own approach." Pierce had assembled his own reference library. "I studied every operation that would be necessary to create such a body from 'spare parts,'" he said. "I studied the physical effect of each, and strove to reproduce them in Mr. Karloff's final character. Every line, every scar, every peculiarity of contour had to be just so for medical reasons." Pierce needed time to achieve these effects, and, though Whale was anxious, Karloff knew that Pierce "was in a position to stall the test. So at the end of a day's work on *Graft* I would stay, and he would stay, and nightly he worked on the makeup until we felt it was ready."

This work continued for three weeks, with Karloff as both subject and collaborator. "We had to surmise," said Karloff, "that brain after brain had been tried in that poor skull, inserted and taken out again." Pierce added:

> There are six ways a surgeon can cut the skull in order to take out or put in a brain. I figured that Frankenstein, who was a scientist but no practicing surgeon, would take the simplest surgical way. He would cut the top of the skull off straight across like a potlid, hinge it, pop the brain in, then clamp it on tight. That is the reason I decided to make the monster's head square and flat like a shoe box and dig that big scar across his forehead with the clamps holding it together.

Using layers of cheesecloth and collodion, Pierce built up Karloff's forehead without a visible line of demarcation.

He also had Karloff remove a partial bridge he wore, which contributed to a sunken, cadaverous look. Blue-green greasepaint covered his face. Studying himself in the mirror, Karloff saw something wrong. "We had the problem that if your eyes were alive and normal—and, I hope, intelligent—it would simply destroy the makeup and it would destroy the illusion. And that's why we used putty over the eyes—to distort them and to veil them a little bit, so they wouldn't be too clear and too sharp." The monster's stance and gait would be equally telling.

Pierce said: "The Egyptians used to bind some criminals hand and foot and bury them alive. When their blood turned to water after death, it flowed into their extremities, stretched their arms to gorilla length, and swelled their hands, feet, and faces to abnormal proportions." Since the Monster was supposed to be made from the corpses of hanged criminals, Pierce put black shoe polish on Karloff's fingernails, shortened the sleeves on his coat, padded it with a quilted undersuit, put steel struts on his legs, and outfitted him with asphalt spreader's boots. Lastly, there were metal studs on his neck, "inlets for electricity—plugs such as we use for lamps or flatirons. Remember," said Pierce, "the monster is an electrical gadget. Lightning is his life force." When Whale saw the test, he was, in Karloff's words, "overjoyed."

Frankenstein went into production on August 24. Karloff's initiation was the birth of the Monster, a display of both literal and cinematic pyrotechnics. "The scene where the monster was created, amid booming thunder and flashing lightning, made me as uneasy as anyone," he recalled. "For while I lay half-naked and strapped to Doctor Frankenstein's table, I could see directly above me the special-effects men brandishing the white-hot scissorslike carbons that made the lightning. I hoped that no one up there had butterfingers."

Karloff began to arrive at 4:00 A.M. for his four-hour makeup sessions. According to Pierce's assistant, "Each day he'd make a new head and then keep it so he could copy it. It wasn't exactly the same each time because it was custom-made—it wasn't done with prosthetics. He despised prosthetics." By the time Karloff walked to the soundstage, his head covered with a white towel, his Chaney-like suffering had begun. The entire costume weighed forty-eight pounds, and September 1931 in the San Fernando Valley was seasonally hot. "After an hour's work I would be sopping wet. I'd have to change into a spare undersuit, often still damp from the previous round. So I felt, most of the time, as if I were wearing a clammy shroud myself."

September 28 was a trying day. Karloff recalled: "I got into the makeup shop at half past three in the morning to be ready to go out on location and we went out and we worked in the hot sun on the edge of the lake for the scene with the little girl." The company stayed longer at Lake Sherwood than expected because Karloff argued with Whale about the necessity of showing the Monster drown a child. Whale overruled his objections. They returned to the studio, ate dinner, and then went onto the back lot to shoot still more scenes. Karloff labored until five in the morning. He had worn his makeup and costume for over twenty-five hours. Having already lost ten pounds and strained his back, Karloff asked the Academy of Motion Picture Arts and

Sciences to intervene; after that, his longest day was sixteen hours.

Karloff could not resist looking at the first footage. Edward Van Sloan recalled: "When he saw the rushes of the picture, he mumbled unhappily to me that the film would ruin his career. But I told him, 'Not so, Boris, not so! You're *made!*'" His misgivings overcome, Karloff found Whale's direction lucid and thorough. Actress Mae Clarke, playing Henry Frankenstein's fiancée, observed: "He and Boris got on well together after the first couple of scenes were done, and they knew they had something. They were so at ease they would just whisper and agree. I remember all the gestures the Monster did were Whale's." Karloff said:

> Whale and I both saw the character as an innocent one. Within the heavy restrictions of my makeup, I tried to play it that way. This was a pathetic creature who, like us all, had neither wish nor say in his creation, and certainly did not wish upon itself the hideous image which automatically terrified humans it tried to befriend. The most heart-rending aspect of the creature's life, for us, was his ultimate desertion by his creator. It was as though man, in his blundering, searching attempts to improve himself, was to find himself deserted by his God.

Indicative of Whale's skill was his handling of the Monster's first appearance. He had Karloff enter the room backward, and awkwardly, as befit a creature only days old. Then, as Karloff turned toward the camera, Whale cut from a wide shot to a medium closeup. Before the viewer could react to the frightening makeup, he cut to a closer shot, accomplished with a longer lens. Then, for maximum shock effect, he cut to a tight closeup made with a telephoto lens. This technique, known as "cutting on axis," made Karloff's entrance the most frightening scene in *Frankenstein.*

At the film's preview in Santa Barbara, patrons walked out, huddled in the lobby, but finally returned. Its December opening night in New York saw sellout crowds ignoring a rainstorm in order to see what the newspapers were now calling the "latest horror film." With *Dracula* still playing countrywide and *Frankenstein* a phenomenal hit, Universal could breathe more easily. The studio ended the year with a $400,000 profit.

A Cycle Spawned

By the end of 1931, with the record-breaking duo of *Dracula* and *Frankenstein*, Universal Pictures appeared to have a franchise. The term *horror film* had appeared as early as April, when *Variety* announced "U Has Horror Cycle All to Self." Other studios had films with similar themes—Paramount's *Murder by the Clock* and Warner Bros.' *Svengali*—and even though they lacked the supernatural elements of the Universal films, they advanced the cycle. In early December, Colonel Jason Joy of the Studio Relations Committee (SRC) was concerned that these films were causing local censor boards to cut expensive release prints to shreds, exactly what his department was supposed to prevent. He wrote to Will Hays, head of the Motion Picture

Producers and Distributors Association, asking: "Is this the beginning of a cycle that ought to be retarded or killed?" The New Year's Eve premiere of Paramount's *Dr. Jekyll and Mr. Hyde* confirmed the cycle, if not the franchise.

To direct its first real horror film, Paramount chose Rouben Mamoulian, the Russian-Armenian director whose *Applause* and *City Streets* had taught Hollywood how to use sound creatively. Robert Louis Stevenson's 1886 novella, *The Strange Case of Dr. Jekyll and Mr. Hyde*, would be the showcase for his bravura effects. Stevenson had written: "All human beings, as we meet them, are commingled out of good and evil. And Edward Hyde, alone in the ranks of mankind, was pure evil." John Barrymore's masterly performance eleven years earlier, in which he effected the transformation from Jekyll to Hyde without makeup or camera tricks, warranted an encore. Paramount offered Barrymore $25,000, but he wanted more, so producer B. P. Schulberg turned to Irving Pichel, who had played a violent halfwit that year in *Murder by the Clock*. Mamoulian refused Pichel, saying that he could certainly look like Hyde but could never pass as Jekyll; the director wanted to change Jekyll from the middle-aged man of the novel to a young leading man. There was a Paramount contractee known for imitating Barrymore. Mamoulian asked for Fredric March.

"You're crazy!" said Schulberg. "Fredric March is a comedian!"

This was not true, and Mamoulian had no trouble telling Schulberg so. The producer gave in. Mamoulian saw in March not only the ability to transform himself into another character, but also the sexual magnetism necessary to convey a new concept of the novel. Working with screenwriters Samuel Hoffenstein and Percy Heath, Mamoulian had turned the book's conflict between good and evil into a struggle between Victorian repression and sexual expression. It was widely known that March, after playing a sensitive scene on a Paramount soundstage, would become a singleminded seducer, luring a starlet into his dressing room. Mamoulian invested the film with March's sexual energy but put it into a pressure cooker. "I wanted a replica of our ancestor," the director explained, "the Neanderthal man that we once were, to show the struggle of modern man with his primitive instincts."

The doorway between the modern Jekyll and the primitive Hyde was a potion. To show its transformative effects was a challenge even for Mamoulian. Paramount cofounder Jesse Lasky sat in with March as Mamoulian explained that he was going to use "subjective camera" to make the audience experience the transformation. March waited until Mamoulian was out of earshot and asked Lasky what that meant. Lasky snapped at him: "My God, if you don't know what subjective photography is, what are you doing in this business?"

"Well, what is it?"

"How the hell do I know?" Lasky sputtered.

Subjective camera, also known as first-person camera, is the use of the camera in place of a character in the film. Mamoulian used it in the scene in which Jekyll first drinks the potion, undergoes a violent transformation, and then sees himself in the mirror for the first time with his evil side unbound, as Mr. Hyde. "I wanted to put the audience into

Jekyll's shoes," he explained, "and make them feel a little sharper this vertigo that Jekyll goes through." To show this primeval release, Mamoulian evoked the drunken phenomenon of the dizzily spinning room. "I had the camera revolve around upon its axis, and all four walls of the set were lit completely. This had never been done on the screen. The cameraman had to be tied to the top of the camera. He had to lean down and control the focus from up there." Fortunately, the sound blimp on the Paramount camera was the largest in Hollywood and the operator was as small as a jockey.

And what would Dr. Jekyll hear during the transformation, other than the echoing voices of the other characters, chiding him for his indecency? "I felt that the sound elements here had to be as unreal as the visual elements," said Mamoulian, who first recorded drums in a heartbeat cadence, and then tried running up and down a staircase and recording his own heart. It worked. In addition, he recorded a gong, then rerecorded it backwards, and even painted on the soundtrack. The finished sequence, of course, needed the payoff of a transformed face.

Cameraman Karl Struss devised a system whereby the first series of changes in March's face would occur without any dissolves or optically printed effects. Struss said: "The Hyde makeup was [applied to March's face] in red and didn't show at all when the red filter was on the lens, but when the filter was moved very slowly down to the green, Mr. Hyde appeared." Then the camera went into its mad montage, ending with a tracking shot to a mirror, where Hyde's face is revealed for the first time, staring back at the camera—and the audience. A gallant young man has devolved into a snorting brute.

Mr. Hyde's face was created by makeup artist Wally Westmore, who had to conceive six progressively grotesque makeups. After consulting with Mamoulian, he made a plaster mold of March's face, onto which he could apply bestial features with clay. He brought the mold to a dentist, Dr. Charles Pincus, who, after several tries, fashioned porcelain fangs that would allow March to speak

clearly. Then it was back to the studio for a four-hour application of makeup. This went on for six weeks, with the makeup graphically showing Hyde's degeneration. When March won the 1931–32 Academy Award for Best Actor, he said: "Wally [Westmore], whom I consider a great artist, is responsible for the greater measure of my success." The success was not only his. Every review praised Mamoulian and Struss's cinematic pyrotechnics. *Dr. Jekyll and Mr. Hyde* made the *New York Times*'s "Ten Best" list and became one of Paramount's top-grossing films of 1932.

The next entry in the horror cycle came from Universal Pictures. *Murders in the Rue Morgue*, released in February 1932, was the project to which Robert Florey was shunted after his unappreciated work on *Frankenstein*. Now he found himself with a smaller budget and the same difficult actor, Bela Lugosi, for whom there was no role in the Edgar Allan Poe short story. To remedy that problem, Florey borrowed the name "Mirakle" from composer Jacques Offenbach and created the character of a sideshow charlatan to manage the murderous ape of the original tale. Allied with cameraman Karl Freund, Florey tried to turn the French story into a German Expressionist piece. It lost much in translation, weakened as much by Florey's limitations as a director as it was by the studio's insistence on haste and economy. Florey always prepared his projects with detailed drawings and notes, and this film was no exception, with foggy street scenes, sinuous tracking shots through a crowded sideshow, and the camera's dizzying ride on a swing. Unfortunately, the horror element was given insufficient play. Only at the very end of the film, after too much time has been spent on unfunny comedy and unconvincing romance, is the ape given his spotlight. Critics called *Murders in the Rue Morgue* a weak follow-up to Universal's horror templates.

While Universal wasted James Whale and Boris Karloff on minor projects such as *Impatient Maiden* and *Night World*, M-G-M's Irving Thalberg hopped on the horror cycle, luring Tod Browning back to the studio to film a weird C. A. Robbins novel, *Spurs*. Thalberg had bought the property for Browning years earlier, but not until he saw what *Dracula* had done for the Laemmles did he have a squad of writers transform *Spurs* into *Freaks*. This sideshow story of gross deformity, unrequited love, and perverted vengeance was perfect for Browning. Its main characters were sideshow "freaks": Siamese twins, a bearded lady, and pinheads, among others. There was a limit to what makeup could accomplish, so Thalberg came up with the idea of casting real-life sideshow veterans. A typically thorough M-G-M casting call produced a full cast, and although they were not allowed to eat in the studio commissary (after then-contract writer F. Scott Fitzgerald regurgitated his lunch), Browning saw to it that the freaks were housed, photographed, and treated like featured players.

Even though M-G-M was one of the few studios still showing a profit in the midst of the Depression, a number of executives began to question Thalberg's judgment. Director Jack Conway defended him: "Irving's right so often he's earned the right to be wrong." And so the filming commenced. "There was a certain glee in the way Tod Browning went about making this picture," recalled screenwriter Budd Schulberg, "that made us think of him as Count Dracula on Stage Ten. Those freaks were all over the set and it sent shivers through us to look at them. But he enjoyed it too much." Film editor Basil Wrangell said: "I think he got a bang out of seeing these crippled characters." Indeed, Browning spent more time with them than he did with the "normal" cast members.

The plot of *Freaks* had a vain, greedy trapeze star, Cleopatra (Olga Baclanova), marrying the sideshow midget, Hans (Harry Earles), then poisoning him so that she and her lover, Hercules (Henry Victor), can abscond with Hans's savings. Baclanova, herself a waning star of silent films, had to adapt to the self-sufficient world of the freaks. "It was very, very difficult the first time," she recalled. "Every night I felt that I am sick. Because I couldn't look at them. And then I was so sorry for them . . . . It hurt me like a human being. How lucky I was. But after that, I started to get used to them." Ultimately, Baclanova became friendly with a number of the freaks, especially the hermaphrodite Josephine Joseph and the legless Johnny Eck, who developed a crush on her. Tiny Harry Earles grasped the implications of the script. "And I make him jump on my lap, and I treat him like a baby," said Baclanova. "But always he say to me, 'You be surprised!'" It was this sort of interplay that fueled Browning's imagination, and he made *Freaks* a catalogue of shocks, with scene after scene of sights and situations for which American filmgoers were totally unprepared.

In one scene, an apparently naked clown (Wallace Ford) is sitting in an outdoor bathtub, having a conversation with a young woman (Leila Hyams) who keeps looking into the tub. Only after the clown climbs out from under the tub is it made evident that he is wearing pants and that the tub is a circus prop. With such ambiguous scenes, Browning creates a feeling of unease—but his scenes with the freaks are designed to shock. An armless and legless black man (Prince Randian) carries on a conversation while lighting a match and propelling a cigarette into his mouth. A wild-eyed pinhead speaks an unintelligible language. Josephine Joseph displays a yen for a male character, who is understandably bewildered. The gulf between "freaks" and "nor-

mals" is unforgettably shown in the wedding-party scene, in which Cleopatra is honored with an initiation ceremony. The freaks chant: "One of us! We accept you! We accept you!" Revolted, Cleopatra throws the ceremonial wine into the face of a midget and screams: "Dirty! Slimy! *Freaks*!"

For the climax, Browning has the freaks punish Hercules and Cleopatra for attempting to murder Hans. While lightning, thunder, and rain turn dusty country roads into rippling pools of mud, a dwarf sends a knife flying into Hercules. He screams in pain, and falls. Then he sees his pursuers. Seven freaks are crawling under a circus wagon, coming toward him, their usually placid faces now grim with anger. Terrified, the wounded man pushes himself along the ground. A pinhead, her dress smeared with mud, crawls from under the wagon, holding a knife, her tiny eyes fixed in a hateful stare. Two dwarfs march forward, splashing water with their feet as they brandish switchblade knives. A dark thing in a mud-stained print dress, its face covered with hair, lurches along. The armless, legless man slithers through the mud, almost swimming in it, a knife clenched in his teeth. Now Cleopatra runs screaming through the night. She stops at a tree. As lightning flashes, four freaks run toward her, bounding over fallen tree branches. They finally catch up with her.

In this scene, Browning created horror without precedent; his achievement was a momentary one. *Freaks* overwhelmed its first preview audience. Most of them hurried from the theater before this scene even played. The initial ninety-minute version showed the results of the freaks' revenge: Hercules a fat, castrated freak, and Cleopatra a mutilated "chicken-woman." After the preview, Thalberg cut the film by thirty minutes (never explaining what happened to Hercules) and filmed transitional scenes to fill some gaps. Even at this length, *Freaks* provoked controversy. Angry letters came from critics, clubwomen, and outraged citizens, all warning that M-G-M was exposing the film industry to the threat of federal censorship. A review in *Harrison's Reports* expressed the feeling of most: "Not even the most morbidly inclined could possibly find this picture to their liking. Saying that it is horrible is putting it mildly; it is revolting to the extent of turning one's stomach, and only an iron constitution could withstand its effects." The film opened in Los Angeles and Washington, D.C., and then abruptly closed two weeks later. It was banned by the San Francisco and Atlanta censor boards, yet it did well in Boston, Cincinnati, and Omaha. M-G-M had never seen such a weird attendance pattern, and, after losing $164,000, pulled the film from circulation, an unheard-of retreat for the most powerful studio in Hollywood.

The second most prosperous studio at the beginning of 1932 was the Fox Film Corporation, and its foray into horror was fittingly extravagant. William Cameron Menzies's *Chandu the Magician* starred Edmund Lowe as a heroic yogi trying to save the world from Roxor, a sinister megalomaniac. As Roxor, Bela Lugosi is an imposing presence, threatening, raving, and kidnapping in order to get his hands on a death-ray machine. "That lever is my scepter," he declares. "All that live will know me as master and tremble at my word!" Before he can pull the lever and melt Paris or London, Chandu bests him in a battle of wills that curiously omits any closeups of Lugosi's superior staring power.

Hal Phyfe made this portrait of Bela Lugosi as Roxor to publicize **CHANDU THE MAGICIAN**. Whether on the set or in the portrait gallery, Lugosi gave his all.

Variety did not take kindly to such lapses of logic. "Chandu carries the fantastic, the inconsistent, and the ludicrous to the greatest lengths yet achieved by the screen. Were it to be taken seriously, there'd be no enjoyment for anyone. If it's accepted strictly as hoke growing out of the horror cycle, it's not so bad, but it's still hoke."

Lugosi did better with *White Zombie*, a film made on such a small budget that it had to shoot at night. It was produced and directed by Edward and Victor Halperin, independent producers who rented space at larger studios and released their product through United Artists. *White Zombie* starred Lugosi as "Murder" Legendre, master of the zombies, dead folk who are magically resurrected to do nighttime slave labor in the cane fields of Haiti. This time, Lugosi was given enough screen time and closeups to create a chilling characterization. His famous stare was better photographed than it had been by Karl Freund in *Dracula*. Instead of trying to match the angle and intensity of two tiny spotlights, cameraman Arthur Martinelli, according to his nephew, Enzo, "just took a cardboard and cut two holes in it about as wide apart as Lugosi's eyes, placed it in front of Lugosi's face and put a light through it." Lugosi's weirdly glowing eyes were scary, but he was absent from the film's most frightening moment.

In the mill where the zombies deliver their nightly harvest, there is a silent, trancelike parade of unseeing, unfeeling zombies. As they carry loads of cane through the building, the only sound is the ominous grinding of the cane shredder. Zombie after zombie walks up to the shredder and drops cane into the maw of the machine, where razor-sharp blades slice it into bits. One zombie has a very heavy load of cane. He stumbles as he drops it in. Unable to regain his balance, he falls into the shredder. There is no scream, only the drone of a machine shredding dead flesh.

White Zombie did well at the box office, prompting Universal to slate a Karloff feature for Halloween. James Whale wanted to avoid a Browning-like label of horror director, but he could not resist the pleasure of adapting

J. B. Priestley's *Benighted,* a novel that spoke to his own ironic sensibilities. *Benighted* was a wry distillation of all the old dark-house stories that had come before, with the obligatory shabby mansion, mysterious occupants, innocent visitors, whispered secrets, booming thunderstorms, and violent climax. Whale had enjoyed Paul Leni's *The Cat and the Canary,* and he now conceived, with screenwriter Benn Levy, a film in which the unwelcome guests would have to confront not only unseen chills but also the unsavory pasts of the other characters.

Renamed *The Old Dark House,* the film presents Karloff as Morgan, the scarred, mute butler of the eccentric Femm family. Horace Femm (Ernest Thesiger) is an effeminate, cadaverous-looking man who uses "the vanity of age" as an excuse not to confront the drunk, rampaging Morgan. His 102-year-old father, Roderick Femm (John Dudgeon), is secluded in a paneled bedroom high in the mansion. His sister, Rebecca Femm (Eva Moore), is a squat, gruff zealot who reluctantly gives shelter to three storm-whipped travelers, one of whom, Margaret (Gloria Stuart), needs to change her wet clothes in Rebecca's bedroom. In Priestley's novel, the bizarre nature of the encounter between the fanatical hag and the elegant lady is described: "Somehow she felt as if the broad road of life were rapidly narrowing to a glittering wire." Whale adapted this scene with deft assurance.

Rebecca sits on the bed, watching Margaret disrobe and muttering:

> My sister Rachel had this room once. She died when she was twenty-one. She was a wicked one—handsome and wild as a hawk. All the young men used to follow her about, with her red lips and her big eyes and her white neck. But that didn't save her. She fell off her horse—hunting—and hurt her spine. On this bed she lay, month after month. Many's the time I sat here, listening to her screaming. She used to cry out to me to kill her. I'd tell her to turn to the Lord. But she didn't. She was godless to the end.

Whale accentuates Rebecca's increasingly deranged speech with a series of closeups shot through a warped mirror, effectively conveying her distorted mentality. "With James," Stuart later said, "every line, every single movement, your whole approach to the character was very meticulously discussed. He was the most prepared director I ever worked for." The care with which Whale mounted *The Old Dark House* went unappreciated. The secret locked in the room at the top of the stairs turns out to be Roderick and Rebecca's brother, Saul (Brember Wills), who is crazy and dangerous, but no monster. After *Frankenstein,* the public expected more than a slight, balding pyromaniac. After all, this was Halloween, and the ads had promised chills! Where was the monster? Before 1932 ended, Hollywood would give its customers more than enough monsters.

In **THE OLD DARK HOUSE**, Boris Karloff's second film with James Whale, the actor portrayed "an uncivilized brute." Halloween audiences expecting a monster were disappointed.

right
In M-G-M's 1932 **FREAKS**, Olga Baclanova marries Harry Earles. While posing on Baclanova's lap for these photographs, Earles made provocative remarks.

below
Tod Browning poses with the cast of **FREAKS**, the only M-G-M film ever to be pulled from release before completing its domestic engagements.

CHAPTER 3
Pre-Code Horrors

Madness Reigns

In early 1932 Hollywood studios took stock of the horror cycle. Each company conceded that while critics at *Film Daily*, *Variety*, and the *New York Times* could barely conceal their condescension, Universal had made millions from *Dracula* and *Frankenstein*, and Paramount had done almost as well with *Dr. Jekyll and Mr. Hyde*. In the midst of an economic depression, as unemployment figures threatened to claim one-third of a nation, citizens were plunking down dimes to be frightened—and titillated. Films that flouted the two-year-old Production Code, sexy sagas such as *Red-Headed Woman*, *No Man of Her Own*, and *Call Her Savage*, competed with horror films for the grandstanding censure of women's clubs, clergymen, and politicians, and all these films made money. Even so, RKO, Paramount, and the Fox Film Corporation were either in receivership or headed there by the end of the year. Some studios closed down for weeks at a time, but while they were open, they took the horror cycle in a new direction. Supernatural monsters were momentarily put on the shelf. In their place were brilliant madmen who mixed sex and horror in gleaming beakers.

A big-budget entry in the "mad horror" cycle was *The Mask of Fu Manchu*, in which Boris Karloff got the M-G-M star treatment. Like Ethel Barrymore, who had come to the studio in a blaze of publicity for *Rasputin and the Empress*, Karloff shot for two weeks and then saw all his work thrown out when Irving Thalberg decided that director Charles Vidor was inept. When filming resumed, Karloff was asked to learn his lines for the day from a freshly typed script, which was handed to him as he sat in the makeup chair. "This is absolute nonsense," he said. "I can't learn this in time to do it." He did not have to because on his way to the soundstage he was given an entirely different set of pages. The *New York Times* reported that several writers (including John Willard, playwright of *The Cat and the Canary*) had "been formed into a shock-troop to get something filmable out in a hurry."

Director Charles Brabin, who had been fired from *Rasputin* for his lack of speed, visualized the scientist Fu Manchu as an "Oriental super brain," but writers trying to keep a day ahead of shooting lost the complexity of Sax Rohmer's original character. Fu Manchu became a racist megalomaniac who, assisted by his daughter (Myrna Loy), drugs, tortures, dismembers, and murders the British archaeologists who stand between him and the tomb of Genghis Khan. In one scene, Loy would have to whip a half-naked young archaeologist (Charles Starrett). "Say, this is obscene," she complained to the film's supervisor, Hunt Stromberg. Jason Joy of the SRC recognized the Freudian import of the scene, and it was cut so that Loy merely supervised the sadistic exercise. The rest of the film was sensationalistic in the extreme. Loy later wrote: "Boris and I brought some feeling to those comic-book characters. Boris was a fine actor, a professional who never condescended to his often unworthy material."

Karloff's first speaking role in a horror film presented a problem. "I could not use any of the many types of false teeth which were such potent parts of disguises in silent days," said Karloff. "Lon Chaney once told me speech had made impossible about fifty of his best makeup devices. In *Fu Manchu*, [makeup artist Cecil Holland] used some thin shell teeth that covered only the front of the natural teeth." Adopting the "snake-like lisp" of Rohmer's character, Karloff speaks such provocative dialogue as: "You accursed son of a white dog . . . I will wipe out your whole accursed white race . . . just before I dispatch you to your cold, saintly Christian paradise!" Karloff's lines were more than matched by the archaeologists' jingoism. The only censorship the film suffered was the temporary elimination of lines such as "You hideous yellow monster!" so that the Chinese consul would approve the film's release. Critics accurately predicted the film's appeal to matinee youngsters, but

In the 1970s, Merian Cooper said of the film he produced: "**KING KONG** was never intended to be anything but the best damned adventure picture ever made. Which it is. And that's *all* it is."

above
A production still shows Claude Rains with his bandages partially removed for the unmasking scene in James Whale's 1933 **THE INVISIBLE MAN**. Also visible are his black velvet underpinnings and his breathing hose. Rains said to Whale: "I want to do a little more. I thought at least I could try to express something with my eyes." Whale replied: "But Claude, old fellow, what are you going to do it with? You haven't any face."

Variety complained that Karloff "makes the doctor a monster instead of the cunning, shrewd fellow that he usually is." More profitable than most films in the grim fall of 1932, *The Mask of Fu Manchu* was also (with *Chandu the Magician*) the most lavishly produced of the cycle thus far.

Warner Bros., which had produced the first all-talking horror film, now one-upped M-G-M by making a full-color horror film. Two-color Technicolor was a red-and-green process typically used to enhance the closing reel of a musical. Musicals had gone out of vogue, but Technicolor owed the studio two more films, so producer Hal Wallis found a mystery play, *Doctor X*, to fit its limited color spectrum. Heeding the dictates of Technicolor adviser Natalie Kalmus, art director Anton Grot colored his sets in muted browns and grays, while designing a laboratory set that suggested "a bird of prey about to swoop down upon its victim." Production head Darryl F. Zanuck and director Michael Curtiz reframed the play as a newspaperman's investigation of a "moon killer" to give it the topical urgency for which Warners was known. They cast the fast-talking Lee Tracy as the reporter, Columbia player Fay Wray as a no-nonsense ingenue, and stage star Lionel Atwill as Dr. Xavier. Speaking so rapidly that he almost spat out his words, narrowing his eyes, and suddenly stopping to punc-

tuate his speech with a chilling half-smile, Atwill ensured his future in horror films. Another character was revealed as the killer, causing capacity audiences to scream when he applied "synthetic flesh" to himself, but Atwill stayed in the public's mind. Fay Wray also made an impression on horror fans, who did not know that, while working on *Doctor X*, she had been making tests at RKO for an untitled jungle film. Mordaunt Hall of the *New York Times* wrote that *Doctor X* "makes *Frankenstein* look tame and friendly."

For its last two-color film, Warners again turned to Curtiz, Wray, Atwill, and madness. *Mystery of the Wax Museum* even returned to the newspaper milieu, but this time made the brash reporter a woman (Glenda Farrell). Disregarding the Code, its script had lines such as: "How's your sex life?" Another reporter talks about a victim in a morgue and her ex-boyfriend: "Everyone knew that they were living together, but he got involved with another twist." In a third scene, a policeman harasses a heroin addict: "Junkie, eh?" Its horror elements were just as raw. *Mystery of the Wax Museum* was the story of a sensitive sculptor (Atwill) driven mad by the destruction of his museum, his artwork, and the maiming of his hands in a near-fatal fire. Years later, apparently confined to a wheelchair, he has rebuilt his collection of sculptures by sneaking bodies from the morgue and coating them with wax. Only his masterpiece, Marie Antoinette, eludes him. When he sees the reporter's friend (Wray), who looks exactly like the long-lost figure, he captures her and prepares her for her fate. "Immortality has been the dream, the inspiration of mankind through the ages," he raves. "And I am going to give you immortality!" At this point, the frightened girl screams and hits the sculptor, whose face literally cracks and falls off, revealing that he has been wearing a wax mask since his face was disfigured by the fire.

The British censor complained to the SRC that Perc Westmore's makeup for Atwill was "nauseating and by far the worst of its type." Farrell recalled: "I used to sit while

we were waiting our turn to go in front of the camera and I
couldn't bear to look at him, it was so frightening." Wray
had more of a problem. "I knew there was going to be an
ugliness underneath," she said, "but somehow, when I did
it and the mask fell away, I just couldn't move for a fraction
of a second. I had such revulsion. I just froze." Director Curtiz, who had been driving the company for three weeks of
fifteen-hour days, blew up.

"Stop the camera!" he shouted. "You should have kept
hitting and hitting until all that was broken away!" Wray
regained her composure and a second mask was applied to

Atwill's already covered head. In a few hours he passed out,
felled by the heat of the intense arc lights needed to
expose the slow Technicolor film. (At that time, it was rated
at an abysmal ASA 2.) *Mystery of the Wax Museum* became
a success, in spite of a dry *New York Times* review: "After
witnessing this unhealthy film, it is very agreeable to gaze
upon a short subject dealing with the wonders of Yellow-
stone Park."

The Vampire Bat was an attempt by a small studio to
cash in on the madness cycle. Following the lead of the
Halperin brothers, Majestic Pictures rented space from Uni-

Clarence Sinclair Bull did numerous portrait sittings of Boris Karloff and Myrna Loy during the making of **THE MASK OF FU MANCHU**. There was plenty of time, for reasons Karloff recalled: "About a week before we started, I kept asking for a script. And I was met with roars of laughter at the idea that there would *be* a script!"

versal, shooting on still-standing *Frankenstein* sets with a promising cast. Wray, Atwill, and Melvyn Douglas could have given the story conviction, but they were weakly directed by Frank Strayer. Only cameraman Ira Morgan gave the film some flair. In one scene, he cranes his camera down the side of an ivy-covered bell tower at midnight as the screen wipes from the vertiginous blur of the wall to the cozy interior of a bedroom where a sleeping woman is devoured by an omnivorous shadow. Dwight Frye, once more typecast as a simple-minded obsessive, is the too-obvious suspect. The actor, who excelled in musical comedy, felt as trapped by the horror cycle as any of his characters, saying that he expected to "go screwy playing idiots, halfwits, and lunatics on the talking screen!" In *The Vampire Bat*, Frye appears to be either a vampire or in league with one, so the citizens of his Middle European village hound him to death. The film's title is misleading. There are no vampiric thrills, only the anticlimactic revelation that Atwill has murdered eight villagers to supply blood for a "vampire" that looks like a surgical sponge. "Mad?" Atwill, eyes bulging, says to Wray. "Is one who solved the secret of life to be considered *mad*?" Edward Lowe's thin script only tests the Production Code's dictum against vulgarity with its final curtain joke. After Douglas translates the Latin on a mysterious bottle, identifying it as Epsom salts, poor Maude Eburne races the fade-out to reach the bathroom.

The success of *White Zombie* prompted Paramount Pictures to offer the Halperin brothers a production deal that included the talents of Carole Lombard. In *Supernatural*, Lombard plays a girl who has been trying to contact her recently deceased brother through a phony medium (Alan Dinehart), only to become the unwitting host for another spirit, a vengeful murderess (Vivienne Osborne). Lombard was the first to see that the Halperins were out of their depth in the big studio. As the intelligent actress watched director Victor Halperin bungle shot after shot, she said to no one in particular, "Who do you have to screw to get *off* this picture?"

Stretching his imagination, Carl Laemmle Jr. tried to envision Karloff's next vehicle. Screenwriter Preston Sturges advised him: "The strange thing about these horror characters is that their effectiveness grows in inverse ratio to the amount of time we see them. Familiarity breeds contempt and too much gruesomeness becomes funny." As if to confirm Sturges's opinion, Universal's next horror film would have a madman who could not be seen and who had a brutal sense of humor. In January 1933 Karloff, the studio's newest star, was now earning the comparatively modest sum of $750 a week. Potential Karloff projects included *The Return of Frankenstein*, *A Trip to Mars*, and *The Suicide Club*. The studio had also purchased the rights to *The Invisible Man* from H. G. Wells for $10,000. In June 1933, when Karloff asked for the $250 weekly raise the Laemmles had promised him, they reneged. Karloff walked out. By this time, *The Invisible Man* script had already passed through the hands of nine scenarists, including Sturges, Garrett Fort, John Balderston, and John Weld. James Whale took on the project, perfectly happy to make it without Karloff. For its adaptor, Wells suggested R. C. Sherriff, who crafted a story with the perfect blend of madness and mirth.

Sherriff changed the 1897 novel in one significant way. The chemical that makes scientist Jack Griffin invisible to his fellow man also unhinges him. Sherriff said: "[Wells] agreed with me entirely that an invisible lunatic would make people sit up in the cinema more quickly than a sane man." At the SRC, an exhausted Joy resigned, leaving former New York state censor James Wingate in his place. Wingate approved the *Invisible Man* script, noting: "This is one picture which should cause no great difficulty in casting the leading role as the man himself becomes visible only for a few minutes at the end, on his death bed." Casting was indeed a problem for star-poor Universal. By the time the studio gave in to Karloff, he had already gone to work on RKO's *The Lost Patrol*. Colin Clive was the next choice, but Whale had a former colleague in mind. He got the studio to run some RKO screen tests. When Claude Rains came on the screen, auditioning for *A Bill of Divorcement*, Whale shouted: "I don't give a hang what he looks like! That's how I want him to sound and I want HIM!"

Rains rushed from his Lambertville, New Jersey, farm and reported to the makeup department, where he was almost asphyxiated by a series of life-mask castings. Then he had to report for work in a black velvet costume so that when he was filmed as the partially invisible Griffin, he would disappear into the walls of a specially designed black room. John Fulton's painstaking special-effects work stretched the shooting schedule to sixty days, and postproduction was prolonged by a corps of photo retouchers who had to hand-paint matte lines from internegatives so that the illusion of invisibility would be uncompromised.

In the end, Whale described *The Invisible Man* as his most challenging project, and the film broke box-office records at the Roxy Theatre in New York. Audiences loved this madman who was both very cruel and very funny. In one scene, he rants: "Power to rule! To make the world grovel at my feet!" In another scene, he skips down a country lane, chasing a terrified old lady who sees behind her nothing but a pair of pants singing, "Here we go, gathering nuts in May!" In a telling review, one critic went so far as to say that Whale had "become the successor to the throne once held by Tod Browning as king of all directors engaged in the pleasant pastime of causing the filmgoing teeth to chatter."

Karl Freund's The Mummy

In early 1932, Boris Karloff told Hollywood columnist Harrison Carroll: "I have been lucky and have received splendid handling. My main concern now is to do good work in my future parts. I believe Universal plans to give me a variety of roles . . . . I understand, however, that I am not to be continuously distorted by makeup, as in 'Frankenstein.'" Inasmuch as the article was entitled "Boris Karloff Is Bespoken for Chaney Mantle," Karloff's statement was a quixotic one. In the fall, he endured the most painful makeup of his career.

Carl Laemmle Jr. knew that the public was still intrigued by the 1922 discovery of King Tutankhamen's tomb—and by the curse that reportedly struck down its plunderers. He asked story editor Richard Schayer to find a literary work that dealt with Egypt. There was none, so Schayer and writer Nina Wilcox Putnam delved into eighteenth-century history to find an alchemist named Cagliostro, around whom they fashioned a nine-page treatment. *Cagliostro* was the tale of a vengeful San Francisco magician who lives 3,000 years by injecting nitrates. This treatment was

In Karl Freund's 1932 film **THE MUMMY**, Ardath Bey (Boris Karloff) and Helen Grosvenor (Zita Johann) gaze into a pool that shows scenes of her earlier incarnation.

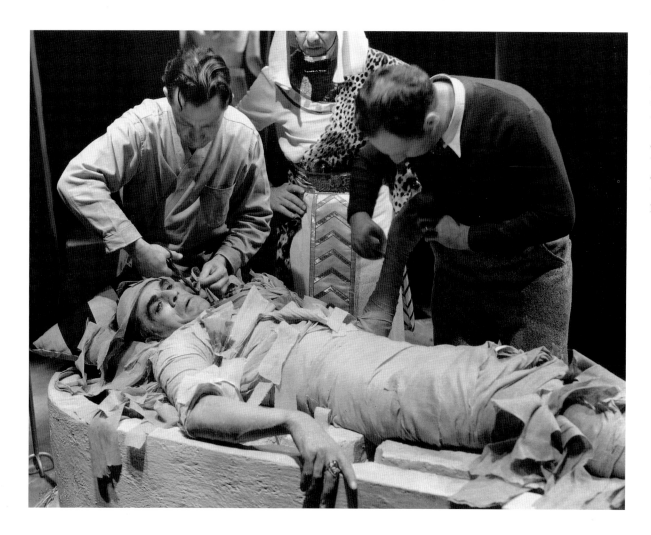

Universal Pictures makeup artist Jack Pierce (at left) and an assistant hurriedly cut bandages from Boris Karloff's face after filming the harrowing scene in which he suffocates.

opposite
To impersonate a 3,700-year-old mummy, "Karloff the Uncanny" endured a seventeen-hour ordeal.

enough for Laemmle to trumpet the upcoming production in the trade papers. He then assigned playwright John Balderston the task of turning the treatment into a screenplay. Few were more qualified than this student of Egyptology. "He worked for the *New York World* as a correspondent," said Balderston's son, John. "And one of his assignments just turned out to be the opening of King Tutankhamen's tomb. So, of course, he was in his element." Balderston moved the setting from San Francisco to Cairo and changed the character's name from Cagliostro to Imhotep, after the third-dynasty architect of the pyramids. In the spirit of his play *Berkeley Square*, he gave Imhotep a journey through time in search of a lost love.

Imhotep is the story of a high priest in ancient Egypt who falls in love with a vestal virgin, Princess Anck-es-en-Amen. When she suddenly dies, he tries to raise her from the dead with incantations in the Scroll of Thoth. Before he can revive her, he is caught. The Pharaoh sentences him to be buried alive, and buries the scroll with him. Thirty-seven hundred years later, a British expedition uncovers his tomb. Ignoring a prominently displayed curse, a brash young archaeologist reads the scroll aloud. The dusty mummy returns to life, comes up behind the young man, and takes the scroll. As Imhotep shambles out of the room, the archaeologist is convulsed with insane laughter. "He went for a little walk! You should have seen his *face!*" Act Two of Balderston's story has Imhotep, disguised as modern Egyptian Ardath Bey, pursue the current incarnation of Anck-es-en-Amen, a young woman named Helen Grosvenor. Wily Egyptologist Dr. Muller knows who Bey is and tries to save Helen. In Act Three Bey outwits Muller

and then prepares to kill Helen, mummify her, and use the scroll to give her immortality. As he starts to penetrate her bare abdomen with a ceremonial knife, a statue of Isis raises its arm. The ankh in its hand sends a bolt of lightning into Imhotep, destroying both him and the scroll.

Balderston's script incorporated the best elements of his work on *Dracula* and *Frankenstein* and created a character that allowed Karloff greater range than *The Old Dark House* or *The Mask of Fu Manchu*. Imhotep would also be more sympathetic than Karloff's recent "monsters." James Whale and Tod Browning were obvious choices for director, but the Laemmles tapped an unlikely talent. Cinematographer Karl Freund wanted to become a director; the Laemmles owed him a favor. In 1930 he had saved the ending of Lewis Milestone's *All Quiet on the Western Front* by suggesting the poignant, simple scene in which the momentary distraction of a butterfly ends the young hero's life. He now promised to bring the same inventiveness to this project. There were only two problems, typical of Universal: time and money. Could the cameraman of *The Golem* and *Metropolis* make this little film in three weeks? Assigned the job on a Saturday, Freund cast it on Sunday and started shooting on Monday.

For the role of the reincarnated Egyptian princess, Universal needed someone quite different from Helen Chandler or Gloria Stuart. Balderston wrote: "For the heroine, a dark girl of Egyptian appearance is essential. She should approximate in type the bust of Nefertiti in the Berlin Museum." They found her in Zita Johann, a Hungarian-born Broadway actress who herself believed in reincarnation. Her wan, otherworldly presence caught the quality of

A behind-the-scenes photograph by Fred Archer shows cameraman Charles Stumar (in dark hat) and director Karl Freund (in light hat) as they catch Karloff in the act of stealing the Scroll of Thoth.

Pierce finished the job at 7:00 P.M., at which point Karloff was taken to the soundstage, where he lay in the upright sarcophagus until he took his "little walk" and was released—at 2:00 A.M. Removing the makeup took only two hours, but prying the dried gum from his face caused excruciating pain. "Physical exhaustion was nothing compared to the nervous exhaustion I suffered," said Karloff, who later described that day as "the most trying ordeal I have ever endured."

His suffering was rewarded by both critical and popular adulation. Sometimes blasé *New York Times* critic André Sennwald wrote that "for purposes of terror, there are two scenes in 'The Mummy' that are weird enough in all conscience. In the first, the mummy comes alive and a young archaeologist, going quite mad, laughs in a way that raises the hair on the scalp. In the second, Imhotep is embalmed alive, and that moment when the tape is drawn across the man's mouth and nose, leaving only his wild eyes staring out of the coffin, is one of decided horror." A *Los Angeles Times* critic wrote: "Surely the mantle of the late Lon Chaney will eventually fall upon the actor Karloff, whose portrayal of an unholy thing in this film, aided by magnificent makeup, establishes him as not just a good character actor, but a finished character star." Karloff was characteristically modest about this recognition. "There will only be one Lon Chaney because he understood so well the souls of afflicted people. None of us can do what Chaney did, because none of us feels it just as he did."

Jungle Horrors

In March 1933 Boris Karloff visited England for the first time in twenty-four years. Born William Henry Pratt, he had turned his back on a career in government service at age twenty-one and sailed for the wilds of Canada. The black sheep of the Pratt family had then learned acting in stock companies, invented a stage name borrowed from some maternal forebears, and spent two decades as a struggling actor. Returning to London after so long, he thought no one would recognize him. Instead, he was "continually mobbed by smiling—yes, actually smiling—youngsters who ran after, instead of away, from me." The horror cycle had made him a star, but eminent diplomat Sir John Pratt still treated him like a younger brother. "Billy," he cautioned, "save every farthing. This can never last!" True, changing tastes and the Depression had littered Hollywood with former stars. Even a new horror star was having a hard time.

White Zombie and *Chandu the Magician* had not done for Bela Lugosi what *The Mask of Fu Manchu* and *The Mummy* had done for Karloff. Without a studio contract, Lugosi got no star buildup, only offers from Poverty Row studios eager to cash in on his name. For this generous, impulsive, and extravagant actor, cash was elusive. Socializing only with other members of Hollywood's Hungarian colony, he chose to relive European escapades rather than learn English. In October 1932 he was forced to file for bankruptcy, listing four suits of clothing and $500 worth of furniture as assets against nearly $3,000 in debts. He tried to work off these debts in low-budget films such as *The Death Kiss*. As a result, he moved notch by notch down the Hollywood totem pole.

mystery Balderston had written for this very old soul.

"Miss Johann! You're not going to make this picture!" said a Universal contract attorney. "It's a horror story!"

"It's more money than you could ever make in the theater!" urged her husband, Broadway producer John Houseman. One of the few contract players at Universal who had script approval, she agreed. Karloff, meanwhile, was billed as "Karloff the Uncanny," and the film's title was changed to *The Mummy*. Johann got along well with Karloff; as she recalled: "Boris was really, truly a great gentleman."

Karloff's first scene was the one in which the mummy awakes in his sarcophagus. To impersonate an ancient corpse, he would have to be wrapped in bandages from head to toe. Due to the extensive makeup and the shortness of the scene, Freund decided to transform Karloff into a mummy and make all his shots on the same day. Jack Pierce began work on the actor at 11:00 A.M., covering his face with layers of cotton and collodion held in place with foul-smelling spirit gum. After two hours, Pierce applied clay to Karloff's hair and, as it dried, put grooves in it to make it match reference photos of the mummy of King Seti II. Then Pierce wrapped Karloff's body in linen bandages that had been treated with acid and scorched in an oven. Karloff's face had already hardened to the point that he could not speak; he had to gesture for a cigarette. Other amenities were a problem. Pierce did not allow that Karloff might want to relieve himself. Karloff said to him later: "Well, you've done a wonderful job, but you forgot to give me a fly!"

The film capital was in thrall to jungle movies. The sylvan bravado of Olympic swimmer Johnny Weissmuller had made a million-dollar hit of M-G-M's *Tarzan the Ape Man* in early 1932, and when SRC censors allowed United Artists to film John Colton's notorious tropical play *Rain*, jungle pictures began to appear on studio schedules. The horror cycle likewise headed for exotic, steamy locales. Its first film was M-G-M's *Kongo*, released in September. This remake of *West of Zanzibar* had Walter Huston reprise his 1926 Broadway performance as Deadlegs Flint. Sound added a new dimension to tropical horror, with atonal chants and weird instruments (recorded in Africa for the 1931 *Trader Horn*) piercing the bamboo walls of his compound. In this version, Huston enacts Flint's rituals of magic and vengeance with a maniacal fervor that surpasses even Lon Chaney's. The new Flint brings more horror to Ann (Virginia Bruce), the innocent girl he has forced into white slavery and alcoholism. At one point, Flint torments her by withholding brandy, then, after giving it to her, forces her to break the glass. "Who wants to drink after *you*?" he laughs. He lets his barking pet chimpanzee, Kong, jump on her, at the last moment yelling, "Back, Kong! Back!" Later, he abandons Ann to an orgy of drugged natives. He also sticks a drug-addicted doctor (Conrad Nagel) in a pond full of leeches. He even starts to wrap a wire around the tongue of his mistress, Tula (Lupe Velez). Though Huston played neither a mad scientist nor a monster in *Kongo*, his bravura performance in a wheelchair gave the film horror status.

Madmen also motivated Paramount's jungle horrors. *Island of Lost Souls* (1933) featured Charles Laughton as the blasphemous scientist of H. G. Wells's 1895 novel *The Island of Doctor Moreau*. Laughton studiously prepared for every role he undertook. While researching Dr. Moreau, he suffered "Klieg eyes" and had to visit an eye doctor for burned retinas. When he saw the doctor, "who had a most peculiar little beard and moustache," Laughton exclaimed: "Dr. Moreau!" In short order, the actor was growing a natty

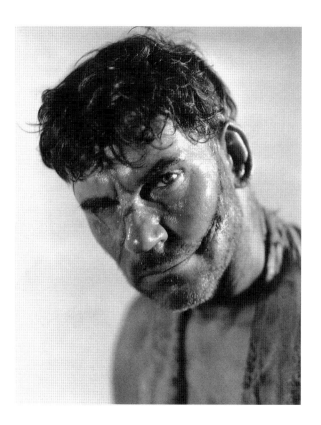

goatee. Another element of his portrayal was a bullwhip. Director Erle C. Kenton planned to use a double for the scenes in which Dr. Moreau cracks the whip over the denizens of his island. Laughton had learned the technique from a London street entertainer while preparing for a play with James Whale four years earlier. "Charles felt very proud when he nonchalantly said he could do it himself," wrote his wife, Elsa Lanchester. What types of natives need to be kept in line with a bullwhip? Dr. Moreau has been driven out of London because of his "unholy" experiments with animals. On a remote island, he has taken these experiments to their illogical but picturesque conclusion. He has vivisected animals into an uncertain state of humanity. There are male "natives" who are part bird, part reptile, and part pig. There is even a Panther Woman, Lota (Kathleen Burke).

To create a proper setting for this menagerie, Kenton collaborated with cinematographer Karl Struss; the two had already been experimenting with wide-angle and zoom lenses. "[Kenton] had been a pictorial photographer," said Struss. "I had met him when I was exhibiting stills in the early Twenties." In *Island of Lost Souls,* they used these lenses (and Struss's lighting) to transport viewers into a world where the line between animal and human is totally blurred. They began on the deck of a tramp steamer, a floating zoo where Struss created a gauzy softness with diffusion filters and Catalina Island fog. A zoom lens rushed in to show the film's first shock when Parker, the hero (Richard Arlen), sees that Moreau's servant (Tetsu Komai) has the ear of a dog. A later confrontation between Parker and Moreau (in which Moreau admits his intent to mate Parker with Lota) uses a subjective camera to give the audience a punch in the face. The wide-angle lens finds its most effective use when the scientist's creations run amuck, their fangs, claws, and hooves lunging into the camera. To Kenton's credit, these effects are never used self-consciously but are seamlessly integrated into an artfully composed design.

Chicago dental assistant Kathleen Burke beat thousands of lovely contestants to win the role of Lota, the Panther Woman in **ISLAND OF LOST SOULS.** A critic wrote: "It must be said for her portrayal of the wistful half-woman that it possesses a certain bewildered, sad-eyed quality." Actress Gail Patrick later said: "The best thing that ever happened to me was not winning as the Panther Woman. I became good friends with Kathleen Burke, and that phrase came to haunt her and ruin her chances for better roles."

Island of Lost Souls upset reviewers. The *New York Times* wrote: "Although the attempt to horrify is not accomplished with any marked degree of subtlety, there is no denying that some of the scenes are ingeniously fashioned." *Variety* called it a "deliberate and mechanical attempt to cash in on the horror cycle which results in gruesomeness rather than blood-chilling fascination." Fourteen American censor boards agreed, rejecting the film in toto; the British censor banned it outright. The scene most often cited to the SRC was one in which a burly "manimal" tries to rape an unsuspecting visitor to the island. Meanwhile, Paramount was readying another jungle horror film.

In Eddie Sutherland's *Murders in the Zoo* (1933), Eric Gorman (Lionel Atwill), the insanely jealous zookeeper, uses snakes (or if they are not available, their venom) to dispatch would-be rivals. Sutherland was known for comedies, but the opening of this film was a departure from form. Gorman leaves a man to die in the jungle, saying, "You'll never kiss another man's wife again!" How has he ensured the man's demise? We see when the man stumbles to his feet and staggers into a grisly closeup—his lips have been sewn shut.

The *Los Angeles Examiner* reported that one audience was "at times driven to a mild state of hysteria by scenes in *Murders in the Zoo*." This was partly due to Atwill's overripe performance. He had come to Hollywood from Broadway, where he had attained matinee-idol status opposite stars such as Helen Hayes and Katharine Cornell. Married to a Washington, D.C., heiress, "Pinky" Atwill nonetheless gained a reputation for attending murder trials and hosting wild parties. He was proud of his ambiguity. "See," he said,

Unidentified actors played an Owl Man and a Pig Man.

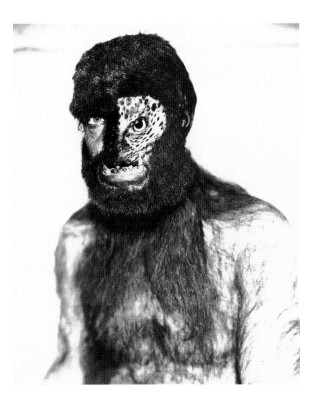

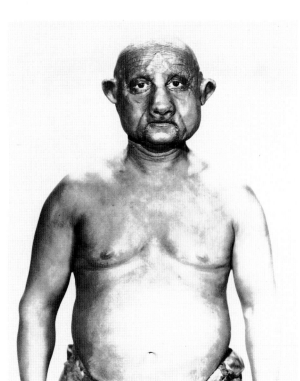

"one side of my face is gentle and kind, incapable of anything but love of my fellow man. The other side, the other profile, is cruel and predatory and evil, incapable of anything but lusts and dark passions. It all depends on which side of my face is turned toward you—or the camera."

Another British actor had an unbalanced countenance, but his was not a reflection of temperament. The left side of Leslie Banks's face was immobilized as a result of wounds suffered in World War I. He used this look to enhance his arch-villain Count Zaroff in the 1932 jungle horror film *The Most Dangerous Game*. Zaroff is a Russian nobleman bored of big game hunting. "When I lost my love of hunting, I lost my love of life, of love," he relates. "What I needed was not a new weapon, but a new animal." He sets misleading channel buoys near a reef, causing shipwrecks. After wining and dining the survivors in his island castle, he throws them into the jungle. If they can elude him until dawn, he will set them free. His "trophy room" is full of grisly evidence that no one has escaped.

Ernest Schoedsack and Merian C. Cooper made *The Most Dangerous Game* for three-year-old RKO–Radio Pictures, Hollywood's newest major studio. "RKO was never a rich company," said producer Pandro S. Berman. "We had to buy cheap stories and create originals." True enough, this studio spawned a "jungle horror" film that transcended both categories by virtue of its originality: *King Kong*. Cooper had been carrying an idea in his head since the days when he and Schoedsack, both decorated World War I veterans, had parlayed their love of danger into the documentaries *Grass* (1925) and *Chang* (1927).

Bela Lugosi in a test shot as the Sayer of the Law in **ISLAND OF LOST SOULS**. Charles Laughton hated making the film. "I remember each horror and monster had more hair than the one before. Hair was all over the place," said Laughton. "I was dreaming of hair. I even thought I had hair in my food."

Having filmed scenes of marauding tigers and stampeding elephants without trick photography, Cooper envisioned a film about giant gorillas, an epic that would "combine the sweep and excitement of the best of silent picture technique with the dramatic possibilities of sound."

Cooper's pipedream floated over his head for three years. The image of gorillas fighting Komodo dragons merged with a childhood fantasy of an ape carrying a screaming woman into a jungle. His own experiences in the mountains of Persia and the jungles of Laos had left him

In Paramount's 1933 **ISLAND OF LOST SOULS**, Parker (Richard Arlen) tours the laboratory where Dr. Moreau (Charles Laughton) accelerates evolution, turning animals into humans. The English censor banned the film because it was "against nature." Elsa Lanchester, Laughton's wife, responded: "Of course it's against nature. So's Mickey Mouse."

with a respect for the power of nature. "All of Schoedsack's and my pictures have had one basic theme: that of man's fight against nature for survival." As his idea evolved, he saw that the documentary form would narrow its scope. It needed the narrative form, so it could be a fable of Beauty and the Beast. There would be one immense ape, who falls in love with a human and then is torn from his habitat and forced to the top of a skyscraper. Instead of man fighting nature to save his life, nature would be fighting civilization to save beauty. Cooper wrote a treatment. Unlike the typical Hollywood yarn, it was original—too original. He could find no studio with the technical ingenuity to film it.

In November 1931, Cooper joined David O. Selznick at RKO in the hope of shepherding the studio through lean times. Among the projects he was told to either revive or shelve was an aborted adventure film called *Creation*. It amounted to no more than a few test scenes, but its special effects—dinosaurs chasing humans through a jungle—revived Cooper's dream. *Creation*'s effects crew had been headed by freelance animator Willis O'Brien. Cooper tracked him down and got to know him. "The only way he could communicate an idea," said Cooper, "was by sketching it out. He could sketch animals, particularly prehistoric animals, better than any man who ever lived. He was certainly the best trick and special effects man that Hollywood had ever seen." O'Brien was, of course, the animator of *The Lost World*, but that film had done little to establish him. Cooper persuaded Selznick to retain O'Brien and his crew. A young Mexican assistant, Marcel Delgado, could translate O'Brien's sketches into movable models. Some of these models had scales and some had fur, but whatever skin they had, the muscles he put under it made them look as if they could breathe. Photographed one frame at a time using the technique of stop-motion animation, the models came to life. Cooper shelved *Creation*, commissioned O'Brien to prepare a test reel, and engaged British mystery writer Edgar Wallace to expand the ape treatment into a screenplay.

The test reel was crucial to the project. For it, Cooper had to direct a fight between a dinosaur and the ape. Delgado's newest creation, "Kong," stood eighteen inches tall and was made of a fully articulated steel armature covered with rubber muscles, poured latex skin, and close-cropped rabbit fur. O'Brien and Delgado could give it movement, but could they give it personality? "It was a helluva thing to direct," Cooper said, "harder than directing people, because you have to get the movements over to the animators." Cooper played Kong, punching and feinting. Then he played the allosaurus, hissing and snapping its jaws. "I tried to give them both a certain human quality, which was hard. The ape wasn't too bad. I got that down pretty good. But I sure as hell don't look like a dinosaur." Eventually O'Brien took over, giving Kong his own grumpy charisma.

Selznick showed the test reel at an RKO sales meeting. The assembled executives were at first perplexed, then awed by the remarkably realistic effects. These were not the jerky movements of earlier animation efforts. The allosaurus moved like a real reptile, swishing its massive tail. Kong beat his chest with believable bluster. Even his fur looked alive. "Hey, Kong is mad!" observed one exec. "Look at him bristle!" Cooper, Schoedsack, and O'Brien breathed a collective sigh of relief; the rippling fur was caused by animators' fingerprints. When the screening room lights came up, the verdict was clear. Selznick was vindicated. Kong had the makings of a star. RKO approved a $500,000 budget.

By the time shooting began in spring 1932, Wallace had died suddenly of pneumonia. Schoedsack's wife, Ruth Rose, finished his script, changing its title from "The Beast" to "The Eighth Wonder of the World," and "using just the kind of romantic dialogue I wanted," recalled Cooper. She made the rugged director the basis for the character of Carl Denham, the Barnum-like character who discovers Kong. Denham says, "I'm goin' out to make the greatest picture in the world, something that nobody's ever seen or heard of. They'll have to think up a lot of new adjectives when I come back!" For Ann Darrow, Kong's love object, Cooper wanted an ideal girl, "innocent and brave." Cooper approached Fay Wray, with whom he was not too secretly smitten, telling her, "You're going to have the tallest, darkest leading man in Hollywood." Wray thought that Cooper meant Clark Gable until she saw artist's renderings of a girl clutched in the furry paw of a giant ape. "It was not too appealing to me to have to work with this big gorilla," she said, "even though it was to be unreal, a manufactured one. I almost backed away from it, but he had the drawings and the concept in such a way and his boyish enthusiasm was so infectious and he was such a giving person that I just decided to go ahead."

The originality of Cooper's concept required this attitude from everyone at RKO. The sound department had to invent cooing sounds for Kong, and the camera and optical-printing departments had to combine live actors with various-sized Kong figures. Large rear-projection screens had only been in use a short time. Wray's first scene in front of one took so long to get right that she had to sit in a treetop in front of a fuzzy image of Kong for twenty-two hours. Since the film was in production (on closed sets) for nearly a year, she and Robert Armstrong had to perform in an even more fragmented mode than the typical film actor, sometimes acting only on weekends and in front of black velvet backdrops. They rarely saw the groundbreaking work O'Brien and his crew were accomplishing on tabletop jungles made of delicate copper trees. The forty-one-year-old Armstrong was a veteran of vaudeville, Broadway, and talkies, but this was something new. "Excuse me, Mr. Cooper," Armstrong said, standing on a jungle set. "If I understood you correctly, you said that I just saw a fifty-foot ape."

"Yes, that's right, Bob," said Cooper from the camera.

"Well, am I supposed to take it big?" asked Armstrong.

"Yes, Bob."

"Well, I've been in this business a great many years, but *you* tell *me* how to take a fifty-foot ape *big!*"

As *The Eighth Wonder of the World* neared completion, Cooper reached the end of his budget. RKO president B. B. Kahane refused him the additional money he wanted for a musical score. Cooper put up $172,000 of his own money, and musical director Max Steiner spent eight weeks composing for the film. "It was made for music," said Steiner. "It was the kind of film that allowed you to do anything and everything, from weird chords and dissonances to pretty melodies."

In early 1932, RKO producer Merian C. Cooper shared a pipedream with Fay Wray. Before long he had her wearing a blonde wig, hanging from a giant paw, and screaming. A year later she sat in Grauman's Chinese Theatre with the premiere audience of **KING KONG**. "I was uncomfortable watching the film that night," she later wrote, "mostly because of my screaming. Too much, too much, I thought." Twenty years passed before the hardworking, literate actress realized what she had helped to give American culture.

On the closed set of **THE EIGHTH WONDER OF THE WORLD**, Marcel and Victor Delgado worked on the full-size head of a giant ape named Kong. Three men could climb into the bearskin-covered ape and work his controls, making him blink, smile, and chew on humans. After achieving stardom, Kong was retired to the RKO ranch, where he sat for more than twenty years, hosting entire cities of fleas, until an unsentimental studio regime set fire to him.

Max Steiner conducts his score for **KING KONG**. Musician and composer Oscar Levant wrote: "Full of weird chords, strident background noises, rumblings and heavings, it was one of the most enthusiastically written scores ever to be composed in Hollywood."

In a 1994 interview, Fay Wray said: "I think I had some quality that made this great animal think a little bit. When we see him on top of the Empire State Building, he becomes something more than a great ape. He becomes an individual of sensitivity. When it comes to the last scene, I still feel sorry for him. And that's kind of miraculous."

opposite

The big Kong had two eighteen-inch alter egos. Marcel Delgado recalled: "I had two Kongs. They were made out of rubber. The rubber sulphurizes in the ozone, you know. It starts to go from the first day. When the air hits it, that's it! Sometimes [the model] only lasted a few hours into the day and then it broke and I had to get the other one. Many times I had to tear King Kong down to the bone and start all over again. And when I finished, it still had to look like the other model!"

As Wray recalled, Cooper was so enamored of the new-born Kong that he imitated him, beating his chest to greet friends. Yet he was uncertain about the film's title. Wray had heard him trying out the euphonious "King . . . Kong." She later wrote: "There was a ring to that, as though a reverberating tone had been struck on a Chinese gong and 'King' and 'Kong' sounded enormous—and enormously right."

On March 2, 1933, as the Great Depression shut down American banks, *King Kong* bravely faced a New York premiere, opening simultaneously in RKO's two mammoth theaters, the RKO Roxy and Radio City Music Hall. Within a week, 180,000 people had watched the colossal Kong beat his chest atop the fluted silver cupola of the Empire State Building. A critic reported that "constant exclamations issued from the Radio City Music Hall" while the film was playing. The Hollywood premiere of *King Kong* took place on March 24 at Grauman's Chinese Theatre. Sid Grauman wired Cooper: "Never saw greater enthusiasm for any picture in my experience of presenting premieres. First time in the history of any picture where applause so frequent and spontaneous. Audience applauded at least twenty times tonight." Within a year, the film had made $2 million, and

science-fiction author Lloyd Arthur Eshbach wrote: "So great is its impact that I venture to predict it will not be forgotten even in 1960—destined to become a living legend, part and parcel of American film lore."

Edgar Ulmer's The Black Cat

While RKO, Paramount, and M-G-M continued to ride the horror cycle, Universal looked in vain for Boris Karloff, who had returned from England to find numerous non-horror roles awaiting him—at other studios. Now involved in the formation of the Screen Actors Guild, Karloff was prepared to hold out indefinitely for a better contract with Universal. Bela Lugosi was in New York, leading a revival of *Dracula*, and intent upon a renewed stage career. In desperation, Universal looked to its story department for an economical project with which to lure Karloff back. *A Trip to Mars* would be too expensive, but there were several treatments based on Edgar Allan Poe's *The Black Cat*, the tale of a drunken fiend who seals his wife and cat behind a wall of bricks. True to Hollywood, no element of Poe remained in the half-baked treatments. One featured a cat with a half-human

The idea of costarring Boris Karloff and Bela Lugosi occurred to Universal as early as 1932, when a savvy publicist arranged a photo session for the benefit of *Weird Tales* magazine.

This Roman Freulich portrait of Bela Lugosi captures the duality of his character in **THE BLACK CAT,** an "avenging angel" who succumbs to the evil he has come to snuff.

To maintain the balance of power between **THE BLACK CAT**'s two stars, Freulich shot them in similar poses. Billed for the first time simply as "Karloff," the star played one of the most wicked characters of his career.

brain. Another had a cat-infested castle whose inhabitant wants to mate his insane son with an entrapped girl who is terrified of cats.

The story that brought both Karloff and Lugosi back to the fold was the brainchild of an uncommonly talented thirty-year-old. Edgar G. Ulmer was working at Universal as assistant art director, in which capacity he had served on, among others, *The Golem* and *Metropolis*. He had recently done some writing for Universal, but he really wanted to direct. He was friendly with Carl Laemmle Jr., to whom he now proposed a low-budget film. Recalled Ulmer: "Junior gave me free rein to write a horror picture in the style we had started in Europe with [*The Cabinet of Dr.*] *Caligari.*" Like Merian C. Cooper, Ulmer had been carrying an idea with him for years, waiting for an opening in the studio assembly line. His idea had originated in 1920 in conversations with the author of *The Golem*, Gustav Meyrink.

Ulmer said: "Meyrink at that time was contemplating a play based upon Doumont, which was a French fortress the Germans had shelled to pieces during the First World War. There were some survivors who didn't come out for years. And the commander was a strange Euripides figure who went crazy three years later when he was brought back to Paris, because he had walked on that mountain of bodies." As Ulmer sat down with screenwriter Peter Ruric, he turned the commander into Hjalmar Poelzig, a sadistic architect. Ulmer modeled him in part after director Fritz Lang but mostly after Aleister Crowley, whose Satanic cult was then being exposed in a libel suit.

The Black Cat told the story of Dr. Vitus Werdegast (Bela Lugosi), a Hungarian psychiatrist who was imprisoned in 1919 after Poelzig (Boris Karloff) betrayed his fortress to the Russians and stole his wife. After fifteen years, Werdegast returns to the fortress; Poelzig, the head of a cult of devil worshipers, has built a mansion on its ruins. Werdegast finds his dead wife in the bowels of the fortress—mummified in a suspended glass casket. His plan of vengeance is momentarily thwarted by the presence of a young American couple stranded at Poelzig's home after an auto accident. The script suggests that the nubile occupants of the numerous glass caskets in his basement were sacrificed during the infamous Black Mass. There is an embalming room, "where he immortalizes the bodies of his women after having immortalized their souls in other, perhaps gentler ways." Now the American girl, Joan, is captured and prepared for sacrifice. After rescuing her from the Satanists, Werdegast learns that his daughter, Karen, is now Poelzig's wife. When Werdegast finds her dead on an embalming table, he becomes totally unhinged. After a scuffle, Werdegast subdues Poelzig in his own embalming room and skins him alive.

Ulmer's script was unprecedented in its perversity, but oddly enough, Joseph I. Breen, the newly appointed head of the SRC, had only token objections to it. Preoccupied with a grassroots campaign to impose a more stringent Code, he got Ulmer's promise to change less than ten items and then let the quirky film go into production. Among his requirements were: "Sequence E-6: This scene of a man in bed with a nude woman and all it implies should be omitted." As shot by Ulmer, Karloff was still in bed with a woman, but she was discreetly draped. Lucille

Lund, who portrayed Karen, recalled: "Ulmer had made for me, especially, a little tiny one-piece bathing suit—made out of the sheerest net. Nothing underneath it!" If titillation was Ulmer's muse, he had no time to indulge it; he had to complete the film in fifteen days—and Karloff was having too good a time. "He got into bed," said Ulmer. "We got ready to shoot, and [then] he got up, turned to the camera and said, 'Boo!'"

When the Laemmles returned and got their first look at the completed film, they were disappointed that Ulmer had mishandled the potentially lucrative costarring of Karloff and Lugosi. Lugosi's character was also a fiend, giving the audience no one with whom to sympathize. Lugosi complained to them that he had been promised a different type of role. Three feverish days of retakes balanced the story.

The Black Cat had a gala premiere at the Pantages Theatre in Hollywood. Reviews were dismal. The *New York Times* described the film as "more foolish than horrible." *Film Weekly* wrote: "Lots of screams, but neither rhyme nor reason." *Variety* decried the skinning sequence: "A truly horrible and nauseating bit of extreme sadism, its inclusion in a motion picture is dubious showmanship. The devil-worshiping cult is also close to the border." Few reviews mentioned Ulmer's bold art direction, roaming camera, fogged lenses, moody lighting effects, or polished editing. Ulmer had created the most stylized horror film yet, but all the reviewers could say was that it was just another spook show. Confounding both critics and censors, *The Black Cat* became Universal Pictures' highest grossing film of 1934, and the last horror film to flout the Production Code.

For Karloff's home in **THE BLACK CAT**, described in the script as "an architectural chef d'oeuvre," Ulmer designed an Art Moderne mansion. "It was very, very much out of my Bauhaus period," Ulmer later said. Happily for Universal, this entire set cost a mere $3,700.

Lucille Lund described the making of this scene: "They had a big hook at the top and they twisted my very long hair (all my own hair) around that hook, so it looked like it was standing straight up. Then they had a little contraption—sort of like a pair of canvas panties— that they put me in, that went up under my long robes. These were suspended by wires, so I was lifted and my feet were dangling . . . there was no way that I could get out of that glass coffin unless somebody lifted me out." As capricious as he was imaginative, Ulmer one day decreed that Miss Lund would spend her lunch break in this "contraption."

Karloff presides over a Black Mass. Joseph Breen of the SRC warned Universal about filming this unprecedented scene: "Throughout this celebration of the Black Mass of Poelzig's rituals, care should be taken to avoid any suggestion of a parody on any church ceremony," Breen wrote. "In this scene, there should be no suggestion of the performance of any sexual rite." The scene passed the censors but raised critics' eyebrows.

opposite
Karloff was never frightening to his director. "My biggest job was to keep him in the part, because he laughed at himself," said Ulmer. "Every time I had him come in by the door, he would open the door and say, 'Here comes the heavy.'"

Gothic Moderne

Variations on a Gothic Theme

André Sennwald was perhaps the most sarcastic movie critic of the 1930s. His reviews in the *New York Times* were a mixture of butterscotch and battery acid. In January 1936, he wrote an article titled "Gory, Gory Hallelujah," which, despite its title, addressed a serious concern. To his eye, Joseph Breen's reconstitution of the Studio Relations Committee in July 1934 as the Production Code Administration (PCA) had cleansed Hollywood of sex, only to make it available for horror. "The screen is providing an acute emotional experience and, what is more important, vast multitudes are enjoying it even in the act of being shocked and revolted by it." Indeed, one of the most frequently cited pieces of evidence in the Catholic campaign had been the book *Our Movie-Made Children*, which quoted a number of dubious studies to prove that Hollywood was hypnotizing children into delinquency and degeneracy. The chapter "Horror and Fright Pictures" was chock-full of hysterical quotations. One girl said: "After seeing [*King Kong*], I was afraid to go into a dark room at night because an ape might just be coming in through a window to carry me off." A boy related: "Sometimes I go to shows and see mystery pictures and after, at night, I dream about them . . . they come nearer and nearer and after I feel like they are on top of me, I holler." A fourteen-year-old girl claimed: "I was so frightened by *The Phantom of the Opera* I could not scream . . . I could not move for two or three minutes . . . it was a mysterious sensation, and my blood became cooler." Box-office receipts told a different story. Even with the new Code, Gothic horror packed theaters.

Unpretentious Columbia Pictures wooed Boris Karloff in 1935 with the promise of an impressive production and the chance to play a dual role. *The Black Room* (1935) was the story of nineteenth-century Austrian twins haunted by a legend that says the younger twin will kill the older "in the Black Room." Anton, the younger, crippled from birth, is

gentle and considerate. Gregor, the older, is depraved and murderous. They compete for the affections of the angelic Thea (Marian Marsh). The screenplay by Arthur Strawn and Henry Myers takes the doomed twins through enough permutations to give Karloff a field day. Essaying a horror role for the first time without elaborate makeup, he differentiated the twins solely with his expressive voice, impressing no less a critic than novelist Graham Greene. "Mr. Boris Karloff has been allowed to act at last," wrote Greene. "He is not quite at ease with virtue, suavity, and good looks, but he gives a very spirited performance as the wicked Count and carries the whole film, so far as acting is concerned, on his own shoulders."

After the *Black Room*, Karloff returned to Universal for a heavily made-up, one-dimensional role opposite Bela Lugosi in *The Raven* (1935). Karloff's attitude toward his home studio was pungently expressed as he walked to the set one morning. Actor Ian Wolfe, new to Universal, accosted Karloff, with whom he would soon be working, and asked him politely: "Where is the toilet?"

"This whole damned studio is a toilet," replied Karloff.

As Dr. Vollin, a demented surgeon, Lugosi had a

showier role than Karloff, yet he was painfully aware that he was only earning half as much as Universal's biggest star. His insecurity began to tell. "He never took the trouble to learn our language," said Karloff. "Consequently, he was very suspicious on the set, suspicious of tricks, fearful of what he regarded as scene-stealing. Later, when he realized that I didn't go in for such nonsense, we became friends." Their collaboration did produce a scary vehicle, but its Grand Guignol aspects—disfigurement by plastic surgery and a torture chamber complete with a pendulum—caused censor boards in Virginia, Pennsylvania, Ohio, and New York to snip such lines as "So you put the burning torch into his face—into his eyes!" *Time* magazine said *The Raven* was "stuffed with horrors to the point of absurdity," but it brought Universal a tidy profit.

Karloff and Lugosi were teamed again in *The Invisible Ray*, a 1936 science-fiction film about a scientist, poisoned by radiation, who metes out vengeance with his fingertips. Instead of the usual harried two-week shooting schedule, Universal allowed director Lambert Hillyer thirty-six days, which he devoted to staging impressive radiation effects.

At M-G-M, Karl Freund embarked upon *Mad Love* (1935), his last film as director. To film Maurice Renard's gruesome novel *The Hands of Orlac* would have been a challenge for Universal, but Freund went further by starring the Hungarian actor Peter Lorre. In 1931, Lorre had shocked the world with his portrayal of a child murderer in Fritz Lang's *M*. In 1935, the cynical André Sennwald wrote: "Peter Lorre's American debut should have been one of the most important events of the season. Yet the producers were content to arrange a vehicle called *Mad Love* for him, apparently under the delusion that the distinguished Hun-

garian actor was a rival of Bela Lugosi." For Metro to hire the controversial Lorre and the faltering Colin Clive for a story about grafted hands showed just how attractive horror films had become.

Working with Guy Endore and John L. Balderston, Freund created a horror film to outdo Universal. Stephen Orlac (Clive) is a concert pianist whose wife Yvonne (Frances Drake) is the star of the Theatre des Horreurs in Paris. Her greatest fan is a voyeuristic surgeon, Dr. Gogol (Lorre). When Orlac's hands are smashed in a train wreck, Gogol grafts the hands of a recently executed murderer onto Orlac's wrists, hoping to take Yvonne from him. Before long, Orlac sees that his hands have a will of their own— and a predilection for knife-throwing. For all its elegant perversity, *Mad Love* was the one horror bomb of the mid-1930s. *Time* magazine called it "one of the most completely horrible stories of the year." A Long Island exhibitor groused: "The producers must have been mad to even attempt such a piece as this. This is certainly a black eye for M-G-M . . . *Mad Love* is the type of picture that brought about censorship." The film lost $39,000.

Warner Bros. borrowed Karloff as box-office insurance and had the prolific, gifted Michael Curtiz direct him in *The Walking Dead* (1936). Producer Hal Wallis, hoping to avoid the bad reviews that had followed *The Raven* and *Mad Love*, emphasized Karloff's humanity. In *The Walking Dead*, Karloff is not a bogeyman or a monster but an unjustly executed man who returns from the dead to punish his murderers. Audiences felt sympathy for a dead man who could sit down to a piano, play the *Kamenoi Ostrow*, and have tears well up in his eyes—before dispatching some nasty gangsters.

Boris Karloff matched glares with Bela Lugosi in **THE INVIS-IBLE RAY,** the story of a scientist poisoned by his own discovery. Universal assigned the top-notch production to Lambert Hillyer, a director of Westerns and B-pictures.

above

In this scene from **MAD LOVE,** Dr. Gogol poses as a patient exhibiting a prosthetic neck. Screenwriter Curt Siodmak said of Lorre: "He liked to go watch operations in the hospital. He really was a freak—he played the same part in life that he played in the pictures."

Meanwhile, Tod Browning, the director who had paved the way for so many other horror artists, sat out a trying hiatus at M-G-M. Since the fiasco of *Freaks* he had been allowed only one film, *Fast Workers,* a wretched low-budget vehicle for John Gilbert, who was as much out of favor as he. Browning tried for a comeback with *The Vampires of Prague,* which he packaged as a partial remake of both *London after Midnight* and *Dracula,* with Bela Lugosi as box-office bait. M-G-M agreed to pay Lugosi more than Universal had, but still gave him second billing to Lionel Barrymore, the curmudgeonly favorite of studio chief Louis B. Mayer. Lugosi also had to share the spotlight with a cheeky twenty-year-old named Carroll Borland. In Guy Endore's original script, the Czechoslovakian Count Mora (Lugosi) had committed incest with his daughter, Luna (Borland). After killing her and shooting himself in the head, he is condemned to spend eternity with her as a vampire. By the time the script became *Mark of the Vampire,* the only evidence of the censored incest was the bloody bullet wound in Mora's temple.

Borland's makeup, accomplished with a little spirit gum on her temples by M-G-M's William Tuttle, was only a slight modification of her own unconventional appearance, but long, dark hair framing a wan face caught the public's imagination. Browning, of course, created numerous spooky tableaux. Cinematographer James Wong Howe said, "We had cobwebs and a low fog on the graveyard achieved (before there were fog machines) with dry ice." Borland recalled the same set. "We worked in mud all the time," she said. "It was really messy. Every night the costume had to be cleaned. It got shorter and shorter." How did Lugosi reprise his vampire role at glamorous M-G-M? "Bela Lugosi was funny," said Howe. "He lived the part of the vampire." Audiences responded to *Mark of the Vampire,* even if it broke its own spell before the final fadeout by revealing its vampires to be vaudeville performers.

Browning used the film's success to launch another project, *The Witch of Timbuctoo.* Again drawing on elements of his silent hits with Lon Chaney, Browning had Guy Endore, Garrett Fort, and Erich von Stroheim concoct a tale of an escaped convict disguised as a woman who shrinks people to the size of dolls and sends them on vengeful missions. Before they had gotten to a shooting script, the British Censor Board warned Breen that if the film had any elements of voodoo, it would never play in England or in any British sovereignty. *Freaks* and *Island of Lost Souls* had been banned, so this was not an idle threat. Like Chaney in one of his own films, Browning had to watch helplessly as his script was truncated. The finished film, called *The Devil-Doll* (1936), had its hair-raising moments, as smartly dressed homunculi used straight pins to stab victims. By the time Browning finished it, he felt as if he, too, had been poked—with censors' pens. In his glory days, Browning could turn to Irving Thalberg for support. Now Thalberg was fighting for his own survival, both artistically and physically. On September 14, 1936, the visionary who had done so much for horror films died a tragically premature death. Before long, Browning left M-G-M and drifted into a suitably reclusive retirement.

Although Lionel Atwill did not play a madman in **MARK OF THE VAMPIRE,** he still projected sex menace. *Motion Picture* magazine writer Faith Service enthused about Lionel Atwill: "Here is a handsome man who makes women's hearts beat faster—until he stops them. . . . Here is a man with the most sardonic mouth I have ever seen, the coldest and most merciless eyes ever set in a man's skull." Portrait by Clarence Bull

MARK OF THE VAMPIRE screenwriter Guy Endore envisioned Count Mora (Bela Lugosi) and his daughter Luna (Carroll Borland) as an incestuous couple whose eternal punishment was to prowl the night in search of victims. Endore was described as "a strange, wispy little man, sensitive as a violin string."

Anything Universal could do, M-G-M could do better. For **MARK OF THE VAMPIRE,** associate art directors Harry Oliver and Edwin B. Willis whipped up a graveyard set that actors found creepy to look at—and to stand in.

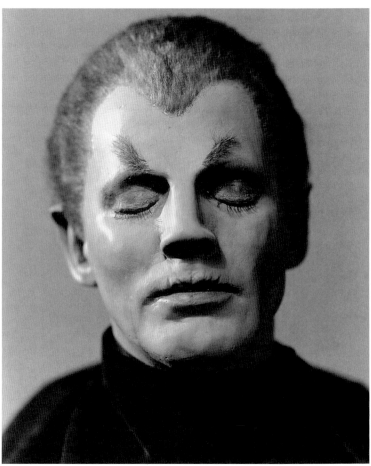
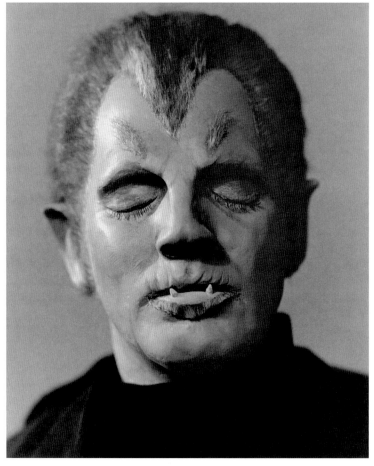

WereWolf of London

The runaway success of Universal horror films in 1935 had Boris Karloff and Bela Lugosi literally running to other studios. In order to populate their own horror films, the Laemmles were forced to cultivate new stars. They looked to Henry Hull, who was still basking in the glow of his Broadway success as Jeeter Lester in the earthy play *Tobacco Road*, but when he arrived in Hollywood, the unconventionally handsome actor fit no cinema mold. He was cast as Magwitch in a modest production of *Great Expectations*. It was only a matter of time before he was offered a Karloff project, *The Wolf Man*. Carl Laemmle instructed his son-in-law, producer Stanley Bergerman, to make Hull a star. "He was, of course, a very good and powerful actor," said Hull's costar, the young British actress Valerie Hobson. "But he didn't photograph very well. He had a snub nose, which is never good for a leading man."

Hull's nose was a moot point once makeup artist Jack Pierce transformed him into a wolf. The novel aspect of this transformation was that, for the first time in a Universal horror film, it had to be shown in progressive stages. Frankenstein and Imhotep had each been a monstrous fait accompli, but Dr. Wilfred Glendon, a man afflicted with lycanthrophobia, had to be shown experiencing the atavistic change from man to beast. Special-effects technician John P. Fulton and his assistant David Horsley collaborated with Pierce to show the initial transformation as Glendon (Hull) walked out of his laboratory. They photographed Hull walking against black velvet, and then used columns separately matted over him and a third image (the laboratory) to effect a smooth transition.

Pierce's ego was slighted by Hull's unwillingness to submit to the same degree of makeup as Karloff. Hull demanded—and got—an additional makeup fee. It was a credit to Pierce that the resulting look was as frightening as it was. Hobson, who was seventeen at the time, later recalled:

> I knew Mr. Hull was supposed to look horrible, but I had no idea he would look like that. I took one look at him and then started to scream. I couldn't stop. He thought I was joking, so he ran towards me and let out an unearthly yell while he reached out a hairy hand as though to grasp my throat. Suddenly he and director Stuart Walker discovered I was in the middle of a fit of hysterics. They rushed me to the studio hospital, where they gave me a sedative. When I quieted down, I was so weak I could not walk. I had to go home for the remainder of the day.

Hull later said: "It was a pretty good getup, wasn't it? Jack had a special talent for turning men into freaks." The film, renamed *WereWolf of London* (1935), was a success. The critics gave Hull and director Stuart Walker good reviews, but no one commented on John Colton's literate and sensitive screenplay, which likened a werewolf curse to episodes of binge drinking. Colton, a homosexual with a penchant for lower-class types, set the monster's attacks in tawdry milieus that he himself was known to frequent. The film was a success for all involved. "The studio liked the job

When Universal first submitted the **WEREWOLF OF LONDON** script to the PCA, Joseph Breen issued a pointless warning: "We understand that you will not show the actual transvection from man to wolf, and that repulsive or horrifying physical details will not be used." Universal negotiated another Jack Pierce triumph.

I had done," remembered Hull, "and they wanted me for similar roles, but I declined because I didn't want to be limited to work in horror films."

Bride of Frankenstein

In 1934, three years after its release, *Frankenstein* was still making money. *Tarzan the Ape Man* had been followed by *Tarzan and His Mate*, and *King Kong* by *The Son of Kong*. A *Frankenstein* sequel was in order, and it could not be entrusted to a minor director. James Whale, perhaps believing that a sequel dishonors the film it follows, feigned indifference. "I squeezed the idea dry with the original picture," he said, "and I never want to work on it again." Only after having two hits in a row (*The Invisible Man* and *One More River*), and enjoying the prestige that such success bestows, did Whale allow himself to be persuaded by the Laemmles. "The producers realized they'd made a dreadful mistake," recalled Boris Karloff. "They'd let the Monster die in the burning mill. In one brief script conference, however, they brought him back alive. Actually, it seems he had only fallen through the flaming floor into the millpond beneath, and now could go on for reels and reels!" *The Return of Frankenstein* became "A James Whale Production." With all of Universal's resources at his disposal, Whale bypassed the various theatrical versions and went back to Mary Shelley's book. *Frankenstein, or, the Modern Prometheus* had episodes in which the Monster attempts to save a drowning girl, encounters a blind man in the woods, and learns to speak. "I demand a creature of another sex," the Monster says, "but as hideous as myself. We shall be monsters, cut off from all the world; but on that account we shall be more attached to one another."

The idea of a female monster intrigued Whale. He confided to his housemate, David Lewis, that he wanted to escape the stigma of the inferior sequel by making the film "a hoot." Lewis recalled: "He knew it was never going to be *Frankenstein*. He knew it was never going to be a picture to be proud of. So he tried to do all sorts of things that would make it memorable." The first script for *The Return of Frankenstein*, written by the usually inventive John Balderston, was not entirely to Whale's liking, so he reworked it, first with R. C. Sherriff and then with William Hurlbut, creating a burlesque for his repertory of eccentrics. His friend Jack Latham watched the film grow from concept to reality. "I think he had great fun with it," said Latham. "He was very amused by Boris and Ernest Thesiger and their characters."

The first character to be refined was, of course, the Monster, and Whale made the controversial decision to have him speak. According to the studio publicist: "At conferences between director James Whale and the psychiatrist of the studio medical staff, it was decided that such a being as the Monster would have the mental age of a ten-year-old boy and the emotional age of a lad of fifteen." Using a wall in the research department for a giant chart, the writers culled simple idea words from the test papers of children under the age of ten who were working at the studio. The forty-four words that became the Monster's vocabulary included: bread, drink, friend, good, smoke, fire, alone, and bad. Karloff was adamantly opposed to a talking

above
Marian Marsh remembered Boris Karloff's special friend. "Boris had a pet pig, whose name was Violet," she said. "Sometimes Boris would be late from the studio. When the pig heard his car, it would start bouncing, forward and back, forward and back. . . . So, in would come Boris. 'How's my little Violet today?' he'd ask, and with his long legs, he would climb into the playpen with the pig, and they would romp together."

opposite
Censor Joe Breen did not like Elsa Lanchester's gown in her Mary Shelley scene in **BRIDE OF FRANKENSTEIN**. "The shots in which the breasts of the character of Mrs. Shelley are exposed and accentuated constitute a code violation," he wrote to Universal. Lanchester had a different feeling. "Mary Shelley's dress," she wrote, "was the most fairy-like creation that I have ever seen before or since in a film. The entire white net dress was embroidered with iridescent sequins—butterflies, stars, and moons. It took seventeen Mexican ladies twelve weeks to make it. The dress traveled around the country and appeared in the foyers of all the big openings of **BRIDE OF FRANKENSTEIN**."

Monster. "They made a great mistake about which I complained," he said. "Speech! Stupid! My argument was that if the Monster had any impact or charm, it was because he was inarticulate—this great, lumbering, inarticulate creature." As the script neared completion, Karloff tried to dissuade Whale. "Time and time again I argued that the monster shouldn't speak. If he spoke, he would seem too much more human, I thought. But the director won his argument."

Whale did not have such an easy time with the formidable Joseph Breen of the PCA. *The Black Cat* had gotten by Breen, but this script, with its religious symbolism, put the militant Catholic on alert. "Throughout the script," he wrote, "there are a number of references to Frankenstein which compare him to God and which compare his creation of the Monster to God's creation of Man. All such references should be eliminated." Whale shrewdly complied, eliminating one layer of Code violations, which allowed him to retain a host of less obvious ones. Furthermore, Breen was not expecting to find homosexual humor in a horror film. The entrance of "Dr. Pretorius" is described as "something to make a witch's skin creep." What the script did not tell Breen was that Pretorius would be played by Ernest Thesiger, the fifty-six-year-old British actor who had been Horace Femm in *The Old Dark House.* According to one coworker, Thesiger was "prissy and bitter," but Valerie Hobson liked Thesiger. "He was one of the first people to make 'almost camp' fun," she recalled. "He did it as a serious thing, you know—ooh, the sort of arched eyebrow and arched nostril." He was fond of needlepoint, referring to himself as "the stitchin' bitch," but never, of course, in the presence of England's Queen Mother, with whom he spent hours sewing.

Reprising the role of the Monster's creator was another homosexual actor, Colin Clive, whose alcoholism had worsened since his first outing as Henry Frankenstein. He was now susceptible to emotional outbursts—or worse, to drinking himself insensate on lunch breaks. He had recently fallen and hurt his leg during one of these episodes. Whale, who was also homosexual (and living openly with Lewis), insisted on using Clive. "He was inclined to be a hysterical actor," said Hobson. "Jimmy Whale held him in reserve, because it was precisely that hysterical quality that he needed."

Having pacified Breen with a series of patronizing, overly polite letters, Whale prepared the film, pursuing his own vision without interference from Junior Laemmle or anyone else at Universal. "He had complete control from beginning to end," said Latham. "I don't believe he could have worked any other way." He certainly could not have worked at M-G-M, where his script would have been reworked by a battery of contract writers. As it evolved, so did his idea of the female Monster. Whale socialized with Charles Laughton's wife, thirty-three-year-old Elsa Lanchester. Looking at her frizzy red hair, widely spaced eyes, and pouting lips, Whale envisioned a dual role, one that would more clearly link the sequel with the original. He would have Lanchester portray not only the female Monster but also the story's scandalous author. "James's feeling was that pretty, sweet people, both men and women, had very wicked insides," said Lanchester. "Evil thoughts. These thoughts could be of dragons. They could be of monsters.

above

Dr. Pretorius (Ernest Thesiger) eyes the Devil (Peter Shaw), one of the homunculi he has grown from cultures. "Certainly, with his wonderful pointed eyebrows, he looked like a devil," recalled Valerie Hobson. "But I don't think I ever saw Ernest Thesiger looking like anything else!"

opposite

Karloff's makeup was a surprise to a visitor to Universal. According to Cortlandt Hull, Henry Hull's great-nephew: "Henry's wife came to visit him on the set [of *Were Wolf of London*] and she was directed to the **BRIDE OF FRANKENSTEIN** set by mistake. A technician told her, 'You don't have to go around the buildings. There's a connecting corridor between the two stages.' The corridor was dimly lit. As she proceeded toward the other end, she heard, 'Thump! Thump! Thump!' Halfway through, she saw Boris Karloff coming down the corridor in full Frankenstein makeup, smoking a cigar. As they met, he said, 'Good morning, Mrs. Hull.' She shrieked, 'Aiee! Aiee! Aiee!' She knew Boris, but in the dark corridor she didn't recognize him."

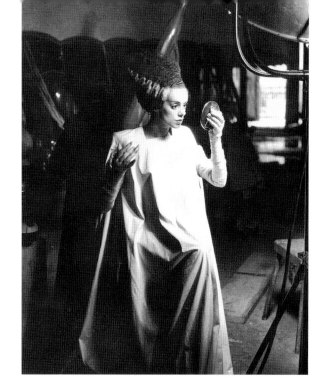

They could be of Frankenstein's laboratory. So James wanted the same actress for both parts to show that the Bride of Frankenstein did, after all, come out of sweet Mary Shelley's soul."

And how would the female Monster look? "I know the Bride's makeup was Whale's conception," recalled film editor Ted Kent. "He was very clever with his pencil and I saw several sketches he made showing details such as how her hair should look." Lanchester recalled: "He and Jack Pierce, the makeup man, knew exactly what they wanted, so I didn't have to do many makeup tests. They had Queen Nefertiti in mind for the form and structure of the Bride's head." As filming commenced, Whale changed the title to *Bride of Frankenstein.*

Lanchester, fresh from the clubby atmosphere of M-G-M's *Naughty Marietta*, found the lordly makeup boss off-putting. "Jack Pierce really did feel that he *made* these people," she said, "like he was a god who created human beings. In the morning he'd be dressed up in white, as if he were in a hospital to perform an operation." Pierce was also at work on Karloff, designing the look of a creature who had survived a fire—singed, sooty, soiled. The Monster was something to behold, especially for a seventeen-year-old girl fresh from England. Valerie Hobson had just been cast as Elizabeth (since Mae Clarke was no longer with Universal and had suffered a series of nervous breakdowns) and was finding her way around the labyrinthine corridors of Universal City. "I had been warned what he was going to look like," she said, "and I thought he was absolutely extraordinary. I hadn't realized his boots were so built up, and he'd be so huge! I was totally amazed!"

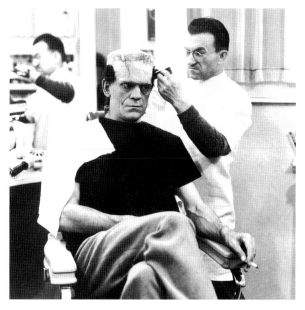

Karloff's first scene required him to surface from the mill pond. Karloff recalled: "The watery opening scene was filmed with me wearing a rubber suit under my costume to ward off the chill. But air got into the suit. When I was launched into the pond, my legs flew up in the air and I floated there like some sort of obscene water lily, while I, and everyone else hooted with laughter." What was not so funny was Karloff's increasing trouble with arthritis, which may have accounted for a fall in which he dislocated his hip not long afterward. Both Karloff and Clive began the film on crutches.

Whale kept the company's spirits up with his customary flair. "I admired Whale's directing and the waiting-for-something-to-happen atmosphere he was able to create around us," Lanchester recalled. What she did not admire was Whale's invidious attitude. "He was very derogatory about Boris Karloff. He'd say, 'Oh, he was a *truck driver.*'" Whale was still insecure about his newly found status, especially as he owed much of it to Karloff. "You don't know how wonderful it is," Whale once said to her, "when you've had nothing, to be able to pour gold through your hair!" Now it was time for Lanchester to have her own exotic hair experience, courtesy of Pierce, who brought Nefertiti to life. "I've often been asked how my hair was made to stand on end," said Lanchester. "Well, from the top of my head they made four tiny, tight braids. On these was anchored a wired horsehair cage about five inches high. Then my own hair was brushed over this structure." Lanchester's performance as a monster began very much as Karloff's had in 1931, wrapped in gauze, lying on a table while Kenneth

Strickfaden's electrical engineering created both chaos and life in Henry Frankenstein's fantastical laboratory. This time, however, the creation scene was the film's climax. The script had built sympathy for the Monster, having him suffer even more loneliness, rejection, and persecution than in the first version, especially when he briefly experiences the joy of friendship with a blind hermit (O. P. Heggie).

Now the waspish Dr. Pretorius has blackmailed Henry Frankenstein into creating a mate to answer the Monster's needs. How will this newly created Bride look? How will she look to the Monster? And how will he look to her? As in the creation sequence, in which Whale and cinematographer John Mescall innovated lighting effects to make the audience feel the power of electricity pushing life into a patchwork cadaver, the Bride's first reaction to the Monster is hammered home with a startling wide-angle shot and an ear-splitting scream. Her second reaction is an even louder scream. The rejected Monster decides to kill himself and the Bride. Lit from below by Mescall's scary spotlight, she closes her eyes, bares her fangs, and hisses! "I've always been fascinated by the sound that swans make," wrote Lanchester. "Regents Park in London has lots of them on the lake. Charles and I used to go and watch them very often. They're really very nasty creatures, always hissing at you." Whale had found the perfect allegory for a woman spurned, and he made sure that the sound technicians got it right. Lanchester remembered: "I did get a very sore throat, what with the long shots, medium shots, retakes and so forth. With those hisses and screams, I lost my voice. It hurt very much and I had codeine." She then took the train to New York with her husband, where the unconventional lady told a reporter: "I had a nice time with codeine on our trip."

Before turning the film entirely over to editor Kent, Whale invited the participation of yet another supremely talented individual. *Frankenstein* had been devoid of any musical score. Franz Waxman was a twenty-eight-year-old refugee from Nazi Germany when he met James Whale at a party in the Santa Monica home of writer Salka Viertel. "Nothing will be resolved in this picture," Whale told him, "except the end destruction scene. Would you write an unresolved score for it?" The somewhat dubious Waxman agreed, producing a composition so carefully wrought that instead of merely being motivated by scenes, it motivated *them*. In the creation scene, a synthetic heart thumps to the beat of a muffled tympanum. "It was a 'super horror' movie," recalled Waxman, "and demanded hauntingly eerie, weird, and different music."

Bride of Frankenstein was ninety minutes long in its first cut. Breen reviewed it and missed all the sexual ambiguity, but refused the film a seal. "This picture seems to us definitely to be a violation of our Production Code because of its excessive brutality and gruesomeness," he wrote, citing twelve violent scenes. These included the Monster drowning a husband and wife in the mill, Karl (Dwight Frye) murdering his uncle, and the Monster throwing Karl off a tower. Whale negotiated to keep half of them and then trimmed the film of killings, subplots, and stray lines. The trims were thrown away, and a seventy-five-minute version was released on May 6, 1935. *Bride of Frankenstein* became that rare Hollywood commodity, a critical and popular suc-

"Ernest Thesiger was a delightful laugh for anybody who saw him or talked to him—a weird, strange character," said Elsa Lanchester. "Very acid-tongued. Not a nasty person at all. Just acid."

"Most monsters have frightening eyes, but Boris, even in makeup, had very loving, sad eyes," said Valerie Hobson.

"Colin Clive was a strange, quiet, buttoned-up, saturnine sort of man," recalled Valerie Hobson. Clive died two years after making this film.

opposite
"It's sometimes pleasant to have very young kids in markets or in the street recognize you as the Bride of Frankenstein," wrote Lanchester in 1983.

cess. There was the occasional quibble about the amount of gallows humor, but most reviews were as keen as *Variety*: "This tops all previous horror pictures in artistry and popular entertainment values . . . . The final action in the tower of doom is the most magnificent mechanical scene within recollection—as awesome as a page from Genesis."

Dracula's Daughter

After the success of *Bride of Frankenstein,* a Dracula sequel was inevitable. Oddly enough, the first move was made not by Universal, but by an ambitious young producer at Metro-Goldwyn-Mayer. In 1933, the newly arrived David O. Selznick wanted to make—along with *Dinner at Eight* and *David Copperfield*—a Dracula sequel. The only problem was that Universal had a proprietary attitude toward the title of its most lucrative film. Though the studio only owned the rights to one Bram Stoker novel, the use of the name "Dracula" in an M-G-M title might constitute trademark infringement, just as the use of the name "Tarzan" would in a Universal title. Fully aware of this, Selznick optioned a short story from Florence Stoker. "Dracula's Guest" was a section of *Dracula* that had been excised because of length. It dealt with a female vampire but was not connected to the plot of the Universal film.

During the production of **DRACULA'S DAUGHTER,** Bela Lugosi visited Gloria Holden for some publicity photos. He sensed a change in the air. "The English censor laws are trying to put a stop to horror pictures," he wrote a fan. "However, if enough of my film friends would write to the studios telling them they would like to see me in good horror pictures, I am sure it would help a great deal towards my success." *Dracula's Daughter* was the last horror film released before Universal's self-imposed hiatus.

At the time when Selznick had purchased the option, the Production Code was being pushed, bent, and broken. He dreamed up a new title, *Dracula's Daughter,* and hired horror craftsman John L. Balderston to rework the property. In this version, vampire fighter Professor Van Helsing goes to Dracula's castle in Transylvania to kill Dracula's three brides. Balderston expanded on these characters, making them dependent on Dracula's daughter, who uses a whip to keep them in line for their dinner, which is a baby in a sack. "We want love as well as drink," the brides implore her. "Give us love. You keep that for yourself. Men. Young men." Van Helsing kills these depraved creatures but inadvertently introduces Dracula's daughter to London, where she enslaves a young aristocrat. Balderston was determined to make the most of both role reversal and the weakened Code. "The use of a female vampire instead of male gives us the chance to play up SEX and CRUELTY legitimately," he wrote. "We profit by making Dracula's Daughter amorous of her victims." Citing *The Sign of the Cross,* Balderston asked: "Why should Cecil B. DeMille have a monopoly on the great box-office values of torture and cruelty in pictures about ancient Rome? I want to see her loathsome deaf mute servants carry into her boudoir savage-looking whips, chains, straps, etc. and hear the cries of the tortured victims without seeing exactly what happens . . . I feel sure that so long as it is a WOMAN torturing MEN, the thing is not TOO unendurable, as it would have been had the man Dracula so treated his female victims."

That Balderston used characters from the 1931 Universal film suggests that Selznick planned to make the most of his option. Since M-G-M could not make a film with the title *Dracula,* he would tailor the project for Universal, who could. By the time Universal took the bait and bought the option from Selznick, Joseph Breen had reconstituted the Production Code; Balderston's script was too much for him. "This story, which was submitted to us 'off the record' by Junior Laemmle," wrote Breen, "contains countless offensive stuff which makes the picture utterly impossible for approval under the Production Code." R. C. Sherriff worked to tone down the sensational elements, but Breen was not satisfied. "There still remains in the script a flavor suggestive of a combination of sex and horror," the censor complained. Apparently Breen had missed the point of the entire cycle. Sex and horror were what paid Universal's bills; there had not been enough of either lately.

In 1935, Universal suffered a loss of $677,186. Carl Laemmle tried the emergency measures that had tided him over before. He cut the payroll, laid off 125 employees, and looked around for a source of ready cash. He found it in the Standard Capital Corporation, a Wall Street firm known for shoring up endangered companies. Standard agreed to a $750,000 loan, but with a string attached. Standard retained a ninety-day option to purchase Universal for $5,500,000. The Laemmles cashed their check and hoped for the best.

Junior Laemmle, preoccupied with the company's uncertain fortunes, announced *Dracula's Daughter* as a James Whale production starring Bela Lugosi, then turned it over to E. M. Asher, associate producer of *Dracula, Frankenstein,* and *The Black Cat.* Where Laemmle's involve-

In **DRACULA'S DAUGHTER,** screenwriter Garrett Fort composed this incantation for Gloria Holden to say over the corpse of her vampire father: "Unto Adonai and Astaroth, and to the keeping of the lords of the flame and lower pits, I consign this body, to be ever-more consumed in this purging fire. Let all baleful spirits that threaten the souls of men be banished by the sprinkling of this salt. Be thou exorcised, O Dracula, and thy body, long undead, find destruction throughout eternity in the name of thy dark, unholy master. In the Name of the All Holiest, and through this cross, be the evil spirit cast out until the end of time."

ment in the project might have interested Whale, Karloff, or Lugosi, Asher seemed incapable of investing the project with star power. Karloff went to England again and Whale declared that he was through with horror. Asher did put Lugosi on salary, but Garrett Fort's screenplay for some reason did not include Lugosi. After earning $4,000 for doing nothing (more than his entire $3,500 *Dracula* salary), the actor accepted an offer elsewhere. Zita Johann had been considered for *Dracula's Daughter*, but at the last minute Asher chose an unknown supporting player under contract to M-G-M.

Gloria Holden was twenty-seven, married to a dance director, and had more than ten years of stage experience.

The studio publicity department described her as "a rather moody, quiet young person who likes fine, artistic things; a homebody who enjoys knowing people of intellect and finds much to study and enjoy in each new day." This morbidly shy woman invested the role of Dracula's daughter with qualities that would have eluded other actresses. Holden had a deep, throaty voice occasionally given to an uncertain quaver, but more often possessed of an icy authority. Cinematographer George Robinson made the most of her high cheekbones and almond eyes, using lighting that recalled William Daniels's treatment of Greta Garbo. Director Lambert Hillyer, here directing a more intimate vehicle than *The Invisible Ray*, elicited a unique per-

In **DRACULA'S DAUGHTER**, Gloria Holden tells all: "It came over me again, that overpowering command . . . wordless . . . insistent. *And I had to obey*."

In **DRACULA'S DAUGHTER,** Lili (Nan Grey) is a girl of the streets who agrees to model for a mysterious artist, Countess Marya Zaleska (Gloria Holden). When Lili pulls down the straps of her brassiere, the Countess evinces strange impulses.

formance from Holden, a psychological profile of a vampire. The scene in which she glides through a foggy London night and entraps an unsuspecting playboy does justice both to Balderston's original concept and to the vaunted opening scenes of Tod Browning's *Dracula*. And there was nothing in any horror film to compare with the scene in which Holden has her slave, Sandor (Irving Pichel), bring a hungry prostitute (Nan Grey) to her artist's loft for a "modeling session." Breen's misgivings about sex and horror were justified.

Variety enthused about *Dracula's Daughter*: "This is a chiller with plenty of ice; a sure-fire waker-upper in the theater and a stay-awake influence in the bedroom later on. Rates top among recent horror pictures and, as such, figures to deliver nice grosses." The film's lengthy preproduction had raised its budget to the point where its nice grosses could not offset its overhead. Even if it had been a blockbuster, it could not have saved Universal for the overextended Laemmles. On March 14, 1936, four days after *Dracula's Daughter* completed principal photography, Standard Capital exercised its option and bought eighty percent of Universal's common stock. Thus the Laemmle family bade farewell to Universal City. Universal Pictures

became the "New Universal." With Charles Cochrane as president, William Koenig as general manager, and Charles R. Rogers as vice president in charge of production, the studio would now emulate Twentieth Century–Fox's Western Avenue studios, concentrating on low-budget films supervised not by producers or directors, but by the front office. And there would be no more horror films.

Chary of problems with the British censor, who determined what could be seen not only in the British Isles but also in British territories, the new regime put the brakes on horror scripts. On May 6, 1936, *Variety* reported: "Universal is ringing curfew on horror picture production for at least a year. . . . Reason attributed by U for abandonment of horror film cycle is that European countries, especially England, are prejudiced against this type of product. Despite heavy local consumption of its chillers, U is taking heed to warning from abroad." The British censor did not actually ban horror films, but in January had instituted the film classification "H" for "Horrific" to keep children out of theaters. With this lucrative market denied it, the "New Universal" began a self-imposed horror ban. Audiences watching a wooden arrow pierce Gloria Holden's heart would wait three long years for their next unearthly thrill.

Son of Frankenstein

The horror hiatus ended in late 1938 when Universal Pictures, now under the leadership of Nate Blumberg, caught wind of a local incident. E. Mark Umann, manager of the failing Regina Theatre in Beverly Hills, had spent $99 to book *Dracula, Frankenstein,* and *The Son of Kong.* Within a week, he was forced to run the triple bill in twenty-four-hour shifts. Bela Lugosi described the scene outside the theater: "One day I drive past and see my name and big lines of people all around. I wonder what [the theater] is giving away to people—maybe bacon or vegetables. But it is the comeback of horror. And I come back." Lugosi did indeed come back, thanks to a horror craze that spread around the country, jamming double-bill theaters in Seattle, Portland, Salt Lake City, New Orleans, St. Louis, and New York. Universal, which had been $1 million in the red for three years in a row, hurriedly struck five hundred new prints of *Dracula* and *Frankenstein.* Before long, there was good news from *Variety:* "Grosses from the key cities indicate the horror revivals are mopping up everywhere." The time had come to end the horror hiatus.

What was needed was a new Frankenstein film for Boris Karloff. James Whale's career was stalled, partly due to a couple of flops and partly due to his indifference. The project went to Rowland V. Lee, who was known for creating big, atmospheric productions such as *Zoo in Budapest* and *Cardinal Richelieu.* Willis Cooper, writer of the radio show *Lights Out,* came up with a script that had the Monster talking, performing brain surgery, and fighting with an army. Lee listened as Karloff voiced his objection to playing a loquacious Monster, and, after Technicolor tests of Karloff revealed that Jack Pierce's makeup looked terrible in color, the director took the project in a different direction.

Lee brainstormed a black-and-white *Son of Frankenstein* and introduced the character of Ygor, the Monster's broken-necked "friend," who was to be played by none other than Bela Lugosi. Because they had just allowed Lee a budget increase of $50,000, Universal executives hoped to skimp on Lugosi's salary, no doubt aware of his financial plight during the horror "ban." According to Lugosi's widow, Lillian: "They cut Bela's salary from $1,000 per week to $500. Then they planned to shoot all his scenes in the picture in one week." Lee had other ideas. "Those God-damned sons of bitches!" he swore. "I'll show them! I'm going to keep Bela on this picture from the first day of shooting right up to the last!" Lee revamped the story to emphasize the friendship between Ygor and the Monster, consequently building up Lugosi's part. This paid off. "The interpretation he gave us was unique, imaginative, and totally unexpected," said Lee. For the first time, the Monster would share the screen with a character as arresting as he, a hunchback with a neck broken by the hangman's noose.

Lionel Atwill also gave a compelling performance as a police inspector who has a prosthetic arm, the result of a boyhood encounter with the Monster. "One night he burst into our house," says Inspector Krogh. "My father took a gun and fired at him, but the savage brute sent him crashing into a corner. Then he grabbed me *by the arm.* One doesn't forget easily, Herr Baron, an arm—torn out *by the*

roots." In an interview, Atwill expanded on the theme that Tod Browning had so often treated: "It would be pretty horrible to have an arm or leg torn off, but you cannot feel horror without an imagination and at the time of such a fatality, the imagination is paralyzed, ceases to function. Pain stultifies conscious thought. Horror is more mental than physical." Atwill improvised a series of creaking, snapping prosthesis movements, creating the impression of an intelligent machine waiting for the chance to wreak vengeance on the Monster.

The shooting got off to a slow start. As Lee lavished attention on every detail of the production, Universal was distressed to learn that he was working from a mental blueprint, not a script. Josephine Hutchinson, who played Elsa von Frankenstein, remembered: "The director had a theory that dialogue learned at a moment's notice would be delivered more naturally. For actors like Basil [Rathbone] and Pinky [Atwill] and myself, trained in theater technique, this is not true. Nevertheless, Mr. Lee did some rewriting on the set. We spent a lot of time in separate corners, pounding

Peter Lorre was originally slated to play the title role in Universal's 1939 film **SON OF FRANKENSTEIN,** but director Rowland V. Lee preferred the elegant Shakespearean actor Basil Rathbone (shown here), who at $5,000 a week was perhaps Hollywood's most expensive supporting player. Boris Karloff, the real star of the film, was making $1,250 less. Rathbone brought a steely fervor to the role, but later referred to the film as a "penny dreadful." This portrait was made by Ray Jones before Lee defined the character as more scientific than mystical.

The Universal publicity department combined three portraits by Ray Jones to make this image. But who steals the show, as he did in **SON OF FRANKENSTEIN?** Bela Lugosi! When asked about his breakthrough role as Ygor, he replied modestly: "God, he was cute!"

new lines into our heads." Lee's unorthodox work habits stretched the shooting schedule from thirty days to forty-six, and inflated *Son of Frankenstein*'s budget from $300,000 to $420,000. Lee completed the film just eight days before its premiere, requiring composer Frank Skinner and his colleague Hans Salter to work in rotating shifts for nearly fifty hours straight. "[Frank] would sit at the piano and compose a sequence and then he would hand it to me," Salter remembered. "I would orchestrate it and he would take a nap on the couch in the meantime. Then, when I was through orchestrating, I would wake him up, and he had to go back and write another sequence while I would take a nap." Sadly, only Skinner received onscreen composer credit.

The beleaguered postproduction department delivered the film on time, and it proceeded to break attendance records in Boston, Los Angeles, and Richmond. Equally important, the film proved that the so-called horror ban was more a matter of public relations than law. A typical British review read: "Forceful narration frankly out to frighten, and abundantly succeeding on wealth of thrilling detail and physical horror." American critics were no less enthusiastic. The *New York Daily Mirror* called the film "a star-spangled horror epic." The *Motion Picture Herald* thought it was "a masterpiece in the demonstration of how production settings and effects can be made [into] assets emphasizing literary melodrama." The *Hollywood Reporter* wrote: "Bela Lugosi is quite horrible, and very impressive as the living dead man, Ygor. And, of course, Boris Karloff as the monster . . . is not exactly a household pet." Lugosi was delighted to be back in the limelight, but Karloff looked askance at *Son of Frankenstein*. "I could see the handwriting on the wall as to what was going to happen to the character of the Monster," he said. "There is just so much you can develop in a part of that nature, and it was a case of diminishing returns. The Monster was going to wind up as he did, a rather comic prop in the last act."

Karloff never portrayed Frankenstein's Monster in another movie, but there were plenty of horror roles for him—and for everyone. *Son of Frankenstein* had touched something in the public consciousness, and it had pushed Universal's yearly profit to $1 million. *Look* magazine observed: "Movie producers attribute the public's current thirst for terror to the war scares of unsettled Europe. Quick to take their cue, they have started a race to produce blood chillers on a more lavish and fantastic scale than they have ever attempted before."

November 23, 1938 was an auspicious day for Boris Karloff. As he began to film a scene with Basil Rathbone and Bela Lugosi, a birthday cake appeared out of nowhere. His fifty-first birthday was not the only reason to celebrate. His first (and only) child, Sara Jane, had been born that morning.

left
Emma Dunn, Basil Rathbone, Donnie Dunagan, and Josephine Hutchinson play a lighthearted breakfast scene in one of the imposing "psycho-logical sets" designed for **SON OF FRANKENSTEIN** by Universal art director Jack Otterson. "The sets were rather an orderly array of planes and masses which at first glance resembled a castle interior," Otterson said, "but the angles and masses were calculated to force an impression of a weird locale, and without intruding too strongly into the conscious-ness of the spectator."

right
Edgar Norton, Karloff, Rath-bone, and Lugosi listen for a telltale heartbeat. The serious-ness of such scenes sometimes gave way to helpless laughter. In the scene where Karloff was lying helpless next to Lugosi, the line "He . . . *does things* for me" took on an adult signifi-cance. According to Karloff: "And there I am, all stretched out on this dais—well, we all just doubled up, including everyone else on the set, the entire cast, crew, and even Row-land, who said he didn't mind the extra takes for the chuckles it gave everyone." Of course, the film went sixteen days over schedule.

opposite
Upon seeing **SON OF FRANKENSTEIN**, the *New York Times* wrote: "Michelan-gelo had his 'David,' Auguste Rodin had his 'Thinker,' and Jack Pierce has profited by their example. He has his 'Franken-stein Monster.' If this be sculp-ture, Pierce is making the most of it." The film had been planned as a Technicolor pro-duction, so the Monster's cos-tume was changed from a black suit to a padded sheepskin. Boris Karloff later said: "In the third film, I didn't like it because they changed his clothes completely, wrapped him up in furs and muck and he became just nothing." The actor never again portrayed the mon-ster in a feature film.

CHAPTER 5

Universal, the Horror Factory

House of Horrors

In late 1938, the Justice Department filed a lawsuit against Hollywood's eight major studios. Owners of independent theaters claimed that the practices of blind-selling and block-booking were preventing them from renting profitable first-run films. If a theater wanted to book a title that promised to be a blockbuster, an all-star M-G-M production such as *San Francisco*, these practices required it to also book four minor M-G-M films. If it wanted to play a prestigious independent film such as Selznick's *Garden of Allah*, it still had to abide by the M-G-M contract. That meant that the theater would have to pass up the Selznick feature or demean it by double-billing it with a M-G-M programmer like *Three Live Ghosts*; there was no alternative. The suit was settled in November 1940, when five majors (Metro-Goldwyn-Mayer, Paramount, Twentieth Century–Fox, Warner Bros., and RKO-Radio) signed a consent decree in which they promised to limit such unfair trade practices. Since they could no longer force-feed B pictures to exhibitors, these studios moved toward bigger productions and left the Bs to the so-called major minors: Columbia, United Artists, and Universal.

Within a year the advent of World War II caused the simultaneous loss of the European market and new demand from the domestic market, and further established the separate domains of the two groups. M-G-M or Paramount could gamble on expensive productions such as *Meet Me in St. Louis* and *Lady in the Dark* because there was now a guaranteed market for them. This left Columbia free to develop low-cost, high-profit "formula" series such as *Lone Wolf*, *Blondie*, and *Crime Doctor*. Universal, with a virtual franchise on Dracula and Frankenstein, saw no reason not to turn them into formulas too. Since 1938 the studio had been headed by RKO veteran Nate Blumberg, whose charm, organizational skills, and feeling for public taste led the company to a net profit of $2 million by 1941.

He and production head Cliff Work, another RKO emigré, did it with a few prestige productions (*Son of Frankenstein, Destry Rides Again, My Little Chickadee*), a few Deanna Durbin films, and a lot of monsters.

Universal wasted no time in putting profits from *Son of Frankenstein* into modest horror projects. The year 1940 saw sequels such as *The Invisible Man Returns,* which introduced writer Curt Siodmak and actor Vincent Price to the studio stable; *The Invisible Woman,* a comedy that featured a supposedly nude Virginia Bruce; and *The Mummy's Hand,* a well-made but puerile effort. There was also *Black Friday,* the last pairing of Boris Karloff and Bela Lugosi at Universal,

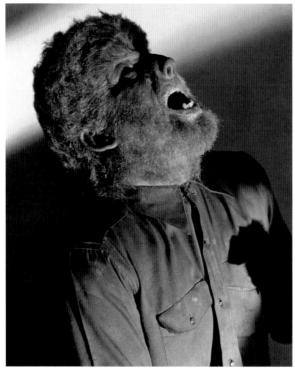

above

Evelyn Ankers and Lon Chaney reprise their first meeting for Ray Jones's still camera. "I was standing on the set," recalled Ankers, "when I felt a tap on my shoulder. Turning around, expecting to see Ralph Bellamy or one of the other production members, I found myself inches away from a snarling beast. He bared his fangs and grabbed me with these hairy claws. I almost jumped right out of my skin."

right

"Even a man who is pure at heart and says his prayers by night may become a wolf when the wolfbane blooms and the autumn moon is bright." Curt Siodmak invented this bit of folklore for his screenplay, **THE WOLF MAN.**

Wolf Man, and we shoot in ten weeks. Get going!'" Siodmak did just the opposite. "I targeted the screenplay to be delivered as late as possible. That gave the front office no time to engage another writer who could mess up my screenplay." This was a vital ploy, since his screenplay had the first original concept for a Universal horror film in ten years. "I studied many books about Lycanthropy, or wolf madness, a mental delusion in a human being believing himself to be a wolf. There was ample material about this in books about psychiatry." Fortunately for Siodmak and for director Waggner, Jack Pierce was on hand to create an equally original makeup. Chaney griped publicly about Pierce's tender mercies. "What gets me is, after work, when I'm all hot and itchy and tired and I've got to sit in that chair for forty-five minutes while Pierce just about kills me, ripping off the stuff he put on me in the morning." For all his crabbing, he knew it was worth it. With *The Wolf Man,* Lon Chaney Jr. became just plain Lon Chaney—a star.

The Wolf Man also made Waggner a producer. In a *Saturday Evening Post* interview, he shared the horror formula:

1) They must be once-upon-a-time tales.
2) They must be believable in characterization.
3) They must have unusual technical effects.
4) Besides the major monster, there must be a secondary character of weird appearance, such as Ygor.
5) They must confess right off that the show is a horror film.
6) They must include a pish-tush character to express the normal skepticism of the audience.
7) They must be based on some pseudoscientific premise.

Karloff encountered the same limitations at Columbia. After playing five mad doctors in a row, he asked the producer Wallace MacDonald, "These things are all right, but don't you think we should perhaps spend a little more on the writing, or change the format?"

"We know exactly how much these pictures are going to make," replied MacDonald. "They cost so much. They earn so much. Even if we spent more on them, they wouldn't make a cent more. So why change them?"

Karloff finished his contracts, then went to Broadway and starred in a historic hit play, *Arsenic and Old Lace.* The actor who had been scaring the world for ten years suddenly developed stage fright. It got so bad that he spent the entire night before the dress rehearsal walking the deserted streets of New York. "Opening night, someone pushed me onto the stage," he said, "and I don't remember a thing—except that I had diarrhea for three weeks!" While Karloff was away, Universal continued to grind out formulaic horror. *Son of Dracula* (1943) was notable for the oddly effective casting of Lon Chaney and for the talky script that resulted when director Robert Siodmak replaced his brother Curt with screenwriter Eric Taylor. Nevertheless, a unique performance by Louise Allbritton and George Robinson's foggy camerawork distinguished the film from the Saturday matinee approach of Universal products such as *The Mad Doctor of Market Street, Captive Wild Woman, The Mad Ghoul,* and *The Mummy's Ghost.*

which was disappointing since they had no scenes together. In 1941, after making a fool of Lugosi in *The Black Cat*—an inane film with no connection to either Poe or the 1934 Ulmer film—Universal struck gold. George Waggner's *Man Made Monster* brought Lon Chaney Jr. to his father's genre, and Arthur Lubin's *Buck Privates* established the vaudeville team of Bud Abbott and Lou Costello as Hollywood's most popular comedians. Universal next assigned Siodmak to combine some of these elements.

Siodmak recalled: "I was told, 'We have $180,000, we have Lon Chaney Jr., Claude Rains, Ralph Bellamy, Warren William, Maria Ouspenskaya, Bela Lugosi, a title called *The*

In 1942, for the first time, another actor portrayed the Frankenstein Monster. In *The Ghost of Frankenstein*, Lon Chaney had Erle C. Kenton as director and Lugosi's Ygor as a sidekick. Their antics were a bit perfunctory, but wartime audiences made the film hugely profitable. Another Frankenstein feature was inevitable. At lunch in the Universal commissary, Curt Siodmak joked to Waggner. "George, why don't we make a picture *Frankenstein Wolfs the Meat Man*, er, *Meets the Wolf Man*?"

Waggner did not respond. Sometime later, after Siodmak had defied the wartime economy to buy a conspicuously new car, Waggner saw him and asked him, "Did you buy the car?"

"Yes, I bought it," answered Siodmak.

"Good!" said Waggner. "Your new assignment is *Frankenstein Wolfs the Meat Man*—er, *Meets the Wolf Man!* I'll give you two hours to accept!" The resulting film had the distinction of bringing Bela Lugosi full circle—he was playing the "idiot" role he had rejected in 1931. "He finally did it because of money," said his wife, Lillian Lugosi. "He wouldn't do it any other way." The Monster's dialogue was a far cry from the monosyllables of yore. "If Dr. Frankenstein were still alive," he says, "he would restore my sight. He would give me back the strength I once possessed—the strength of a hundred men—so that I could

right
A Ray Jones portrait of Susanna Foster and Boris Karloff in character for
THE CLIMAX

below
Russell Schoengarth's editing made this scene the most frightening in **PHANTOM OF THE OPERA**.

live forever!" For all his good intentions, Lugosi could not muster the strength to make the Monster convincing. Carrying thirty-five pounds of makeup and costume for fifteen hours at a time tired the sixty-year-old actor to the point where he collapsed on the set. Equally sad was the reaction to his line readings. After laughing hysterically at the rough cut of the film, the producers cut all of Lugosi's lines. "It sounded so Hungarian funny," explained Siodmak, "that they had to take it out!" Without dialogue, the characterization made no sense. After *Frankestein Meets the Wolf Man*, the once proud Shakespearean actor departed Universal City. This was also Dwight Frye's last film there. A few months after its premiere, just as he was about to escape the typecasting that had plagued him since *Dracula*, the forty-four-year-old actor was felled by a heart attack on Hollywood Boulevard.

Karloff did not find much interesting material when he returned to Universal in January 1944 after a two-year absence. Hoping for the best, he signed a two-picture deal in the wake of Arthur Lubin's Technicolor hit *Phantom of the Opera*, which starred Nelson Eddy. Why did a horror film star "the singing Capon"? Producer Waggner had decided that this version should emphasize opera. He cast Claude Rains as the phantom "Enrique Claudin" and let the audience know from the beginning that the Phantom was not a monster in the Chaney mold, but a victim of chemical scarring. Then, too, Rains was unwilling to wear a full mask,

left
Blonde Louise Allbritton and beefy Lon Chaney overcame unlikely casting in Robert Siodmak's misty **SON OF DRACULA.** "It was great fun making this film," Allbritton recalled, "but I had to wear a black wig and I got constant headaches from it."

above
Lon Chaney, Bela Lugosi, and Maria Ouspenskaya made **FRANKENSTEIN MEETS THE WOLF MAN** one of Universal's biggest wartime hits. The *Hollywood Reporter* wrote: "Roosevelt meets Churchill at Casablanca, Yanks meet Japs at Guadalcanal, and yet these events will fade into insignificance to those seemingly inexhaustible legions of horror fans when they hear that Frankenstein meets the Wolf Man."

Lon Chaney as Count Alucard in **SON OF DRACULA**.
Portrait by Ray Jones

fearing that it would interfere with the leading-man status to which he aspired: "He didn't want to follow in the footsteps of Lon Chaney," said Lubin. "We had been in the war for just over a year," recalled Susanna Foster, who played Christine. "They were worried about boys coming back with terrible injuries on their faces. So they decided not to make a fantastically horrible makeup." Though the unmasking was rather anticlimactic and the concept vague, the film wooed audiences with color and song. It was no surprise, therefore, that Waggner offered Karloff *The Climax*, a Technicolor project set in an opera house. Badly written and

hastily directed, it was a poor welcome home for horror's greatest star. In fact, it was a conspicuous flop. Lubin, who had bailed out early, said, "It was the picture that finished off George Waggner's career."

Karloff's last performance in Universal's classic horror cycle was *House of Frankenstein*, the studio's idea of an all-star film. Its "stars" were franchise monsters played by whomever they could get to sit in a makeup chair. John Carradine played Dracula, Lon Chaney was once again the Wolf Man, and Glenn Strange played the Frankenstein Monster. Karloff was a vengeful scientist who linked the

left
Boris Karloff, no longer playing Frankenstein, and John Carradine, now playing Dracula, were part of the ensemble in **HOUSE OF FRANKENSTEIN.**

below
A saturnine Lon Chaney stands with director Reginald LeBorg on the set of **THE MUMMY'S GHOST**. Chaney thought audiences were crazy to spend money on mummy films. "It was usually kids and teenagers that went to see that kind of a picture," LeBorg said.

above
Rondo Hatton and Martin Kosleck as model and artist in **HOUSE OF HORRORS**; at one point in the film, Robert Lowery says: "The hungry maw of the cinema is always waiting to devour new beauty." By the time audiences saw this film, Hatton had died of complications from acromegaly.

right
Sensing the limitations of his acting ability and physicality, the hard-drinking Lon Chaney became the most temperamental horror star.

Bud Abbott, Lou Costello, Bela Lugosi, and Glenn Strange go through their preposterous paces for the end of Universal's classic horror cycle, the 1948 **ABBOTT AND COSTELLO MEET FRANKENSTEIN.** Director Charles T. Barton found the comedians more frightening than the creatures. "The real monsters were Abbott and Costello. Bud and Lou had quite a chip on their shoulders about doing [the film] and they'd fight me like hell," the director recalled. "We never had any trouble with Lon [Chaney] or Bela or Glenn. The 'monsters' were as sweet as little babies."

individual monster episodes that comprised the film. Strange knew he was working in Karloff's shadow. "He was sick during some of the filming," recalled Strange. "He had finished his scenes and could have gone home, but he stayed on and worked with me. He showed me how to make the Monster's moves properly, and how to do the walk that makes the Monster so frightening." At this point, Karloff was as sick of Universal as he was with back ailments. A studio that could exploit the acromegaly of actor Rondo Hatton in *House of Horrors* was no place for the director of the Screen Actors Guild. Karloff quietly departed. He was not the only one. In 1946, after writing both *House of Frankenstein* and *House of Dracula*, Edward T. Lowe decided that he, too, was through. The screenwriter of the 1923 *Hunchback of Notre Dame* turned in his guild card, went home, and, in what he called "the great cleansing," burned thirty-five years' worth of scripts and memorabilia.

Within two years the Universal horror cycle rolled to its inevitable end: self-parody. In 1948 the studio spent a meager $792,000 to make *Abbott and Costello Meet Frankenstein.* Lugosi was asked if he thought that his appearance as Dracula in this comedy would sully his image. "There is no burlesque for me," he replied. "All I have to do is frighten the boys, which is a perfectly appropriate activity. My trademark will be unblemished." Universal asked Karloff to help publicize the film, in which he did not appear. He agreed, but added: "As long as I don't have to see the

movie!" Proving the adage "All's well that ends well," this collision of slapstick and spooks rang down the curtain with a resounding $3.2 million gross.

In the Gothic Tradition

In 1939 RKO–Radio Pictures trotted out a new version of the story that had launched horror films sixteen years earlier. Irving Thalberg had hoped to remake *The Hunchback of Notre Dame* at M-G-M with Charles Laughton, but after the mogul's death the epic fell to Pandro S. Berman and William Dieterle. "Naturally, I won't play it as Lon Chaney did," said Laughton. "Any actor who understands his stuff always plays to catch the tempo of the moment." Laughton was, if anything, more self-torturing than Chaney, and given to bizarre rites of preparation. On *I, Claudius,* he had irritated his coworkers by endlessly playing a gramophone record of Edward VIII's abdication speech in order to put himself in character. He had also required that a muscular young stagehand kick him in the rump repeatedly before enacting a scene of humiliation for Josef von Sternberg.

To make Laughton's portrayal of Quasimodo endurable in the late summer heat, makeup artist Perc Westmore molded a hump that would weigh six pounds instead of twenty. Laughton refused to wear the foam-rubber prosthesis, saying that he could not be convincing unless he was "suffering under the same weight Chaney had carried." Westmore told him to try acting. An incensed Laughton

In Paramount's **THE MONSTER AND THE GIRL,** a scientist (George Zucco) pops a human brain into the head of an ape (Charles Gemora). Zucco's wife and mother were attending one of his films when an elderly woman in the row behind them said, "I bet *he's* a son of a bitch at home!"

As portrayed by Basil Rathbone, the lead in **THE MAD DOCTOR** was not a scientist trying to create life or dominate the world. He was an effete psychiatrist marrying and murdering rich women with the help of his boyfriend. Rathbone said: "All characters should be kaleidoscopic." With him in this Eugene Robert Richee photo are Ellen Drew and John Howard.

Perc Westmore's brother Frank, "Laughton only grunted a monosyllabic approval." Westmore had a revenge of sorts when it came time to attach the hump to Laughton's back. As Frank Westmore watched, Laughton got on his hands and knees. Perc prepared the belts and straps, and positioned the hump. Laughton began to sweat. "Give me a drink, Perc."

Westmore shook a bottle of quinine water, sprayed it in Laughton's face, and then kicked him in the rump. "That's for all the grief you've given me."

The filming of the *Hunchback* was not much easier. Laughton insisted that Dieterle have a brawny young man twist his ankle just out of camera range to give added motivation to the scene where the whipped Quasimodo cries out for water. Laughton ruined take after take, saying that he could not feel the pain. Dieterle, wondering who was really being punished, whispered: "Charles, listen to me. We'll do one more take, and I want you—I want you to *suffer*." The young man twisted very hard this time, and Laughton finally managed to get through the shot.

The suffering on the RKO ranch in that hot September of 1939 was intensified by the knowledge that families and friends of the European emigrés making the film were embroiled in a new world war. "When England and France declared war on the Third Reich," Dieterle recalled, "the tension on the soundstage was unbearable." The scene in which Laughton rings the huge cathedral bells became a catharsis. "It developed into something so powerful that everybody, including myself, forgot that we were shooting a film. Something superdimensional happened at that moment, so that I forgot to call 'cut.'" After moments of silence, Laughton spoke. "I couldn't think of Esmeralda in that scene," he whispered. "I could only think of the poor people out there, going to fight that bloody, bloody war! To arouse the world, to stop that terrible butchery! Awake! Awake! That's what I felt when I was ringing the bells!"

As World War II raged in Europe, America quietly prepared for its eventuality, and Hollywood produced a spate of films about mad scientists. The first was directed by Ernest Schoedsack of *King Kong* fame. Paramount put the big-budget Technicolor *Dr. Cyclops* into production in mid-1939, but its release was delayed until April 1940 by the complexity of its special effects, which were literally planned on blueprints by cameraman Henry Sharp and effects director Gordon Jennings. This story of a deranged biologist who shrinks human beings in an Amazon laboratory was filmed on closed soundstages so that no one would see its outsized sets and tiny rear-projection screens.

Dr. Alexander Thorkel was played by Theater Guild alumnus Albert Dekker, who had ingeniously won a supporting part in M-G-M's *Marie Antoinette* a year earlier by submitting an elegantly posed photograph taken by his wife on the balcony of their Hollywood Hills apartment. Producer Dale Van Every cast unknowns as Thorkel's guinea pigs. "It naturally will be difficult," the producer explained, "to make the audience believe that our characters have been reduced to a point where they are only twelve or fourteen inches high. It would be impossible to make an audience believe it, for example, if we had Fred MacMurray and Barbara Stanwyck in the boy and girl roles." What he meant was that movie stars had been presented since silent-

called Westmore a hired hand, and said, "You're going about this makeup all wrong. I must look like a pig, with a very heavy hump."

"You look like a pig *without* a very heavy hump," replied Westmore.

Berman mollified the two artists, only to have another fracas occur when Laughton rejected twelve test makeups in a row. Westmore swallowed his pride and went on to create a makeup that combined a false eye, a movable copper eyelid disguised with rubber and paint, and a thread of catgut to make the lid on the false eye blink in unison with Laughton's real eyelid. "While everyone on the lot was raving over what seemed an almost impossible task," wrote screen days as larger than life. In this film, only the villain was supposed to be huge. Dekker's grand style and booming voice made him so.

Dekker played a psychotic in another offbeat Paramount production, Stuart Heisler's *Among the Living* (1941). Lester Cole and Garrett Fort wrote a dual role for Dekker. One twin, Paul, is an unshaven recluse made unstable in childhood by witnessing spousal abuse. The other twin, John, is an upstanding, stable scion of a small-town fortune. Dekker made the scenes in which Paul is inflamed by sexy hoyden Susan Hayward unpleasantly real. *Variety* said his performance was "somewhat akin to the sensational *M* that came out of Germany just prior to the Hitler regime."

Tim Whelan's *The Mad Doctor* (1941) was another Paramount thriller that trod the outer limits of the Production Code. In it, Basil Rathbone is not a mad scientist but a New York psychiatrist with a penchant for murdering infatuated wives. Aiding him in these crimes is a possessive henchman, played by Martin Kosleck as if to imply that their relationship is something more than that of employer and employee. The PCA's Joseph Breen passed the film without grasping the implications of Kosleck's jealous ranting or the lavender flavor of Rathbone's speech as he grumbles about the wife he has just murdered: "These atrocious paintings! This absurd wallpaper! These pathetic antiques! They all breathe her spirit. I can almost see her now, coming down those stairs—with that foolish smile and the love light in her eyes." The *Hollywood Reporter* praised Rathbone's performance as the "half-baked soul meddler" of the title. "Never once losing sight of the brooding, neurotic demands of his murderer role, Rathbone creates a character of staggering stature, dominating the film with the finesse and skill of his portrayal." Rathbone once said that audiences like the heavy because "usually the hero and heroine have no character, while the heavy is a real human being. And when, as it sometimes happens, he is led to prison or death, they don't hate him. He is a man who has failed—and most people have failed."

George Zucco was another distinguished Broadway actor lending his considerable talents to "low A" and "high B" pictures at Paramount. In *The Monster and the Girl* (1941) the actor who had played Disraeli to Helen Hayes's Queen Victoria now used his orotund histrionics to transplant a man's brain into the cranium of a gorilla. Breen passed the film after producer Jack Moss and director Heisler changed the plot so that the gorilla's friend (Ellen Drew) was not forced into white slavery, only into a sort of gray indebtedness. This was not enough for some censor boards, who complained that the film did indeed depict white slavery. The Milwaukee Board also warned that *The Monster and the Girl* defamed the medical profession. A letter to Breen said that the film "makes scientists appear as egomaniacs using our laboratories for a purpose which brings them in ill repute. The transferring of a human brain to a gorilla is very obnoxious and fantastic. The gruesomeness of this picture does not seem to set very well with the public." It set well enough to establish Zucco as a popular villain. Having already made Sir Arthur Conan Doyle's Dr. Moriarty his own, he went on to make a dozen more horror films, eventually describing himself as "Hollywood's unhap-

Ingrid Bergman pleaded with Victor Fleming for the role of the barmaid Ivy in M-G-M's **DR. JEKYLL AND MR. HYDE.** Lana Turner had already been cast, but Fleming made a screen test of Bergman. Portrait of Bergman as Ivy by Clarence Bull

piest actor, because I am always being cast as a bloodletting, law-breaking, evil old man."

Another actor who could not escape typecasting was the extravagant former director Erich von Stroheim, whom Universal had dubbed "the man you love to hate" in 1921. Yet here he was in 1943, working on Poverty Row—at Republic Pictures, which he promptly dubbed "Repulsive Pictures." The studio needed a vehicle for the dramatic debut of ice skater Vera Hruba Ralston. Someone saw the popular new novel *Donovan's Brain*, written by the prolific Curt Siodmak, which was transformed into the film *The Lady and the Monster*. "I didn't know anything about money," Siodmak recalled. "I sold everything cheaper than I should have. For $1,900 they bought the rights. The boss calls me in and says, 'Siodmak, you're crazy. A scientist of

Spencer Tracy was embarrassed by the makeup he wore in M-G-M's **DR. JEKYLL AND MR. HYDE.**

The deranged scientist (Albert Dekker) examines one of his experiments (Charles Halton) in **DR. CYCLOPS.**

A nightmare image from Ernest Schoedsack's **DR. CYCLOPS.**

that size [and of Stroheim's vaunted reputation], he can't live in a hut in the desert. He must live in a castle.' So they changed it."

In 1941, M-G-M producer Victor Saville took a good look at Rouben Mamoulian's 1931 *Dr. Jekyll and Mr. Hyde*, bought the rights (and the camera negative), and assigned it to Victor Fleming, who had finally recovered from making *Gone with the Wind*. The unlikely choice for the blasphemous scientist was the M-G-M star esteemed by his colleagues as the best actor on the lot, if not in the entire industry. Spencer Tracy later said:

> When they first mentioned *Jekyll and Hyde*, I was thrilled. I had always been fascinated by the story and saw it as a story of the two sides of a man. I felt Jekyll was a very respectable doctor—a fine member of society. . . . But there was another side to this man. Every once in a while, Jekyll would go on a trip. Disappear. And either because of drink or dope or who knows what, he would become—or should I say "turn into"?—Mr. Hyde. Then in a town or neighborhood where he was totally unknown, he would perform incredible acts of cruelty and vulgarity. The emotional side of Jekyll was obviously extremely disturbed.

Tracy, whose reticence was legendary, said a great deal in this synopsis. He himself had been dropped by the Fox Film Corporation in 1935, at a point when it could ill afford to lose a star. The reason was that Tracy, after repeatedly disappearing on binges, had quarreled violently with studio head Winfield Sheehan. According to makeup artist Frank Westmore, Tracy "went on such a drunken rampage that he had to be locked inside a huge studio sound stage. . . . Before he reached the blessed state of unconsciousness, he tore down sets and systematically smashed thousands of dollars' worth of lights." If he thought that *Dr. Jekyll and Mr. Hyde* might exorcise his demons (or win him a third Academy Award), he was disappointed. Saville and Fleming wanted horror makeup. The idea was abhorrent to him. "It's like constructing a dummy and then trying to breathe life into it," he said. "I like to be the dummy myself, and then make people—force people—to believe that I'm whatever I want them to believe. Inside out instead of outside in. No makeup."

Dr. Jekyll and Mr. Hyde was a sterling M-G-M product, with a startlingly sexy performance from Ingrid Bergman, a provocative Freudian montage by Peter Ballbusch, and shimmering cinematography by Joseph Ruttenberg. Though Tracy did not feel right in monster makeup, driving from his dressing room to the sound stage with the window shades pulled down, the *Hollywood Reporter* liked it. "Tracy wisely chooses to play Hyde with the smallest application of makeup, and his face, though radically altered with the assistance of Jack Dawn's creations, is no longer a visage designed to haunt little children. . . . His Jekyll and Hyde is the top portrayal of a top actor's career." The public agreed, showing M-G-M that horror was not a Universal monopoly.

The Psychic

CHAPTER 6

Big-Budget Chills

Glossy Hauntings

In 1936, Boris Karloff said: "Humor is to horror as sunshine is to shadow. And without one, you can't very well have the other. Actually, the one is emphasized all the more by the other. I can be my most menacing a few seconds after another character has done something to make the audience laugh. It is a matter of contrast—and the greater the contrast, the better the effect." Arthur Hornblow Jr., one of the more erudite producers at prosperous Paramount Pictures, must have read this interview. In 1939 he resurrected *The Cat and the Canary* and, with director Elliott Nugent, made it a roller-coaster ride of laughs and screams. The film also created the first new horror star since Karloff, although this star was not, strictly speaking, a monster. But the suggestion of unseen menace, of ghosts, of madness hiding behind blandness intrigued adult audiences in a way that the traditional monsters no longer did. Sensing this, the major studios looked for properties that would evoke terror by depicting psychic phenomena. Paramount was the first, and it turned out to be a lucky trend for one languishing contract player.

Thirty-six-year-old Bob Hope had been under contract to Paramount since 1937, when director Mitchell Leisen lured him from a busy Broadway career. After six second-tier films, he needed a chance and he got it. "*The Cat and the Canary* was the turning point for my movie career," wrote Hope. "Paramount apparently got the message about my radio show and decided to put me in an A picture tailored for me." The Pepsodent Show was still establishing Hope's persona when *The Cat and the Canary* went into production. Hope was a trifle unnerved to be working with Paulette Goddard, who was married to his childhood idol, Charles Chaplin. Hope ran into the couple at the racetrack in Santa Anita. Goddard casually asked him, "You know Charles, don't you?" Hope was face-to-face with Chaplin after twenty years of watching him and imitating

him. He did not know what to say. Chaplin broke the awkward silence. "Young man," he smiled. "I've been watching the rushes of *The Cat and the Canary* every night. I want you to know that you are one of the best timers of comedy I have ever seen."

The Cat and the Canary was something of a throwback to the silent-era idea of horror, but the chills were genuine, and Hope's terror of them was too. The final scene, in which the mysterious murderer is exposed, deftly balanced Hope's "brave coward" act with the menace of a madman bent on gouging Hope to death with a large metal hook. Frank S. Nugent, writing in the *New York Times*, said:

> Streamlined, screamlined and played to the hilt for comedy, *The Cat and the Canary* is more hare-brained than hair-raising, which is as it should be. Panels slide as menacingly as ever; Paulette Goddard's screams would part a traffic snarl in Times Square; the lights dim and an eerie wail rises when the hopeful legatees assemble in the manse in the bayous for the reading of Uncle Cyrus's will. Over them all broods Bob Hope, with a chin for a forehead and a gag line for every occasion.

Nothing succeeds like success, and Arthur Hornblow's follow-up to *The Cat and the Canary* was an example of Paramount at its glossy best. From Walter DeLeon's sparkling script to Hans Dreier's glowing white Cuban settings to Charles Lang's creamy photography of them, *The Ghost Breakers* (1940) was a top-notch production. Directing it at an appropriately breathless pace was George Marshall, whom actor Macdonald Carey remembered as "a great director for staging business." Some of the business involved a zombie played by Noble Johnson, who, in addition to his work in films such as *King Kong* and *The Mummy*, had a career as a producer of Harlem-based race films. Interestingly enough, neither DeLeon nor Marshall

overleaf

In **THE LODGER,** Laird Cregar portrayed a madman who wanted to cut the evil out of beautiful women.

opposite

In 1940 a jury of artists chose Paulette Goddard as the actress with the most beautiful body in the world. All the better to see it, Paramount insisted on having psychopaths and zombies tear off her clothes. "Every film I ever made had a bathtub scene," exaggerated Miss Goddard. This "cheesecake horror" pose was made for the 1939 Paramount film **THE CAT AND THE CANARY.**

ever say if the zombie is real or a hoax. Likewise, the ghost who rises from a sarcophagus and transparently walks the grounds of "Castillo Maldito" is similarly unexplained; this would never have happened in a silent horror film. Hope and Goddard are allowed to make jokes at the expense of the spooks, but only because they are so obviously afraid of them. The best joke of the film is Hope's line upon seeing a thunderstorm shut off all the power in New York: "Basil Rathbone must be having a party."

With *The Uninvited,* Paramount put its considerable resources behind a ghost story that was not played for laughs. *Uneasy Freehold* was a novel written by Anglo-Irish journalist Dorothy Macardle while she was in prison for siding with the Irish republicans during the "Troubles." Paramount head B. G. ("Buddy") De Sylva purchased the property after its mass publication as *The Uninvited* in 1942 and made Billy Wilder's writing partner Charles Brackett its producer. Brackett brought in Charles Lang to work his visual magic, which this time meant creating a ghost with effects specialists Farciot Edouart and Gordon Jennings. Macardle's story told of an eighteenth-century seaside house haunted by two female spirits who are vying for the attention of an insecure young woman. One of the spirits may have been her mother, and one of them may be quite malevolent. As Joseph Breen saw it, one of them may also have been perverted. He requested that the mannish character played by Cornelia Otis Skinner not use the term "dearest" in reference to a deceased woman because the audience might infer an "unacceptable relationship"

between the two. Brackett removed the word but Lewis Allen directed the scene so that there was no doubt as to the nature of their relationship. More unusual for a horror film was the introduction of a song as a plot device, in this case Victor Young's "Stella by Starlight," which the hero (Ray Milland) is composing. Another unconventional touch is that the hero and heroine are brother and sister.

The sister was played by Ruth Hussey, who (unlike some actors) read the novel in preparation for her role. She was on a train headed for Hollywood, snuggled in her sleeper compartment. "I had just got to the point where the ghost bursts through the door," she recalled, "and I began to feel really eerie. I didn't feel as if there were spooks around or anything, but I felt funny . . . so I thought, 'I'll finish this tomorrow!' and I left the light on all night." Director Allen was able to transmit this feeling to the audience, both in the scenes where the ghostly presences are first felt and in the apparition that climaxes the film. Actress Elizabeth Russell had been working at RKO on a series of talked-about horror films, so Brackett thought that she should essay the role of a ghost. This necessitated having her portrait painted for two props to be used in the film. Paramount was footing the bill, so her portraits were done from life by a British artist named Kitchen, rather than from photographs (as was the case in Twentieth Century–Fox's *Laura*). Next she had to be photographed floating down a staircase. "I was suspended on wires, like Mary Martin in *Peter Pan*," remembered Russell. "Unfortunately, they had wrapped me in some kind of gauze for the special effect

An honest-to-goodness zombie (Noble Johnson) menaces Paulette Goddard in "Castillo Maldito" (Cursed Castle) on "Black Island," her fictitious Cuban estate, in the 1940 George Marshall film **THE GHOST BREAKERS.**

they wanted and I couldn't bend any of my joints—my knees, my arms, nothing. I was stiff as a board, which would never do. They were finally able to modify the gauze wrapping and get the shot, but it took days to work it out."

Released in 1944, *The Uninvited* was another wartime hit, so Paramount felt secure in preparing a second suspense film, at first titled *Fear*. Raymond Chandler collaborated on the screenplay, and Allen directed a cast that included Gail Russell, Joel McCrea, and Herbert Marshall. The film, retitled *The Unseen*, did mild business, and after De Sylva's early retirement because of a heart attack, Paramount lost interest in the newfound genre of psychic terror.

Music and Madness

The notoriety of *The Wolf Man* and *The Ghost Breakers* was not lost on Twentieth Century–Fox cofounder William Goetz. He had Bryan Foy, his B-picture specialist, buy the rights to a cheap British novel, *The Undying Monster*. The 1942 film got off to a rocky start when its star, George Sanders, went on suspension rather than "report for work . . . dressed as a gorilla." Sanders was replaced by John Howard. The resulting werewolf story was directed by forty-nine-year-old John Brahm, a distinguished refugee from Nazi Germany who had run his own classical theater in Berlin but was now making B pictures in Hollywood. Collaborating with cinematographer Lucien Ballard, he elevated *The Undying Monster* from a double-bill programmer to a chiller that could stand on its own. One of its highlights was the depiction of a murder from the werewolf's point of view. He and Ballard accomplished this by tracking the camera across a craggy seaside terrain without trying to minimize the jolts and bumps to the camera. The result was the impression of a panting animal stalking human prey.

Darryl F. Zanuck, the other cofounder of the studio, was so pleased with Brahm's work that he assigned him a three-star project. *The Lodger* was a 1913 novel by Marie Belloc Lowndes about Jack the Ripper, who in 1888 killed and disemboweled at least five prostitutes in London's Whitechapel district. Alfred Hitchcock's 1926 version had starred the dreamily handsome Ivor Novello. To play the friendless Victorian lodger, Zanuck cast a contract player who was admittedly unconventional. "I am, after all, a grotesque," said actor Laird Cregar. "That is, an actor who doesn't fit readily into parts . . . I am too big, too tall, too heavy. I don't look like an actor." At six foot three and 252 pounds, "Sammy" Cregar could not compete with Tyrone Power or Victor Mature, but he had gotten raves for supporting them in *Blood and Sand* and *I Wake Up Screaming*. Zanuck thought him ready for stardom, in spite of his occasional imprudence. "Sammy had a little boyfriend who was a dancer in a musical in Hollywood," recounted actor Henry Brandon. "One night the boyfriend was sick, so Sammy went on for him . . . . And he was incredibly graceful, floating like a balloon. Still, it was incongruous to see this great fat man among those little chorus boys. Well, Zanuck found out about it and put his foot down with a bang!"

For the second star of *The Lodger*, Zanuck cast George Sanders as the wily detective. For his third star, Zanuck cast Merle Oberon, who, after entertaining the troops in

Europe, had been felled by a serious case of makeup poisoning. Acclaimed for her flawless beauty, she was recovering from both plastic surgery and depression. The prospect of a horror film was especially distasteful, since she now had facial scars. "I had been very ill during that period and I didn't want to work any more," Oberon remembered. "The war and everything had gotten to me." Zanuck spoke to her. "You're so silly," he said. "You've got to work." He promised that cinematographer Ballard would use filters, lighting, and angles to render her scars invisible. Ballard would then turn the same effects upside down to make the Lodger ugly, shooting bands of light from below into the heavy hollows of Cregar's eyes.

Creating a bizarre yet believable Lodger was a challenge for screenwriter Barre Lyndon. "The first problem with him was to get him sympathetic," he said, "because he was in it all the way through. He was really the leading man. You couldn't have just a plain and simple murderer. That's one of the reasons I had him quote the Bible. He read it constantly. I liked that touch. Though a maniac, he wasn't thoroughly wicked. He had the feeling that he should punish people." The people being punished were changed from prostitutes to actresses, in accordance with the dictates of the PCA, who, strangely enough, missed the Lodger's real motive. He is mourning a brother who died after degrading himself with beautiful actresses. "I can show you something more beautiful than a beautiful woman!" says the Lodger as he hands his landlady his brother's self-portrait. "Isn't that a marvelous piece of work to come from the hands of a man—a young man?" This androgynous youth has obviously engendered something more than sibling affection in the Lodger.

Zanuck was famed as a story editor. At a story conference with producer Robert Bassler, he said: "In all the killings, we must [put] over the fact that when these women find themselves face to face with the Ripper, and know that they are to be murdered, their great fear of what is about to happen paralyzes their vocal cords, so although they try desperately to scream, they can't do it." Lyndon's script followed suit: "Jack the Ripper has come into the room, and although we cannot see him, Jennie realizes who he is, and

Charles Lang's lighting conveyed the not-quite-right atmosphere of a haunted house on the Cornish coast in **THE UNIVITED**. Inviting an apparition in this scene are Alan Napier, Ray Milland, Gail Russell, and Ruth Hussey.

she knows why he is there. She slowly starts to back away. We see the dread in her eyes, and hear her gasping voice as she pleads in terror. She is so afraid that she cannot find her voice. She is looking into our eyes as she looks into the eyes of Jack the Ripper." To translate these words, Brahm and Ballard paraphrased their stalking shot from *The Undying Monster*. Hand-held cameras had been used as recently as 1941's *Citizen Kane*. In this scene, though, the filmmakers kept the camera on wheels, making its moves jerky with actual physical blows to the camera blimp. The murder of Jennie (Doris Lloyd) was so startling that a fan wrote her, saying that he had seen *The Lodger* thirteen times because her murder scene "gave him a tingle."

Shortly before the premiere, Cregar told an interviewer: "*The Lodger* is the most sadistic picture of all [the recent crime films], with the brutal multiple murders of the famous criminal. I tried to work in contrast and just a touch of sympathy by making him shy, apologetic, and polite. Maybe you'll get what I mean when you see it." *The Lodger* premiered at the Roxy Theatre on January 19, 1944. Cregar sat with *New York Times* critic Thomas Pryor. When nervous tittering greeted his onscreen ranting, Cregar said softly to himself several times: "Interesting reaction." Pryor tried to shrug off Cregar's unsettling performance, but the *New York World Telegram* reviewer wrote: "Without the aid of any fantastic makeup he conveys [the] intensity of evil fascination to his audiences. None of his crimes needs be seen. His presence is sufficiently malign and revolting to make it almost painful to wait for his demise."

Lyndon was at one of the film's first Hollywood showings. "The theater was full," he said, "and we had to sit at the back among the college crowd. To my astonishment, they were all excited and they loved it. When George Sanders came on, they applauded and laughed before he

said anything at all. They really were with it." Sanders, Oberon, and Cregar were pleasantly surprised by the reviews and by the film's box-office pull. "Now I don't try to be modest about that picture at all," Cregar gloated. "I think it's a wonderful picture, no matter how I am in it . . . And I may be doing something non-villainous for the motion pictures one of these days. I have the feeling the studio is almost beginning to consider me an actor now, instead of a type."

Cregar's hopes were realized very soon, for Bassler and Lyndon were already remolding Patrick Hamilton's novel *Hangover Square*. It was the psychological study of an unemployed dreamer, George Harvey Bone, sentimental about stray cats and sad movies, who becomes obsessed with Netta, an avaricious actress. When his "dead moods" take over, he is powerless to resist homicidal impulses. Lyndon had reservations about the book. "I read about half of it and thought, 'This is a weird one. I can't understand it at all,' and gave it to the guy at the garage to read." Five drafts later, it was ready for Zanuck to package. While the thirty-one-year-old Cregar was torturing his body with a crash diet, Zanuck was twisting Hamilton's weird story into something awfully familiar. "The story is entirely overwritten from the standpoint of sets, and it will have to be radically confined to a budget of $850,000," wrote Zanuck. "I see no reason why we cannot use all of the streets and sets as they are from *The Lodger*." After moving the story from the twentieth century to the nineteenth, Zanuck considered casting. "We must get a very sexy woman, possibly a foreigner, for the role of Netta. She should have the same lure that Marlene Dietrich had in *The Blue Angel*." The tantalizing chemistry that might have occurred between Dietrich and Cregar never saw a camera.

When Cregar learned that his leading-man role had become another *Lodger,* he went on suspension. Dietrich, sensing trouble, withdrew from the project. Cregar, having already shed eighty pounds, continued to diet and refused to negotiate. Zanuck could be persuasive—and threatening. Cregar feared that the vindictive mogul would not

Laird Cregar played a tormented composer in John Brahm's 1945 film **HANGOVER SQUARE.** Actor Alan Napier said: "He was fundamentally shy and insecure as a human being, behind a front of talent and success. Sadly, on *Hangover Square,* he was playing— offstage—'the great Laird Cregar.' But, tragically, he didn't really believe in it." This schism of selves made a great film but caused a real-life tragedy.

Actor Cregar and director Brahm faked smiles for the unit still man on the set of **HANGOVER SQUARE.** Brahm said: "I have been called many things by many people—stubborn, difficult, temperamental, overexacting. Maybe they are all true. I know I will do a scene one hundred times if necessary to get what I want on the screen."

renew his contract. He returned to work after two weeks. "They tell me at the studio I will be a great leading man," he wrote his niece. "My size is the only disadvantage. I've got a picture coming up called *Hangover Square,* which is one of those thrillers you like . . . I play a tormented and deranged killer who is a concert pianist." To his friends, Cregar confided otherwise. "A tragic resolve was born in Laird's mind," wrote Sanders, "to make himself over into a beautiful man who would never again be cast as a fiend. He confessed this to me on the first day of shooting. He told me he was going to have an operation on his eyes and make various other changes. And that above all, he was going to reduce until he became as slender as a sapling." Cregar began taking drugs, which perhaps amplified his self-loathing and affected his judgment. "It was not only his desire to play heroic roles that made him diet," said his friend DeWitt Bodeen, "but the hope that he would attract a young girl."

Bassler and Brahm cast Linda Darnell as Netta. The voluptuous nineteen-year-old sensed that she was walking into a hornet's nest. "Miss Darnell wanted to do the part," said Brahm, "and felt instinctively that here was a new role for her of greater depth, but she was frightened to death and at first refused. I argued with her, pleaded, showed her the marvelous drawings of Toulouse-Lautrec, who so admirably caught the demimonde of the music halls." Like directors Robert Florey and Lewis Milestone, Brahm prepared his films with detailed storyboards. *Hangover Square* especially required this approach, since its key scenes had so many shots that they resembled the montages of Slavko Vorkapich, famed specialist in this transitional technique. George Bone's character was a complex one, and Brahm used a dazzling array of cinematic techniques to express it. Unfortunately, Cregar could not see past his need to look good and be liked. One of the montages had a very short shot of Cregar strangling Darnell. "I hated to do it!" said Cregar. "I tried to convince them that it shouldn't be done before the cameras! Those are the kinds of things that have me looking for a different kind of character to create." Drugs and fatigue began to take their toll. "The thermometer on Stage 14 registered 104," wrote a reporter, "and Laird Cregar, who, in spite of his dieting, is still a mighty fat boy, was blaming the heat for his repeated blow-ups." The most frustrating was his continued inability to say a simple line of dialogue, "I am enormously complimented." On Take 11, he slipped and said, "I am enormously *complicated.*" The entire company laughed at him. A concerned Bassler called lunch.

The spectacle of an actor unraveling before the eyes of his coworkers was hardly unknown in Hollywood, but seldom had the process been more suited to the performance. George Bone is a high-strung composer who goes into a homicidal blackout whenever he hears a loud, discordant sound. As the hot August job dragged on, the look of desperation in Cregar's bulging eyes was more and more convincing. "Shooting was exhausting to him," Brahm recalled, "and the hot lights didn't help matters." Sanders soon gave his own show of temperament, refusing to say a simple line like "He's better off this way." Bassler found him sitting in a canvasback chair at the edge of the set, holding up the fiery (and expensive) climax scene. The producer

confronted Sanders and, when he did not reply, shouted: "How dare you, you arrogant son of a bitch!" Sanders blithely reached forward and punched Bassler, knocking him out. The two soon compromised.

By the end of the filming, Cregar had become so difficult that the crew wrote a letter to the *Hollywood Reporter* in support of Brahm. "Laird wanted so badly to do *Hangover Square* that the story was bought especially for him," Brahm said. "Yet all through the film he behaved so badly, like a naughty little boy, whereas he'd been charming when I directed him in *The Lodger.*" Cregar was now 102 pounds lighter and recovering from a failed attempt at a "conventional" romance. He had no more time for Brahm. "Well, I think we've worked long enough together to know that we never want to work together again," he said to Brahm, and then turned on his heel and walked off.

Cregar had spoken too soon, for Brahm's perfectionism now called for a month of retakes. Cregar made arrangements for an unspecified abdominal surgery, and then gave the performance of a lifetime. "Cregar saw himself one hundred percent in those characters, being a Victorian at heart," Brahm recalled. What the two artists had created was, if not a masterpiece, the most cinematically virtuosic film of the year. The scene in which Bone plays his "Concerto Macabre," a haunting composition by Bernard Herrmann, was one of the high-water marks of psychic horror, blending fogged lens effects, bold lighting changes, a camera crane choreographed to the music, staccato cutting, and Cregar's fevered playing. Said Brahm: "I defy anyone to tell me that the photographed music, expressing the musician's thoughts, is not equally as engrossing as any of the romantic sequences; as truly exciting as a chase!" Before any reviewer had a chance to concur—or to validate Cregar's sufferings—this item appeared in the *Hollywood Reporter*: "Laird Cregar . . . Twentieth Century–Fox star, passed away Saturday afternoon at 4:52 P.M. of myocardial failure following an operation at Good Samaritan Hospital."

Brahm eulogized Cregar. "For all his obstinacy and childishness, he attended to every necessary detail—such

John Brahm's **THE UNDYING MONSTER** gave Twentieth Century–Fox a reason to bankroll horror projects. John Howard was an earnest Englishman afflicted with a furry curse. Howard recalled: "It started off with a good premise but just sort of petered out." Audiences did not mind as long as they got their fright ration.

as retakes, dubbing, stills—before going to the hospital, even though I suggested that many matters could be left for his return. . . . He insisted on finishing up, and then he made a will, carefully disposing of all his personal belongings. No doubt he had a premonition that he would not return."

The Terror of Evil

In the 1940s, Universal had its monster rallies, Paramount had glossy humor, and Twentieth Century–Fox had evocations of the nineteenth century. The other major studios—RKO–Radio Pictures, Warner Bros., and Metro-Goldwyn-Mayer—approached the genre with a new understanding of the mechanics of fright. The goal of a horror film would no longer be horror. It would be terror. Terror did not come from the disfigured face or twisted body of an undead being. It emanated from a diseased soul. It was the product of evil. And it often wore the disguise of Hollywood's most potent product, glamour.

William Dieterle's *The Hunchback of Notre Dame* had made so much money that RKO granted him an independent production unit. His first film under this arrangement was the 1941 *All That Money Can Buy*, based on Stephen Vincent Benet's short story "The Devil and Daniel Webster." In it, the great statesman (Edward Arnold) must save the soul of a farmer (James Craig) by debating Satan (Walter Huston), who is here called "Mr. Scratch." Grinning, leering, profanely sure of himself, Mr. Scratch steals the show, taunting the farmer who is hesitant to sell his soul. "A *soul*?" grunts Mr. Scratch. "A soul is nothing. Can you see it? Smell it? Touch it? No!" In keeping with the new trend, Huston's portrayal is as attractive as it is frightening. Howard Barnes wrote in the *New York Herald Tribune*: "Walter Huston plays Mr. Scratch with such consummate skill that it will be hard for me to ever think of Mephistopheles again without recalling his roguish and malignant portrayal."

The same studio gave Peter Lorre a terror outing in a creepy little B picture called *Stranger on the Third Floor*. Lorre went to town as a furtive, mannered crank who punctuates his exits by flipping a scarf over his left shoulder. This gesture eventually allows the heroine to track him down and save her fiancé from the electric chair, a fate that the viewer has been shown in an expressionist dream sequence created by special-effects director Vernon L. Walker and cinematographer Nicholas Musuraca. This was one of Lorre's first spook roles after a series of seven Mr. Moto films. Lorre acted strangely on the set too. On lesser projects than *The Maltese Falcon* and *Casablanca* he affected airs, refusing to do retakes. He once told director Vincent Sherman: "That's all, Brother Vince. I can only do this kind of crap once a day."

"You've done crap before," Sherman fumed. "How the hell did you do all those Mr. Motos?"

"I took dope," answered Lorre, and he was not kidding. He had been addicted to heroin and painkillers for fourteen years, since the days in Berlin when he was lighting up such Bertolt Brecht–Kurt Weill plays as *Happy End*. His last scary role of the 1940s was in *The Beast with Five Fingers*. In this 1946 Warner Bros. shocker, Robert Florey invoked Tod

Browning's amputation imagery, showing a severed hand chasing Lorre around an Italian mansion. In a sensationally grisly scene, Lorre nails the hand to a board but it eventually breaks loose and strangles him. The studio's special-effects department had fun creating a "gloved hand with stump," a "mechanical hand to crawl on floor," and a "mechanical hand to claw at face."

Robert Siodmak, meanwhile, had left Universal after a series of successful thrillers to direct an RKO film in which he perfected his favorite scenario, that of a handicapped person trying to solve a crime. In Dore Schary's 1946 production *The Spiral Staircase,* Siodmak had a bevy of afflicted characters, foremost of whom were a traumatized mute girl, Helen (Dorothy McGuire), and a bedridden invalid, Mrs. Warren (Ethel Barrymore). A shadowy killer in a small town is murdering one disabled girl after another, unseen and undetected, until he finally corners Helen on the staircase of a gingerbread mansion during a thunderstorm. Siodmak fulfills the promise of his work on *Son of Dracula,* using fluid camerawork and optical zoom effects to take us into the mind of the killer. George Brent is a textbook psychopath as he calmly explains to the terrified girl: "You looked in this mirror once before today. I watched you. You had no mouth then, just as you have none now. . . . And there's no room in the whole world . . . for imperfection."

Brent gave the delicious performance that only a seasoned leading man could, shocking his fans by playing against type. Robert Montgomery, who had also spent the thirties as a leading man, pioneered this kind of role in 1937's *Night Must Fall,* in a psychopathic turn that Louis B. Mayer warned would destroy his career; it expanded it. Franchot Tone took Montgomery's cue and played a glacially cool killer in Siodmak's 1944 *Phantom Lady.* Siodmak, unlike most of his horror contemporaries, devoted as much care to performances as to cinematic engineering.

The regal Miss Barrymore (who shocked audiences by killing her stepson in the film's climax) praised Siodmak as "the only movie director who gave me the same feeling I had when working on the stage."

If a mature leading man could fascinate audiences with a repellent portrayal, what could a handsome unknown do? The director who answered this question was Albert Lewin, an alumnus of both Irving Thalberg's M-G-M and Harvard. "They hate me here because I have a college education," he was known to say. He had just scored a hit with Somerset Maugham's *The Moon and Sixpence,* a faithful adaptation made noteworthy by George Sanders's coldly misogynistic painter. According to actor Hurd Hatfield, the bookish Lewin "used Sanders several times in films because I think Sanders was his idol, what he wished he could be." Lewin was five feet tall, deaf, and impressed by tall, unavailable women. Sanders was a cynical, sneering Lothario, cruel to his long-suffering wife and condescending to his coworkers. Lewin saw him as the necessary ingredient in his next project.

In *The Picture of Dorian Gray,* Sanders would be the ideal Lord Henry, the pithy snob who plants an ungodly notion in the mind of the impressionable Dorian Gray. To cast the title role, Lewin auditioned scores of Adonises. Montgomery Clift turned down the part of the surpassingly handsome degenerate, instructing his agent to say that it was "not the type of role or script for his debut in pictures." Lewin settled on a twenty-five-year-old Broadway actor. Hurd Hatfield had the aesthetic good looks, but had not acquired the requisite elegance. "Albert Lewin cast me because he thought I looked the part," said Hatfield. "But in reality I had never worn evening clothes. I had never had to be icy, to underplay." Beyond that, he had to convey the paradox of a debauched soul masked by ephebic beauty.

Lewin wanted *The Picture of Dorian Gray* to be a horror film—and then some. When the *Hollywood Reporter* tittered at the idea that M-G-M would consider filming a story

William Dieterle's 1941 **ALL THAT MONEY CAN BUY** was a prestige project that suffered the same treatment by RKO as Orson Welles's *The Magnificent Ambersons*. After several unfriendly previews, the anxious studio cut twenty-two minutes from it. Fortunately, most of Walter Huston's sulphurous performance as Mr. Scratch survived. Portrait by Ernest Bachrach

famous for its "abnormal sex theme," the PCA's Joseph Breen put the studio on notice. "There will be no possibility of any inference of sex perversion anywhere in this story," he warned. M-G-M in 1944 was an unlikely place for this project, catering as it did to the middle class with Judy Garland, Mickey Rooney, and Lassie. Lewin had left the fold after Thalberg's death, sensing correctly that he would not fit into Mayer's M-G-M. Now the Hollywood Rajah welcomed him back, teamed him with Pandro S. Berman (who had produced *The Hunchback of Notre Dame* at RKO), and gave him a budget of $1 million. Mayer said proudly to a nervous young actor, "I'm delighted to be making a prestige film again, Mr. Hatfield."

As adapted by Lewin, Oscar Wilde's Dorian Gray is spellbound by Lord Henry's false values:

> The gods have been good to you, Mr. Gray . . . because you have the most marvelous youth—and youth is the one thing worth having. . . . What the gods give, they quickly take away. . . . Live! Let nothing be lost upon you. Be afraid of nothing. There's such a little time that your youth will last—and you can never get it back. As we grow older, our memories are haunted by the exquisite temptations we hadn't the courage to yield to. The world is yours for a season. It would be tragic if you realized too late, as so many others do, that there is only one thing in the world worth having—and that is youth.

The picture of the title is a painting that captures the essence of Gray's youth. Looking upon it, he has an unsettling thought. "As I grow old, this picture will remain always young. If it were only the other way. If it were I who was always to be young—and the picture was to grow old." In the rarefied air of the artist's studio, Gray conceives of a parallel universe where he can retain the most evanescent of possessions. "If only the picture could change and I

could be always what I am now. For that I would give anything. Yes, there is nothing in the whole world I would not give. I would give my soul for that."

The Picture of Dorian Gray does not have a Mr. Scratch to answer Gray's blasphemous prayer, only a statue of the Egyptian cat goddess, Sehkmet, but it is answered. His epicene features remain unchanged as he pursues a life of unspeakable (and unspecified) depravity. Only the painting, locked away in his childhood schoolroom, betrays the state of his soul. Lewin took every conceivable pain to create a credible adaptation of Wilde's morality tale, and then worked tirelessly with cinematographer Harry Stradling and art director Hans Peters to create a suffocating aura of decadence. "Lewin was intellectual, bright, kind," said Hatfield. "I must mention Lewin's assistant, Gordon Wiles; he was continually at Lewin's side, with matters of taste—moving objects and things. . . . The film is full of things they had fun with, giving it a subtext, and making it very rich."

The dissipated painting was the work of the renowned artist, Ivan Albright, who, with his twin brother Malvin, was hired to paint a series of four portraits. Their preparation was deemed newsworthy by *Life* magazine. "Masters at portraying decaying flesh, the twins made the rounds of the local insane asylums, alcoholic wards, and hospitals for the incurably diseased." Malvin eventually dropped out, and the first portrait of Gray was made by Henrique Medina.

The film was allotted fifty-two shooting days. It soon became obvious that Lewin would push the schedule far beyond that. Berman came to the set to see what was taking so long, and he spent one impatient day watching Lewin blocking a sinuous camera move. "Al, I don't see why you're complicating things for yourself," said Berman. "This guy's telling his friend the very sad and tragic news that his girl has died. Why don't you do it in a nice two-shot on the sofa, with over-the-shoulder closeups?"

"Well, Pan, this is my style, you see."

right

After using various chemicals to age the fabric on a dummy supplied by M-G-M, Ivan Albright earned more than $35,000 by painting the "bestial, sodden, and unclean" portrait of Dorian Gray. When the painting appeared onscreen, the film changed from black and white to Technicolor.

above

Angela Lansbury received an Academy Award nomination for her portrayal of fallen angel Sibyl Vane in the lavish 1945 M-G-M production **THE PICTURE OF DORIAN GRAY.** Harry Stradling's cinematography won the Oscar, a rare demonstration of respect for a horror film. The film was also nominated for Best Art Direction and Best Set Decoration.

right

In **THE PICTURE OF DORIAN GRAY,** director Albert Lewin implied the wantonness of Oscar Wilde's character without upsetting the PCA. This was due in part to Hurd Hatfield's silky performance. He played a thirty-eight-year-old sybarite who looks like an unspoiled teenager, and whose childhood alphabet blocks now show the initials of his victims. "The film didn't make me popular in Hollywood," Hatfield later said. "It was too odd, too avant-garde, too ahead of its time. After all, Lewin always said he made it for six friends! The decadence, the hints of bisexuality, and so on, made me a leper. Nobody I knew had a sense of humor and people wouldn't have lunch with me!"

"Style, style," clucked Berman. "People are always talking about style. What is this style?"

Lewin explained that, in the cinema, style was the difference between Lubitsch and Ford, just like turning on the radio and telling the difference between Mozart and Bach.

"Oh, so *that's* style. Well, I don't want it in any of my movies." said Berman, who had produced the elegant Astaire-Rogers vehicles—with compliant contract directors. After spending a staggering 127 days and $1,918,168, Lewin finally completed his portrait of evil. The M-G-M publicity department decided to sell it as a horror picture, and everyone awaited the reviews.

"His is a passive, dreamy mask," wrote the sometimes incomprehensible Parker Tyler in *View*. "Not only does Hurd Hatfield create the first male erotic somnambule who is a beauty rather than a Dracula, or such as the denizen of Caligari's cabinet, but he is the first Great Lover who, despite Hollywood's handicaps, manages to seem more loved than loving." The eminent film critic James Agee was tart. "Albert Lewin's version is respectful, earnest, and, I am afraid, dead," wrote Agee. "The movie is just a cultured horror picture, decorated with epigrams and an elaborate moral, and made with a sincere effort at good taste rather than with passion, immediacy, or imagination."

After these reviews, Hatfield was afraid to go to the premiere at New York's Capitol Theatre. As it turned out, he was mobbed by enthusiastic fans. The film broke house records in its first week. A friend told him that the audience "laughed at the right places, was properly silent, and gasped and shrieked at [the decayed portrait] and the dummy on the floor. A woman behind me—after the murder of the painter—kept saying 'Uh, uh!' at each twist of the plot." The tragic ending garnered this reaction: "A very young fellow, obviously an intellectual, seemed lost in thought as the last of the picture faded out, and then murmured 'Excellent!'" *The Picture of Dorian Gray* vindicated Lewin. It grossed $2,975,000 worldwide. The expensive "prestige picture" could do little more than recoup its cost, but it was M-G-M's highest-grossing horror film to date—and became one of Mayer's favorite films. However, the strain of fighting with every department at Hollywood's biggest studio took its toll on the professorial Lewin; he decamped to United Artists, where he could film Guy de Maupassant's *Bel Ami* without interference.

THE BEAST WITH FIVE FINGERS was director Robert Florey's 1946 variation on Tod Browning's dismemberment themes. In this scene, Andrea King confronts what may or may not be a hallucination.

left and opposite
In the opening sequence of Robert Siodmak's *Some Must Watch*, a handicapped girl sits in a room of people who are mesmerized by a flickering silent film. The eye of the movie projector becomes an analogue for . . . the eye of a killer who is obsessed with physical perfection. In a hotel room above the screening, he hides in a closet, watching a crippled girl dress. Siodmak explained how he got away with such material in 1946: "There was a strike on in Hollywood when I was cutting *Staircase*, so they let me alone." Not entirely; the studio changed the title from *Some Must Watch* to THE SPIRAL STAIRCASE.

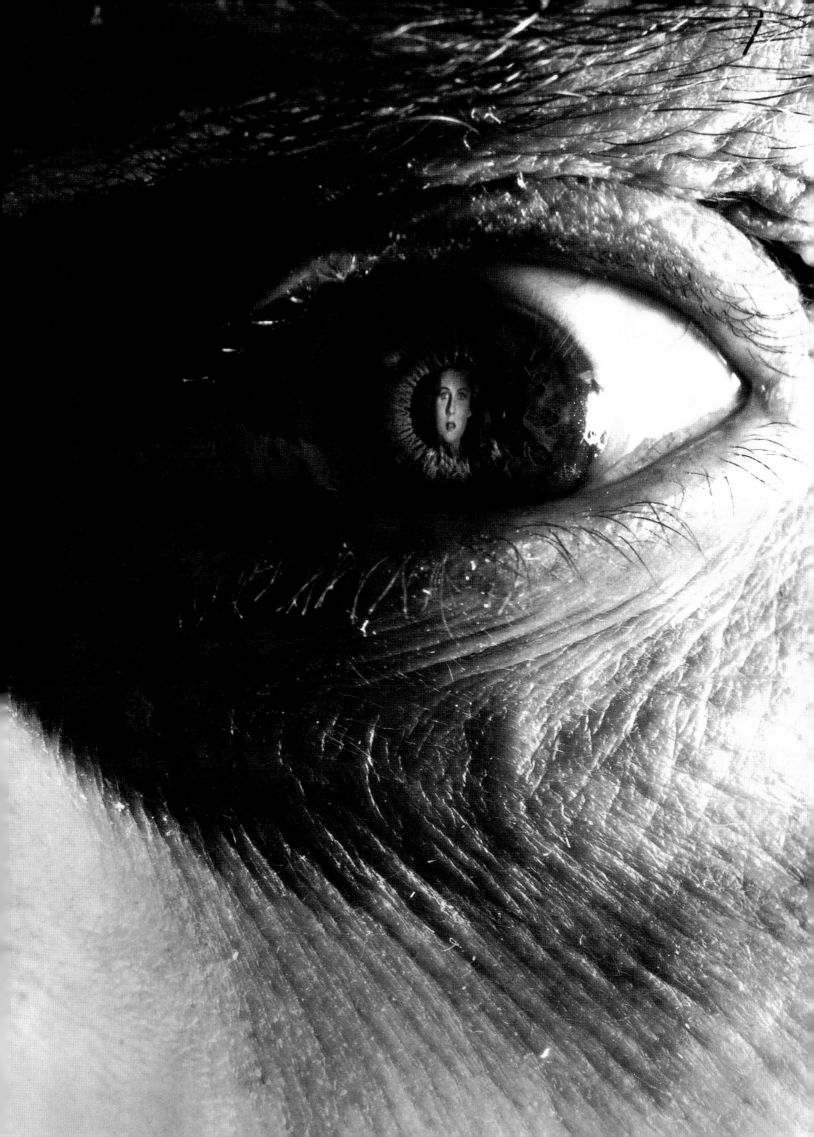

CHAPTER 7

Val Lewton and the Psychology of Fear

Poetry and Danger

RKO–Radio Pictures was the smallest of the majors in 1939, an odd little studio that had barely survived its first ten years. To radio star Orson Welles, RKO was "the greatest electric train set a boy ever had." The studio had just stabilized itself after a series of flops when its president, George Schaefer, gave the headstrong Welles a multimillion-dollar contract. Within three years, Welles's brilliant, uncommercial films had nearly derailed the studio, and both he and Schaefer were out on their ears. World War II was in progress; next door, at Paramount Pictures, someone had scrawled on a wall: "In case of an air raid, go directly to RKO. They haven't had a hit in *years*!"

Joseph Breen stepped down from his post at the Production Code Administration (PCA) and took over the shaky studio for a time in 1942, followed by a dark horse named Charles Koerner, who, according to writer DeWitt Bodeen, "had managed a lot of first-class movie theaters and was brought into RKO to manage the studio because his sense of exploitation was so acute." Breen suggested to Koerner that he hire David O. Selznick's affable story editor, Val Lewton, so Koerner offered Lewton his own production unit at RKO. There were, however, certain conditions.

Lewton could have "artistic freedom" if he: (1) produced "horror programmers"; (2) kept their budgets within $150,000; (3) accepted titles arrived at by a system of marketing research; and (4) agreed to a salary of only $250 a week. Lewton agreed but confided to Bodeen, "They may think I'm going to do the usual chiller stuff which'll make a quick profit, be laughed at, and be forgotten, but I'm going to fool them . . . I'm going to do the kind of suspense movie I like." Bodeen recalled: "Mr. Koerner, who had personally welcomed me on my first day at the studio, was of the opinion that vampires, werewolves, and man-made monsters had been over-exploited and that 'nobody has done much with cats.'" At a Hollywood party, some giddy

person had tossed him a catchy title: *Cat People*. "Let's see what you can do with that," Koerner told Bodeen the next day. Lewton was crestfallen. "There's no helping it," he said to Bodeen. "We're stuck with that title. If you want to get out now, I won't hold it against you." Bodeen needed RKO's $75 a week—and wanted to work with Lewton. "When I first knew Val," said Bodeen, "he was only thirty-seven, a huge, burly, kindly man with a quick sense of humor. He was extremely shy, and easily hurt if his superiors failed to go along with him on story and production plans."

Lewton knew the value of teamwork from his years at Selznick International, so he built a team in which each member had an artistic stake, whether writer, art director, or assistant. In less than three weeks, Bodeen wrote a script inspired by a magazine layout that showed fashion models wearing cat masks. The new team sat in Lewton's office, tore the plot apart, and put it together again. At times, Lewton took the stage. Bodeen recalled: "He would move to the light switch of his office, turn off the lights quickly, and continue recounting the story in the darkened room." After the conference, Lewton would plop himself down at his old Royal typewriter and, with two fingers, rewrite most of the script. "My wife and I would be driving back to the San Fernando Valley at half past one or two in the morning," director Jacques Tourneur remembered. "And always as we passed the studio, we'd see a light in that corner office of his, and he'd be alone, working, correcting what the writer had written. He could only work at that time of night. Next day, he'd hand the work to us."

According to Lewton's wife, Ruth, he dredged his own Russian Jewish psyche to write the first film. He was terrified of cats. "He had a folk fear," she said, "an atavistic kind of fear of something going way, way back. Of course, he knew better. He was a very intellectual man and not a superstitious person—and so he was both frightened and fascinated by his fear." The plot of *Cat People* was not so different from Universal's werewolf fables. A Serbian girl,

In Jacques Tourneur's 1943 **THE LEOPARD MAN,** Mexican actress Margo portrayed a dancer in a small Southwestern town. She was the typical female character in a Val Lewton production—independent, assertive, thoughtful. "I think that came from his being raised by women," said his son, Val Lewton Jr. "They were such a strong influence in his life." Lewton was raised by his aunt, the Russian actress Alla Nazimova, and by his mother, an M-G-M story editor.

Irena (Simone Simon), turns into a panther when jealous of her husband's coworker, Alice (Jane Randolph), or sexually aroused by an unethical psychiatrist (Tom Conway). Lewton's approach to the material, though, was quite different.

"We tossed away the horror formula right from the beginning," Lewton said. "No grisly stuff for us. No mask-like faces, hardly human, with gnashing teeth and hair standing on end. No creaking physical manifestations. No horror piled upon horror." What he counted on to frighten his audiences was something more elemental than the fear of a walking mummy. "The stories he produced," said Bodeen, "are dramatizations of the psychology of fear. Man fears the unknown—the dark, that which may lurk in the shadows. . . . That which he cannot see fills him with basic and understandable terror." What Lewton finally conceived was a format in which to tap this well of fear. "Take a sweet love story," he said, "or a story of sexual antagonisms, about people like the rest of us, not freaks, and cut in your horror here and there by suggestion, and you've got something." Suggestion meant not showing the source of terror. This was unthinkable for Universal, but essential to RKO's low-budget strictures. Bodeen's script met those terms. "In the darkness," he wrote, "to one side of them, there is a sound like a snarl. . . . From the darkness, following them, there is a whisper of light, padded feet, a delicate tick, tick of claws scraping the floor. . . . Now there comes again, pursuing them, the whispering tread of soft paws."

The director on Lewton's team was his friend Jacques Tourneur, with whom he had filmed the Bastille sequences for Selznick's *A Tale of Two Cities* seven years earlier: "Val was the dreamer and I was the materialist," Tourneur recalled. "We complemented each other. By himself, Val might go off the deep end, and I, by myself, might lose a certain poetry." Lewton knew what he wanted. "If you make the screen dark enough," he said, "the mind's eye will read into it anything you want. We're great ones for dark patches." Tourneur had a flair for creating shadowy sequences, perhaps inherited from his father, Maurice Tourneur, who was the silent cinema's first master of chiaroscuro. "We believed in suggesting horror rather than showing it," said Tourneur.

One of the standout sequences in *Cat People* had Alice in a deserted indoor swimming pool late at night, splashing contentedly until she becomes uncomfortably aware that something is prowling along the edge of the pool. "The shadow you saw of the big cat on the wall of the swimming pool was actually my fist," Tourneur admitted later. Another "terror spot" was Alice's solitary nighttime walk through Central Park, an increasingly nervous stroll accented by alternating sounds of high heels and feline growls, and climaxed by an ordinarily innocent noise. Film editor Mark Robson described it: "From the other side of the park, a bus came by and I put a big, solid sound of air brakes on it, cutting it in at the decisive moment so that it knocked viewers out of their seats. This became the 'bus,' and we used the same principle in every film."

A less frightening but equally unsettling scene called for a glamorous stranger in black to unnerve Irena's wedding party by staring at her and saying in Serbian, "Moja sestra? (My sister?)" Lewton was a frequent visitor, along with Aldous Huxley, Christopher Isherwood, and Greta Garbo, to Salka Viertel's Santa Monica salon. He asked her son, Peter, to help him cast the Serbian part. When Viertel met actress Elizabeth Russell, the roommate of his girlfriend, Maria Montez, he said: "I have a friend at RKO who needs a woman for his new movie that looks like a cat."

"You mean you think I look like a *cat*?" asked Russell.

"Well, they'll talk about your looking like a cat, so the audience will accept it," said Viertel, trying not to offend her. Russell went on to make the scene "a strange, mysterious thing."

When Koerner saw the first cut of *Cat People*, he felt that Lewton had let him down. There were not enough shots of the black panther that the studio had paid to rent. Yet the film had been completed in a mere twenty-four days and $7,000 under budget. Lewton apprehensively took it to a sneak preview at the Hillstreet Theatre in downtown Los Angeles, a rowdy blue-collar haunt. Bodeen remembered:

> The preview was preceded by a Disney cartoon about a little pussycat and Val's spirits sank lower and lower as the audience began to catcall and make loud mewing sounds. "Oh, God!" he kept murmuring, as he wiped the perspiration from his forehead. [Our] picture's title was greeted with whoops of derision and louder meows, but when the credits were over and the film began to unreel, the audience quieted, and, as the story progressed, reacted as we had hoped an audience might. There were gasps and some screaming as the shock sequences grew.

At the Rialto Theatre in New York, *Cat People* became a holdover sensation. "It was with a sense of elation that one sat in the back row of the Rialto," recalled writer Don Miller. "[I] watched the concerted scream of the packed house when a bus pulls alongside the girl with the hiss of air-brakes. An optical illusion, perhaps, but it seems that the entire theater audience rose and fell in one rippling wave of fear." Bodeen recalled that "although the café meeting scene of Simone and Elizabeth Russell was very brief, some audience members read a lesbian meaning into the action." Lewton's feline females eventually scared more than $3 million out of audiences. His secretary, Verna De Mots, said, "*Cat People* saved RKO when it was practically bankrupt."

Lewton's next film was called *I Walked with a Zombie*. He overcame his initial aversion to the title by adapting *Jane Eyre*—one of his favorites—to a modern setting in Haiti. Curt Siodmak and Ardel Wray adapted it. "We were all plunged into research on Haitian voodoo," Miss Wray recalled, "every book on the subject Val could find. He was an addictive researcher, drawing out of it the overall feel, mood, and quality he wanted, as well as details for the actual production." Lewton sent her to buy a doll for a sequence in which voodoo animates a figurine. Through the collaborative process, a department-store toy became a charged icon.

Lewton imbued his collaborators with a sense of shared inspiration. "We'd work late," Wray said, "go to dinner at the Melrose Grotto, back to the studio, work some more, then walk out, enjoying and talking about the eerie, half-sinister quality of an empty lot at night." Indeed, it was a nighttime walk that gave this film its most memorable "terror spot," when Frances Dee and Christine Gordon traverse the Haitian jungle in the dead of night to attend a voodoo ceremony. "*I Walked with a Zombie* was the best of Val's films," Robson said, "an absolutely beautiful movie." Credit for this was partly due to the dramatic moonlight effects of Nick Musuraca's cinematography, with its glistening tropical leaves and inky black shadows. And Tourneur, in keeping with the title, kept his agile camera on the move. It was all part of the formula. "After a horror sequence," said Robson, "we always tried to give the audience relief by going to something very beautiful, lyrical if possible. We tried to make the films visually interesting." The team had another hit.

Lewton condensed the formula. "A love story, three scenes of suggested horror and one of actual violence. Fadeout. It's all over in less than seventy minutes." At sixty-six minutes, *The Leopard Man* was his third success story, although he and Tourneur again faced the issue of how not to show the movie's menace, a psychopathic museum curator. In one of his most disturbing set pieces, Lewton has a young Mexican girl tracked by an unseen "leopard" as she runs an errand for her angry mother. What makes the scene almost unbearable is that the errand is unnecessary, the girl is in real danger, and the mother—to punish the girl—refuses to let her into the house, even as she screams for help. Only when blood trickles under the door does the heartless mother realize what she has done. Tourneur later observed that these exercises in terror were "made during the war, and, during war, for some mysterious reason, people love to be frightened. Subconsciously we all enjoy being afraid . . . and in wartime, people had money from the plants, money to burn, and they loved that kind of film." Lewton's tight little team could now take pride in having outdistanced Universal's horror films, both critically and financially.

The surprising profits of the first three Val Lewton films made RKO–Radio Pictures greedy. According to Tourneur: "We were making so much money on our films together that the studio said, 'We'll make twice as much money if we separate them.' So they pulled us apart." Koerner rewarded Lewton by promoting him to A pictures. When Lewton in turn promoted Robson from film editor to director, the studio told Lewton that he could not have an untried director on his first A film. To ensure his own independence and to keep his promise to Robson, Lewton asked the studio to put him back on Bs. He got his wish, as well as another pretested title: *The Seventh Victim*. Charles O'Neal began to write Lewton's idea of an orphan trying to find a murderer before she becomes his seventh victim. Then Lewton changed his mind and hired DeWitt Bodeen to write a script in which the orphan goes to Greenwich Village to find her older sister and save her from a vengeful group of Palladists. "See if it's possible for you to get to a devil-worshipping society meeting," Lewton told Bodeen.

To Bodeen's surprise, RKO quickly located such a group on New York's West Side. He was allowed to attend a meeting, but only as an anonymous, silent observer.

> It was during the war and I would have hated to be Hitler with all the spells they were working against him. They were mostly old people and they were casting these spells while they knitted and crocheted. A bunch of tea-drinking old ladies and gentlemen sitting there muttering imprecations against Hitler. I made use of the experience in that the devil-worshipers in *The Seventh Victim* were very ordinary people who had one basic flaw, an Achilles heel which had turned them against good and towards evil.

In his first draft, Bodeen had a character named Natalie Cortez explain why she has become a Palladist. She is a tall, faded brunette whose black party dress cannot disguise that she has only one arm. "Life has betrayed us," she says. "We've found that there is no Heaven on Earth, so we must worship evil for evil's own sake." *The Seventh Victim* (1943) became Lewton's darkest story, a quest by innocent Mary (Kim Hunter) to save fatalistic Jacqueline (Jean Brooks), the sister who does not want to be saved.

Lewton's team made Mary's search suspenseful with the usual techniques. "Horror spots must be well planned and there should be no more than four or five in a picture," said Lewton. "Most of them are caused by the fundamental fears: sudden sound, wild animals, darkness. The horror addicts will populate the darkness with more horrors than all the horror writers in Hollywood could think of." There were more than enough in this picture. The young heroine accompanies a timid middle-aged detective through a deserted office building; as the suspense of the walk wears off, he falls to the floor, dying of a scissor wound. Later, Jacqueline is almost forced to drink poison by the Palladists but escapes. As she runs through pools of light in grimy alleys, a knife-wielding man creeps behind her. She finally reaches the safety of the brownstone where she has a room. It is furnished with two items: a wooden chair and a noose hanging over it. "*The Seventh Victim*," said Robson, "had a rather sinister quality, of something intangible, but horribly real. It had an atmosphere. I think the actors and the director had to believe very strongly in the possibilities

Mark Robson's **THE SEVENTH VICTIM** was an unlikely wartime film about a cult of devil-worshipers in Greenwich Village. The 1943 Val Lewton production featured the enigmatic Jean Brooks as a renegade Palladist walking a tightrope between life and death.

of disaster, that something *was* there. We believed it ourselves. We talked ourselves into believing it."

Jacqueline, sleek and dark in a Cleopatra wig and a mink coat, tiptoes to her room. A blowzy woman in a bathrobe startles her. "Who are you?" asks Jacqueline.

"I'm Mimi," replies the thin woman with the bony face and tangled hair (Elizabeth Russell). "I'm dying."

"No," says Jacqueline, staring at the neighbor.

"Yes," says Mimi. "I've been quiet. Oh, ever so quiet. I hardly move. And yet it keeps coming all the time, closer and closer. And I rest and I rest. And still I'm dying."

"And you don't want to die. I've always wanted to die. Always."

"I'm afraid," says Mimi, clutching her robe. "And I'm tired of being afraid. Of waiting."

"Why wait?" asks Jacqueline softly, one eyebrow raised.

"I'm not going to wait," says Mimi with a new determination. "I'm going out. I'm going to laugh and dance and do all the things I used to do."

"And then?"

"I don't know." Mimi trails off, distracted, and walks into her room, closing the door.

Jacqueline stares after her and whispers, "You will die." Then she walks slowly to her own room, where the chair and noose await. Mary, waiting with a friend, is relieved to know that Jacqueline has escaped the Palladists. While she is planning a new life for the two of them, we see the hallway outside Jacqueline's room. Mimi's door opens and she comes out, dressed to the nines, her golden hair now elegantly piled atop her head, her sequined cape sparkling in the gaslight.

As she closes her door, ready for a final night of fun, she hears something behind Jacqueline's door—the sound of a chair falling. Mimi shrugs and hurries into the night as Jacqueline's disembodied voice quotes John Donne's *Holy Sonnet VII*: "I runne to Death, and Death meets me as fast, and all my Pleasures are like Yesterday."

Lewton's son, Val Edwin Lewton, said, "I think my father was really very pessimistic, and I think that comes out in his films. They may look cheerful and hopeful enough, but I think the real effect behind them was a dark pessimism and hopelessness. This whole dialogue of death—he was obsessed with it." *The Seventh Victim* did not get the reviews that Lewton had come to expect, and its box-office receipts lagged behind its predecessors.

Lewton's next film was planned around a single standing set, a ship built for the 1939 film *Pacific Liner*. "We were interested in single source lighting," Robson explained. "We chose sets that were suitable for single source. It made setups and characters very interesting. It was important for us to use light for dramatic purposes." *The Ghost Ship* (1943) was another of Lewton's waking nightmares. A sailor (Russell Wade) finds himself the only crew member who knows that the captain (Richard Dix) is a psychopathic killer. "We thought everything out," said Robson. "We had to do this to accomplish what we did with such low budgets. Val emphasized detail. I remembered that Orson [Welles] had said, 'Detail is the most important thing. The big things take care of themselves.'" The film was doing well when it was stopped by what appeared to be a nuisance suit, a claim that Lewton had plagiarized the story from an unsolicited manuscript. Lewton later lost the suit, and the film was pulled from circulation, the first of the series of bad turns that doomed his career.

As 1943 ended, though, Lewton was still making films that were both personal and profitable. Bodeen recalled: "When he was given the assignment to make the sequel to *Cat People*, he groaned because he was told to call it *The Curse of the Cat People*. So he said, 'What I'm going to do is make a very delicate story of a child who is on the verge of insanity because she lives in a fantasy world.'" Lewton assembled his repertory of players—Kent Smith, Jane Randolph, Simone Simon, Elizabeth Russell—and replaced a slow director, Gunther Fritsch, with film editor Robert Wise. Russell, who played a frustrated actress in the film, recalled that Lewton "was constantly on the set, and had the worried look all the time. He was always in there, perfecting the script the night before." He also oversaw such details as the main titles and publicity. "Val had been involved in publishing," said Robson, "and had a great sense of typography, so the lettering of the main titles was gone over very carefully. We used Caslon Old Style—very clear, lovely, wonderfully stylish lettering—and we would italicize caps for the first letter of each word." There was also a concern that the RKO publicity department not misrepresent the film. "We would ask the heads of the advertising unit to please not use the goddamned 'fur' letters and other trick lettering that gave one a supposed sense of horror," Robson recalled. Still, the publicists insisted on ballyhooing the film as if it were a Universal monster movie. The press book trumpeted: "Sensational Return of the Killer Cat Woman." Exhibitors were advised: "Send out a group of men and women wearing cat masks to walk through the streets with cards on their backs reading: 'Are cats people?'"

When Lewton's bosses finally saw the film they were less than happy, according to Bodeen. "I remember after *Curse of the Cat People* the front office thought Val had betrayed them because they wanted more horror." But the audience would be the judge. James Agee sat with a New York audience in March 1944. "And when the picture ended," he wrote, "and it was clear beyond further suspense that anyone who had come to see a story about curses and were-cats should have stayed away, they clearly did not feel sold out; for an hour they had been captivated by the poetry and danger of childhood, and they showed it in their thorough applause." Agee was becoming one of Lewton's biggest boosters. In the January 20, 1945, issue of *The Nation*, he summed up Lewton's oeuvre to date. "I esteem them so highly because for all their unevenness, their achievements are so consistently alive, limber, poetic, humane, so eager toward the possibilities of the screen, and so resolutely against the grain of all we have learned to expect from the big studios."

To compete with the big studios, or even with a "major minor" like Universal, RKO needed more than poetry and imaginary cat people. It needed someone to boss Lewton, and where else to turn *but* Universal?

Horror Meets Terror

As a unique combination of producer and writer, Val Lewton had grown accustomed to dealing directly with RKO-Radio head Charles Koerner. After the diminishing returns of *The Seventh Victim*, *The Ghost Ship*, and *The Curse of the Cat People*, Lewton ran afoul of an executive named Sid Rogell. At Lewton's request, Koerner replaced Rogell with an emigré from another studio. "I now find myself

top
Screenwriter DeWitt Bodeen suggested veteran actress Julia Dean to Lewton for his 1944 film **THE CURSE OF THE CAT PEOPLE**. Dean gave a memorable performance as a reclusive former actress who lives in a dream world of colored spotlights and echoing applause, and Lewton's masterly mise-en-scène gave her an animated backdrop.

above
Much of the power of Lewton's dreamlike films can be credited to cinematographer Nick Musuraca, who used spotlights to paint calligraphic shadows on the walls of otherwise unremarkable sets. The controlled, intelligent performance given by Frances Dee was another asset of **I WALKED WITH A ZOMBIE**.

working for an abysmally ignorant and stupid gentleman
called Jack Gross," Lewton wrote to his mother, "the man
who has been making those Universal horror films and so
had a particular grudge against me, as our pictures had
shown up his films, not only from an artistic viewpoint, but
also from a standpoint of profits." This was not entirely
accurate. Jack J. Gross came from Universal to RKO in
early 1944 with a rather impressive portfolio, having produced *My Little Chickadee*, *The Wolf Man*, and *Son of
Dracula*. Mark Robson said, "In a way, I think [Val] was a
man who needed an enemy." Lewton may have imagined
envy, but not self-importance. "Jack Gross called Val into
his office for a conference," recalled Robson. "Gross had
come to RKO from Universal, where the prevailing idea of
horror was a werewolf chasing a girl in a nightgown up a
tree." Also at the meeting was a taciturn exhibition executive named Holt.

"O.K.," said the peremptory Gross. "We've just signed
Boris Karloff to a [two-picture] contract and you're going to
use him in your next film."

Lewton was less than thrilled to hear that his subtle
exercises in terror would be compromised by what he considered a hammy bogeyman. There was no title yet, so the
meeting was awkwardly adjourned.

As Lewton and Robson headed for the door, Holt
spoke up. "Remember!" he said, pointing at Lewton. "No
messages!"

Lewton turned and left without a word, but by the time
he got to his office he was furious. He had his secretary get
Holt on the line. "I'm sorry, but we do have a message, Mr.
Holt. And our message is that death is good!"

What Lewton did not know was that Boris Karloff had
signed with RKO because he was fed up with Universal's
horror act. "I dislike the word 'horror,' yet it is a word that
has been tagged to me," said Karloff. "It is a misnomer, for
it means revulsion. The films I have made were made for
entertainment, maybe with the object of making the audience's hair stand on end, but never to revolt people. Perhaps 'terror' would be a much better word to describe
these films." The decline he had predicted for the Frankenstein Monster had indeed taken place. "When it started to
become *Frankenstein Meets the Wolf Man*," he said, "it
was done from hunger." Perhaps RKO, which was paying
him $6,000 a week, would be a little more imaginative.
Soon it was time for him to meet the reluctant Lewton.

"It was strange, the first meeting," Robert Wise
recalled. "Boris came to the studio for a meeting with Val,
Mark, and me. I had never seen him except on the screen,
and this was before [I had seen him in a] color film. When
he first walked in the door, I was startled by his coloring,
the strange bluish cast—but when he turned those eyes on
us and that velvet voice said, 'Good afternoon, gentlemen,'
we were his, and never thought about anything else."
Someone was thinking about Universal monster rallies
because Bela Lugosi's name came up. Karloff, ever tactful,
agreed to work with him. At this point, Lugosi was eking
out a living in Poverty Row programmers and occasionally
doing scenes from *Dracula* in summer-stock productions.
He was preparing for one such tour when his ongoing
financial anxiety took the form of ulcers. A sympathetic
doctor treated the pain as well as the gastric distress.
Lugosi was soon addicted to morphine.

Lewton endured the indignity of presenting script pro-
posals to RKO. The first project to be approved was a story
he dreamed up as a child while staring for hours at Arnold
Böcklin's painting *Isle of the Dead*. The film commenced
shooting on July 14, 1944, but Karloff began to suffer
severe back pain. "Between shots, he was in a wheelchair,
but he made no complaints," recalled writer Ardel Wray.
"He managed to be wryly humorous about it—not falsely,
in that obnoxious 'See how brave I'm being' way.'" Lewton
shut down production and Karloff entered Good Samaritan
Hospital for a spinal fusion. The operation was a success,
but his recovery took six weeks. *Isle of the Dead* was post-

poned because of other cast members' commitments.

Another proposal was *The Body Snatcher.* Lewton had written to Gross on May 10, outlining the reasons why Robert Louis Stevenson's 1884 short story would make a Karloff vehicle. His reasons were: (1) a good title; (2) the exploitation value of a classic; (3) its public-domain status; (4) a period setting that could still be filmed cheaply; and (5) a character that could be adapted for Bela Lugosi. Stevenson's story made anecdotal use of the 1829 case of Burke and Hare, two Edinburgh "resurrectionists" who murdered eighteen people in order to supply cadavers for the anatomy lab of the infamous Dr. Knox. Burke's claim to fame was suffocating each victim by forcefully holding his hand over the nose and mouth.

Lewton and writer Philip MacDonald expanded Gray's character to fit Karloff's stature and loaded the script with scenes of dissection, mayhem, and death. Alas, Joseph Breen refused to pass the script "because of the repellent nature of such matter, which has to do with grave-robbing, dissecting bodies, and pickling bodies." Lewton hurriedly rewrote the script, but a nervous MacDonald worried that the hasty rewriting might reflect badly on him, so he insisted that Lewton share credit; Lewton used the pseudonym "Carlos Keith." One of the first scenes he cut showed a bereaved woman trying to locate a loved one in a laboratory littered with spare parts. While Lewton strove to make the script acceptable to Breen, Gross pushed him to write more horror. "It breaks my heart to see Val come home night after night late and so discouraged," wrote Lewton's wife, Ruth. "You know his temperament. It's hard for him to throw off slights, fancied or otherwise." Breen, who respected Lewton, approved his revisions.

"Boris was very keen to do this film because he felt it gave him an opportunity to show that he could act as well as play the monster," said director Robert Wise. "He was fascinated by the duel between him and Henry Daniell, one of the great character actors of the time." Daniell was known for his sardonic, showy roles in *Camille*, *The Sea Hawk*, and *Jane Eyre*. "Henry Daniell was a nice man," recalled actor Alan Napier, "but he was a crazy man. Believed in the devil and that sort of thing. He had a belief in the powers of evil." Karloff called him "a pro, a real honest-to-goodness pro. There was no rubbish with him, no faking." Karloff rose to the occasion in spite of ongoing pain. "He had back problems," recalled Wise, "but he never let that interfere a bit, and was determined to show that he could hold his own with Henry Daniell."

As anticipated, their scenes crackled with the electricity that only two great performers can generate. The well-structured script gave each successive encounter between Karloff's insolent grave robber and Daniell's guilty doctor an additional charge until Karloff's final speech: "I am a small man, a humble man, and, being poor, I have had to do much that I did not want to do. But so long as the great Dr. MacFarlane jumps at my whistle, that long am I a man. And if I have not that, I have nothing."

Karloff's scenes with Lugosi were a different matter. "Lugosi was quite ill," recalled actor Robert Clarke, "and he was not very communicative. He talked very little to anyone. He was off by himself, and he spent a lot of time lying on his back in his dressing room." Lugosi was playing the

doctor's half-wit assistant, so he did not have long speeches to memorize. However, illness, narcotics, and alcohol debilitated him. "He was a little vague," said Wise. "He was not quite on it, which was all right for the role, because he played a not-very-bright guy." There was one juicy scene, though, in which Lugosi tries to blackmail Karloff and is knocked to the floor, suffocated, and thrown in a vat of brine. The physical demands of the scene could have harmed Lugosi. "I always appreciated Karloff's sensitivity," said Wise. "Boris was very gentle with him." Indeed, the big horror star began to win many admirers at RKO, including visiting servicemen who watched him carry a cadaver onto the set. When Wise called cut, they were amazed to hear Karloff say to them, "God damn it, this thing is heavy!" Overjoyed that he was not playing a monster or a mad scientist, Karloff invested his performance with his own intellectual humor. No one ever had so much fun being "bad." The results showed on film, earning both financial and critical rewards. The *Hollywood Reporter* called *The Body Snatcher* "an unqualified lulu, certain to satisfy the most ardent chill-and-thrill craver, for this is about as grisly an affair as the screen has ever ventured to offer."

Isle of the Dead went into production on December 1, 1944. Koerner was ill, so Lewton had to argue with Gross about how much horror to film. As a result, last-minute rewriting caused much of the film to be overexpository and episodic. What worked, however, was the scene in which Mrs. St. Aubyn (Katherine Emery), terrified of being buried alive, succumbs to the plague and is interred. "After the pallbearers have gone," James Agee wrote, "the camera coldly, tenderly approaches the coffin in a silence so intense as to be almost unbearable. When the shriek of the prematurely buried woman finally comes, it releases the rest of the show into a free-for-all masterpiece of increasing

In Val Lewton's 1945 **ISLE OF THE DEAD**, Karloff was supported by Helene Thimig, the wife of theatrical legend Max Reinhardt. With director Mark Robson, they made this tale of suspicion, plague, and madness a hit. Film critic James Agee called the film "as brutally frightening and gratifying a horror movie as I can remember."

as she is trapped with them forms the story that Robson cowrote with Lewton. "The stories of his pictures are not half so important as the experiments and innovative effects he tried," said Robson, "and his ideas about shock and beauty in motion pictures."

Chamber of Horrors, ultimately called *Bedlam* (1946), had a slickness that belied its budget; it used standing sets from *The Bells of St. Mary's* and a hand-me-down gown from *Gone with the Wind*. Lewton made the most of each set piece and Karloff threw himself into the part of Sims with gruesome relish, dishing out cruelty with a lisp and a smile. In one scene, he makes his patients perform for the rich guests at a Vauxhall masque. After beating one lunatic (Glenn Vernon) into memorizing a sycophantic speech, he then paints him gold so he can portray Reason. The disoriented young man cannot recite his speech because his skin is starting to suffocate. When he collapses and dies, Sims makes obsequious jokes with the uncaring nobility.

"Boris used to get quite annoyed when people referred to it as a horror picture," Lee remembered. "He said, 'It's not a horror picture. It's a *historical* picture.'" Karloff explained:

> Horror too often is played for revulsion. Val used to say that the audience is the best actor in theater, if you give it a chance. Let the audience fill in the details, Val said. If you do everything for them, the power of the imagination doesn't come into play.

Master Sims (Boris Karloff) shows off Dorothea the Dove (Joan Newton), one of his prize "loonies" in Mark Robson's 1946 **BEDLAM**, a harrowing journey into the St. Mary of Bethlehem asylum. Producer Val Lewton re-created the eighteenth century with studio remnants and a lively imagination.

Karloff enjoyed himself as he mugged for Ernest Bachrach's portrait camera after finishing **BEDLAM**. Karloff found Lewton a liberating influence.

terror." A West Virginia exhibitor concurred. "The first part of the picture is boring, but the last part had my patrons screaming and shouting their heads off."

Lewton had hardly finished *Isle of the Dead* when Charles Koerner died of leukemia. His death in February 1945 left RKO in disarray and Lewton without an advocate. Karloff was interested in working with Lewton again, but first had to honor a promise to entertain troops in the Pacific for several months. When Karloff returned, Lewton had to compete for his services. Universal was offering Karloff a three-picture contract. "I came home and we went to the studio," said Karloff, "and, to my horror, I found that the first film was a Frankenstein." He tried to be polite, but an unnamed producer forced the issue.

"Don't ask me to feel sorry for you," said the producer. "You can quit after your next picture. I have to keep making them."

"But you'll have to get another Monster," smiled Karloff, ending the negotiations.

Lewton could breathe a sigh of relief about Universal, but when he saw M-G-M's *Picture of Dorian Gray*, he was envious. "We make horror films because we have to make them, and we make them for little money and fight every minute to make them right," wrote Lewton. "Here's a man who makes a bawdy horror story out of a classic, with no compulsion upon him to do so and with every facility that money and time can provide for the making of a good film. Mr. Lewin just hasn't got it. He must be a poop."

With Robson again directing, Lewton got to work on *Chamber of Horrors*, a project inspired by Plate Eight of William Hogarth's "The Rake's Progress." Karloff would portray Master Sims, an inhuman bureaucrat who runs the St. Mary of Bethlehem asylum ("Bedlam"). Nell Bowen (Anna Lee) is a rich man's toy who comes to despise Sims for his treatment of the "loonies." Her struggle to help them even

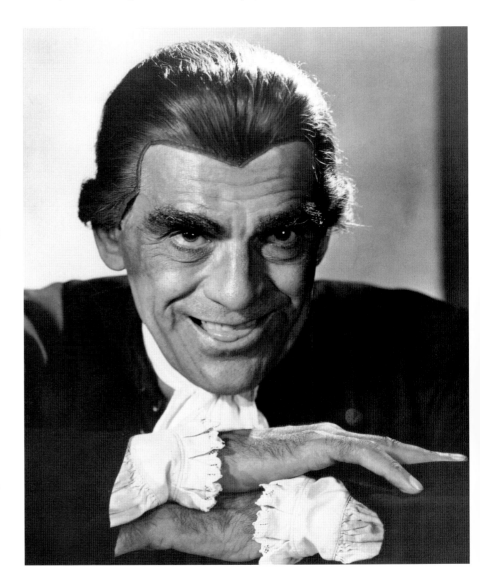

Suggest things. [They] need suggestions to stimulate their imaginations. . . . Only outline the details.

The scenes in the asylum had contrasty images of stark white arms shooting out from opaque shadows and a soundtrack vibrant with the cacophony of madness. Together they conveyed the filth and misery of the notorious institution. Once again, Agee had praise for Lewton: "I think that few people in Hollywood show in their work that they know or care half as much about movies or human beings." As the 1946 film became yet another Lewton hit, Karloff was interviewed for a *Los Angeles Times* article titled "Farewell to Monsters." In it, Louis Berg wrote a touching sentence: "Mr. Karloff has great love and respect for Mr. Lewton, as the man who rescued him from the living dead and restored, so to speak, his soul."

Perhaps some sort of transference had occurred between the two artists, because *Bedlam* was the beginning of the end for Val Lewton. "Pressure was placed upon him to get out of B pictures and into something better, something which Val never really wanted to do," said Wise. "But he was not immune to the pressures of this town—more money, more status, the urgings of his agent. He was pushed out of his home at RKO and couldn't deal with what he found elsewhere." In November 1946 Lewton suffered a heart attack. He then left RKO, and at one studio after another—Paramount, Metro, Universal—tried to make A films that would have the vitality of his Bs. "Fighting for what he wanted wore Val out, and failure to get it broke his heart," said Napier. "He should have been an independent producer, [yet] he needed the protection of a big studio."

In the late 1940s the studio system—assaulted by the Supreme Court, hostile senators, and television—was beginning to sag under its own weight. Lewton had had trouble playing the game when he knew the rules. Now, ignored by an industry that was making new rules, he grew despondent. He sat in a silent office, sometimes sobbing behind its closed door. "The whole aspect of such waiting is just too corrosive," Lewton wrote to his mother. "One even begins to doubt one's own abilities." Bodeen said, "I never knew anybody who was so desperately unhappy, who lost all faith in himself." If he had been able to hold out a bit longer, he might have benefited from the cataclysmic changes that were roiling the motion-picture industry, but he could not. Val Lewton suffered a second heart attack and died on March 13, 1951. He was forty-six years old.

above
The *New York Daily News* lauded Karloff's performance in **BEDLAM** as "the personification of evil genius." In his three films with Val Lewton, he was allowed to create rounded, textured characters. Portrait by Ernest Bachrach

left
This Bachrach portrait shows Karloff with one of the cadavers he had to carry in **THE BODY SNATCHER.** "Karloff was not particularly well at the time," Wise recalled. "He was having a lot of back problems, but he didn't let that stop him at all. He was in there, working."

"They torment me. I wake in the night and the tread of their feet whispers in my brain. I have no peace. I have no peace . . . for they are in me." The thirty-one-year-old French actress Simone Simon played a Serbian dress designer in Jacques Tourneur's 1942 film **CAT PEOPLE**, the first of the nine legendary "terror" films Val Lewton produced for RKO. Lewton's films were populated with characters that had real jobs and lived in recognizable settings. "If you're going to have horror," said Tourneur, "the audience must be able to identify with the characters in order to be frightened." When casting the film, Lewton said, "I'd like to have [for] the girl a little kitten-face like Simone Simon, cute and soft and cuddly and seemingly not at all dangerous." This duality was odd, according to Lewton's wife. "He was very unhappy about cats," she said. "I think it stemmed from an old folk tale he remembered from Russia—that cats were peculiar creatures that you couldn't trust." Portrait by Ernest Bachrach

The Atomic

CHAPTER 8

Poisoned Air

Kiss Me Deadly

overleaf

THEM! was a 1954 Warner Bros. film about the possible side effects of nuclear testing. Instead of animated miniatures, technicians used ants at one-and-a-half human size. "They had people in them," said actress Sandy Descher, "working the legs, you know, much like a float in the New Year's Day Parade. They were aluminum with netting all over them, and the hairs were glued on."

opposite

Robert Aldrich's 1955 **KISS ME DEADLY** was a Cold War hybrid of the detective, horror, and science-fiction genres. In this scene, Gaby Rodgers becomes an atomic Pandora.

Mickey Spillane was the son of a Brooklyn bartender, a veteran of World War II who read Dumas and then got the itch to write. His formula was to seclude himself for two weeks, writing toward an ending he already knew, and to aim his exercises in sex and violence at the paperback audience. By 1965, seven of his Mike Hammer novels were among the top thirty books written since 1895—not bad for an author who never revised a manuscript.

One of Spillane's biggest fans was Victor Saville, producer of big-budget M-G-M films such as *Dr. Jekyll and Mr. Hyde*. Robert Aldrich, meanwhile, was one of the new generation of directors at Saville's home base. He had come up through the ranks by working as production manager to renegade directors Abraham Polonsky and Lewis Milestone at the well-intentioned but short-lived Enterprise Pictures. Seeing the "alternative to the big studios" founder under the big-studio expense of *Force of Evil* and *Arch of Triumph* proved a valuable lesson for this admirer of Orson Welles. He learned how to shoot quickly and cheaply by directing filmed television in New York. This, of course, made him desirable to the big studios. "Victor Saville, who owned rights to all Mickey Spillane, came to me and asked if I would direct one," Aldrich recalled. "I agreed to do it, provided he would let me make the kind of movie I wanted and provided I could produce it."

Aldrich formed a production company and read Spillane's *Kiss Me, Deadly*. It was one of the multimillion-selling Mike Hammer detective stories, and it was lurid. In it, Hammer breaks open a drug ring, sneering, slugging, and shooting his way from one vicious situation to the next. In the messy climax, he corners the malevolent art collector, Dr. Soberin. "He was quiet in his chair. The quiet that terror brings and for once he was knowing the hand of terror himself. I said, 'Doc . . .' and he looked at me. No, not me, the gun. The big hole in the end of the gun. And while he was

looking I let him have what came out of the gun. Doctor Soberin had only one eye left." Then Hammer learns that Lily, the girl whom he has been trying to save from the gang, is one of them. "The gun pressed into my belt as she kneeled forward, bringing the revulsion with her. 'You're going to die now . . . but first you can do it. Deadly . . . deadly . . . kiss me.'" Knowing she has just taken an alcohol bath, Hammer pushes a lit cigarette lighter against her, turning her into a shrieking human torch.

Aldrich was not impressed. "We just took the title [minus the comma] and threw the book away." Joseph Breen had just retired from the Production Code Administration, but his successor, Geoffrey Shurlock, told Aldrich that the drugs were off limits. Aldrich changed the "Great Whatsit" that all the characters in the book were pursuing to an element that moved the film out of the detective category and into the atomic.

Less than ten years earlier the United States government had learned the destructive power of science. In early 1945, President Harry Truman wrote: "We have discovered the most terrible bomb in the history of the world. It may be the fire destruction prophesied in the Euphrates Valley Era, after Noah and his fabulous Ark." In August 1945, he made the decision to use two atomic bombs to pulverize Japan's resistance and end World War II. The bombs killed more than 200,000 people instantly and left a legacy of pollution, mistrust, and death. When the Soviet Union began testing its own nuclear devices, the world was polarized in a new type of conflict, a "Cold War." Its chill first reached Hollywood in the form of the "Red Scare" that had rabid Senator Joe McCarthy looking for suspected communists in every sound stage, then vilifying them and destroying their careers. The Cold War next reached its frigid fingers into Hollywood scripts, imbuing them with a miasma of fear. Routine horror films began to portray science as a tool more evil than Dr. Frankenstein had ever anticipated.

In keeping with the temper of the times, Aldrich moved Spillane's nasty detective story into a universe ruled by the "darkness and corruption" cited in "Remember," the Christina Rossetti poem that holds the clue to finding the Great Whatsit. *Kiss Me Deadly* (1955) became an amalgam of horror, terror, and science fact, evoking fears that could be neither ignored nor discussed. Aldrich, who had lost friends to both war and blacklisting, later said of his film: "It did have a basic significance in our political framework that we thought rather important in those political times: that the end did not justify the means." Spillane's out-of-control detective was the perfect character with whom to preach this idea, a sex-and-violence machine whose quest for the Great Whatsit brings him face-to-face with a device of apocalyptic power.

"The scriptwriter, A. I. Bezzerides, did a marvelous job," said Aldrich, "contributing a great deal of inventiveness to the picture. That devilish box, for example—an obvious atom bomb control—was mostly his idea." In the film, Mike Hammer (Ralph Meeker) uses wit, coercion, and graphic violence in order to find out what a gallery of bizarre Los Angeles characters is so desperate to hide. It turns out to be a leather-covered box stashed in a locker of the Hollywood Athletic Club. When he gingerly starts to open it, it emits a blinding light and an ungodly noise. "We worked a long time to get the sound it made, the ticking and hissing," Aldrich recalled. "We finally used the sound of an airplane exhaust overdubbed with the sound made by human vocal cords when someone breathes out noisily, so that it became a subdued jet roar, a 'sonic box' type of thing." Having established that this is no ordinary box, the

film snatches it from Hammer, who must endure yet more violence to reach it. The box is now at the beachfront house of the urbane, mellow-voiced Dr. Soberin (Albert Dekker). With Soberin is Lily Carver (Gaby Rodgers), the seemingly dizzy waif who is actually Gabrielle, a treacherous siren who has betrayed Hammer to Soberin. As Soberin and Gabrielle stand over the mysterious box, Bezzerides's dialogue improves on the book.

"You have been misnamed, Gabrielle," says Soberin. "You should have been called Pandora. She had a curiosity about a box and opened it, and let loose all the evil in the world."

"Never mind about the evil," Gabrielle dismisses him. "What's in it?"

"Did you ever hear of Lot's wife?" When his biblical allusion fails, Soberin tries mythology. "The head of the Medusa. That's what's in the box. And whoever looks on her will be changed, not into stone, but into brimstone and ashes . . ."

"Whatever is in that box, it must be very precious. So many people have died for it."

"Yes," replies Soberin. "It *is* very precious."

"I want half," says Gabrielle flatly.

Soberin tries to humor her, but finally says, "Unfortunately, the object in this box cannot be divided."

"Then I'll take it all," Gabrielle says softly. "If you don't mind." She pulls out a gun and shoots Soberin.

"Gabrielle," gasps Soberin, sinking to the floor. "Listen to me, as if I were Cerberus, barking with all his heads at the gates of Hell. I will tell you where to take it. But don't . . . don't open the box." Soberin collapses on the floor,

The villains in **KISS ME DEADLY** come from walks of life usually accorded respect in Hollywood films. In this scene, a morgue director (Percy Helton) asks detective Mike Hammer (Ralph Meeker) and the peculiar "Lily Carver" (Gaby Rodgers) for a bribe. All he gets are his fingers jammed in a drawer. Robert Aldrich had originally intended Rodgers's character to be a drug-addicted lesbian but could have no explicit scenes due to the Production Code. He changed the character but kept the look. Rodgers said: "Hollywood's idea of having you portray a lesbian at that time was to have your hair all chopped off and to be dressed in a tuxedo."

dead. Gabrielle steps over him to loosen the straps that enclose the outer case of the box. She is interrupted by the arrival of Mike Hammer.

"Hello, Mike," she politely points the gun at him. "Come in," she says to the wary Hammer. She suddenly becomes kittenish. "Kiss me, Mike. I want you to kiss me. Kiss me . . . the liar's kiss, that says 'I love you,' but means something else. You're good at giving such kisses. *Kiss me.*"

Before Hammer can accede or refuse, Gabrielle shoots him too. He falls to the floor. She redirects her attention to the box, now loosening the straps and opening the outer case. A gray metal box is inside. She touches the top. It is hot. Undaunted, she slowly raises the lid. A roaring, hissing sound emanates from it, followed by a white-hot light. Gabrielle's clothing ignites.

Hammer rouses himself and manages to escape what is turning into an inferno. He rescues his secretary, Velda (Maxine Cooper), and together, they stumble onto the beach. As they splash into the Pacific Ocean, the entire beach house explodes in a nuclear fireball.

Stage actress Gaby Rodgers played Lily-Gabrielle. "It was really Aldrich's show," she remembered. "He was a very good-natured, easy-going man, and had a large family. [I] couldn't believe that such a nice man had made such a sadistic film." Neither could CBS-TV censor Ed Nathan. He refused to air commercials for *Kiss Me Deadly*, saying that the film had "no purpose except to incite sadism and bestiality in human beings." Nathan's attempt to silence the messenger proved that the noisome events of the mid–twentieth century were inspiring works of art, hybrids that could not easily be classified as horror, crime fiction, or science fiction.

Lab Work

The atomic bomb was quietly resting and the Red Scare was still on the horizon when, from out of nowhere, another kind of bomb fell on Hollywood. On May 4, 1948, the Supreme Court handed down a ruling that declared the five major studios in violation of antitrust laws. The ruling abolished block-booking and ordered these studios to divest themselves of their theater chains. Harry Warner urged his peers to fight the ruling, but any hope of solidarity was lost when maverick mogul Howard Hughes signed a consent decree that cut RKO's theaters loose. In short order, the other studios fell like dominoes, scattering theaters in all directions. Exhibitors who had been forced to take any old B picture in order to get an eagerly awaited A now had a choice. The majors tried to adapt, but it was obvious that the era of the independents had begun.

United Artists had been the first studio to distribute independent productions. Samuel Goldwyn, David O. Selznick, and Stanley Kramer had all enjoyed UA's hospitality in the forties. As in-house studio financing became trickier, independent producers began to find open doors at studios that once would have told them to go to UA. One producer who stayed with UA was Allan Dowling, who packaged a new version of Curt Siodmak's novel, *Donovan's Brain.* Siodmak had not gotten along with his brother Robert or with Val Lewton, but he now wanted to direct his

The 1953 version of **DONOVAN'S BRAIN** was a story of mind control. Actor Gene Evans remembered that Nancy Davis (later Reagan), shown here with Lew Ayres, also espoused the theme of control. "She was always telling the director how the thing should be done," said Evans. "He'd have to tell her, 'Nancy, this is a fifteen- or twenty-day shoot. These walls are put up, and we have to live with them. We can't move things around.' Now, Lew had no problem with her. He just paid no attention."

own story. Once again, his ego got in the way. Herbert L. Strock, assistant to coproducer Tom Gries, recalled: "It seems that in discussion of how things were going to be done, Curt became the stiff, Germanic, immobile person, and would not listen. Gries and the producer, Allan Dowling, became very upset. I pleaded with them to keep Curt on, that I would guide him through, but behind my back they bumped him."

As scripted and directed by Felix Feist, the new *Donovan's Brain* (1953) had a well-meaning scientist, Patrick Cory (Lew Ayres), preserving the brain of a nasty millionaire killed in a plane crash. With the assistance of a boozy country doctor (Gene Evans), Cory keeps the brain alive, unaware that it will soon be controlling him and everyone else in his sphere. The brain makes Cory think and act like the ruthless businessman that Donovan was, using coercion and blackmail to quash his competitors. The concept of mind control was, of course, topical in an industry nervous about communist infiltration. How the low-budget film materialized the evil brain was something else. "We're leaning over this fish tank, and the brain's floating in it," Evans remembered. "It's this big, globby piece of rubber with this green light under it." The two actors contained themselves until Feist instructed them.

"All right now," he said. "I really want a reaction here, Gene. And Lew, keep up your energy." The camera rolled. "We'll soon know," intoned Ayres.

As Evans recalled: "All of a sudden this green light starts glowing and the brain starts puffing up and throbbing. We cracked up, because it was the funniest-looking thing we'd ever seen. It looked like a big, pulsating pussy. I got hysterical and had to go sit down."

Stanley Kramer had made hits for United Artists of *Champion* and *High Noon*. No wonder, then, that the redoubtable Harry Cohn allowed him to produce a strange project for Columbia Pictures. "For years I'd imagined something like a cheap British Gothic horror film," said Kramer. To enter this genre, Kramer chose an unlikely property. *The 5,000 Fingers of Dr. T.* was a children's story by the beloved Dr. Seuss, whose real name was Theodore Geisel. In it, a child has a nightmare that his piano teacher, Dr. Terwilliker (Hans Conried), is a megalomaniac who imprisons five hundred boys so that he can control their minds—and hands. Geisel had once taken piano lessons "from a man who rapped my knuckles with a pencil whenever I made a mistake. I made up my mind I would finally get even with that man. It took me forty-three years to catch up with him. He became the Terwilliker of the movie."

None of Kramer's previous projects had cost even $1 million to make. Columbia, while denying him the budget of a Rita Hayworth musical, gave him Franz Planer's Technicolor camerawork, Frederick Hollander's songs, and Rudolph Sternad's expressionistic art direction, all of which came to $2.75 million. A visiting journalist reported: "They have built a gigantic piano with a double-tier keyboard curving in a gigantic S across two adjoining sound stages. Above it is the podium where the tyrannical Dr. Terwilliker instructs his little charges in his 'Happy Fingers' piece." Most of this bizarre imagery was courtesy of Geisel, whose La Jolla, California, home was "decorated with the stuffed heads of monsters that never existed, such as a unicorn with a horn made of a spindle-chair leg, or a walrus with a mustache made up of shaving brushes."

Translated to the screen by choreographer Eugene Loring and director Roy Rowland, Geisel's childhood nemesis became a pompous queen lording it over not only his hapless students but also a bevy of strategically uncovered chorus boys whose writhing and posing was uncomfortably evocative of sadomasochistic homosexual literature. Even the *Los Angeles Times* noticed the scent of lavender. "The teacher—Dr. Terwilliker, played by the actor Hans Conried—is a fabulous character, too," wrote Louis Berg. "He wears various getups which are a combination of a circus band drum major, Carmen Miranda, and Herman Goering." Hardly kiddie fare, the film disturbed children and revolted adults. After this 1953 bomb, Cohn had to wait two years for an atomic hit. It came from an ascetic young animator named Ray Harryhausen.

The control of young minds was the theme of **THE 5,000 FINGERS OF DR. T.**, in which a reluctant student (Tommy Rettig) finds himself in the nightmare domain of the foppish pedant, Dr. Terwilliker (Hans Conried). The film was a tour de force of art direction and three-strip Technicolor cinematography, but its homosexual subtext repelled 1953 audiences.

CHAPTER 9
Poisoned Waters

CREATURE FROM THE
BLACK LAGOON (1954) was
Universal International's first
new monster since 1941's *The
Wolf Man*. The concept of a
fish-man had a curious connection with another film made that
year, *Citizen Kane*. This photograph shows Ben Chapman
relaxing between shots.

Modern Inconveniences

In 1933, a boy barely thirteen went to see *King Kong*. Ray Harryhausen recalled: "I came out of the theater stunned and haunted." Once he recovered, he set himself to emulating Willis O'Brien's techniques and turned his parents' garage into a miniature movie studio. To animate a cave bear, he built a fully jointed wooden skeleton and "found" its other ingredients. "My mother's fur coat provided the exterior," Harryhausen later admitted. Fortunately, his parents encouraged his unusual talent, as did one of his few young friends, a budding writer named Ray Bradbury. As Harryhausen added skill to talent, he eventually realized his dream of working with his idol.

In 1949 he joined O'Brien and master model maker Marcel Delgado on RKO's *Mighty Joe Young*, a nostalgic revisiting of Kong territory. The hero of the piece was an oversized gorilla, so Harryhausen, using a gorilla skeleton, designed and constructed four models, assisted by machinist Harry Cunningham. "Every joint that a real animal would have was duplicated, right down to the little finger," said Harryhausen. Delgado built the muscle system of foam rubber, dental dam, and cotton, and taxidermist George Lofgren implemented a lifelike new process of rubberizing fur. "I had my favorite model of the four," recalled Harryhausen. "It was the only figure I really felt at home with, and which I could successfully manipulate into the many complicated poses I visualized. . . . It is really quite fascinating how one can become attached to a mass of metal and rubber." Harryhausen did more than eighty percent of the animation. The film gave him a name in Hollywood, but, as O'Brien had learned, outlets for these unique skills were scarce in the studio system. Moreover, union regulations constantly intruded on the monklike solitude in which he was accustomed to working. He found that he could not touch up a model's fur or adjust a spotlight without stepping on someone's toes. Disillusioned, he returned to his parents' womblike garage. Only when a tiny independent company took on an oversized project did he find a more agreeable situation.

Hal Chester was a former child actor who joined two partners, Bernie Burton and Jack Dietz, to create Mutual Films, a studio with neither stages nor stars. Armed with $285,000 and a few story outlines, they approached Eugene Lourie, the distinguished art director of Jean Renoir's *Grand Illusion* and Charles Chaplin's *Limelight*. "One outline was amusing to me," said Lourie. "It was a subject that very seldom was done. It was the dinosaur coming out of the water." The story was called "Monster from Beneath the Sea." Lourie offhandedly said to his would-be employers, "I doubt that anybody will know how to direct this picture. But if you like, I feel capable to do it, and I will do it." As coincidence would have it, Harryhausen's pal Bradbury had recently sold the *Saturday Evening Post* a short story, "The Beast from 20,000 Fathoms" (later republished as "The Foghorn"). It featured a sea serpent who destroys a lighthouse when it does not return his romantic attentions. Bradbury was not interested in writing for Mutual, but sold his story to them for $2,000. In a fated convergence of talent, Harryhausen was introduced to the fledgling company. As he helped them refine their concept, he found a way of adapting his solitary work methods to the restrictions of feature filmmaking. He became an independent assembly line, a one-man department whose assistants answered only to him. In this way he was able to give each project the best of his talent without being hamstrung by the politics that had worn down many a studio artist.

The Beast of the story began to take shape. *The Beast from 20,000 Fathoms* was the first film to treat the idea that nuclear radiation could change a living organism. Should the creature, thawed from its primordial slumber by an atomic test, be a textbook dinosaur? "We did a lot of research among prehistoric beasts," Lourie said. "But most of them, like the allosaurus and the brontosaurus, are too familiar from geology book sketches. And anyway, they don't look half fierce enough or powerful enough to scare anybody." The solution was to invent a new species of dinosaur, the Rhedosaurus, which was designed and constructed by Lofgren. Its face was more expressive and its teeth more ferocious than any prior screen dinosaur.

While Lourie filmed live-action sequences with actors Paul Christian, Kenneth Tobey, and Paula Raymond, Harryhausen struggled with Mutual's limited budget. Out of necessity, he devised a cheaper way to combine live-action footage with animated miniatures. The rear-projection technique in use since *King Kong* required an expensive miniature projector playing onto the back of a small translucent screen on a tabletop set. Harryhausen found it cheaper to creat the illusion of people shrinking from giant creatures by having a standard projector shoot at the set from alongside the movie camera. The images would fall on a specially coated reflective screen; hence the term *front projection*. With typical modesty, he wrote: "I found it an interesting challenge to try to find new ways (and less expensive ways) of achieving a spectacular pictorial effect." Harryhausen dreamed up a number of stunning set pieces, including an attack on a diving bell, a rampage on the docks of New York, and a scene in which a brave policeman is picked up by his head. After catching the cop, the Beast gulps and swallows him. As mean as the Beast was, Harryhausen still gave him a certain appeal. "The scene of the Beast in the burning roller coaster was like a big opera act, like a tenor who dies in a very dramatic scene," said Lourie.

The finished film far surpassed Mutual's expectations and Dietz offered it to Jack L. Warner for a distribution deal. The crafty mogul (no doubt aware that the 1952 reissue of *King Kong* had grossed $3 million) offered the cash-poor Dietz $450,000 for a buyout. *The Beast from 20,000 Fathoms* became one of the highest-grossing Warner Bros. films of 1953, eventually earning almost $5 million. Every time Dietz glanced at *Variety*, he said, "Oh, am I stupid!"

Harryhausen's star was on the ascendant, and so the offers began to roll in. He accepted the one that would allow him to work in his own way. Charles Schneer's independent Clover Productions gave him the freedom to continue his one-man animation unit. Under the new arrangement, Harryhausen would decide on a theme and then find a startling image to express it. "The picture is built around the fantasy sequences," he later said. "It has to be." He and a writer would then develop them into a full-length script, all the while allowing for budget limitations. Prompted by Schneer's desire to make "something new and different from the normal type of adventure films," he revisited the theme of man-made weapons vs. nature. Nature in this case was an octopus so large that it could imperil the Golden Gate Bridge. The title was *It Came from Beneath the Sea*.

Location filming was begun in San Francisco by director Robert Gordon. When it came time to film scenes on the bridge, the city's film-permit office refused, on the grounds that the creature might also imperil faith in the bridge's structural integrity. Undeterred, Gordon sent a car equipped with a concealed camera to capture the necessary background footage. Meanwhile, the actors were at the Embarcadero, reacting to offscreen tentacles. "The assistant director would walk around with something on the end of a stick," Kenneth Tobey recalled, "and you would follow that with your eyes. I tried to visualize what the monster might look like. We'd never even seen the giant octopus up 'til then." When they did see it, they counted only six tentacles. Building and animating all those suckers had turned out to be too costly. "If the budget had been cut any more, we might have ended up with an undulating tripod for the star villain of the picture," mused Harryhausen. Part of the cheapness may have originated with Columbia, which was distributing for Schneer. Having lost so much on *Dr. T.*, Harry Cohn was not about to pay top dollar for another fantasy film. *It Came from Beneath the Sea* did well enough in 1955 to cement the partnership between Harryhausen and Schneer, and they continued to make films together, destroying city after city. "At that period of filmmaking," recalled Harryhausen, "it was important to include the ultimate in mass devastation if one even hoped to sell an idea."

Mass devastation was on the mind of screenwriter Ted Sherdeman when he wrote *Them!* for Warner Bros. On August 6, 1945, when this army colonel had learned of the dropping of the atomic bomb, he had knelt in the gutter and vomited. He brought this visceral immediacy to a script that made atomic testing the villain. Its first surviving victim was a little girl, shown walking in the desert, her eyes blank with the numbness of horror. What has she seen? When pressed for an answer by police and doctors, all she can whisper is: "Them!"

"Them" are eventually revealed to be a colony of ants mutated to a twenty-foot height by radiation from test bombs. They are powerful, vicious, and determined to take over Los Angeles. The child actress who played this harrowing scene was eight-year-old Sandy Descher. "It was very hot in the desert," she recalled, "and we had a lot of sand that was supposed to be blowing. It was difficult for me to maintain that catatonic state. I had to keep my eyes open, and sand was always blowing in them." There was another distraction as she played her scene. Director Gordon Douglas had set up the shot so that the camera would track backward from her as she walked in her trancelike state. To better direct her, Douglas crouched next to the camera at her eye level. As the camera started to roll, the dolly grips pulled it on its tracks. Douglas remained on his haunches, but walked backward on the balls of his feet in order to stay out of camera range, all the while repeating, "Don't blink." Of course he could not see what was behind him: a cactus plant. He fell right into it, gritted his teeth, and kept going. Descher saw it all. "I didn't ruin the scene, and he didn't cry out until the shot was over," said Descher. "He wound up with a number of stickers in his rump, and he had to have them pulled out by the makeup man with tweezers." For their pains, Descher and Douglas could have the satisfaction that this talked-about scene helped make *Them!* the highest-grossing Warner Bros. film of 1954.

The highest-grossing science-fiction film of that year came from Universal-International, as the studio had been known since 1946, when it was taken over by William Goetz, formerly of Twentieth Century–Fox. The confusion of the late 1940s kept Universal-International in the red until a

A large, irradiated creature could be seen in Columbia's **1954 IT CAME FROM BENEATH THE SEA.** Animator Ray Harryhausen used light, perspective, and composition to give the illusion of an octopus wreaking havoc in the City by the Bay.

surprising change of ownership improved its fortunes. Decca Records acquired a controlling interest in it; under its aegis, a raft of young producers exerted their influence. One of them was William Alland, who had started on Broadway at the Mercury Theatre and portrayed the reporter Thompson in 1941's *Citizen Kane*. He went to Universal-International in 1952 and, after a few routine projects, made a big splash with *It Came from Outer Space*.

The idea for Alland's biggest hit originated at a dinner party hosted by Dolores Del Rio and Orson Welles during the filming of *Citizen Kane*. Mexican cinematographer Gabriel Figueroa told Alland about a region along the Amazon River where dwelt a race of creatures that were half fish and half human. Ten years later Alland wrote a memo, putting a fish-man into a beauty-and-beast story called "The Sea Monster." It was expanded into a treatment in December 1952 by Maurice Zimm, then by Harry Essex and Arthur Ross as *The Black Lagoon*. "The whole idea was to give the Creature a kind of humanity," said Essex. "All he wants is to love this girl, but everybody's chasing him!" As the project developed, Hollywood was in the throes of a 3-D craze caused by Arch Oboler's runaway hit, *Bwana Devil*. In 1953, no less than twenty-four films were released in 3-D. *House of Wax*, a 3-D remake of *Mystery of the Wax Museum*, made Vincent Price a horror star and made

Warner Bros. a staggering $9.2 million. Not surprisingly, Alland hired Jack Arnold to direct *Black Lagoon* in 3-D. Now it was time for Universal to create the first new monster since the Wolf Man.

Jack Pierce's autocratic bearing and disdain for faster techniques had resulted in his ouster in 1947. Bud Westmore, the new manager of the makeup department, was, if more congenial than Pierce, no less regal. He thrived in the Hollywood social scene, using every function as an opportunity to trumpet his department's latest achievement. When it came to the often messy business of designing, molding, and applying makeup, he routinely delegated. He assigned freelance artist (and former Disney animator) Milicent Patrick to do preliminary sketches of the Creature. Jack Kevan, who had done makeup for *The Wizard of Oz* and made prosthetic appliances for World War II amputees, executed the foam-rubber body. Chris Mueller Jr. sculpted the Creature's head. Since the Creature was to be portrayed by one actor underwater on location and by another actor on land at Universal City, two costumes were made. Ben Chapman was the in-studio actor. "I'd report to makeup every day," he remembered. "[There were] plaster of Paris impressions of my body, testing various pieces and so on. It was tedious but I enjoyed it. The suit was literally built right onto my body, to make sure that everything fit

For Joan Weldon in **THEM!** the most distressing aspect of a giant ant attack was sartorial; her wardrobe comprised a wool suit, a wool hat, and high heels. "We're in the Mojave Desert, it's 110 or 115 degrees, and I've never been so hot in my life," she recalled. "And running up and down sand dunes in heels—that's an adventure!"

properly." He was advised to maintain his physique. "If I lost weight, the suit would crinkle all over, and if I gained, of course, I'd have trouble getting into it." The transition from human to fish was a tactile one for Chapman. "It fit perfect, like it was part of my body, my skin." It could also be uncomfortable, since he had to wear the costume for fourteen-hour stretches without removing it or sitting down. "I would heat up, because I had a body stocking on and then the foam rubber outfit over it." On the sound stage, he would ask to be hosed down. On the back lot, he would stay in the lake that was doubling for the Amazon.

While Chapman and Arnold began filming at the studio, second-unit director James C. Havens was in Wakulla Springs, Florida, directing underwater footage of Ricou Browning, a college student who had staged and performed in water shows in the area. Former Warner Bros. portrait photographer Scotty Welbourne took an underwater 3-D camera into the spring to make the balletic shots of Browning and swimming double Ginger Stanley. As sometimes happened during the making of fantasy films, Browning forgot the impact his appearance might have on the unsuspecting. He recalled:

We were shooting in the middle of the spring, and I had to go to the bathroom. They were going to take me ashore in a boat, but I said, no, I was gonna swim over. I swam underwater . . . to the ladder that was on the dock next to shore. I came up the ladder, and there was a lady with a little girl standing there. I came out, and this little girl started screaming. She started screaming and running and the mother went after her, and I went after both of 'em, trying to say, "Hey, hey, it's okay, it's okay!" But me saying "It's okay!" didn't do a thing. They took off, and that's the last I saw of 'em!

The collaboration of Browning, Stanley, Welbourne, and Havens yielded outstanding images, shimmering black-and-white visions of an unselfconscious woman enjoying a solitary swim and a subaqueous being who, as he mimics her graceful motions, becomes infatuated with her. "I made sure [that Welbourne shot] it with the sun directly overhead so the girl was almost in silhouette," said Arnold. "I wanted to create a feeling of mystery and romance, but also a sense of terror. The scenes where the girl is swimming above while the monster watches from below play on the basic fear we all have about what might be lurking below us in the water. Being scared of something unseen is basic to our nature."

On the Universal back lot, on an old boat called *Rita*, Arnold directed Chapman to move, gesticulate, and walk. "I want him to glide," Arnold told Chapman. "He glides in the water and also on land." In order for a six-foot-five Tahitian dancer to walk gracefully, he needed to see where he was going. This was a problem of the headpiece's design. "The eyes of the Gill Man popped out," Chapman said, "like contact lenses. For closeups, we had eyes that were 'complete,' that looked like regular eyes. These eyes I really could not see through and they would have to direct me with flashlights." His vision was only slightly better with the pinhole eyes designed for medium shots. While wearing these, he enacted a scene in which he carries the unconscious heroine (Julia Adams) into his lair. Adams remembered: "The day we shot on the stage where they had the Creature's underwater grotto, we were in this huge tank of

water. They had forgotten to heat the tank . . . I was trying not to shiver as I was lying in this poor guy's arms." Chapman recalled: "I was wearing those 'medium' eyes, trying to carry her through there, when all of a sudden, *clunk*!" Adams said: "He scraped my head against a plaster rock." Chapman added: "And she let out a yelp, let me tell you!"

Mishaps and physical discomfort aside, Arnold had a happy troupe, primarily because he communicated so well. "I wanted to make the Creature ('my little beastie' as I called him) a sympathetic character because I liked him," Arnold explained. "Here he was being chased and killed in his own environment when he just wanted to be alone. He was only violent because he was provoked to violence. So we were trying to say something about human nature, though not in a polemical way—in a way that would be entertaining and acceptable to an audience."

What began as an anecdote over cocktails became *Creature from the Black Lagoon* and, thanks to Arnold's vision, a knockout hit for Universal. Adams pointed out the scariest part of filmmaking. "When a picture is finished shooting, basically it's just all this exposed film," she said.

Since the prehistoric beasts in Roy Chapman Andrews's *All about Dinosaurs* were deemed too tame, **THE BEAST FROM 20,000 FATHOMS** of 1953 featured an invented species, a Rhedosaurus. Director Eugene Lourie took his six-year-old daughter to see the film. She was silent until she got into the car. Then she started to cry: "You are bad, Daddy! You killed the big nice beast!"

"The director had to have a picture of it in his mind, to know what's telling and what isn't. Jack really put together a picture that touched people."

Cheap Thrills

In the late 1940s atomic bombs were not the only things exploding. American soldiers had come home from the war, and suddenly a million more children were being born each year. From 1946 to 1964, the baby boom produced more than 78 million children. One of these became film historian Harvey Stewart. "My uncle owned two theaters in George-town, South Carolina, the Strand and the Palace," he recalls. "From the time I was five, I saw everything. And my friends saw everything. It didn't matter what it was. We watched it. Especially anything creepy."

To feed this voracious, uncritical audience, atomic horror radiated from the major-majors all the way down to the quick-and-dirty indies. At the top of this pulsating pyramid was Universal-International, which quickly decided that the Gill Man had not really died. "The only natural thing to do was to capture him and bring him back alive," said director Jack Arnold. As the human hero of *Revenge of the Creature* (1955), Arnold cast John Agar, a bland young actor who had recently started at the top in prestigious John Ford films. Agar was at first amenable to working in the atomic genre. After all, *Revenge* was a fairly expensive 3-D movie. But the inevitable corner-cutting began to occur. Here and there, Universal prevailed upon producer William Alland to rein in Arnold. Given less direction, Agar could not compete with Ricou Browning's expressive Creature. A mediocre performance resulted and Agar found himself in a strange new territory. "Any time a science fiction picture would come up at Universal," he recalled, "Bill Alland would say he wanted me in it. The studio at that time was grooming a lot of young actors—Rock Hudson, Tony Curtis, Jeff Chandler, and George Nader. I was part of that group, but the studio only seemed to want to put me in science fiction."

Tarantula (1955) was the story of another innocent animal blown up to monstrous proportions by errant science and then blown apart after much chewing of both scenery and people. Trying to temper creativity with economy, Arnold scouted locations with which to tell his less-than-original story. He found one just north of Los Angeles, at the edge of the Mojave Desert. "It was a place called Dead Man's Curve," said Arnold, "where there was an outcropping of rocks that I particularly wanted to use. I would just go into the desert and look for something that looked eerie, and if it gave me the shivers, I would say, 'Right! Let's shoot here!'"

Arnold brought his actors there and put them through their carefully measured paces. "When Mara Corday and I were out in the desert," Agar recalled, "of course there wasn't any tarantula out there, climbing over those hills or mountains. We just had to react to that and use our imagination." Back at the studio, Arnold filmed real tarantulas. "What we did was match the rocks in the studio to the actual rocks out there in the desert, then shoot them in perspective," Arnold said. "We'd push the spider about with air jets until I got the shot I wanted." Both negatives were

turned over to the optical-printing department, which then had the unenviable task of combining the two images into some semblance of reality. Despite their best efforts the creature was unconvincing, perhaps because a one-hundred-foot-tall tarantula would not move in the feather-light way that Arnold had filmed. Surprisingly, the public did not question either the concept or the execution. "When we were making it, I had no idea how it would turn out," Agar said. "But it really caught on. I think *Tarantula* cost a total of $750,000 to make. It turned out to be the fifth-biggest money grosser for that year."

Alland went underground for his next cut-rate creeper, *The Mole People* (1956). Agar was now less sanguine about life at Universal. "Bill Alland, for some reason, wanted me in all his science-fiction pictures, and when they came up with this one, well, the story just didn't jell with me at all—people coming up out of the ground, looking like moles, and an underground civilization." Agar bypassed first-time director Virgil Vogel and went to Alland, saying, "This won't work. People just don't talk like this."

"I paid a writer good money to write that dialogue," replied Alland.

"Well, you got cheated," said Agar, completing the affront.

Contract player Cynthia Patrick felt that her role as a Sumerian did not give her enough dialogue to create a characterization, and, worse yet, "they did not tell me I had to fall through the mole hole." Each mole hole was a sort of vertical revolving door through which the Mole People, oppressed slaves of the albino Sumerians, could travel up and down. "There were two main holes that the Mole men would crawl out of on the set," said stunt man Bob Herron. "At first they were called the 'A Hole' and the 'B Hole,' and that caused a lot of laughs on the set, so we changed it to 'One Hole' and 'Two Hole.'" To go back through the holes, the Mole People had to depend on a hydraulic lift and some clever set decoration. "We had very stiff rubber across the top of an empty swimming pool," explained Vogel. "We slit the rubber and covered it with ground cork. That way, when the monsters pulled a body down through the slit, the rubber was so thick and stiff that it split just

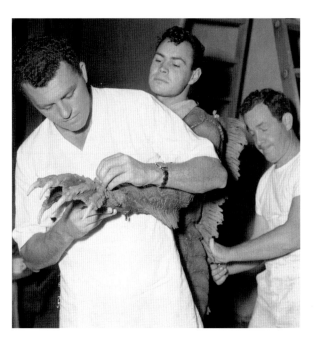

opposite
The Creature was introduced in each scene by a distinctive three-note "signature." Composer Herman Stein recalled that musical director Joe Gershenson "wanted some kind of theme, some kind of a little striking thing, a motif or something." The strident chords frightened many a child under a theater seat. "The Creature scared people, but there was also a sort of sweetness about it," said actress Julia (later Julie) Adams. "In the real classics, there always is that feeling of compassion for the monster. I think maybe it touches something in ourselves, maybe the darker parts of ourselves that long to be loved and think that they really can't ever be loved."

The Creature was played on land by Ben Chapman, here shown in the final stages of costuming. Chapman said: "Jack Arnold and I worked together a bit to try and breathe life into the character, rather than make him a cardboard cartoon." Chapman was a Tahitian dancer in the Islander Room of the Hollywood Roosevelt Hotel when a Universal producer discovered him. "Every graceful, fantastic move [Chapman] made inside his monster suit, and what he did with his face inside that head, made the whole ridiculous thing believable," said actor Richard Carlson.

wide enough for the body. The cork couldn't all run through." The best efforts of the special-effects and stunt departments could not convince Patrick. "I'm not going down through that hole," she told Vogel.

"Well, of course not, darling," Vogel assured her. "A stuntwoman will do that. All I need you to do is run across there." When she was out of earshot, Vogel ordered a stunt man in a Mole costume: "When she hits that goddamned hole, you grab her legs and pull!" Patrick got her cue and ran across the set. As she hit the spot, she suddenly felt as if she were "falling through a bottomless pit." Vogel said, "She screamed and yelled as she went down, but it was probably the best acting she did in the picture."

Agar began to have a different kind of sinking feeling. "There were all these guys around us with Mole Men masks on. All of a sudden I heard this voice say, 'Agar, what did you get yourself into this time?' I turned around, and it was Rock Hudson. I don't know if he meant anything by it, but just the way he said it bothered me."

Exhibitors played the film on a double bill with *Curucu, Beast of the Amazon.* "Science fiction in *Curucu* and *The Mole People* reaches its lowest common denominator," wrote *Cue* magazine, "which is to say, approximately six and a half years old." A *Los Angeles Times* review was equally wry about a plot contrivance in which Agar defeats the Sumerians with a flashlight. "Like the story line, the Albinos can't stand much illumination." After three such films, Agar was ready for a change. He met with Jim Pratt, vice president of Universal. "I told him I wanted to do other things. He told me flat out he couldn't make any promises, so I decided it was time to move on."

When he moved, though, it was not on—or up. Like a victim of the Mole People, Agar was sucked downward; and, when he landed, it was in another zone of filmmaking, at low-rent outfits like Howco, Medallion, and Allied Artists.

But he was not alone in his fall from grace. Low-budget filmmakers grabbed whomever they could, former stars and notorious has-beens, exploiting their names and profiting from their professionalism. A case in point was the 1954 Ivan Tors production, *Gog.* Emblazoned on its 3-D credits was the name of one of Hollywood's most distinguished actors, Herbert Marshall. Director Herbert L. Strock had the sixty-three-year-old Marshall walking all over a subterranean laboratory set, using his velvety voice to invest Tors's plodding dialogue with a sense of urgency. Marshall had overcome a traumatic leg amputation in World War I to become a star of stage, screen, and radio. Now he was working to pay medical bills caused by a prosthetic maladjustment. The consummate professional, Marshall asked Strock, "Herb, is my limping too obvious?"

Without thinking, Strock replied, "Oh, no, no, it's a good gimmick."

"Gimmick?" snapped Marshall. "With this pain, I'd hardly call it a gimmick."

"I felt terrible," Strock recalled. "I apologized, and he, being the charming Englishman that he was, understood." Strock also tread lightly around the elegant blonde beauty who was playing the lead. Constance Dowling was Mrs. Ivan Tors, but only a few years removed from a major scandal. After being dumped by director Elia Kazan, Dowling and her sister Doris (who had been dumped by director Billy Wilder) essayed the real-life roles of international playgirls. Constance became involved with an Italian writer, Cesare Pavese. When she left him, he committed suicide. "She was a sweet, lovely woman," Strock recalled, "probably not the finest actress in the world, but very competent, easy to get along with." Sharing the screen with two robots, she had slid a long way from lavish Samuel Goldwyn productions, so it was with some irony that she spoke her dialogue. "So much has changed," she says sadly. "This place is so inhuman. The machines took over. People aren't important. We live here like ground hogs."

Neither Dowling nor Marshall was the most uncomfortable actor in *Gog*. "The twin robots, Gog and Magog, were operated by a midget named Billy Curtis," Strock recalled. "He got inside and was able to walk around, move the arms about, and fire the acetylene torch which was in one arm. Billy was inside of those damn robots until I thought he would die." For all its inanity, *Gog* was a legitimate United Artists release. It did respectable business and propelled Tors on a long career.

Equally profitable were offbeat projects such as *Tobor the Great*, *Kronos*, and *The Monolith Monsters*, all of which showed man fighting out-of-control science, and all of which were produced or released by major studios. As numerous as these films were, they were not enough for a nation of bored baby boomers. Drive-in theaters and television stations demanded a constant supply of scary movies. Miles from the deeply carpeted offices of Universal-International, at the bottom of the Hollywood heap, grubby independent producers were eager to provide them. It was here, in the smoggy, nondescript jumble of cut-rate rental studios and sleazy apartments, that one such filmmaker offered a tatty mattress to cushion the crash landing of a great horror star.

In 1953 Ed Wood Jr. was an unemployed twenty-eight-year-old with a fleshy face, luxuriant, perfectly parted hair, and eyelashes too long for a heroic ex-Marine. Wood was a confirmed heterosexual, but he was given to wearing women's clothes. Actor Paul Marco, a regular in Wood's troupe, remembered: "If he was sitting at home with his negligee on, and a wig, *and* a mustache, smoking a cigar, with a bottle of vodka nearby, pounding on his typewriter in a most unladylike fashion, and somebody walked in, he'd say, 'Hi! Sit down. I'll be right with you.'" Wood's eccentricity poured from no wellspring of genius. He had neither the talent nor the connections needed to enter even the lowest echelons of the industry. He did have the charm needed to recruit actors and crew from the nether regions of the Hollywood social order. Investors were another matter. Securing backing for something called *Glen or Glenda?* was not easy in 1953. He would approach anyone who would listen, then order drinks and make an impassioned pitch for money. As often as not, he would soon be cruising down tawdry Las Palmas Avenue to buy raw stock at Eastman Kodak. This was his thrill: to create a production from the ground up. The results, of course, were mixed. His movies were not low budget; they were "no budget."

Whether in a great film or a humble one, sometimes a director crafts a stirring set piece or a memorable moment of fright and the plot is momentarily beside the point. Wood's plots were not beside anything. They could not be summarized, criticized, or even located. They did not exist. In truth, the process of making a film was more important to him than the finished product. "He enjoyed playing the role of the Director," said one of his recruits. "This meant that the Director sat there on his chair like De Mille, shouting out orders with this megaphone, and he would have this person doing that, and everybody running all over the place." In this coterie of fruits, there was one actor at whom Wood did not wave his megaphone.

At seventy-two, Bela Lugosi was a brittle vestige of the tall, elegant actor who had made audiences gasp in 1931. His wife of twenty years had divorced him and taken their teenage son, leaving Lugosi in the crippling grasp of addiction. When the reality of his fragmented family and desperate finances began to eat at him, he would sit in a shabby apartment on Harold Way, a block from the monolithic soundstages where he had once worked for the Fox Film Corporation, and gulp his favorite drink, the "boilermaker." When this potent mix of whiskey and beer began to lose its edge, Lugosi sought help from a newfound friend, the ebullient Wood, who also had a propensity for the bottle. "Ed used to drive him around to this place on La Brea Avenue to get paraldehyde," recalled Charles Anderson, a Wood familiar. "Lugosi was in bad shape by this time. He had gotten past the point of being affected by liquor."

Working on Wood's *Glen or Glenda?*—a quasi-documentary about transvestites—did nothing for Lugosi, who slipped back into morphine addiction. Then the British producer Alex Gordon, who had been helping Lugosi, offered Wood a dusty screenplay called "The Atomic Monster" as a vehicle for the aged actor. With $800 in hand, Wood began shooting it at Ted Allan Studios in October 1954 under the title *Monster of the Marshes*. In typical form, Wood soon ran through the money, but after a few fundraising forays he resumed filming in March 1955. His new angel was Arizona rancher Donald E. McCoy, owner of the Packing Service Corporation. McCoy bankrolled the film on the condition that his son, Tony, play the hero and act as associate producer.

In the film, now known as *Bride of the Atom*, Lugosi played a scientist trying to create an atomic woman. Wood nursed Lugosi through it, but barely. "One night we were shooting in Griffith Park," Marco recalled. "It was very

A subterranean being menaces John Agar in Virgil Vogel's 1956 production **THE MOLE PEOPLE**. It was not easy being a Mole Person. Stunt man Bob Herron said, "The Mole man mask would bunch up and we groped around a lot."

damp and a black night up there in the hills. Bela walked over to Ed and said, 'Eddie, take me home. I've got to take my medicine.'" After some back and forth, Marco drove Lugosi to his apartment, where the actor's flagging energy was revived by a ritual injection of morphine. Now Lugosi was able to fight a prop octopus left over from Republic Pictures' *Wake of the Red Witch*. No one could figure out how to operate the mechanical prop, so Lugosi's double pulled its flaccid tentacles over him in a pathetic attempt to animate it.

On a cheap rental stage called Centaur Studios, Lugosi was now reduced to playing his scenes in small pieces. Wood could not afford to shoot so much film. He copied Lugosi's one big speech onto cue cards so that the frail, sick actor could complete it in one take. Wood respectfully helped Lugosi to a couch. Lugosi suddenly said, "Oh, take those cards away. *I'm* going to *do* it!" He took a deep breath, regained a bit of his old presence, and declaimed: "I was classed as a madman, a charlatan, outlawed in the world of science which previously had honored me as a genius. Now, here, in this forsaken jungle hell, I have proven that I am *all right*." On April 22, 1955, the *Los Angeles Examiner* printed a poignant headline: "Bela Lugosi Surrenders Self as Narcotic Addict." Three months later, Lugosi emerged from Metropolitan State Hospital in Norwalk; in short order, he was giving interviews. "I cannot describe the tortures I underwent. My body grew hot, then

cold. I tried to eat the bed sheets, my pajamas. My heart beat madly. Then it seemed to stop."

Bride of the Atom premiered at the Paramount Theatre in May 1955. "This re-hashed version of a story which was old hat years ago is an amateurish effort," wrote a reviewer in *Variety*. "Even the least discriminating audiences will find it dull. Bela Lugosi's histrionics are reduced to the ridiculous through over-direction." (A year later, the film was sold to Filmakers Releasing Organization for general release as *Bride of the Monster*.)

Beaten down but not defeated, Lugosi rallied long enough in February 1956 to act the part of a mute servant in another low-budget independent, *The Black Sleep*. Director Reginald LeBorg noted that Lugosi was still full of ideas. "Herr Director! I'm a star. I'm a star! Give me some lines!" LeBorg tried to explain that the character's tongue had been cut out. Lugosi was adamant. "But I'm a star!" he gasped. "Give me closeups!"

After completing the film, Lugosi sank to his lowest physical and emotional ebb, lamenting, "I am now more resurrected than real." In the summer of 1956 Wood asked him to work on yet another fanciful project, *The Vampire's Tomb*. Wood helped Lugosi put on his Dracula cape, gently put him into a car, and, in an overgrown cemetery, filmed silent footage of the feeble old man striking the poses that had made him world famous. A few weeks later, on August 16, 1956, Bela Lugosi died. An undated, unsigned note

To publicize the 1954 film **GOG**, the glamorous Constance Dowling cavorts with a robot in a posed scene that (unfortunately) has nothing to do with the finished film. An international playgirl trying to live down a scandal, she was one of many falling stars who made 1950s science fantasies more appealing to adolescent boys.

was found in his apartment. It read, in part: "Perhaps some day . . . after all the struggle, you will anchor at the harbor of your dreams."

But what about Wood's vampire film? Marco recalled: "We were all sitting around, having a few drinks and talking about what to do with this Lugosi footage that Ed had shot. Ed said, 'Let's make a monster movie!' We all laughed." A determined Wood beat the bushes, only to find financing in his own building, the Mariposa Apartments. His landlord, J. Edward Reynolds, was a leader of the Baptist Church of Beverly Hills. Reynolds agreed to bankroll the film if he could baptize the entire cast and crew. The massive Swedish wrestler Tor Johnson, known for routinely cracking Wood's toilet seats, had to be baptized separately because the church's baptismal tank was too small for him.

Wood's newest "guest star" was Finnish-born ex-model Maila Nurmi, better known as Vampira, Channel 7's horror-movie host. After Wood offered her $200 to appear in his film, the recently unemployed Nurmi pulled her contrasty costume out of the closet. "I made myself up at home," she recalled. "And since they couldn't afford a chauffeur, I took the bus to the studio." Wood's current rental studio was a Quonset hut next to a bar called Gold Diggers. Nurmi slinked past the bar and down an alley, entered the cramped stage, and surveyed Wood's attempts at art direction. "They had a cemetery set there," she recalled, "that consisted of paper yard grass, cardboard tombstones, and a little plywood crypt. And some dead bushes and dead twigs which were serving as shrubbery. I thought, Hmmm . . . this is about what I expected." Nurmi's wordless performance and Lugosi's posthumous footage were only a small part of the cinematic jumble that was eventually released as *Plan 9 from Outer Space*. More amazing than its flying saucers, grave robbers, and jump cuts were its ongoing profits, none of which went to Ed Wood. He had sold the entire production to the Baptists.

In 1955, the great Bela Lugosi found himself in a No Man's Land outside the studio system. He gained a new notoriety when an eccentric named Ed Wood mounted **BRIDE OF THE ATOM** around him. "He was a gentleman of infinite dignity and refinement," said actress Maila Nurmi. In 1956, **BRIDE OF THE ATOM** was renamed **BRIDE OF THE MONSTER**, but it was too late to help Lugosi's career.

Criswell, the narrator of Ed Wood's **PLAN 9 FROM OUTER SPACE**, asks: "My friends, can your hearts stand the shocking facts about grave robbers from outer space?" The only fact Maila Nurmi found shocking was that she had to take a city bus to the movie studio looking like this.

The Cosmic

CHAPTER 10

The Science-Fiction Film

overleaf
This 100-foot-wide saucer sat expectantly on the Twentieth Century–Fox back lot between takes of **THE DAY THE EARTH STOOD STILL**. Years later, after the lot had become Century City, producer Julian Blaustein drove by and reminisced. "Every time I pass the place, I can still imagine that I see our spaceship sitting there, a specter of the past glories of Fox."

opposite
One of the stars of M-G-M's 1956 **FORBIDDEN PLANET** was Robby the Robot, a 6'11" machine that could be inhabited by no one taller than 5'6". The robot was top-heavy, hot, and claustrophobic. Actor Frankie Darro animated Robby until the strain pushed him to drinking five martinis at lunch one day. Anne Francis recalled: "He almost took a nosedive, if three grips hadn't grabbed him in time. Robby was the most expensive actor on the show . . . so the young man who was working him from the inside was replaced."

Unearthly Subversion

For all its vaunted normality, America in the 1950s was a scared and scary place. The 1940s had ended with a proliferation of atomic weapons. Fear was palpable, making itself felt in the most unlikely places. In a jazz song, "Atomic Cocktail," Slim Gaillard sang: "You push a button, turn a dial/Your work is done for miles and miles/You're small as a beetle or big as a whale—BOOM—Atomic Cocktail." As testing spread, Robert Oppenheimer, who had played a starring role in the A-bomb's development, pleaded for pardon. "In some sort of crude sense, which no vulgarity, no humor, no overstatement can quite extinguish," Oppenheimer said, "the physicists have known sin, and this is a knowledge which they cannot lose." With A-bombs being detonated on American soil, the public began to question the culpability, indeed the sanity, of the scientific world. Even so, the madness spread.

In 1949, the Soviet Union trotted out an A-bomb. The Red Scares of thirty years earlier came back with a vengeance, and, in short order, America came up with a hydrogen bomb. Confirming right-wing admonitions, communists moved into Europe, seizing the remnants of the Austro-Hungarian Empire and installing governments in Albania, Bulgaria, Czechoslovakia, Hungary, Poland, and Romania. What Winston Churchill called the Iron Curtain slammed with a clang. In 1950, not long after communists had seized power in China, the Cold War came to a steely standoff in Germany. As the war heated up in Korea, there was one question: Is America next? Senator Joe McCarthy thought so and began to investigate alleged communist sympathizers, first in the State Department, and then in Hollywood. Edward G. Robinson and John Garfield were accused. When McCarthy could not prove his wild charges, his committee intimidated studios into blacklisting these stars, along with 1,500 other film-industry employees. Concurrent with the Red Scare was a "flying saucer" scare.

On June 24, 1947, an Idaho businessman and pilot named Kenneth Arnold spotted a formation of nine silvery crescent-shaped objects flying in tight formation near Mount Rainier, Washington. The objects were estimated to be fifty feet wide and flying at a speed of 1,200 miles per hour, which was more than twice the speed of any contemporary aircraft. Almost before a reporter could invent the term "flying saucer," there were hundreds more reports of "unidentified flying objects." A retired Marine, Major Donald Keyhoe, took to the pages of *True* magazine in January 1950 to aver that flying saucers were not a hoax, not American test balloons, and not to be dismissed. They were real! Soon after, more than 5,000 people in Farmington, New Mexico, witnessed a spectacular display of aerial phenomena. One witness described "a total of twenty to thirty disc-shaped objects, including one red one substantially larger than the others, moving at high velocity across the Farmington sky on the late morning of March 17." A country still healing war wounds did not know what to believe. A *New York Times* reviewer aptly described this as "an age of A-Bombs, B-pictures, cold wars and science fiction." To capitalize on this malaise, Hollywood prepared paranoid fantasies that showed space beings coming to subvert the American way of life.

Ray Bradbury had recently written the science-fiction novel *The Martian Chronicles*. "The secret of science-fiction writing," he explained, "is in exploring the human element rather than the mechanical. Science writing is really sociological studies of the future, things that the writer believes are going to happen by putting two and two together. 'Fantasy' is dream-world stuff you can't believe ever has a chance of happening." *Red Planet Mars* (1952) was an independent production released through United Artists. John L. Balderston, who had contributed so much to the Gothic horror genre with *Dracula* and *Frankenstein*, coauthored a script based on his own play, *Miracle from Mars*, which was about a young married couple, Linda and Chris, who discover an interplanetary intercom. In a reflection of her times, Linda says, "The whole world's scared. It's become our natural state."

The film's solution to this is the reassuring voice of a superior being. He sends coded messages to them from—of all places—Mars, exhorting Russian Christians to overthrow communism. Apparently the Russians have forgotten about Rasputin because they install a priest as their new

Andrea King and Peter Graves communicate with a cosmic intelligence who speaks in the parlance of conservative screenwriters John Balderston and Anthony Veiller in the 1952 United Artists release **RED PLANET MARS.**

leader. The film ends with Russians and Americans marching to church, while on the screen appears the quixotic legend "The Beginning." Although *Red Planet Mars* was well directed by Harry Horner and handsomely lit by Joseph Biroc, it was science fantasy, too far-fetched to reassure anyone.

Tapping into the fear of communist infiltration was another independent production, *Invaders from Mars* (1953). William Cameron Menzies applied the skills he had used as the production designer of *Gone with the Wind* to make the rented Normand Stage at Republic Pictures look like Selznick International. His script told the story of a boy, David (Jimmy Hunt), who looks out his bedroom window and sees a spaceship burrowing into the ground. Later he sees familiar townspeople disappear into a mysterious sand pit. When they reappear, they are somehow different—subdued, distant, almost robotlike. He sees a telltale scar on the back of each changed person's neck and deduces

that someone has implanted a radio transmitter there. He tries to alert his family, friends, and even the police, but no one will believe him. He alone knows that his town is being subverted. Only when he falls through the sand does he learn that Martians are responsible. Their leader is an octopuslike creature with a human head and tiny tentacles, a sexless, voiceless being that communicates only by telepathy and must be transported by giant goons.

Menzies's limited budget precluded Technicolor, so he used a one-negative color process called Cinecolor, which made *Invaders from Mars* suitably garish. The head Martian was played by a female midget named Luce Potter, who had to sit her head atop a tiny prosthetic body in a glass globe. To play her mute myrmidons, Menzies hired two former circus giants, Max Palmer and Lock Martin. At eight feet and 450 pounds each, they found any exertion difficult; playing Martians was a trial. "It was hot," Hunt said, "and because of the slits in their eyepieces, they couldn't really see. These guys would always complain about them. They could only wear them for so long before they had to take them off. The poor guys would be crying."

Menzies was an inspired designer, but, coming from the era of studio extravagance, he had a hard time adjusting to the budgetary restrictions of this period. "He was the best," said Lee Sholem, who had assisted Menzies on *Our Town.* "He was always lost in thought, like he was far away someplace," said actor William Phipps. "He had a problem, and that was drinking," explained Sholem, who had learned to keep Menzies "off the booze, or to keep him off it at least long enough to get the job done, and then let him go out and have his drinks." Menzies did manage to fit twelve sets on one sound stage, including the sand pit, which was a reprise of the famous picket fence set he had designed for *Our Town.* He also made the sand pit more frightening by having musical composer Raoul Krushaar use an a cappella chorus to underscore the shots in which the humans are pulled underground. On a more practical level, he made a space gun out of an auto headlight, and cave wall bubbles out of condoms. What he could not do was make a coherent film out of several impressive sequences. Nonetheless, coherence was not that important to his audience; the film's frightening images—the sand pit, the needle scars, the skeptical police officer—reflected the country's paranoia.

The ultimate in infiltration nightmares appeared between the glossy covers of *Collier's* magazine in late 1954 with the serialization of Jack Finney's novel *The Body Snatchers.* It began: "I warn you that what you're starting to read is full of loose ends and unanswered questions. It will not be neatly tied up at the end, everything resolved and satisfactorily explained." In simple, unadorned prose, Finney tells the story of Mira Vista, a small California town that is quietly and systematically taken over by aliens who use a most insidious method of subversion. While the victim sleeps, a sinister intelligence replaces his or her body with a duplicate that has been gestating in the leaflike shell of a large green pod. The "new" person is emotionless, impassive, and deadly. Its only goal is to propagate more of its own kind. Miles Bennell, the hero of the story, spends the story trying to save himself and his girlfriend, Becky Driscoll, from the inevitable "death" of sleep.

left

The pods that motivated the **INVASION OF THE BODY SNATCHERS** were molded in clay and then cast in plaster. "Liquid latex was used to make the 'skins' of the pods, and these skins were, in turn, mounted on mechanized frames," said a studio release. "During actual operation, hydraulics were used to manipulate the action of the pods. Compressed air and chemicals were employed to cause the pods to pulsate and emit frothy substances, as well as [to push] the embryos from the pods."

above

King Donovan, Carolyn Jones, Kevin McCarthy, and Dana Wynter look at a dummy of Donovan in Don Siegel's 1956 **INVASION OF THE BODY SNATCHERS.** The dummies of Donovan and company were cast directly from the actors in a claustrophobic process that cost $30,000.

Producer Walter Wanger grabbed this unique property and carried it to Allied Artists (AA), the low-rent releasing outfit he was calling home since his release from prison. Wanger, one of the most literate producers in town, had nearly been excommunicated from filmdom in 1948, when he had fired a pistol into what was euphemistically described as "the groin" of talent agent Jennings Lang, who may have been having an affair with actress Joan Bennett, Wanger's wife. According to director Edward Bernds: "He needed a job, and the studios where he had been such a big man didn't want to give him a break." A producer of Wanger's caliber could not float around Hollywood forever. Steve Broidy, the head of AA knew a good thing when he saw it, and hired Wanger. After a few B pictures, Wanger hit his stride with *Riot in Cell Block 11*. With Don Siegel, that film's director, and Daniel Mainwaring, screenwriter of Jacques Tourneur's *Out of the Past*, Wanger visited author Finney in bucolic Mill Valley, California, pronouncing it a perfect place to film *The Body Snatchers*. But Allied Artists was a funny outfit. Spawned by the quick-and-dirty Monogram Pictures, AA was only slightly less cheap. Wanger would have to film Finney's novel for less than $350,000, which meant that a northern California location was too expensive. Mainwaring tailored his script to more familiar Los Angeles locations: Bronson Canyon, the Los Feliz district, Glendale, and, most prominently, the tiny burg of Sierra Madre.

John Delgatto was in Sierra Madre grammar school when filming began, and he saw what many citizens saw at some point in the 1950s. "They'd gathered a bunch of people from the town, local people, and had them all running down the street," he recalled. "Just townspeople. My dad was one of them. I remember people running, guys with

change in their pockets falling out, all supposed to be running from . . . we didn't know from *what*." This was the mood of the film, although this alarming shot would appear only in the film's preview trailer. What ended up in the film was frightening enough.

"Wanger and I decided to reduce special effects to a minimum," Siegel said. "We had something to say, for the invaders in our film were pods, cocoons which grow to resemble people, but who remain alive without feelings or hope. They are, they drink, they breathe, and they live, but nothing more—like a lot of people, after all." That is what makes the invaders so terrifying. They look exactly as they did in the earlier part of the film, but are devoid of emotions or conscience. In a pivotal scene, Miles (Kevin McCarthy) and Becky (Dana Wynter) are trapped by one of the pod people, Dr. Dan Kaufman (Larry Gates), who imparts their chilling philosophy. "Less than a month ago, Santa Mira was like any other town. People with nothing but problems. Then out of the sky came a solution." He gestures to a room full of pods. "Your new bodies are growing in there. They're taking you over, cell for cell, atom for atom. There's no pain. Suddenly, while you're asleep, they'll absorb your minds, your memories, and you're reborn into an untroubled world."

"Where everyone's the same . . . ?" asks Miles. "I love Becky. Tomorrow will I feel the same?"

"There's no need for love," answers Kaufman.

Miles is alarmed. "Then you have no feelings, only the instinct to survive. You can't love or be loved. Am I right?"

Kaufman is condescendingly patient. "You say it as if it were terrible. Believe me, it isn't. You've been in love before. It didn't last. It never does. Love, desire, ambition, faith—without them, life's so simple. Believe me."

"I don't want any part of it."

"You're forgetting something, Miles."

"What's that?" asks Miles, holding Becky close to him.

"You have no choice."

As originally shot by Siegel, *The Body Snatchers* had Miles and Becky pursued through the woods, almost escaping. Thinking that they have once again reached an uncontaminated area, Miles leaves the exhausted Becky alone for a moment. When he returns, she has been taken over by her duplicate and she is now one of the enemy, calling them to capture him. He escapes to a busy highway, where he tries to flag down the speeding, indifferent drivers. No one will stop. The final shot shows Miles looking into the camera in total desperation, screaming, "They're coming! You're next!" Eager for an audience reaction to this awful ending, Wanger and Siegel spirited a work print to Long Beach for a sneak preview. The audience was overwhelmingly impressed—and scared. When Wanger and Siegel came back to AA with the good news, Broidy was irate. "Nobody gave you guys permission to take the film down there and run it!" he yelled. "We don't do sneak previews! We make programmers, exploitation pictures!" Worse yet, Broidy wanted changes. "That ending is too downbeat," he carped.

McCarthy recalled that "Broidy insisted on shooting a prologue and epilogue, where my character is brought to a skeptical psychiatrist who eventually believes me when he learns that a truck carrying these strange, huge seed pods was involved in an accident, and he calls the FBI." The added scenes drove the film's cost up to $416,911. Equally irksome to Siegel was Broidy's decision to rename the film. Since the Val Lewton *Body Snatcher* was still playing "somewhere," and Siegel's preferred title, *Sleep No More*, was not provocative enough, the film was now called *Invasion of the Body Snatchers*. "Don hated the title *Invasion of the Body Snatchers*," said McCarthy, "especially the 'invasion of' part. Thought it made the film sound like a cheap horror picture." Wynter asked Wanger: "How can I admit to my parents that I'm doing a picture called *Invasion of the Body Snatchers*?" In an interview before its release, Wynter tried to distance herself from the film, saying, "I suppose it will appeal to the science-fiction kids." It appealed to a lot of people, touched a lot of fears, and finally grossed $1.2 million. Siegel would not say if he had intended the pod people to represent communists or communist-hunters. He would only say that he had intended it to be a thriller. It was.

The Good Neighbor Policy

America, already watching the skies for atom bombs and flying saucers, had something else to look for in the late 1940s. At the end of World War II, Soviet leaders had appropriated Nazi missiles and German scientists. Their goal was a rocket that could leave the earth's atmosphere. America faced a grim reality. Within a few years, Russia would be able to launch an orbital satellite and spread communism throughout the universe. In short order, the United States enjoined its own group of refugee physicists to surpass Russia. The race for space was on. Meanwhile, another phenomenon beamed from the sky.

In 1948, television made a surprise incursion into the entertainment market. The little round screen and its wavering charcoal images at first looked harmless enough. Darryl F. Zanuck said, "Oh, television doesn't mean a thing. It's just a passing fancy." The novelty of hearing and seeing programs for free and at home soon proved him wrong. Weekly movie attendance, which had reached 82 million in

Kevin McCarthy, exhausted from a grueling shooting schedule, risked his neck to play the climactic scene in **INVASION OF THE BODY SNATCHERS**. He frantically tries to warn apathetic motorists, but he cannot penetrate their glass-and-metal carapaces.

The first major studio to make a cosmic movie was Twentieth Century–Fox. When its boss, Darryl F. Zanuck, saw the finished cut of **THE DAY THE EARTH STOOD STILL**, he exclaimed: "That's it! Don't touch it! Don't do anything to it!" The 1951 film drew crowds like this one.

1946, began to drop. By 1948, it was plummeting below 60 million. By 1949, studio revenues had dropped from $87.3 million to $48.5 million. By 1952, Americans were buying 7 million television sets a year. Milton Berle, *Your Show of Shows*, and *Robert Montgomery Presents* had become a habit. Television was not going to go away.

In desperation, panicked moguls looked for ways to bring back their lost sheep. They began by cutting costs, but what they really needed was something new to offer audiences, something that could not be seen on the TV tube. The Production Code was still in full force, so the sexy movie ploy of the early 1930s was not an option. What was possible was the introduction of technologies that would alter the moviegoing experience. The technology already existed for single-strip color film, wide-screen projection, stereophonic sound, and three-dimensional viewing, but there had never been a pressing need to standardize such processes. The transition to talking pictures had been costly enough. Now TV was nipping at the studios' heels, and these gimmicks were newly attractive. Studio engineers began to work with the fevered speed of American scientists, also hoping to outdistance "the other side."

The first Hollywood film to tackle the space race was 1950's *Destination Moon*, which was produced by the renowned animator George Pal at a small new studio called Eagle Lion. Famous for his animated "Puppetoons," Pal had been contemplating a "documentary of the near future" when science fiction novelist Robert Heinlein approached him with a script that he and Alford ("Rip") Van Ronkel had adapted from his own novel, *Rocket Ship Galileo*. The script told the story of a space expedition funded by American business interests because "the first country that can use the moon for the launching of missiles will control the earth!" After detailed technical explanations of rocket construction and space travel, the story follows the first three space pilots through a successful flight to the moon, where they encounter a major problem. They do not have enough fuel to return to earth, so they rip out everything they can from the ship, lessening the fuel required. Should they sacrifice one crew member for the sake of science?

To ensure the scientific accuracy of this project, Pal recruited "space artist" Chesley Bonestell. The sixty-two-year-old matte painter had recently collaborated with German scientist Willy Ley on a book, *The Conquest of Space*, and was thus qualified to design the lunar landscape. A crew of one hundred men built the sets to his specifications, including the crater Harpalus, which is situated in the high northern latitude of the moon, facing Earth. "High latitude was necessary so that the Earth would appear near the

In **THE DAY THE EARTH STOOD STILL**, director Robert Wise cast Michael Rennie as Klaatu, "the tall, thin, ascetic, almost unreal-looking visitor from the heavens." It was Zanuck's idea to have the robot Gort respond to the password:

"Klaatu barada nikto." Gort was played by Lock Martin, the 7'7" doorman at Grauman's Chinese Theatre. The giant found the costume as frightening to wear as to look at. After five hours of standing still for one scene, he began to shake.

horizon (where the camera could see it) and still pick up some lunar landscape," said Heinlein. Though Bonestell was familiar with the lunar paintings of Lucien Rudaux, he chose to give the moon romantically craggy hills and dramatically cracked valleys. Part of the reason was practical. His budget would go farther if he used forced perspective to blend the reticulated floor of the set with a painted backdrop. Cinematographer Lionel Lindon used Technicolor to capture startling vistas, and director Irving Pichel did a respectable job of keeping tension alive during the film's many expository stretches; Pal and Heinlein were determined to explain every aspect of the subject, using the animated character Woody Woodpecker as a tutor. Even before it was finished, *Destination Moon* was the talk of Hollywood.

Independent producer Robert Lippert, the former exhibitor who had helped popularize drive-in movies, had a script called *None Came Back* that could benefit from Pal's publicity. He told composer Albert Glasser that it had been making the rounds for two years. "No one wanted it," Lippert said. "Why? It's science fiction. Who gives a shit about science fiction? But now, that big idiot, that asshole George Pal is making one about going to the moon." Lippert's plan was to rush a film called *Rocketship X-M* into production and finish it in four weeks. "We'll do it real cheap, and get ahead of him," he said, rubbing his hands together. Lippert's copycat show did indeed beat Pal to the theaters, but, to Glasser, the best thing about it was orchestrating the score written by noted American composer

Ferde Grofé. When *Destination Moon* arrived in August of 1950 the cheap imitation was pushed aside; Pal's $586,000 investment yielded $5.5 million.

If there was some question about which American feature film was the first to deal with space travel, there was none about what was the first to deal with visitors from another planet. It was another low-budget independent production, *The Man from Planet X*. Writing partners Jack Pollexfen and Aubrey Wisberg had enjoyed a middling success in the B level of the studio system, but, in 1950, when they saw the public's fascination with flying saucer reports, they decided to go out on their own. They wrote a script in two weeks, got six investors, and came up with the laughably small budget of $38,000. Undaunted, they formed a company called Mid-Century Films and rented offices and an editing suite at Hal Roach Studios. Happily for them, the studio was still full of the impressive sets built by Richard Day for the 1948 Walter Wanger production *Joan of Arc*. Where Ingrid Bergman and a cast of hundreds had crossed swords, a space craft would soon be landing, thanks to the ingenuity of a rogue director who had a reputation for doing his best work under pressure.

Edgar G. Ulmer's career had not done too well since *The Black Cat*. Perhaps it was because of his difficult personality, or perhaps it was because he had lured one of the Laemmle clan away from her husband. In any case, he had spent the past sixteen years working on Poverty Row, where he overcame every penny-pinching mandate to create personal films such as *Detour*. Now Ulmer had to turn

An astronomer contemplates a crashed spaceship in the 1953 film **IT CAME FROM OUTER SPACE.** Science-fiction writer Ray Bradbury and director Jack Arnold made the film a study in xenophobia.

abandoned sets into a rocky, fogbound Scottish island. Actor Robert Clarke, who played the film's hero, remembered visiting Ulmer's home. "The door opens," said Clarke, "and here's this dark, wild-haired Austrian with these big, piercing eyes. And he leans over with this big, booming, deep voice: 'Ya! Come in!' He could be very intimidating." His talent could be too. It was not enough for Ulmer to pool Pollexfen and Wisberg's meager resources into a watchable product; he also had to put his visual stamp on it. "Ulmer showed us this magnificent drawing of the tower for *The Man from Planet X*," recalled Clarke. "He actually did it himself. It was a charcoal drawing of the Broch [the castle], out on the Scottish moors." The artwork ended up as a matte shot in the film, and Clarke ended up as a new kind of hero, a xenophobic reporter who rescues a visitor from outer space. Ulmer called his film a "science-fiction 'terror' story." He explained: "An alien being arrives in a spaceship from a faraway planet in order to find a new world in which to live. Sent as a conqueror, the alien becomes a friend; then, soon, the target of persecution from thinkers on our planet who absolutely refuse to allow him to explain what it is he wants to do." The first film to show a visitor from space was sympathetic to the visitor, not to the hosts.

The visitor was portrayed by Pat Goldin, a short forty-eight-year-old man who had to work tough hours wearing a bulky costume and a helmet with a photoflood bulb inside

it. "He complained constantly about how little money he was getting," Clarke remembered. "He didn't like wearing that suit, and the mask was hot and uncomfortable." Screen Actors Guild minimum at the time was $175. "We worked from six thirty in the morning 'til eight or nine at night every day, six days straight," said Clarke. "*With* overtime, I think my check was for $210!" *The Man from Planet X* was completed in six days and cost just $41,000. Released through United Artists, it grossed more than $1 million.

Science fiction was obviously profitable, so the big studios opened their doors to space ships. The first was Twentieth Century–Fox, where producer Julian Blaustein had been cogitating. "The idea of tackling a political theme in science-fiction form struck me during the summer or early autumn of 1949," said Blaustein, who reasoned that an audience would listen to a theme woven into an exciting narrative, even if the theme was controversial. "Our theme is that peace is no longer a four-letter word." After searching though years of pulp and science-fiction magazines, Blaustein found a novella in a 1940 issue of *Astounding Stories* magazine. "Farewell to the Master," written by the magazine's founder, Harry Bates, was an almost religious tale of a spaceship that lands in Washington, D.C. Its commander, Klaatu, has come to earth on a mission of peace. As soon as he raises his arm in a gesture of greeting, he is shot by a sniper. Klaatu is resurrected by a wordless giant,

Gnut, and they leave earth with their mission unfulfilled. "The thing that grabbed my attention," Blaustein said, "was the response of people to the unknown. Klaatu holds up his hand with something that looks unfamiliar to them and he is immediately shot. It was a terribly significant moment for me in terms of story."

There were many advantages to making a science-fiction film at a major studio. Twentieth had the biggest back lot and the best story editor in town, its boss, Darryl F. Zanuck. When Blaustein and screenwriter Edmund North met with Zanuck in August 1950, they feared that he would cancel their pacifist project because of the recent hostilities in Korea. Zanuck brought up the war, and then said: "To hell with it! Let's go ahead anyway. It's a good piece of entertainment. I believe in it." He did, however, feel that the film would be better served if it started in Washington rather than inside an alien spacecraft. "When you open a picture on something that does not 'exist,' you have great trouble in capturing your audience," said the veteran of twenty-five years of story conferences. He also suggested casting an unknown British actor as the spaceman who had a face that "radiated kindness, wisdom, the purest nobility." Michael Rennie later said, "I was picked to play this part because Hollywood's movie makers apparently thought I was odd enough looking to have come from anywhere in the universe."

Because RKO was also preparing a science-fiction thriller, *The Thing*, Zanuck and Blaustein needed someone who could make a big film in a big hurry. The logical choice was a Val Lewton alumnus, Robert Wise. "We were starting to feel the pressure and the impact of television in the box office," Wise recalled. "Costs were going up and there was constant discussion as to where the theatrical market was going." He was confident that he could turn this offbeat story into a crowd pleaser. "It was a picture that would hold an audience and fascinate them," said Wise, "while at the same time get a point over about our world and where we were going with it."

With a mighty studio behind them, Blaustein, North, and Wise spun an enthralling yarn from Bates's story. The giant Gnut was changed to a robot called Gort, who was, in turn, played by Lock Martin. The sympathetic newsman was changed to a war widow, Helen (Patricia Neal), who is engaged to an unsympathetic insurance agent, Tom (Hugh Marlowe). Most importantly, Helen was given a young son, Bobby (Billy Gray), who represents the innocence and promise of the human race.

Outside the story conferences, North injected his own message into the script, making Klaatu something of a Christ figure. "I had originally hoped that the Christ comparison would be subliminal," he later said. "It gave the film a kind of form, and it was there for anyone who wanted to see it, but . . . I didn't want to make the audience aware of it." Oddly, it was not this symbolism that bothered the PCA, but rather Gort's blasphemous resurrection of Klaatu. In a "nasty confrontation which had us all boiling over," recalled North, Breen refused to approve the script until North agreed to revive Klaatu only temporarily, and by giving credit to "the all-mighty Spirit." Said North: "The Breen Office certainly made life difficult for us." The other big change to the film came from Zanuck. "We must have an exciting, provocative title that will tell the audience what to expect," he said. "Has the title *The Man from Mars* been used?" That title may have been available, but fortunately the title that stuck was *The Day the Earth Stood Still.*

The production rolled like the well-oiled machine that it was, benefiting by art directors Lyle Wheeler and Addison Hehr, who designed an imposing $20,000 spaceship, and by Bernard Herrmann, who added the Theremin to his distinctive musical flavoring. After running up a cost of $960,000, *The Day the Earth Stood Still* opened in September 1951. "It's more than simply a thriller," wrote Edwin Schallert of the *Los Angeles Times.* "It has a sociological and philosophic side, besides being vastly interesting and exciting." *The Day the Earth Stood Still* was not the first big-budget science-fiction film from a major studio; RKO's *The Thing from Another World* beat it by five months. Even so, it became a cosmic hit.

Universal-International's big hit of the summer of 1953 boasted four "firsts." *It Came from Outer Space* was the first science-fiction film to use: (1) an anamorphic wide-screen image; (2) stereophonic sound; (3) 3-D; and (4) a desert setting. It was produced by William Alland and directed by Jack Arnold, who perhaps chose the desert because of the large number of UFO sightings in the Southwest. Harry Essex adapted its script from a Ray Bradbury story about a space craft that crash-lands in Arizona. Its alien passengers must subvert hostile locals (by assuming their identities) in order to repair the craft and make a safe departure. The theme of xenophobia was again explored, and, once again, disguised by "chills and thrills." The one earthling who sympathizes with the aliens is an astronomer (Richard Carlson). His attitude was a risky one to espouse, even in science fiction.

"This was the height of the McCarthy era, when we were running scared of everything, and you didn't have to be a communist to be suspect," said Arnold. "The whole political climate was one of a witch hunt. And if there were important things to be said about our society and its mores, they weren't being said in the film fare of the time." One of Arnold's thought-provoking scenes shows the astronomer entering the open hatchway of the stranded craft. Instead of making the appearance of the alien the point of the scene, Arnold puts his camera inside the craft. The subjective camera shows the anxious alien's point of view. To the alien, this human is a scary thing, so the alien closes the door on him! To the astronomer's neighbors the aliens are scary, fit only to be hunted and killed. In an unpublished essay written to publicize the film, Bradbury wrote: "We have stepped on too many spiders in the last 2,000 years without stopping to look if we are not also stepping on our dreams."

In 1954, Metro-Goldwyn-Mayer was still Hollywood's biggest studio, and the only one that had not tried science fiction. "Control of the picture business was in the hands of five men," actor Richard Anderson recalled, "and what they decided to make was what the audiences saw. They saw pictures in very simple terms: love stories, high adventure, 'scary pictures.' . . . If anybody could come up with something new and it worked, they'd jump on it and make ten of 'em." Autocratic Louis B. Mayer had been ousted from his studio in a 1951 coup. In his place was Dore Schary, who had a liberal attitude about many things but not about science fiction, which he referred to as "the type of picture that was then being mass-produced by everyone else." Still, Metro was not categorically opposed to the genre. "There was no total anti-science fiction sentiment among the executives," said Schary. "That would have been stupid. We were simply waiting for the right project."

It came from two low-echelon studio technicians, painter Irving Block and writer Allen Adler, who used Shakespeare's *The Tempest* as a basis for a twenty-third-century thriller called "The Fatal Planet." Their script changed Prospero the Magician into the philologist Dr. Morbius; the magical Ariel became Robby the Robot, and Prospero's evil assistant, the hunchbacked witch-child Caliban, became the "Id monster," a powerful, invisible presence. Block and Adler targeted their project at lowbrow Allied Artists. Fortunately, their agent thought enough of their script to push them at M-G-M, where producer Nicholas Nayfack asked them how they planned to film the invisible Id monster. "You can't," Block answered. "That's the point. It's very scary. When you see something, it's not half as frightening as your imagination."

"But how will you know it's there?"

Block acted out the sound and dimensions of the monster, holding Nayfack's attention. "The great thing about this is that it won't cost you a cent to make the monster," said Block. After all, an invisible monster would not need to be designed, constructed, or filmed. Nayfack presented the project to Schary, who okayed it—as a B picture. But a B picture at this studio was the equivalent of an A almost anywhere else. Every department, every fiefdom of creativity got involved. Some of them—the miniatures department, for example—had been idled by slowing production.

Many a baby boomer found this a perplexing image in 1953. The androgynous leader of the **INVADERS FROM MARS** was portrayed by a female midget.

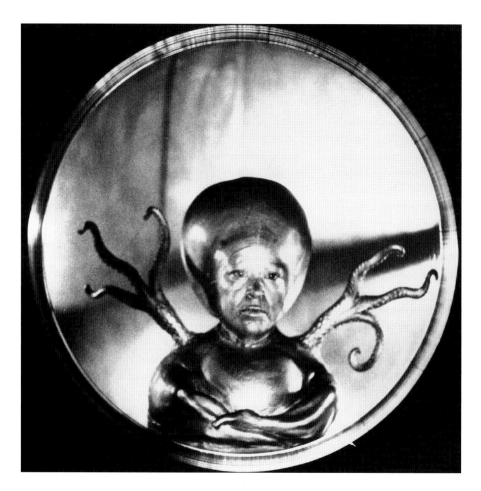

"Metro was funding those people even when they weren't working," said Anderson. "If you worked in special effects, and there was nothing to do, you would stay there and tinker around and experiment with new things. It was an extraordinary operation." Now they had a project in which to put these new things to use.

The result was *Forbidden Planet*, expanded by veteran screenwriter Cyril Hume into the story of Cruiser C-57D, which makes a routine landing on the far-off planet Altair IV. Commander Adams (Leslie Nielsen) meets its sole inhabitants, Dr. Morbius (Walter Pidgeon), his daughter, Altaira (Anne Francis), and Robby the Robot. After learning about the Krell, the advanced civilization that inexplicably disappeared from Altair, Adams and his crew are threatened by a huge invisible monster. Only when he discovers that Morbius's subconscious has created the same type of Id monster that destroyed the Krell can he save Altaira and his ship. "It was a science-fiction fairy tale, and I was the sleeping princess awakened by the prince who landed in his flying saucer," said Francis, who played Altaira in a series of what designer Helen Rose later claimed were the first miniskirts. "I got that part because I was under contract to M-G-M and had good legs," said Francis.

While the premise was a classically simple one, its execution grew complex and increasingly costly, especially when the invisible monster needed to have an outline. The only way to accomplish that was with animation, and M-G-M's animation department had its hands full with Tom and Jerry cartoons. Walt Disney's animators, however, were available, so the Id monster was subcontracted to them, in a curious echo of the film's theme. "At the time it didn't seem dumb to me that collective thinking could create a monster," Francis later said.

The film's most appealing character was Robby the Robot. Unit art director Arthur Lonergan and special effects head A. Arnold Gillespie wanted something new. "Up to that time," Gillespie said, "robots in science-fiction films looked like men in starched aluminum suits." Deciding on a pot-bellied stove as a model, he turned the job over to production designer Mentor Huebner, who put jointed balls on the robot's legs, and to draftsman Bob Kinoshita, who later said: "The total concept for Robby came from different areas. . . . I had something like six people to satisfy." There was also studio production manager J. J. Cohn. "We wanted to keep the budget down," he said. "We didn't have much faith in the picture." Lonergan and Gillespie felt otherwise. "We decided we'd go ahead and design the picture the way it *should* be done," said Lonergan, "regardless of the damn budget." Gillespie agreed. "This gave us a chance to create a new world outside our own solar system. It represented a wonderful opportunity. Nobody could prove us wrong."

With the tacit approval of the debonair Cedric Gibbons, head of the industry's most respected art department, *Forbidden Planet* began to look like an M-G-M movie from the Golden Era. When every department exceeded its budget, Schary paid a call. He surveyed the 98,000 square feet of Altair taking shape on Stage 30 and caught the fever. "I was fascinated with what they were doing," he recalled. "Just fascinated." After fifteen months of work, the film ended up costing $1.9 million. It was released in the spring of 1956, oddly enough, when children were still in school. A spirited publicity campaign failed to attract either children or adults to this intelligent, expansive, and yet detailed film. Sad to say, *Forbidden Planet*, perhaps the most expensive B picture ever made, barely managed to break even, contributing to Schary's eventual ouster from M-G-M.

Green Meanies

In the fall of 1948, director Howard Hawks was in Heidelberg, Germany, filming *I Was a Male War Bride*. During a break in an army post exchange, Hawks picked up an old issue of *Astounding Science Fiction*, one of the many magazines that had surfaced in the wake of the "pulp" craze. *Weird Tales* specialized in fantasy and horror, and *Amazing Stories* had "scientifiction," but *Astounding Science Fiction* published only stories based on proven science. Its editor, John W. Campbell, while discovering authors Isaac Asimov and Robert Heinlein, published his own writing under the nom de plume Don Stuart. It was his story, "Who Goes There?" that caught Hawks's attention. Reading about a spaceman who was frozen in Antarctic ice for 20 million years, Hawks wondered, "What are people from another planet like? I don't see why they should be so entirely different." Stuart's spaceman was four feet tall, with three red eyes, blue hair, and tentacles. Unlike Klaatu or the Man from Planet X, he was evil. He multiplied, assumed the identities of the humans he was visiting, and attacked them, decimating an expedition one by one.

Two years later, with a three-picture obligation looming at RKO-Radio, Hawks looked at the current UFO scares and at magazines such as *Fantasy and Science Fiction*. "Forgetting that almost every Hollywood studio has at least one science-fiction story on its production agenda," he said, "one need only check the growing popularity of the science-fiction magazine to learn of the ever-increasing demand for this type of literature." Hawks promptly bought "Who Goes There?" for his independent production company, Winchester Pictures, and then offered the legendary screenwriter Ben Hecht a thousand dollars a day to do an uncredited adaptation with Charles Lederer, his collaborator on the sarcastically anti-Soviet *Comrade X*. "I thought it would be fun to take a stab at science fiction," said Hawks. He was wary, though, of association with a tired genre. "It is important that we don't confuse the *Frankenstein* type of picture with the science-fiction picture. The first is an out and-out horror thriller based on that which is impossible. The science-fiction film is based on that which is unknown, but is given credibility by the use of science-fiction facts which parallel that which the viewer is asked to believe."

Hecht and Lederer's script, "The Thing," moved the story's expedition to the North Pole, which hinted at anti-Soviet surveillance; gave it snappy, realistic dialogue; added a smart, sexy, tomboyish heroine (Margaret Sheridan, a Hawks discovery in the mold of his earlier find, Lauren Bacall); and gave the spaceman a more human form. Hawks cast a 6'7" young actor named James Arness as the Thing, and then had makeup artist Lee Greenway mold seventeen versions. After the eighteenth, Hawks relented: "Make him look like Frankenstein." Greenway spent $20,000 to create a green foam-rubber skull complete with plastic veins and colored water, and hands that had thorn-like claws on their knuckles and fingertips. Perhaps taking a cue from Val Lewton, Hawks then decided never to show the Thing in high key lighting or in closeup. Still, the impression of a monster was needed to motivate the plot.

The Thing is a vegetative fiend, intent on draining blood from every mammal in sight. This is the threat that divides the expedition. The military faction, led by Captain Hendry (Kenneth Tobey), wants to destroy the creature. The academic faction, led by Nobel Prize–winning Professor Carrington (Robert Cornthwaite), wants to study it. Hecht, a Zionist supporter, was similarly divided from conservatives Hawks and Lederer, but his ambiguous plot could be read as an allegory about either a McCarthy threat or a communist threat. Either way, it was a horror story that called for a master's touch. Some people thought that John Brahm or Robert Siodmak should direct it.

"We all thought this was the dumbest thing we'd ever heard of," said Hawks's script clerk, Richard Keinen. "What is Howard Hawks doing making this stupid horror film?" Hawks confounded his fans further when he gave film editor Christian Nyby the job of director, a risky proposition for a million-dollar film. Hawks knew what he was doing. He was repaying a debt to Nyby, who had saved the jumbled continuity of an earlier film, *Red River*, and, as Cornthwaite said: "On a Hawks picture, there was only one boss. He was an absolute autocrat." Nyby discreetly added: "When you are being taught to paint by Rembrandt, you don't take the brush out of his hand." The master did indeed have his own method. Known since 1940's *His Girl Friday* for overlapping dialogue, he added to the innate tension of each scene by rewriting dialogue so that there were lines that could be "stepped on" without losing exposition. The result was a soundtrack that crackled with an orchestrated chaos. "We'd come in in the morning, and no one knew what we'd be doing that day," Keinen remembered. "We sat around in a big circle and Hawks would read off the lines, but with no character assigned to them. He'd talk it out and get suggestions and write it out while everyone waited around." The tension in the air was not merely creative. "It was weird for the actors, because they never knew when they would be gotten by the Thing, so they never knew when they came to work if it would be their last day."

Just as Nyby was the titular director, so also was Tobey a reflector for the pivotal character, Dr. Carrington. "I was getting the top money in the picture," Cornthwaite recalled. "I don't think Ken [Tobey] ever knew that." Carrington dominates his every scene, a brisk intellectual on a reckless mission. Cornthwaite had to reconcile these conflicting aspects. "I thought to myself, 'The man believes what he says, and therefore in his own mind, he's not the heavy at all. He's doing the right thing.'" In the script, the expedition is under siege in a remote polar outpost. As arctic winds howl outside, the Thing picks off sled dogs and expedition members with equal relish, savagely attacking them, hanging them from the rafters, and draining them of blood. The film builds to a showdown between the invader and the defenders, who have finally hit on a way to destroy it—with electricity. Carrington sabotages their plan by dousing the power, and then runs up to the Thing

Martians vandalized the Los Angeles City Hall in George Pal's 1953 production of H. G. Wells's **THE WAR OF THE WORLDS.** The structure was a six-foot plaster miniature blown up by special-effects master Gordon Jennings.

and pleads with it. "Don't go any farther. They'll kill you. They think you mean to harm us all. But I want to know you, to help you. Believe that! You're wiser than anything on earth. Use that intelligence. Look at me and know what I'm trying to tell you! I'm not your enemy! I'm a scientist!"

Hawks asked the thirty-three-year-old Cornthwaite, a stage actor in his first year of film work, if he wanted to rewrite his dramatic final speech. The surprised actor tried a few changes, and then nervously approached the director. "I can't improve this," the actor said. "Can we do it just the way it's written?" Hawks acceded, so they left Hecht and Lederer's work alone. As they were shooting Cornthwaite's speech, Arness innocently said, "They'll have to come in for a big closeup of you here." Hawks did not shoot a closeup of the scientist because it would make the audience expect a closeup of the Thing; the scene played perfectly without it. The script contributed a catchphrase to American culture. In the curtain speech, a flustered

newspaper reporter (Douglas Spencer) says: "I bring you a warning. Every one of you listening to my voice, tell the world. Tell this to everybody, wherever they are. Watch the skies. Everywhere. Keep looking. *Keep watching the skies.*"

Shortly before its release, the film's title was changed to *The Thing from Another World* to avoid confusion with the Phil Harris novelty song, "The Thing." Tobey attended the Pasadena preview. "I almost fell out of the balcony at the scene where the airmen open the door and the Thing is right there on the other side of it," he said. "I'd forgotten all about it, and the scene scared *me!*" It also scared a woman at the preview; she fainted. Cornthwaite was pleasantly surprised when he saw it for the first time in a theater. "The audience just whooped it up and liked it enormously," he recalled. Released in April 1951, the film grossed $1.95 million, slightly more than *The Day the Earth Stood Still.*

With RKO and Twentieth both doing well in the saucer

sweepstakes, Paramount Pictures decided to take a flyer. Cecil B. DeMille was finishing yet another epic, *The Greatest Show on Earth*, when he agreed to act as executive producer on a George Pal project, *When Worlds Collide*. Philip Wylie had cowritten the novel with Edwin Balmer in 1933, not long after Paramount had filmed both Wylie's screenplay for *Island of Lost Souls* and DeMille's *The Sign of the Cross*. Now, almost twenty years later, the acclaimed cinematographer Rudolph Maté would focus these proven talents on a story of mankind's response to the end of the world. There were no atomic bombs or spacemen in this story, just an out-of-orbit planet coming closer and closer.

The villain of the story, if he could be characterized as such, was Sydney Stanton, a wheelchair-bound billionaire determined to escape the end of the world by constructing a rocket. As portrayed by the wonderfully watchable John Hoyt, Stanton is the high priest of the Cult of Money, mercilessly impatient with anyone and anything that does not do his bidding. The film's awe-inspiring scenes of ecological disaster—tidal waves in Times Square and ocean liners lying capsized alongside submerged skyscrapers—were the combined efforts of advisor Chesley Bonestell, matte painter Jan Domela, and special-effects master Gordon Jennings. The only dereliction of quality occurred when exhibitors pressed Pal for an earlier release than he had planned. Instead of allowing time for a first-rate matte painting of the planet to which forty fortunate earthlings have escaped, Pal hastily substituted a concept painting by Bonestell, a rough rendering that was never intended for a screen-filling finale. Paramount released *When Worlds Collide* in August 1951. Within a year, it was upstaged by some real out-of-this-world weirdness.

On July 19 and 26, 1952, a reported seven UFOs violated restricted airspace above the White House and the Capitol building. Air Force jets went after the craft but could not catch them. On July 29, Major-General John Samford, Air Force Intelligence Chief, held a press conference to blame the incidents on temperature inversions and "radar mirages," which were supposedly ground lights reflected on the undersides of clouds. Major Donald Keyhoe announced that the government was instigating a cover-up and then wrote a book, *Flying Saucers from Outer Space*. This looked like a propitious moment for Paramount to dust off a devalued H. G. Wells property that DeMille had purchased in 1925.

"*The War of the Worlds* was no longer as ancient as Wells had once believed," Pal said. "With all the talk about flying saucers, it had become especially timely." Wells's 1898 novel depicted an attack on London by creatures from Mars. DeMille and Pal hired another former cinematographer to direct it. Byron Haskin, who had been special-effects director at Warner Bros, was now a freelance feature director and the ideal candidate for the complex technical requirements of Wells's nightmarish story. For the screenplay, Pal chose Barre Lyndon, a Wells aficionado who had just written *The Greatest Show* for DeMille, and whose *Lodger* and *Hangover Square* were high-water marks of terror. Pal and Lyndon soon encountered problems.

Paramount's vice president in charge of production was Don Hartman, who had made his mark as writer-producer of the Bob Hope and Bing Crosby "Road" pictures. He thought that he knew more about plot lines and box office than Lyndon and Pal, and he ordered them to add a love interest to the plot. Lyndon spent three months updating Wells's story to present-day Southern California, while striv-

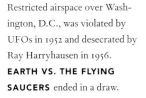

Restricted airspace over Washington, D.C., was violated by UFOs in 1952 and desecrated by Ray Harryhausen in 1956. **EARTH VS. THE FLYING SAUCERS** ended in a draw.

ing to retain its integrity. The result was a fine piece of work. Pal met with Hartman, who looked scornful. "George, this script is a piece of crap," he sneered, "and *this* is where it belongs." With that, he tossed the script into a wastebasket. Pal leaped from his chair, pulled Hartman up by his coat lapels, and began to curse him in Hungarian. The yelling could be heard in the hallway, where it reached the ears of Paramount president Y. Frank Freeman. He burst into the office, broke up the fight, and asked for an accounting. After hearing both sides, Freeman consulted with DeMille, who said, "You're crazy if you don't do this." So Freeman told Pal: "Go ahead and make your film. Do anything you want."

What Pal wanted to do was to capture the human drama, the scope, and the fright of a real invasion. He was aided in this by art director Albert Nozaki, a Japanese American who had his own insights on invasion. At the outset of World War II, he had been forcibly removed from his job at Paramount and carted off to an internment camp. Now Nozaki had regained his position in the studio's prestigious art department. His job was to find an alternative to the water-towerlike Martian craft of Wells's book. "We wanted the machines to be highly mobile," said Nozaki, "but with stilted marching machines it was impossible to be smooth while crashing across gullies and wrecked streets." After numerous tries, Nozaki took off his thinking cap. Then, on a Sunday afternoon, out of nowhere, he found the image: "It came from something like [a] Manta Ray," he recalled. "It was one of those ideas that you instantly know is right." The finished design was forty-two inches wide, made of copper, and suspended by piano wires from an

above
After seeing Martians ravage Los Angeles, Gene Barry and Ann Robinson take shelter in church in the 1953 George Pal production **THE WAR OF THE WORLDS**.

below
Matte painter Jan Domela made this rendering of a swamped New York for the 1951 George Pal production **WHEN WORLDS COLLIDE.**

In the 1951 Howard Hawks production **THE THING FROM ANOTHER WORLD**, a polar expedition investigates a submerged flying saucer. This scene was shot in a March heat wave at RKO's Encino ranch, where the sky was a painted background (with a vertical seam slightly visible) and the frozen lake was made of tempered Masonite, sodium hyposulfite (photographic fixer), and rock salt. These chemicals contaminated the irrigation systems of nearby orchards, the saucer explosion broke windows, and the artificial snow hurt the actors. "A bit of the Styrofoam stuck in my right eyeball," said Robert Cornthwaite. "We got the shot, but I couldn't see out of that eye for twenty minutes afterwards." Cornthwaite retained a permanent scar as a souvenir.

overhead track. Each of the three craft had a cobralike neck that shot a heat ray simulated by burning welding wire. The scenes of the craft moving down the deserted streets of downtown Los Angeles, relentlessly firing on everything in sight, had a grim verisimilitude; Berlin and Hiroshima, after all, were still being rebuilt.

The Martian invasion scenes also had some of the best screaming yet heard in a science-fiction film. Ann Robinson, in her first and only starring role at the studio, did not have to enact the romance mandated by Hartman. Pal had dumped that in favor of a more believable friendship with costar Gene Barry. The script called on him to rescue her from numerous close calls with Martians. Each time, the teenage Robinson managed totally convincing terror. "Byron taught me lots of little camera tricks," she recalled, "like how to use my eyes in a suspenseful manner, and not to over-mug. He taught me how to move my eyes first, and then my head—things that would add suspense to a scene, but things that an inexperienced young girl wouldn't think to do." In one scene, she is hiding with Barry in a deserted house. As she looks for him, three long, wizened sucker fingers lightly tap her on the shoulder. She turns and sees a five-foot being staring at her with one large eye. It is a Martian (played by Filipino sculptor and "ape actor" Charles Gemora). She starts screaming. Barry throws a well-aimed axe into its chest, and it scurries away on spindly legs.

With scenes that included the destruction of the Los Angeles City Hall, *The War of the Worlds* was one of 1953's major hits. Only Ray Harryhausen destroyed more civic landmarks. In his 1956 Columbia film *Earth vs. the Flying Saucers*, nasty discs sliced the tops off the Washington Monument, the Lincoln Memorial, and the Capitol dome. "When you're trying to tell a tale such as we do in the saucer picture," said Harryhausen, "you either spend the time trying to develop characterization, or you spend time developing the destruction, which is what these pictures are all about."

After a slew of films in which the spacemen were either all good or all bad, it was left to Universal-International to make a film in which the invaders could be both. Studio manager Jim Pratt looked at the big picture. "Universal had had its run on *It Came from Outer Space*," he noted. "We'd done very well and had a lot of fun with it, so we thought it'd be damn good business to make another picture in this genre." The opportunity presented itself when agent Vic Orsatti noticed a lime-colored book with an intriguing title on a newsstand. *This Island Earth* had begun life in 1949 as a Raymond F. Jones novelette, "The Alien Machine," in the sometimes sensational magazine *Thrilling Wonder Stories*. Orsatti showed the book to his client, director Joseph Newman, who had been looking for a science-fiction project. "I'd never been associated with science fiction," said Newman, "but I'd been interested in it as a kid. Jules Verne was probably my greatest influence." Newman then engaged screenwriter Edward G. O'Callaghan, who brought an untrammeled imagination to the project. The problem with the book was that the spacemen used only their minds to fight. It was literally too

In **THIS ISLAND EARTH**, Jeff Morrow played Exeter, a sympathetic envoy from a dying planet. "There was a sense of hope," Morrow said, "that if we do ever come to meet people from another planet, in some way we'll be able to communicate on a human level."

cerebral to film. O'Callaghan made the power photographable by translating it into subatomic particles called *neutrinos*. These could control an airplane's flight and burn a hole through lead. His other improvements—an embattled planet, spacemen desperate to leave it, and a race of Mutants—resulted in such an original script that Pratt assigned the project to William Alland.

As soon as O'Callaghan finished his first draft, Alland brought in a staff writer named Franklin Coen. "It was not a practical script," Coen recalled. "There obviously was something about the material that made the studio want to do it, so O'Callaghan's work certainly had value . . . but it certainly was not filmable." One of the first actors to be hired for *This Island Earth* was Jeff Morrow, who also had reservations about the script, and especially about the ruthless spaceman, Exeter, who comes to earth looking for both scientists and uranium. "You had no idea why Exeter was doing any of this stuff," said Morrow, "except that he was an ornery character." Morrow suggested to Alland that the character be given some shading. Walking between soundstages after the meeting, Morrow was surprised to hear Coen say, "I'm so glad you were there, because I've been trying to sell them on that concept for a month!"

The new script had Exeter kidnap nuclear scientists Ruth (Faith Domergue) and Cal (Rex Reason) to help him save his dying planet, Metaluna. When they realize that its leader, the Monitor (Douglas Spencer), is a despot intent on ruling Earth, they try to escape. But Metaluna is in the final stages of destruction by meteor warfare, so Exeter defies both the Monitor and hostile Mutants to send Ruth and Cal back to Earth. Creating spacemen, Mutants, a spaceship, and a planet took two soundstages and the better part of two years. "This was a totally different period from the days when I was changing Lon Chaney Jr. into the Wolf Man," recalled special-effects technician Stan Horsley.

"Television was in competition with the movies and the cost of making pictures was going up. I had caught hell by going over budget on an Abbott and Costello picture, so they were keeping an eye on me." Horsley got around the bean counters by experimenting at home on weekends. Supervising a little army of technicians at the studio, he created a pockmarked planet beset by constant meteor explosions.

Alland had opposed the idea of Mutants, but the front office insisted on having a monster to sell the film, so makeup artists Bud Westmore and Jack Kevan got to work. Even so, the budget only allowed for one foam rubber Mutant, and, when it appeared that its legs were going to be too costly, the Mutant (Regis Parton) was promptly put into pants. The costume included a thirty-inch cerebral cortex, a fiberglass hunchback, a veined breastplate, and lobsterlike pincers. "We didn't have the problems with it like we had with the Creature [from the Black Lagoon] because it didn't have to go in the water," said makeup artist Beau Hickman. "All the Mutant had to do was clack his claws and bleed a lot." But Stein's Stage Blood presented a problem. "It stained the rubber and we'd have to repaint it. So we finally figured, Let's use ketchup. It'll wash right off. So poor Reggie, he's in this thing, and after a while it starts to stink!" Domergue, who was tussling with Parton and dodging meteors, said: "If the space world materializes in my lifetime, I'll be more than ready for it."

Universal was determined to squeeze every last drop of ketchup from the film's $750,000 budget. When the studio refused Horsley the services of Chesley Bonestell, he quit. The sixty-man crew completed the film without him, and it was released on June 1, 1955, garnering the most unanimously positive reviews of any science-fiction film yet. The *Hollywood Reporter* raved: "Science fiction done as well as this presents more than a few of the elements that made *Paradise Lost* and *Faust* so appealing to past generations."

The climax of **THE THING FROM ANOTHER WORLD** was shot on a duplicate set built inside the California Consumers Icehouse in East Los Angeles. Hawks wanted his freezing actors to produce real vapor when they spoke. This still shows the clearest view that audiences had of the Thing, who was played by James Arness.

CHAPTER 11
Drive-in Terror

Tom Tryon and Gloria Talbott costarred in Paramount's **I MARRIED A MONSTER FROM OUTER SPACE**, an imaginative production in which director Gene Fowler's wife and dog helped save the world.

The Last of the Epics

On October 4, 1957, the real outer space eclipsed Hollywood's renderings of it. On that day, the Soviet Union successfully launched a satellite called Sputnik into the space beyond the earth's atmosphere. Four months later the United States launched its own satellite, Explorer I. With the creation of the National Aeronautics and Space Administration (NASA) in July 1958, the race for space had officially begun. Audiences would no longer have to rely on Chesley Bonestell's ideas of how the earth looked from space; satellites would show them. To even the most near-sighted citizen, the world was a changing place. Nowhere was this more obvious than in the insecure kingdoms of Hollywood.

Of the original studio moguls, only sixty-six-year-old Jack L. Warner was still on his throne. L. B. Mayer had just died, and his successor, Dore Schary, had been forced out of M-G-M. (It had also lost its hyphens, and was now known simply as MGM.) In 1957, with movie attendance down twelve percent from the previous year, the company showed a half-million-dollar loss, its first ever. "It needed a person to make decisions," said producer Pandro S. Berman. "I would call the president of the company in New York on some important matter and not get a phone call back for a week." At Twentieth Century–Fox, Darryl F. Zanuck, fed up with his own company president, resigned as head of production. "It became almost impossible to make a good picture after that," said writer Philip Dunne. "All of a sudden, the studio was a place where people were frightened. They were saying, 'What will the censors say to that?' or 'How will this play in Peoria?' They were not thinking of the quality of the picture, simply how much it would cost." RKO-Radio's eccentric boss, Howard Hughes, had led the pack in unloading theater chains. When he sold his studio to General Teleradio in July 1955, he started a new stampede.

Knowing that the studios were obliged to pay residuals to actors only for broadcasts of films made after 1948, RKO's new owners immediately leased the studio's 740 pre-1948 films to C&C Television for $15 million. Swamped with 16mm prints of *Carefree*, *Citizen Kane*, and *Cat People*, local TV stations introduced programs such as "Million Dollar Movie," "The Late Show," and "The Late, Late Show." In May 1956, almost ninety percent of Manhattan television sets were tuned to a weeklong telecast of *King Kong*, instantly eclipsing its 1938, 1942, and 1952 reissues. Neither Fay Wray nor anyone else who had made the landmark film got a penny from its new financial windfall. For the owners of these films and their lessees, it was as if income tax had been abolished. Within months, Jack Warner sold every pre-1950 Warner Bros. film to Associated Artists Productions for $21 million. In February 1958, Paramount upped the ante by selling its pre-1948 library to the Music Corporation of America for $50 million. Paramount head Barney Balaban noted sadly, "When a family starts to sell its silverware, it's the end of the family." Twentieth and MGM held onto their libraries, creating their own syndication packages. Vintage movies now accounted for twenty-five percent of sponsored programming. With this in mind, Columbia's telefilm arm, Screen Gems, leased fifty-two horror films from Universal and created a package called "Shock!" Suddenly there were hundreds of Shock! Theater formats on local TV stations, many with hosts dressed as ghouls or vampires. Creative hosts such as New York's Zacherley attained celebrity overnight.

All this TV watching had an effect on the entertainment industry. At first, TV pulled audiences out of movie theaters and into living rooms. Weekly movie attendance dropped to a new low, just over 30 million; as a result, more than 3,000 theaters closed between 1952 and 1958. With *TV Guide*, TV trays, and TV dinners, teenagers were virtually eating horror movies. Repeated exposure to Shock! Theater had an effect on impressionable young minds. It made

Herbert Marshall and Vincent Price needed twenty takes to film the climax of **THE FLY**. The surprise hit made Price the darling of the drive-in screamers.

them crave horror. In February 1958 a pictorial magazine, *Famous Monsters of Filmland*, capitalized on this appetite. Its first issue—a risky 150,000 copies—sold out almost instantly and made its pun-happy editor, Forrest J. Ackerman, a celebrity. If the teenage boys who pored over it for hours in their suburban bedrooms wanted to see newer, bigger monsters, there was still the neighborhood movie theater, which was now free to book horror films from every level of studio. There was also a new environment, the drive-in movie.

Seventy-two percent of moviegoers were now between twelve and twenty-five years old. Few of them wanted to watch horror films with their parents, and many of them were enjoying the mobility of privately owned automobiles. As the number of young drivers increased, so did the number of drive-in movies. By 1958 there were 4,063 drive-ins—a healthy twenty-five percent of American movie theaters. For frisky adolescents, the drive-in, with its rows of glass-and-metal cocoons, was the next best thing to a motor hotel. "Drive-ins were opening up all over," said producer Samuel Z. Arkoff. "They were known as 'passion pits,' and they didn't give a damn about the pictures they showed. A picture was a way to attract the kids who had wheels." According to an exhibitor quoted in *Playboy* magazine, a drive-in horror movie offered all kinds of thrills. "The girls yell and hang on to the boys, and sometimes you've really got to keep an eye on those cars." When (and if) teenagers looked at the giant outdoor screen, what did they see? The Twentieth Century–Fox fanfare? The Paramount mountain? Leo the Lion?

In **THE FLY**, David Hedison played the victim of an experiment gone wrong. The actor had to wear a twenty-pound fly's head. "Trying to act in it," said Hedison, "was like trying to play the piano with boxing gloves on."

Twentieth Century-Fox built a huge Atlantis set for **JOURNEY TO THE CENTER OF THE EARTH**. James Mason, Pat Boone, Arlene Dahl, and Peter Ronson sat in an altar stone, listening to director Henry Levin. "That's the head of the monster. Look up *there*," said Levin. "And we had to cringe," Boone recalled, "and pull back and brace ourselves against this guy on a ladder with a rag on the end of a pole. We felt like idiots."

By the late 1950s more than sixty-five percent of all Hollywood features were independent productions. True, some of them were made either in or with the major studios, but every year, these "indies" pulled more box-office dollars away from the majors. With production costs constantly rising and immense facilities to support, the majors needed to make films that would regain both the big-city trade and the drive-in market. This meant making films that looked big but cost nothing. The first place to cut costs was in the script. No horror film could now afford an expensive literary property or an original screenplay; only public-domain stories or unknown authors were allowed.

In June 1957 *Playboy* magazine published "The Fly," a short story by George Langelaan about a scientist who shares his molecular structure with a housefly. Twentieth Century–Fox snapped it up, gave it a parsimonious $350,000 budget, and assigned it to director Kurt Neumann, who announced: "The day of the shoddy-looking, cheap exploitation feature is over. There have been too many of them and the public is wise to this type of film. Today, science-fiction films must be believable. They should impart a sense of plausibility and be backed by solid production values."

In addition to this studio's trademarked CinemaScope and Color by Deluxe, these "solid production values" consisted of a $28,000 laboratory set built from army surplus equipment. In the center of this lab was an early computer, an "electronic integrator." Technical advisor on *The Fly* was Dr. Frank Creswell, a pupil of General Electric's Dr. Hugo Steinmetz. Creswell's job was to ensure the accuracy of the integrator, which was based on IBM's famous "brain." Creswell explained: "It has the celebrated 'quick look'

panel on the front, composed of 396 lights which tell whether the primary integration system is functioning properly." In case anyone in the audience could read it, Creswell made sure that the panel flashed only acceptable messages. He had run into trouble on an earlier film, *A Dispatch from Reuters*. When told to type Morse code by a rude assistant director, he had spelled out what was in his mind. Eight people in the preview audience understood his message: "This assistant director is a slob."

In James Clavell's script for *The Fly*, high-minded scientist André (David Hedison) is perfecting the transmission of matter through space when he inadvertently locks a fly in the transmitting booth with him. His supportive wife Helene (Patricia Owens) is naturally shocked to learn that the botched experiment has left him wearing the fly's head and leg. Helene spends several suspenseful scenes trying to find the fly so that André can undo the mistake. After André begins to lose control of his mind and destroys the transmitting machine, Helene follows his last request and squishes him under a huge metal press. In a plot twist reminiscent of Alfred Hitchcock, poor Helene is now accused of murder. (The script does not explain why investigators do not see the fly goo under the press.) Despite the best efforts of André's brother François (Vincent Price), Helene is about to be carted off by police inspector Charas (Herbert Marshall). Just then, the fly wearing André's head is spotted in a spider web. As a spider moves hungrily toward the fly, François and Charas debate what to do with it.

This climactic scene consisted of cuts between closeups of the trapped André, the advancing spider, and the two astonished observers. As the spider's pedipalps wave in

Irwin Allen's **THE LOST WORLD** promised young audiences epic science fiction. It turned out to be an upstaging contest between Jill St. John's poodle and some tricked-up lizards. A critic wrote: "It is left to the heroine's poodle, surprised by a diplodocus, to yap with apposite scorn."

$3 million gross and firmly identified Price with the horror genre. Before Adler could rush Price into a sequel, the fifty-year-old actor began to receive offers from horror producers of all stripes. *Return of the Fly* had to wait until Price fulfilled commitments with Allied Artists and William Castle. In the meantime, profits from *The Fly* launched two science-fiction epics. The first was based—not surprisingly—on a public-domain property, Jules Verne's 1864 novel *A Journey to the Center of the Earth.* Adapting it were Charles Brackett and Walter Reisch, coauthors of *Ninotchka, Niagara,* and *Titanic.*

With the youth audience in mind, producer Brackett approached twenty-five year-old Pat Boone, the singing star of *Bernardine* and *April Love.* Brackett offered Boone the role of a young explorer, Alec, who accompanies his teacher and a lady scientist on an expedition beneath the earth's surface. "I sing songs," said Boone. "I don't want to be in science fiction." Brackett then offered Boone fourteen percent of the film's profits. Boone still said no. When offered four songs and seventeen percent of the gross profits, after expenses, Boone accepted. Brackett then hired James Mason, fresh from Hitchcock's *North by Northwest,* to play the intrepid Professor Lindenbrook. The scientist Carla would be played by Arlene Dahl, the glamorous Norwegian-American actress who had been writing a syndicated beauty column for nine years. Their strong and silent guide, Hans, was played by Peter Ronson, a University of Southern California student who was also the decathlon champion of Iceland. As many a film company learns, the most exotic locales are sometimes found at home. After traveling to Iceland, Scotland, and New Mexico's Carlsbad Caverns, Boone and Dahl had the toughest time on the Hollywood sets of *A Journey to the Center of the Earth.*

Special-effects director L. B. Abbott designed a scene in which Boone would be sucked into a quicksand pit made of salt. When director Henry Levin filmed the scene, Boone fell into the pit and was buried by hundreds of pounds of gypsum crystals. While Levin checked each of several cameras to make sure that they had gotten the scene, Boone began to suffocate. The crew suddenly remembered that their star needed to be dug out, and they retrieved him. After this, Dahl was ready for rough treatment; in fact, she anticipated it, and insisted that a studio nurse wait in attendance. Her big moment came in the sequence when the explorers unexpectedly find the earth's center (a scene not in the book).

Their raft is pulled into a whirlpool and begins to spin violently. Special effects required a rear-projection screen, a raft on casters, a crew to rock it from beneath, and a crew to spray water on it. The actors climbed an eight-foot ladder to reach the raft, which then started revolving. Boone, Mason, and Ronson held on and tried to look brave. With water shooting at her from every direction and the raft spinning like a Disneyland teacup, Dahl lost her usual reserve. "She began to scream," said Boone. "She told Henry to stop the scene, that the nurse had to come and get her; she was getting sick from all the motion and the jerking around. James said, 'Ah, shut up, woman! Hold on, shut up, and do the scene!' I began to laugh. I had to be alert to where the cameras were because I couldn't be seen laughing!"

hungry anticipation, André cries out: "Help me! Help me!" Unfortunately for the two actors, the director had chosen to give the hapless fly a falsetto voice that sounded as if it came from an early talkie cartoon. Price and Marshall were playing the scene in a two-shot framed above the web and had no real actor to react to. There was not even a miniature fly on the web. A script clerk had to feed them the lines "Helppp meee! *Helppp meee!*" Price had been acting for twenty years and had played in genre films such as *The Invisible Man Returns* and *House of Wax.* Marshall, a star of stage and screen, had been acting for forty years. While shooting the arrest scene, he had started to chuckle. This was worse. Something about the plaintive, disembodied voice of the script clerk ruined the mood. "We were playing this scene," Price recalled, "looking at the fly, saying, 'Should we kill it? Should we save it?' and we could never quite get the lines out, because every time that little voice of the fly would say, 'Help me. Please *help me,*' we would just scream with laughter! It was terrible! We ended up doing about twenty takes." *The Fly* was released in July 1958. *Newsweek* wrote: "The last scene, with the human-headed fly caught in a spider's web is as chilling as anything Hollywood has ever compounded."

Buddy Adler, head of production at Twentieth Century–Fox, hoped that *The Fly* would find an audience. It found a

The second epic made by Twentieth was based on a fairly inexpensive property, Arthur Conan Doyle's 1912 novel *The Lost World*. Fans of *King Kong* hoped that producer Irwin Allen would again use Willis O'Brien. The father of stop-motion animation had created a memorable dinosaur sequence with his former protégé, Ray Harryhausen, for Allen's 1956 *The Animal World*, albeit under constant pressure from Allen. O'Brien, now in his early seventies, spent his mostly unemployed time writing treatments and painting storyboards for fantastic projects that he could not sell. Every call from a would-be producer fueled his hopes for his pet project, a CinemaScope and Technicolor *King Kong vs. Frankenstein*. There were not many calls.

O'Brien was hired for *The Lost World*, only to see his hopes dashed again. Allen had no intention of making a film on the scale of the 1925 version. He only wanted O'Brien's name on the credits as "Technical Advisor" to dignify the so-called animation of iguanas and gators. O'Brien accepted a much-needed salary and went back to his drawing board. His was a tragic story, that of an artist so specialized that few projects warranted his art and no studio could afford it. Harryhausen had prospered by allying himself with a sympathetic producer, Charles Schneer, securing British backing, and delving into classical mythology. O'Brien spent his last years trying to interest someone—anyone—in his King Kong project. The only taker was

a small-time producer who bought an option from O'Brien and then tried to peddle it in Japan. O'Brien was working with Marcel Delgado on Stanley Kramer's *It's a Mad Mad Mad Mad World*, again fighting an uphill battle, when he learned that Toho Studios had turned his Kong remake into a vehicle for the Japanese science-fiction creature, Godzilla. O'Brien was disgusted to see a man in an ape suit portraying his brainchild, but there was nothing he could do about it. O'Brien died in 1962, his dream unrealized.

The dinosaurs in *The Lost World*, which was released in 1960, were portrayed by iguanas and alligators with horns glued to their heads, rolling around and biting each other in fight sequences that went nowhere. "I hated the style of the thing," actor David Hedison later said. "Dramatically, nothing in it was real. It was summed up for me with Jill St. John running around in pink tights with that silly little poodle. How could dinosaurs stand up to that?"

On another level that year was George Pal's production of *The Time Machine*. Pal had been offered the rights to H. G. Wells's 1895 novel after the Wells estate saw his *War of the Worlds*. Paramount did not appreciate his work, so he went to MGM, where a success with the 1958 *Tom Thumb* made another Wells project possible. Pal encouraged screenwriter David Duncan to expand on Wells's anecdotal glimpse of the future. The Time Traveler (Rod Taylor) goes from 1899 London to World War I, then to an atomic attack in 1966, and finally to the year 802,701, where he finds that the human race has devolved into two tribes. The bestial Under-grounders (the cannibalistic Morlocks) cultivate the docile Upper-worlders (the slim, blond Eloi) for food. The Time Traveler falls in love with an Eloi named Weena (Yvette Mimieux), foments an Eloi revolt against the Morlocks, and then returns to his own time to bring back three (unspecified) books with which to educate the Eloi.

Pal's film was rich with imaginative detail. The passage of time was shown by rapidly blossoming flowers and trees, and by the frenetically changing fashions on a shopwindow mannequin. The time machine itself was a marvel of originality, created from an antique barber chair by MGM art director George Davis. In a sign of the times, the film's effects were not done by the studio's dwindling special-effects department. The work was farmed out to Project Unlimited, a company formed by veterans of Pal's Puppetoon days. They informed Pal that the only way he could make *The Time Machine* for $827,000 and in twenty-nine days was to have every effect work on the first take.

One effect did not. The script called for lava to flow through the streets of London after an atom bomb triggers a volcanic eruption. The miniature street set was covered with polyethylene, and two bins equipped with trap doors were positioned above it. The night before the scene was to be filmed, technicians cooked oatmeal, stirring red dye into it. Then they poured the oatmeal into the bins. The next morning, effects technician Don Sahlin watched the crew prepare for the scene. Lights were aimed, multiple high-speed cameras were focused, but no one stopped to look in the bins. The cameras started rolling, and the effects team opened the traps. In an instant, it was obvious that hundreds of gallons of oatmeal had undergone an unpleasant change. The oatmeal was supposed to creep like lava; instead, it made a nauseating charge. "This foul-smelling,

Rod Taylor starred in George Pal's 1960 MGM film **THE TIME MACHINE.** Asked why he is so preoccupied with time, the Time Traveler answers: "I don't much care for the time I was born into. It seems people aren't dying fast enough these days. They call upon science to invent new, more efficient weapons to depopulate the earth."

In **THE TIME MACHINE**, the future is a two-level world peopled by two very different tribes, the Eloi and the Morlocks. MGM discovery Yvette Mimieux poses for poster art with a man in a Morlock costume created by William Tuttle.

fermented mess came rushing down over the cameras," recalled Sahlin. "I just went home."

All in all, Pal's production was a model of efficiency, courtesy, and kindness—rare for a Hollywood producer-director. Mimieux remembered: "George Pal went out of his way to make me feel comfortable and explain things to me. He treated us all like human beings, not like cattle." *The Time Machine* was another fulfillment of his vision, praised by even aloof publications such as *Time* magazine.

> *The Time Machine* deserves a place on the very short list of good science-fiction films partly because its hokum is entrancing, its special effects expertly rigged and its monsters sufficiently mon-

strous. But the picture's major virtue is that its human characters are compounded not of green cheese or ground-up Dracula scripts, as is customary in such ventures, but of flesh, blood and imagination.

While MGM searched for more hokum to tap the new market, Universal went through a metamorphosis to equal the Wolf Man's. The so-called second-rate studio became the property of the entertainment conglomerate MCA and transformed into the most frighteningly efficient factory in Hollywood, turning out TV shows such as *Leave It to Beaver* and *The Virginian* with cookie-cutter regularity. Its yearly profits climbed past $10 million; no one in Universal City seemed to care that it was no longer, in the classic Hollywood definition, a movie studio. An MGM producer, William Kozlenko, said: "The movie business can be compared, in a sense, to living in New York. Only very rich or very poor people can live in New York. Only very expensive or very cheap pictures can succeed here." While very expensive pictures like *Cleopatra* were destroying Twentieth Century–Fox, some very cheap pictures about teenage monsters were creating American-International Pictures.

Those Monsters Next Door

In the early 1950s, before the Universal monster movies had been sold to television, they were given a new lease on life by an old distribution company called Realart Pictures. Edgar Ulmer's *The Black Cat*, for instance, was reissued as *The Vanishing Body*. Realart's owner, Jack Broder, had a penchant for renaming movies. When he changed Lon Chaney's *Man Made Monster* to *The Atomic Monster*, he ran into trouble. A young filmmaker named Alex Gordon had left him an unsolicited screenplay with that very title. Gordon paid a visit to Broder, bringing along a heavyset lawyer named Samuel Z. Arkoff. The meeting ended with a settlement of $500. Watching in awe was Broder's lanky sales manager, James H. Nicholson, who had never seen his boss surrender cash so quickly. Before long, Nicholson and Arkoff were meeting to discuss a partnership. Both had paid their dues on the fringes of the industry. At one point, Nicholson and his wife were living on the premises of their Hollywood Boulevard theater, the Markel. A few blocks away, in the Lawyer's Building on Selma Avenue, Arkoff was

eking out an existence by representing his wife's relatives and Ed Wood's friends.

In 1954, Nicholson and Arkoff formed their own distributing company, American Releasing Corporation (ARC). They got their first release from a twenty-nine-year-old producer named Roger Corman, who could put a film in the can in ten days for less than $50,000—and make a profit of $850,000. When Corman found that he liked directing, Nicholson and Arkoff took Corman on as a silent partner. It soon occurred to them that they could make more money by both distributing and producing. Within a year, ARC became American-International Pictures (AIP).

The new company's first films had titles like *The Fast and the Furious, Five Guns West*, and *Apache Woman*. Westerns were cheap and profitable, but after a rocky year AIP had only to talk to veteran theater owners to find out what really made money. The savvy Arthur L. Mayer was owner of New York's venerable horror showcase, the Rialto. He knew his audience. It was young, and it wanted "red meat," said Mayer. "With justifiable lack of faith in the wisdom of their elders and the competence of their contemporaries, the young people are frustrated, purposeless, bitter." He had expected two Billy Wilder films, *The Spirit of St. Louis* and *Love in the Afternoon*, to fill his theater, but James Stewart, Audrey Hepburn, and Gary Cooper had left the kids cold. "They find it easier to identify themselves with the sons of Frankenstein or the granddaughters of Dracula than with Lindbergh soaring across the Atlantic, or a well-constructed young lady of twenty pursued by the sixty-year-old wreck of a once-popular leading man."

American International Pictures monopolized the burgeoning youth market with films such as **I WAS A TEENAGE FRANKENSTEIN.** The black-and-white production had a color climax in which the title creature (Gary Conway) is electrocuted.

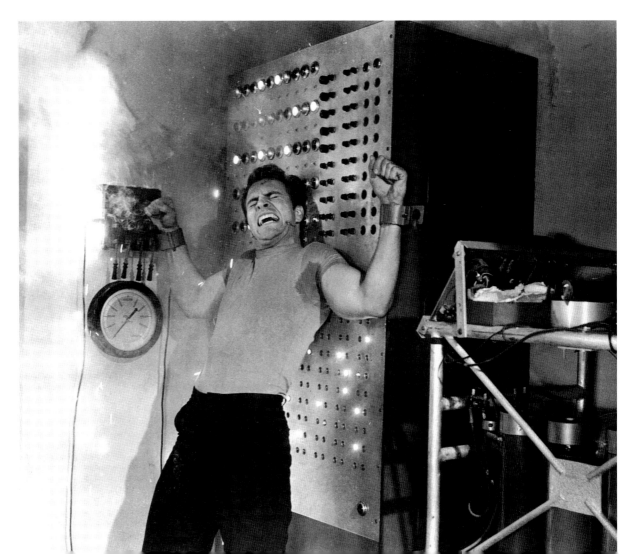

Mayer was not making this up; in 1956, both RKO-Radio and Republic Pictures went out of business. "Young adults were getting married and moving out into new housing in the suburbs," remembered Arkoff. "They were sitting out in their millions of new homes, having babies and watching TV. The only real constant audience which Jim Nicholson and I recognized—one which the majors didn't—was the youth, who didn't *want* to stay home, who had to get *out*." Nicholson agreed: "The majors have been aiming at an audience that's there, but it's an infrequent audience. They've forgotten the people that like to go to a show every week." To fill the gap, AIP came up with attractions such as *The Beast with a Million Eyes*, *Voodoo Woman*, and *The Undead*. Reviewers were unimpressed. *Boxoffice* reviewed *The Phantom from 10,000 Leagues*: "As this hodgepodge draws to a merciful close, a character intones: 'What a mess.' If it weren't for the fact that a prescribed amount of space has to be filled [here], that line of dialogue could aptly serve as the beginning and end of a critique of this offering."

Critics did not pay to see these movies. The kids who did looked at the titles and the posters, and then made up their minds. AIP's posters were colorful and lurid. Nicholson believed that advertising art had to instill a feeling in the onlooker, a sense of urgency. "In my advertising," said artist Albert Kallis, "there was always an understanding of the elements of what we were playing with and whom we were playing to." Part of this derived from each film's title. "We do our planning backwards," said Nicholson. "We get what sounds like a title that will arouse interest, then a monster or gimmick, then figure out what advertising is going to consist of. Then we bring in a writer to provide a

script to fit the title and concept." But there had to be truth in advertising. "The worst thing you can do is to mislead a teenager in your ads by not having the same elements in the picture," Nicholson admitted.

While it courted youth, AIP respected maturity, hiring industry veterans such as cinematographer Floyd Crosby, who had shot *Tabu* in 1931 for F. W. Murnau. At one point, Crosby pointed out to Corman that the microphone boom had been visible in the last shot. Should they reframe it? "I don't care whether the mike is in the shot or not," Corman snapped. "Let's just finish the thing." Another AIP recruit was Edward L. Cahn, a sixty-year-old director who had edited *The Man Who Laughs* at Universal in 1928 and worked at every major studio since. Like so many other skilled veterans, he was at loose ends. When AIP put him to work on *The She-Creature*, he grew suddenly bigger than life. "Sitting in his chair, waving his pipe, he came on like Roosevelt with a cape," recalled screenwriter Charles Griffith. "He was the first one who gave me a cold chill of what it must be like to be a has-been. He was a real puffball, a blowhard." After directing seven more cheapies for AIP, Cahn was in demand and spent his last years at United Artists.

AIP was doing so well that its owners could afford to lease the cozy, half-timbered Charlie Chaplin Studios at Sunset and La Brea. Arkoff eventually sold the lease to comedian Red Skelton, saying, "You don't need studios to make pictures." What they needed—and had—were no-nonsense producers such as Herman Cohen, another Realart alumnus, with whom Nicholson often had lunch. "Herm, can you do a picture for us?" Nicholson asked Cohen one day. "I thought of doing a teenage werewolf picture," said Cohen. "I felt that for a fledgling company which was trying to get the teenage market, it could be ideal. I came up with the title *Teenage Werewolf*, and Jim Nicholson added *I Was a*." Cohen wrote the script with a screenwriter friend, Aben Kandel, who used the pseudonym Ralph Thornton to keep his moonlighting a secret from the majors. Cohen found his director in an adjoining office. Film editor Gene Fowler Jr. had directing aspirations, but Cohen thought he might not want to make his debut on this film. "It's got the worst title in the world," said Cohen, "but it's a very good script." Fowler took it home and read it in the bathtub. It was the story of a high-school boy who expresses his infantile rage in sudden acts of violence. The psychiatrist who is supposed to help him instead injects him with an experimental serum that makes him turn into an adolescent lycanthrope.

Fowler finished reading and said to his wife, "I can't do this goddamned thing!"

"Look," she said. "Why don't you do it anyway? You'd like to do a feature, and nobody will see it."

Fowler decided to do the film if he could make it more than a mere exploitation film. "I was trying to do something with a little substance to it," he said. In the finished film, the boy (Michael Landon) is less nasty and the psychiatrist (Whit Bissell) is less maniacal. To make the film look better than the average AIP product, Fowler asked his friend Joseph LaShelle, who had photographed *Laura*, to help him out. "You're kidding!" exclaimed LaShelle. "I don't want to do something like that." Fowler asked him to do it

Jack Kevan intended his makeup for Universal-International's **MONSTER ON THE CAMPUS** to be covered with a shirt, but the unit still man did not wait for stuntman Eddie Parker to put one on, so actress Joanna Moore was unable to suspend her disbelief—or her giggles.

below

I WAS A TEENAGE WERE-WOLF was a breakthrough film for AIP's Jim Nicholson and Samuel Z. Arkoff. In his first film, Michael Landon played a youth troubled by fits of violence. Young audiences could identify with his alienation from adults and his betrayal by a duplicitous psychiatrist.

as a favor. The combination of LaShelle's lighting and Fowler's direction made the ambivalent young hero an appealing presence. Of course, Landon's acting helped.

The film's standout scene took place in a gymnasium, where the boy watches a girl (Dawn Richard) doing calisthenics on the parallel bars. The classroom bell suddenly goes off, aggravating his sexual excitement. The camera rushes in for a closeup as he turns into a wolf. The girl is now hanging upside down on the bars. A series of subjective upside-down angles show him coming toward her. She screams and tries to escape. He collides with a stack of folding chairs. "We thought he had almost killed himself in that gym scene, when he ran after Dawn," recalled Cohen. "It's funny, but when he had that makeup on, he said he felt like he *was* a werewolf."

AIP released *I Was a Teenage Werewolf* in June 1957, just in time for summer vacation. "Then all of a sudden, Jack Benny, Bob Hope, and various other comedians got ahold of the title and they started making fun of it," said Cohen. "Then people from *Time* and *Newsweek* and *Life* started calling the office." The title that had given everyone

pause turned out to be its biggest asset. "It has a haunting quality about it," wrote the *Los Angeles Examiner*, "and I ought to caution you that if you let it pierce your consciousness, it will echo in your brain in a constant refrain." *I Was a Teenage Werewolf*, shot in five and a half days for $82,000, grossed more than $2 million.

Before AIP could even start counting receipts, a sequel was under way. The owner of a Texas theater chain lamented that he would have to pay a huge rental to the majors for Thanksgiving weekend features. Nicholson offered to supply him with a horror double bill, as yet unmade. *I Was a Teenage Frankenstein* and *Blood of Dracula* were each made in a four-week rush from typewriter to film can. In Cohen and Kandel's script, the teenage Frankenstein is pieced together from the remains of a track team killed in a plane accident. "All those fine, young, athletic bodies, all those hours of training for strength, speed, endurance . . . gone to waste," says Whit Bissell, again playing a mad scientist, but this time without any redeeming traits. In fact, his character shows a perversity increasingly evident in Cohen's films.

above

I WAS A TEENAGE WERE-WOLF was shot in five and a half days. Given the demanding schedule, Landon's transformation was accomplished by makeup artist Phil Scheer while other scenes were being shot around him.

Dr. Frankenstein is obsessed with controlling his muscular young creation (Gary Conway). When his fiancée (Phyllis Coates) becomes jealous of his "experiment," he manipulates the monster into killing her. She is portrayed, as are most of the women in his films, as unintelligent, avaricious, and possessive. In the context of the already slight narrative, the murder is gratuitous. When asked why a similarly pointless death occurs in another of his films, Cohen replied: "She was a very pretty girl, and very sexy, and I thought the audience would get a kick out of seeing her killed." Scenes of the teenage monster show him flexing his shirtless torso, his expanding pectorals dominating the screen. The sexual undercurrent in teen horror films was increasingly noticeable, but, unless there was some overt violation of the Production Code, there was nothing that Geoff Shurlock could do about it. A New York producer named Robert Newman played armchair psychologist. "Horror movies are sexually stimulating to people, whether they know it or not," opined Newman. "The monster itself is usually a symbol of sexual power unleashed." Herbert Strock, who directed *I Was a Teenage Frankenstein* for Cohen, had a more succinct explanation for Cohen's titillating imagery. "I think he'd film a garbage can if he thought it would make money." There was a lot of money to be pulled out of teenage pockets in the late 1950s, and these films were doing it.

Paramount Pictures hoped to cash in on AIP's formula, so they got Fowler to write, produce, and direct *I Married a Monster from Outer Space* (1958), a title with the requisite blend of horror and sex. A $175,000 budget and the Paramount back lot gave the film the quality that AIP could not, but Fowler still had to cut corners. He needed lots of monsters but had a limited costume allowance. "We had two costumes," he recalled, "which we used over and over to make it seem like there were a bunch of them." His design was ingenious. "I gave them a vulnerable spot, those tubes on the outside of their bodies, which gave the dogs something to grab hold of. Having dogs kill off the aliens was probably the cheapest thing we could think of." Getting the dogs to attack was not as easy. "They took one look at the monsters and hid behind the trainer's legs. It scared the living hell out of them. So the monsters had to stand there in their suits and play with the dogs until they got used to them." By the time the attack scene was ready, the dogs were too fond of the monsters to rip out their tubes, so the actors had to guide the dogs' muzzles. Fowler's dog, Anna, helped out, and so did his wife, Marge. "For the dissolving of the monster at the end," he said, "my wife made me about five gallons of Jell-o."

In a departure from the "cheapie" trend, producer Albert Zugsmith convinced Universal-International to do a big project about a small person. Richard Matheson's novel,

Grant Williams narrowly escapes the clutches of his own house cat in Jack Arnold's 1957 hit, **THE INCREDIBLE SHRINKING MAN.** Most of the film's virtuosic special effects were supervised by Clifford Stine, head of the Universal-International special-effects department, but director Jack Arnold solved the problem of simulating giant drops of falling water: a treadmill dropped hundreds of water-filled condoms. At the film's completion, the production office asked Arnold why he had ordered 1,200 contraceptives. "Fellows, it was such a hard picture," Arnold answered, "and we all worked so hard, we decided to have a big party at the end of it."

The Shrinking Man, was the story of a man who is exposed to a radioactive cloud and then starts to diminish in size. The special effects needed to capture this on film would be unprecedented. *The Devil-Doll* and *Dr. Cyclops* had featured tiny characters, but of stable size. This was something new for the studio, which also had to approve a story that did not have a neatly resolved ending. Matheson's novel ends with the character shrinking to infinitesimal size. There is no last-minute rescue; the man just keeps shrinking. In spite of these problems, Zugsmith managed to secure a budget of $750,000. According to Matheson, Zugsmith was "typical of the ten-inch-cigar-smoking executive of the time." Zugsmith told him: "I'm gonna give ya a scriptwriting lesson, kiddie!" Matheson listened politely, then adapted his novel as he saw fit. Zugsmith assigned the film to Jack Arnold, who felt that Matheson's flashback structure weakened the story's suspense. He had Richard Alan Simmons rework the script; but, when Matheson insisted on a solo credit, Simmons graciously stepped aside. Arnold drew the storyboards, designing a film in which "the commonplace becomes bizarre and threatening."

In *The Incredible Shrinking Man* (1957), Scott Carey (Grant Williams) shrinks at a constant, terrifying rate. His wife, Louise (Randy Stuart), does all she can to preserve his safety and dignity. Finding himself unexpectedly handicapped, Scott becomes depressed, doubting his own worth. The plot takes a hopeful turn when an antidote momentarily halts the shrinking. In a poignant sequence, Scott tries to relate with a sympathetic circus midget (April Kent), only to see his symptoms suddenly return. When he is six inches tall, the best Louise can do is hide him in a dollhouse. It is there that the real terror begins. A house cat becomes a dinosaurlike predator when it discovers the tiny human.

"The shot where the cat shoves its paw through the dollhouse window was particularly difficult," said Arnold. "I got a shot of the cat fiercely reaching out for a little bird that was just off camera, and back-projected it through the window. I also had a giant fake paw that I would stick in and out fast." Arnold's most imaginative set piece was the cellar where Scott finds himself trapped without food or a means of escape, as a tarantula approaches and a water heater leaks. "I wanted to make the audience realize that their own cellars were potential hells, that the familiar could become horrible if the circumstances were changed," said Arnold.

Arnold filmed a Panamanian tarantula. He put the film of the tarantula in the ground glass of the camera, moved Williams into a matching position on oversize sets, and then had him count to the beat of a metronome to match his movements to those of the tarantula. For these giant-scale scenes, Williams had to run, climb, fall, and be swept away by a torrent of hot water. When Matheson visited the set, he saw an actor in an exceedingly strenuous role. "That guy looked beat!" said Matheson. "He nearly killed himself. He was almost blinded by an arc light. He was nearly electrocuted. He was half-drowned. Boy, did he work hard." Furthermore, Williams had to play most of his scenes with imagined creatures. "In that situation, a director's only insurance is an actor who is intelligent and knows his craft," said Arnold. "[The film] was almost three-quarters silent and required real acting. Grant gave a truly outstanding performance."

As both Matheson and Arnold expected, Universal wanted a happy ending. "To the studio executives a happy ending meant that the doctors find a serum to reverse the shrinking process," said Arnold. "I had quite a to-do with them, as such an ending is not right for this film. I wouldn't stand for it. I refused." With the Black Lagoon series to his credit, Arnold got the studio to agree to a test preview. What the audience saw was startling—but they liked it. The film ends with Scott so small that he can escape the cellar by passing through the wires of a mesh screen. He stops and looks up at the heavens. "All this vast majesty of creation. It had to mean something. And then I meant something, too. Yes, smaller than the smallest. I meant something, too. To God there is no Zero. I still exist."

The Incredible Shrinking Man became a multimillion-dollar hit for Universal. Instead of rewarding Arnold and Williams with A-picture projects, they rushed them into mediocre Bs. Arnold found himself assigned to something called *Monster on the Campus* (1958). "The science-fiction craze was dying out and I really didn't want to do this kind of picture," Arnold said. "But as a contract director, I had little choice. I had to do it or risk being suspended." Hampered by the title and by an unconvincing Neanderthal Man makeup, Arnold still delivered the goods. The film capitalized on the 1952 discovery of the coelacanth, the so-called living prehistoric fish. Arnold did what he could with the story of a professor whose life is ruined by the toxic blood of one such fish. *Variety* liked the film. "Its premise is logically developed without any great strain on the imagination, acting is convincing, and there's a general professional air about the unfoldment. Film is a good entry for its particular exploitation market."

That market was a thriving one. One exhibitor raised his eyes to heaven in gratitude: "Thank God for the horror pictures. They've saved us. Before this kick, we were thinking of shutting down two nights a week. Now, with all the monster stuff, the place starts filling up at three o'clock." Obviously, the market was broad enough to support any number of entries. Like the monsters in these films, they kept coming.

Don't Step on It!

In early 1956, two mysterious men walked into the Los Angeles Museum of Science and Industry. Dressed in dark suits, they did not have the casual, carefree appearance of most of the museum's visitors. They looked as if they were on a mission. Their expressions were serious, and they moved from display to display with an impatient energy. They rushed through the dinosaur dioramas, barely glanced at tarantulas in amber, and shook their heads at mounted ants. When they came to a preserved praying mantis, they stopped. A moment of silence ensued. The men looked at each other, then back at the mantis. They began to whisper, and one man scribbled on a spiral notepad. Then they turned away from the display cases and hurriedly left the museum.

The two men were producer William Alland and screenwriter Martin Berkeley. Their mission was to find a creature that had not already served as the basis for a science-fiction film. A praying mantis could be their new "it." Back at Universal-International, Berkeley sat down and typed out a "formula sheet," a story breakdown based on the Warner

Bros. film *Them!* This insect fit the requirements of the formula, and in mid-1956 Universal announced a production called *The Deadly Mantis*, starring Rex Reason. Fresh from *This Island Earth*, Reason read the script and did not like the purloined formula. "To me it was very corny," said Reason. "I knew that the monster would be the star, and I knew I was worth a little more than just to support a praying mantis." Reason asked to be released from the film. He was released and then dropped from Universal's payroll, along with most of its other contract players. In the world of low-budget horror and science fiction, a praying mantis was worth more than a whole roster of stars. Teenagers did not care who was killed by the insect as long as someone was and they could scream afterward.

Another genre film released in the summer of 1957 was Bert I. Gordon's *Beginning of the End*. Instead of a giant mantis scaling the Washington Monument, the script called for giant grasshoppers to climb Chicago's Wrigley Building. Animation was deemed too costly, so real insects would be used. Gordon needed two hundred grasshoppers, and not just any species would do; they had to be non-hopping and non-flying. "I had to get my grasshoppers from Waco, Texas," said Gordon. "They had the only species large enough to carry focus. I could only import males because they didn't want the things to start breeding. They even had someone from the agricultural department or someplace like that come out to take a head count—or a wing

count." Duncan Parkin was an uncredited special-effects technician on the film. When he received the shipment from Waco, he made a grisly discovery. The grasshoppers had not adapted to their cramped quarters. During the trip, they had grown restive, quarrelsome, and hungry. "They began to cannibalize one another and eventually we were left with only about a dozen of them," said Parkin. The remaining troupers were filmed walking on dry-mounted still photographs of buildings, which were cheaper than three-dimensional miniatures.

The film was produced by American Broadcasting–Paramount Theaters, a company formed to supply more product to film-hungry exhibitors. "If AB-PT and its fellow theatermen regard *Beginning of the End* as the answer to the product shortage," wrote *Variety*, "the motion picture industry might as well shut its doors this very moment." Did audiences agree? Did they complain? No, they laughed. "Many in the audience finished the last ten minutes of this gripping drama in near hysterics," wrote a critic. Gordon didn't care, as long as they had paid to get in. "The movie audience these days consists almost entirely of teenagers," he said. "Either they're naïve and go to get scared, or they're sophisticated and enjoy scoffing at the pictures. There isn't much a teenager can scoff at these days, you know."

Seeing how profitable these cheap films were, a Pennsylvania distributor named Jack H. Harris thought he could make something better than the ones he was shipping to

A visit to the Museum of Science and Industry resulted in **THE DEADLY MANTIS**, a 1957 Universal film that was shamelessly copied from the Warner Bros. film *Them!* Teenagers did not care.

A dozen well-fed Texas grasshoppers portrayed the invading force in the 1957 **BEGINNING OF THE END.** The cast had originally numbered two hundred, but twelve grasshoppers could not wait to eat Chicago; they ate the other 188 grasshoppers.

local theaters. He buttonholed his friend Irvine Millgate, who was a consultant to the Visual Aids Department of the Boy Scouts of America. They had contacts, they had skills, and they had seen these formulas over and over. Why not raise the money and make their own horror film? "Listen," said Harris to Millgate, "what I want to think up is a movie monster that is not a guy dressed up in a suit—not a puppet—but some kind of form that's never been done before. I want it to do things that will undo mankind if it's not arrested or destroyed." Of course, money was an issue, so the monster would have to be inexpensive. "I want the destruction to be something that Grandma could cook up on her stove on an experimental Sunday afternoon."

Harris pitched his concept to a Methodist filmmaking group, Valley Forge Film Studios, convincing them that they could make better religious films with the returns from a secular film. A minister named Irvin S. Yeaworth Jr. agreed to direct, and Harris raised $240,000. His cast included Steve McQueen, a relatively unknown TV actor, and Olin Howlin, a veteran character actor. His monster was born of another brainstorming session with Millgate. Reducing horror to a chemical composition, Millgate suggested a "mineral monster." After consulting with the Union Carbide Corporation, Harris gave birth to the Blob, a rolling space monster made of silicone.

"We discovered that we could achieve varying degrees of consistency, from that of running water to hard glue," said Harris. "Vegetable coloring gave it the red color. It got redder and redder as it grew and consumed more people.

One thing we never resolved was, how do you keep the color in there? We just had to keep mixing it, like cake batter. Otherwise it would all settle to the bottom." The scenes between McQueen and Howlin, in which the cheeky teenager comes to the aid of an elderly man whose arm is being devoured by the gelatinous Blob, were well played, but most of the film's acting and production values were substandard. Harris's audience did not care. He had purposely made teenagers the heroes of the film, and teenagers were his audience. *The Blob* ultimately grossed one hundred times its cost.

As a distributor, Harris was, of course, aware of the shift in audience demographics. Theater owners would tell him before they would tell the trade papers. In July 1958, just before the film's release, *Newsweek* magazine canvassed a number of exhibitors. Their opinions were illuminating: "I'll say one thing for the horror pictures. The kids stay in their seats—none of this wandering around up and down aisles the way they do during a fancy drawing room opus"; "My audience—I hate to call them juvenile delinquents—but they seem to quiet down a bit when you give them a fairly good thriller. They really seem to be curious about what makes a monster, and how it works"; "As far as I'm concerned, a well-made horror film is better entertainment than a lot of the classy stuff I get. We get plenty of adult trade along with the youngsters. You see kids dragging their parents in for the show." Some of these parents must have cast longing glances at the exit when forced to sit through the inane movies that were oozing from the screen.

In 1957 Sam Katzman, who had been supplying Columbia pictures with an average of ten B films a year, followed his successful *Earth vs. the Flying Saucers* with another airborne menace. This time it was a huge bird. He could not impose upon Columbia's special-effects department for *The Giant Claw*, so he shopped for a cheap alternative. "When I first met the film's producer, Sam Katzman," recalled actress Mara Corday, "he was so excited about the 'Bird,' and it seemed like something to look forward to. The special effects were being done in Mexico and the Mexican crew had given him the impression the 'Bird' would be very frightening, with superior special effects." Costarring with Corday was Jeff Morrow, who brought conviction to his scenes with the as yet unseen creature. "We poor benighted actors had our own idea of what the giant bird would look like," said Morrow. "Our concept was that this was something that resembled a streamlined hawk, flying at such speeds that we could barely see it." The film was nearing completion when Katzman's "Bird" arrived from Mexico. It did not look like a hawk; it looked like a turkey. "Well, Katzman was shocked," said Corday, "but he opted to accept the thing as a joke, because it was not economi-

cal to create a more realistic monster." Morrow saw the finished product, not in a studio screening room, but on the big screen. "I went to a sneak preview in Westwood Village," he recalled. "When the monster appeared on the screen it was like a huge plucked turkey, flying with these incredible *squawks*! And the audience went into hysterics."

The Milner Brothers' 1957 film *From Hell It Came* was the strange story of a South Sea Islands prince who is executed by a witch doctor for fraternizing with American scientists. He then rises from the grave in the form of a tree to seek vengeance. Actor Gregg Palmer's one scene as the prince would require him to lie in the center of the village, staked to the ground, with three chickens standing guard. In a hallway outside the producers' offices, Palmer stared at his agent, Jack Pomeroy, and then asked him: "You want me to lay down and be staked out and have chickens around me? And then I turn into a tree? Come on!"

"Gregg, do this," urged Pomeroy. "A lot of people are going to see this. Science fiction is coming around."

As Palmer related: "The next thing I know, I was staked out on the ground and the chickens were all around me." Palmer was lucky. He finished his role in one day. Someone

Lon Chaney tries to attack Richard Crane in Roy Del Ruth's 1959 **THE ALLIGATOR PEOPLE**. "This picture has as asinine a plot as you will see in a long time of movie going," wrote *New York News* critic Maxine Dowling. "You will have to see it to believe it—and then you won't."

In **THE WASP WOMAN**, Susan Cabot attacks Lani Ward with a mouthful of Hershey's chocolate syrup.

else had to play the tree, though, wearing an eight-foot-tall costume. Former wrestler Chester Hayes was approached by director Dan Milner. "The producers needed someone who could walk in the costume as well as take the overall weight of it," said Hayes. "I don't know how much it weighed, but . . . it was not designed for casual movement or walking, even at the most reasonable pace." As Tabanga, the tree monster, Hayes had to kill natives and carry women, all of whom had to help him balance and see where he was going. To complicate matters, the wire mesh inside the hot, heavy costume lacerated Hayes's face, and its rubber legs started to tear. Between scenes, the tree monster languished on the sidelines while actors recited pages of plodding dialogue. "They would unintentionally forget me for a while," said Hayes. "I'd be standing in that costume, waiting for my next call." When Allied Artists released *From Hell It Came*, Hayes could not resist seeing it. "I was disappointed in the scenes that had Tabanga walking," he said. "It appeared more comical than scary." As his costume split its seams, audiences split their sides—laughing.

Hayes had his chuckles after filming was completed. Actress Beverly Garland could not wait that long. Having survived Roger Corman's quickies at American International Pictures, she thought she had finally made the grade in *The Alligator People* (1959), a wide-screen film that would be distributed by Twentieth Century–Fox. She was working with famous veterans; actors George Macready and Lon Chaney, cinematographer Karl Struss, and director Roy Del Ruth. Garland was unfazed by the film's title. "Filming *The*

Alligator People," she said, "was like working on a 'Double A Movie' compared to working for Roger Corman." She did not mind splashing and falling through a swamp, but she had trouble with the scene in which she goes to a clinic where Macready is trying to help the Alligator People, the victims of a serum meant to reverse limb loss. "I walk in," she recalled, "and here they have these guys in these long white robes with this kind of hat thing on their heads. And I tell you, they all looked like they had urinals on their heads! I started to laugh. Then Roy Del Ruth looked at them and it started to get to him, too." The crew took three hours to film the simple scene because every take was ruined by someone bursting out laughing. "The hardest thing to do in that movie," she remembered, "was simply to keep a straight face."

Garland was portraying the wife of a man (Richard Crane) who is in the early stages of transformation into an alligator. The script called for her to be sympathetic, in spite of his reptilian appearance. "I just played her the way you would if you were married to an alligator," said Garland, who got through her scenes successfully until, once more, something triggered her sense of the absurd. "I had to be a bit romantic and console my poor husband," she said. "This was when he was pretty much an alligator and I had to say to him, 'I'll love you no matter what,' which I think took me a good half day to say. Laugh? I thought I'd die! They almost had to film that on the back of my head." She did better in the film's finale, when Crane, now a full-fledged Alligator Person, dashes heedlessly into the swamp

Allison Hayes made **ATTACK OF THE 50 FOOT WOMAN** a 1958 drive-in hit with an implausible but watchable costume.

and drowns in quicksand. Some viewers criticized the film's sudden ending. "What were they going to do?" asked Garland. "Were they going to have us live happily ever after and raise baby alligators?"

Susan Cabot was part of Corman's repertory when he started a new company called Filmgroup, and she starred in its first film, 1959's *The Wasp Woman*. She played a cranky forty-year-old cosmetics executive who discovers a youth serum made of wasp enzymes. As an energized twenty-two-year-old, she is no easier on her employees. In fact, she turns into a wasp and assaults them. "I was supposed to bite their necks and draw blood," said Cabot. "Roger wanted to see the blood. And so, as I attacked everybody, I had Hershey's chocolate in my mouth, which I proceeded to *blurp*, right on people's necks." Writing in the *Saturday Review*, critic Arthur Knight had some harsh words for the genre. "The real horror is that these pictures, with their bestialities, their sadism, their lust for blood, and their primitive level of conception and execution, should find their greatest acceptance among the young."

Not surprisingly, the most primitive of these films cast women as monsters—and the films were widely booked, as shown by the increasing involvement of the exhibitor in production. This was not the ivory-tower producer trying to raise the masses to his level. This was the bar making its

own booze. One of Louisiana's most prosperous drive-in theater chains was owned by the Woolner brothers. Bernie Woolner came up with an idea that he knew his young patrons would eat up, *Attack of the 50 Foot Woman*, and hired cinematographer Jacques Marquette to produce it. The first thing Marquette did was to hire himself as director of photography so that he could get into the cameramen's union. Then he hired Academy-Award-winning art director Nathan Juran to direct. Juran asked if he could direct under a pseudonym, Nathan Hertz. "He didn't want people to know that he would make that cheap a picture," Marquette explained.

Attack of the 50 Foot Woman was cheap indeed, filmed on side roads and in a private Hollywood home. The special effects were not unconvincing; they were risible, especially the scenes of the wealthy giantess (Allison Hayes) stalking the countryside. Marquette's third-rate matte shots let the background show through her head. Her costume, supposedly made from bed sheets, looks like a beat-up diaper, and her best dialogue is an echoing refrain as she tears off the roof of a café to catch her absurdly unfaithful and abusive husband (William Hudson): "Harry! Harry! *Harry!*" Actress Yvette Vickers described the cheapness of the production: "When the fifty-foot woman started wrecking the café, I ran and hid under a table. All the people were screaming, lumber was falling into the room, and so on. As soon as the scene was over, one of the prop men came up to me and said, 'Don't . . . *move*.' I looked around slowly, and there was a board with a nail through it, right at my ear." Released in May 1958, the film's bookings could barely satisfy the vacationing teenagers who wanted to see a giant rubber hand slide into the café and pull Harry to his doom. *Attack of the 50 Foot Woman*, made for $88,000, grossed $480,000.

The woman scorned was a popular subgenre, as evidenced by the 1958 *Queen of Outer Space*. In this widescreen color cheapie, producer Ben Schwalb and screenwriter Charles Beaumont tried to inflate a ten-page Ben Hecht outline into a Venusian epic. Hecht had written "Queen of the Universe" after a party joke gave him the idea of a planet ruled by women. The Queen of the title was a scarred, man-hating tyrant played by Laurie Mitchell. The actual star of the film was forty-year-old Zsa Zsa Gabor. The Hungarian beauty could not exactly be described as an actress, but she had decorated numerous films with her sloe-eyed indifference. Her real claim to fame was her tempestuous love life. While still married to her third husband, George Sanders, she had carried on a highly visible affair with the Dominican playboy, Porfirio Rubirosa. A much-printed photo showed her wearing an eye patch the morning after Rubirosa punched her in a jealous rage. "The fact that he hit me proves that he loves me," Gabor rational-

ized. "A woman who has never been hit by a man has never been loved." This type of publicity could not be bought, especially by a cut-rate outfit like Allied Artists.

When Director Edward Bernds escorted Gabor to the Western Costume Company, it dawned on her that her wardrobe would be rented, not designed for her. The prestige she was bringing to this dubious project was to be matched with secondhand costumes! She told Bernds that she would not wear them; she had to have a designer. He tried to placate her with a more elegant selection. She threatened to quit unless her demands were met. Bernds turned her over to a company executive and headed for the nearest telephone.

"This is our chance to dump her," he told Schwalb. "If she wants to walk, let her walk."

"No," said Schwalb. "We need a star. Without a star, we haven't got a picture. Look. Stars are that way. Humor her."

Bernds eventually got some second-tier designers to keep Gabor happy, but only momentarily. The population of Venus was played by beauty contest winners, all of whom were decades younger than Miss Hungary of 1936. When their miniskirted forms attracted more attention from the crew than hers, she grew testy. "Ben went to the hospital with ulcers halfway through the picture," recalled Bernds. "I was left to cope with her alone, and she damn near gave *me* ulcers." The combination of a resentful star, a cast of non-actors, dirt-cheap sets, and a preposterous

In the 1958 **QUEEN OF OUTER SPACE**, Venusian scientist Zsa Zsa Gabor and a miniskirted posse capture earthlings Eric Fleming and Patrick Waltz. Gabor brought her Hungarian modulation to lines such as "I hate zat queen." Director Edward Bernds said: "Here on this planet Venus, she was the only one who spoke with a foreign accent."

appeared in 1957, and it played
lots of theaters, providing
unexpected mirth when its rubber legs started to split.

script overwhelmed any hope of creating a genuine genre piece. One exchange sums up the film's attempts at wit.

"You're beautiful," says the Venus girl.

"You're handsome," replies the Earth man.

Said Bernds: "Trying to paste satirical material onto a creaky melodramatic structure just didn't work very well." *Queen of Outer Space* worked well at the box office. Perhaps it was to see the newfangled miniskirts. Perhaps it was to hear the only woman on Venus who spoke with a Hungarian accent. Perhaps it was the country's newfound taste for ineptitude. If so, there were many more inept films. One of the poorest came from Universal's shrinking feature-film calendar.

The Leech Woman (1960) was another look at a woman pushed to monsterhood by the fountain of youth. In this case, June (Coleen Gray), the wealthy, aging, alcoholic wife of yet another uncaring husband (Phillip Terry), goes with him to Africa, where they discover that the fluid from a man's pineal gland will temporarily reverse her aging. She forgets all about making her husband love her again. Suddenly, all she cares about is his pineal gland. She jabs a magic ring into it, rejuvenates herself, and takes off. Back at home, she almost succeeds in ensnaring her handsome lawyer (Grant Williams), but his fiancée (Gloria Talbott) shows up in the foyer with a gun. A scuffle ensues, and June dumps the fiancée in the hall closet.

While the two women were rehearsing the scene, the diminutive Gray said to Talbott, "I'm little, but I *am* strong." Talbott had just done an episode of *Wanted: Dead or Alive* with Steve McQueen. In a fight scene with him, she had flipped him over her back. By comparison, the tiny leech woman hardly looked threatening. "But, by God, this little bitty person wasn't kidding!" Talbott recalled. "She picked me up, threw me in the closet! Incredible. But she was very much a lady. I liked her and she was very good to work with." Gray and Talbott both gave their roles more than the script or direction warranted, but the film's most captivating performance came from seventy-three-year-old Estelle Hemsley, who played the wizened, inscrutable African, Old Malla, with dignity and intelligence. There was little of either in the horror genre as the 1950s ended. Difficult financing and an easy audience had ruined it. A few miles away from the silly antics of *The Leech Woman*, on the MCA Revue lot, stood an old, dark house, where an eminent director was inventing a new type of horror film.

In Universal's 1960 film **THE LEECH WOMAN**, Jerry (Arthur Batanides) has found out that the wealthy June Talbot (Coleen Gray) is not interested in his mind, but in his pineal gland.

In 1954, Barbara Rush said: "My role in **IT CAME FROM OUTER SPACE** required me to register frightened facial expressions so convincingly that I left the set at night with a sore jaw and with eyes that felt as though they had been yanked from their sockets. Furthermore, the frightened reaction is here to stay. Now we'll have to figure out some way to combat the wrinkles that come with the new facial expression!" As the decade wore on, horror and science-fiction players learned to make these faces not only for the movie camera, but also for the portrait camera. Here is a representative sampling. Counterclockwise from top left: Barbara Rush in **IT CAME FROM OUTER SPACE**; Janet Leigh in **PSYCHO**; Alix Talton in **THE DEADLY MANTIS**; Vera Miles in **PSYCHO**; and Brad Jackson in **IT CAME FROM OUTER SPACE**

CHAPTER 12
Last Hurrahs

Alfred Hitchcock

Tippi Hedren and Rod Taylor ward off an attack in Hitchcock's 1963 **THE BIRDS**. The film's electronic sound effects were created by Remi Gassman and Oskar Sala. Hitchcock told them that the "overall sound in this sequence should have a quality of shrill anger, as though the birds in their own particular way were invading the room and almost screaming at the occupants."

"Sex in films should be only for the purpose of explaining a situation or advancing the story. Give audiences too much sex, or in bad taste, and subconsciously they will rebel." Thus spoke Alfred Hitchcock, the world's most famous movie director, assuring his public that it was safe to see his newest film, *Psycho*. Few directors spent the time, energy, and money that Hitchcock did to court his audience, but few directors had as intimate a connection to their work. "The Master of Suspense" managed every aspect of a film's production, from story searches to theatrical presentation, and the films themselves were so carefully crafted that they could bear dissection by scholars and critics. Hitchcock was not making films for critics but for a market, and by 1959 he could see that this market had changed as much as Hollywood had.

Hitchcock had come from England in 1939 at the invitation of David O. Selznick, who wanted the rotund, deliberate director to film the story of the *Titanic*. When the maritime project fell through, Selznick prepared another property, *Rebecca*. While Hitchcock waited, he and his wife Alma acclimatized themselves to Los Angeles. The warm, fragrant region was dotted with orange groves, splashed with yellow jacarandas, and perfumed by Victorian box trees. Its population was a little more than 1.5 million, which meant one verdant square mile for every four people. There were hazy days—indigenous tribes had named it "The Valley of Smokes"—but for most of the year the green Hollywood hills were backed by a cyclorama of deep blue. The air pollution known in Britain as *smog* had not yet appeared in southern California. This was the land of milk and honey. Twenty years later, it had changed.

The population of Los Angeles, booming with babies, the aerospace industry, and the auto industry, had swelled to two and a half million. A swarm of real estate had eaten up the last of the orange groves, leaving nothing but autos and smog. Hitchcock's fellow countryman, actor David Niven, wrote: "From my sun-drenched home on a hillside near the ocean I had looked down with dread upon a yellow-brown, stagnant haze hanging over the distant, restless city, and by the time I reached Western Avenue, the sun above me was diffused to a brassy glare, my chest felt encased in a lead vest, my eyes were prickling, my nose was dribbling, and even the wheezing birds were walking." In this fetid environment, the tasteful entertainments of years past had no more chance than a Victrola playing "To a Water Lily" did against a transistor radio blaring "Poison Ivy." The horror films of American-International proved this, and Hitchcock knew it.

In April 1959 Hitchcock, a few months short of sixty, was enjoying a celebrity beyond even that of the legendary director Cecil B. DeMille. Since 1935 DeMille had amplified his renown by producing and hosting the weekly Lux Radio Theatre. In 1955 Hitchcock had taken this idea to television with a mystery and suspense show, *Alfred Hitchcock Presents*. Introducing each episode with a drawled "Good even-ning" and a morbidly humorous monologue, the roly-poly Hitchcock had become a household word and a brand name. He had his own book series, *Alfred Hitchcock Presents*; his own television company at Revue Studios in North Hollywood; his own film company at Paramount; and he had just finished a $3.3 million MGM film, *North by Northwest*. "Mr. Hitchcock was the biggest thing around, especially on TV," said his script clerk, Marshall Schlom. "He was a hands-off client who got anything he wanted." What he wanted now was a new kind of project, something that would both reflect the culture and have an impact on it.

In his wide-ranging search for material, Hitchcock customarily read the *New York Times*. It was there that he saw the April 19 review of a novel called *Psycho*. Its author, forty-two-year-old Robert Bloch, used sparing prose to tell the story of a motel keeper named Norman Bates. This unprepossessing character is an alcoholic voyeur who appears to be covering up murders of young women committed by his psychopathic mother, but the gruesome climax of the story reveals that there is no mother. If this sounded familiar to Hitchcock, there was a good reason. The plot was inspired by the real-life Wisconsin psycho Ed Gein, who between 1955 and 1957 had murdered and dissected ten women, storing their organs in freezers, hanging dried body parts around his kitchen, and wearing their skins and faces as he indulged in cannibalism and necrophilia. The novel added another angle. "I made Norman Bates a transvestite who dressed up as his mother with a wig and dress whenever he committed these crimes," said Bloch. "Much to my surprise, I discovered that the actual killer dressed up also, but he allegedly wore the breasts and skins of his mother."

The book had already been reviewed by a reader in the Paramount story department. "Too repulsive for films," said the report, "and rather shocking, even to a hardened reader." In a book full of shocking scenes, one stood out, the murder of a young woman, Mary Crane, in a motel shower. Although she is portrayed as an amateur embezzler, she is a sympathetic character. The scene is a vicious one. "Mary started to scream, and then the curtains parted further and a hand appeared, holding a butcher knife. It was the knife that, a moment later, cut off her scream. And her head."

Hitchcock was taken with the novel. "The thing that appealed to me and made me want to do the picture," he said, "was the suddenness of the murder in the shower coming, as it were, out of the blue." Hitchcock's agents, the Music Corporation of America, which also owned Revue Studios, bought the novel for $9,000. After preparing a budget, Hitchcock met with Paramount boss Barney Balaban and vice-president George Weltner. They liked neither the title nor the plot of *Psycho*. Hitchcock dismissed their objections; after all, he had been responsible for a string of hits. When the executives still declined to finance the project, Hitchcock grew steely and determined. He wanted to do this film.

"Well," Balaban told him. "You're not going to get the budget you're used to."

At his next meeting with Paramount, Hitchcock presented an alternative. The film would only cost $800,000. He could prepare it in his Paramount offices and then bring in his Revue television crew, which was used to turning out a half-hour episode in three days. The executives dissembled, saying that all the soundstages were booked. Hitchcock made another offer. If Paramount would agree to distribute the film, he would defer his $250,000 director's salary and shoot the film on the Revue lot; he would, however, retain sixty percent ownership of the film's negative. A deal was made.

Hitchcock assigned one of his TV writers, James Cavanagh, to do a screenplay, but was disappointed when the first draft was a humorless dud. Instead of introducing Hitchcock to Bloch (who was available and interested), MCA recommended Joseph Stefano, an agency client who had written *The Black Orchid* for Sophia Loren. Hitchcock declined; he did not want another intense young writer he did not know. MCA persisted; a meeting finally took place. The jovial Stefano took Hitchcock by surprise, making him laugh and then telling him that he did not like the characters, especially Norman, who is "a middle-aged man, a reprobate, [who] drinks, [is] overweight, wears big thick glasses, peeps through holes." The character needed to be somewhat sympathetic, especially if he has center stage after Mary's murder. "I wish Norman were somebody else," said Stefano.

"How would you feel if Norman were played by Anthony Perkins?" asked Hitchcock.

"Now you're talking," said Stefano, who then turned his attention to Mary's character. He thought she was written as a cipher. "I wish I knew this girl." Now Stefano was warming up, and Hitchcock, in a series of meetings, threw ideas at him.

"What if we got a big-name actress to play this girl?" teased Hitchcock. "Nobody will expect her to die!" Stefano liked the idea, and, in turn, Hitchcock liked Stefano's idea of making her a likable young woman driven to steal by love. Stefano gave life to the characters and imbued the story with two elements that Hitchcock relished: mordant humor and aberrant sex. Stefano was under the impression that *Psycho* would be made on the scale of *Vertigo*. Hitchcock corrected him. "I cannot make this picture in color," said the director. "It will be too gory." Although only a third of Hollywood films were then being shot in color, Stefano was crestfallen. He had hoped for something bigger.

When Alfred Hitchcock was making **PSYCHO** in 1960, he did not allow unit still man Bud Fraker to shoot any key scenes for fear that still photos would give away the film's shocking surprises. Publicity director Herb Steinberg had no option but to tell gallery photographer Ray Jones to shoot old-fashioned "poster art" with quaintly symbolic tableaux. Here are Vera Miles and Janet Leigh, who have no scenes together, with John Gavin, doing their best to be scared by a rocking chair.

"When I asked him why he had bought the book," said Stefano, "he said he noticed that American-International was making movie after movie for under a million dollars, yet they all made ten or thirteen million. And without too much conversation, we decided that this was going to be a picture of Gothic horror, something he really had not done before."

Most of this "Gothic" story took place neither in Europe nor Wisconsin, but in central California, where Hitchcock decided that the "old dark house" overlooking the Bates Motel would be a Victorian. "They're either called 'California Gothic,'" he said, "or, when they're particularly awful, they're called 'California gingerbread.'" In spite of this visual nod to a venerable genre, Hitchcock was wary of association with it. "I did not set out to reconstruct an old-fashioned Universal horror-picture atmosphere," he said. The house was built off a Western street on the Revue lot, but many of the other *Psycho* sets were built on Universal's Stage 28, where Lon Chaney had portrayed the Phantom of the Opera and Bela Lugosi had portrayed Dracula.

At one point, Stefano told Hitchcock, "I would like to see the toilet in the bathroom. In every movie I've ever seen of a bathroom, there's no toilet. And I would like to see that toilet. I think the audience will be unsettled by the sight of it. Do you think they'll let us do that?" Hitchcock said that the way to handle the staff of the Production Code Administration was to put elements in the script that would grab their attention, and, when they raised their objections, say, "Tsk-tsk. All right, I'll take *that* out, but you've got to give me *this*." The only problem with *Psycho* was that Hitchcock wanted to keep too many controversial things: the opening scene with Mary and her boyfriend lying partially undressed on a bed in a Phoenix hotel room; the bloody shower sequence; transvestism; and a detective stabbed in the face. To distract the censors in the Shurlock office from these items, Hitchcock had Stefano play up the suggestion of incest between Norman and his mother. Surprisingly, it worked. After he removed those elements, the script came back rubber-stamped: "Approved, subject to seeing the product."

Hitchcock had gotten his start in the British film industry as a silent-film title artist and art director. All these years later he still drew a picture of each shot, joking that he did not need to improvise on the soundstage because he had already done so on paper. "You had an entire, cohesive picture laid out before you on storyboards," said costume designer Rita Riggs. "You knew every angle in the picture." To cast the role of Marion (the name was changed because a real Mary Crane lived in Phoenix), Hitchcock looked at film of Hope Lange, Martha Hyer, and Lana Turner, then sent the novel to Janet Leigh, who had worked with Orson Welles in *Touch of Evil*. Leigh, thrilled to be working with another master, accepted without seeing the finished script. Hitchcock admitted, "It's rather unusual to kill the star in the first third of the film."

Leigh worked three weeks, one of which she spent on a cramped shower set, as Hitchcock shot seventy-eight carefully composed angles of the stabbing montage. "I used my TV unit because of speed," recalled Hitchcock. "The entire picture took thirty-six days to make, including retakes. I only slowed up when I came to something cinematic, like the shower scene. You could never have shot

that under TV conditions—seven days' work for forty-five seconds' screen time!" On the average, according to Schlom, "We did between fourteen and eighteen setups a day, which, for a major motion-picture director, is a lot."

The first people to see the film were the staff of the Shurlock office. Luigi Luraschi, who was the liaison between Paramount and the censors, thought that he saw a breast in the shower montage. The other staff members were not sure. Hitchcock said he would cut the shot and send them the reel. The next day, he packed up the same reel—untouched—and sent it to their office on La Cienega Boulevard. They said it was better, but that other scenes needed cuts.

"I will take out the nudity if you will allow me to keep the two people in bed in the opening," said Hitchcock, losing patience.

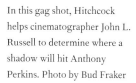

In this gag shot, Hitchcock helps cinematographer John L. Russell to determine where a shadow will hit Anthony Perkins. Photo by Bud Fraker

Another publicity still that gives an incorrect impression of **PSYCHO:** in their one scene together, Janet Leigh wears a white bra, John Gavin is shirtless, and there are no shutters. Universal was one of the last studios to have a functioning portrait gallery, complete with the giant wooden 8x10 camera that Ray Jones used for this artful portrait. In the film, Leigh played a conflicted middle-class woman who succumbs to the temptation of $40,000 in cash. Hitchcock decided against casting Lana Turner in this role. "He wanted someone who could actually look like she came from Phoenix," Leigh later said. "I mean, Lana Turner might not be able to look like she came from there."

Anthony Perkins in a Ray Jones portrait that hints at the complex nature of his performance as Norman Bates. "It was my idea that I should eat candy throughout the film," said Perkins. "I thought it would be more interesting if the killer were a compulsive candy eater."

"No," said the censors.

"All right. If you leave the shower sequence as is, I will reshoot the opening, but I want you on the set."

The censors agreed and a date was scheduled for retakes. When the day arrived, the censors did not. Shortly thereafter, they passed the film. Meanwhile, Hitchcock met with Bernard Herrmann to decide on a musical score. "Hitch was nervously pacing back and forth, saying it was awful and that he was going to cut it down for his television show," Herrmann recalled. "He was afraid it was going to be a flop." The composer tried to reassure him that he was not going to lose his investment, then remembered his own early days as a violinist.

"Wait a minute," Herrmann said. "I have some ideas. How about a score completely for strings?"

Films in Review critic Page Cook described the result: "The prologue opens with two startling stabs from the double bass, a perfect intimation of the jolting nature of the

film to come." When Hitchcock screened the film for the cast and crew, he did not expect it to jolt industry veterans. Schlom recalled: "When Mother's knife came in and Bernie Herrmann's music started shrieking, everybody came off their seats a good six inches!" Janet Leigh screamed. Afterward she told Hitchcock, "When that knife went into me on the screen, I could feel it!" Realizing that he had something special, Hitchcock persuaded Paramount to take an unprecedented step. Exhibitors had to sign contracts agreeing to admit no one to the theater after *Psycho* had begun. Equally newsworthy was Hitchcock's requirement that no critic could see the film before it opened; they had to review it on its opening day, June 16, 1960. Predictably, the reviews were peevish. Bosley Crowther called the film "a blot on an honorable career." *Time* magazine sniffed: "Director Hitchcock bears down too heavily in this one, and the delicate illusion of reality necessary for a creak-and-shriek movie becomes, instead, a spectacle of stomach-churning horror." Their grumbling was overwhelmed by another noise. *Psycho* was opening with a bang.

Schlom was at Revue when the news broke. "We got these stories from theater owners about people going berserk in the audience, running up and down the aisles," he said. "It was mayhem. They had to call the cops." There were reports of traffic jams, of near-riots outside theaters that would not admit patrons to in-progress screenings, and of women fainting. Stefano attended the Hollywood opening. "I saw people grabbing each other," he said, "howling, screaming, reacting like six-year-olds at a Saturday matinee." An unexpected by-product of the hysteria was laughter. A car's hesitant sinking in a swamp got tremendous laughs, drowning out dialogue in the next scene. "I've always been able to predict the audience's reaction," Hitchcock confided to Perkins. "Here, I haven't been able to." Within a year, *Psycho* had grossed $15.5 million worldwide. MCA head Lew Wasserman sent Hitchcock a telegram asking: "What will you do for an encore?" The ever-practical Hitchcock eventually answered, "I have to hurry up and do another picture because of taxes!"

The master did not have to look far for his next subject. While on vacation in Santa Cruz, California, Hitchcock read a bizarre headline: "Sea Bird Invasion Hits Coastal Homes." According to the article in the *Santa Cruz Sentinel*, gulls had violently attacked homes, cars, and pedestrians. This rang a bell. Daphne Du Maurier's 1952 short story *The Birds* had been reprinted in one of his own *Alfred Hitchcock Presents* books. Du Maurier (who had provided stories for Hitchcock's 1939 *Jamaica Inn* and 1940 *Rebecca*) here wove a fantasy of Cornwall farmers attacked by harmless-looking birds. This intrigued Hitchcock. "If the story had involved vultures or birds of prey," he said, "I might not have wanted it. The basic appeal to me is that it had to do with ordinary, everyday birds." In September 1961, he hired writer Evan Hunter, who had already written for his TV series. Hunter was the prolific author (as Ed McBain) of the *87th Precinct* novels.

Hunter found Hitchcock warm and affable, a raconteur who enjoyed talking about wine as much as he did about mayhem. Hitchcock suggested moving *The Birds* from England to northern California so that the special effects could utilize clear blue skies. Other than that, he gave Hunter a free hand. There was, however, the issue of genre. "We did not want this to become a science-fiction film," Hunter recalled. "We did not want this scene where the guys are all peering into a microscope examining a bird feather and they decide the movement of the polar cap or an underground explosion or a low-flying saucer has caused a change in metabolism." Hitchcock later explained: "I was interested in making the film because it was a horror film—horror coming from a different quarter. It wasn't science fiction at all." They decided that the best way to avoid association with the prevailing science-fiction formula was not to explain the bird attacks. "We would offer possible reasons," Hunter said, "but we would never tell the audience *why*." Hunter was, of course, curious to know for what stars he should tailor the script. "There are no stars in this film," answered Hitchcock. "The birds are the stars. I'm the star."

While Hunter spent ten weeks writing a script, Hitchcock sought to answer Wasserman's question about an encore to *Psycho*. He saw a girl in a Sego weight-loss commercial. He had MCA track her down and bring her to Universal City. She was a professional model named Tippi Hedren. After a three-day series of screen tests that cost $25,000, Hitchcock awarded Hedren the lead role in *The Birds*, then began working with designer Edith Head to make her a star. "Hitchcock loved to challenge himself," said camera operator Leonard South. "Creating a new star was the one thing he hadn't done." Riggs recalled: "The sort of education one got from Mr. Hitchcock and Miss Head in publicity and the presentation of a new personality, one could not get anywhere else in the world." Was this kind of buildup necessary to tell the story of a bird attack? "Hitchcock was the real star of *Psycho* and he knew it," said South. "It was as if he now believed that anything he touched—a novice performer, a not-good-enough project—he could turn into gold. It may have been understandable after the success of *Psycho*, but his judgment was badly clouded."

Hunter finished his script in November. As submitted to the Shurlock office, *The Birds* devoted more than a third of its plot to the budding romance between a spoiled playgirl, Melanie Daniels (Hedren), and a San Francisco criminal lawyer, Mitch Brenner (Rod Taylor). Melanie follows Mitch to his home in the California seaside town of Bodega Bay, where she must cope with his possessive mother, Lydia (Jessica Tandy), and his ex-girlfriend, Annie (Suzanne Pleshette). Before this conflict can play itself out, a series of inexplicable bird attacks escalates into a blitz that kills numerous townspeople, including Annie. Melanie, Mitch, his mother, and his sister hide in his boarded-up house while birds lay siege to it. When Melanie unwittingly walks into an attic full of birds, Mitch rescues her. The film ends with the four humans creeping out of the house while thousands of birds sit nearby, quietly and ominously watching.

Shurlock was concerned about "the gruesome details of the several attacks by the birds on the human beings. As we envision this action, we feel it could be presented in such a shocking, brutal, and bloody way as to be unacceptable motion-picture fare." Hitchcock was too preoccupied with technical concerns to pay attention to a weakened censorship office. "*The Birds* posed so many problems that I didn't even bother bringing them up before we started making the picture," said Hitchcock. "I did not ask, 'Can you do this? Can you do that?' The scenes were written and we had to discover how to do it afterwards." The first job was to capture more than 3,000 birds—seagulls, crows, ravens, sparrows—which animal trainer Ray Berwick then taught to attack people. There was the obligatory storyboard, which soon tallied more than 400 special-effect shots. After tests and consultations, Hitchcock decided to forego the conventional blue-screen process for a yellow muslin screen lit by sodium-vapor lights. This process produced superimpositions of superior sharpness. Walt Disney Studios had the only sodium-vapor lamps and "beam splitter" prism in Hollywood, so Hitchcock had to rent an old three-strip Technicolor camera and pay Disney cofounder Ub Iwerks to supervise all of the film's special effects. The mattes of Bodega Bay were the work of Albert Whitlock, who spent a year completing twelve extraordinary paintings.

In February 1962 Hitchcock took his cast and crew to Bodega Bay for two months of location shooting, which he

"I don't care about the subject matter," Hitchcock later said of **PSYCHO**. "I don't care about the acting. But I do care about the pieces of film and the photography and the soundtrack and all of the technical ingredients that made the audience scream." Portrait of Anthony Perkins by Bud Fraker

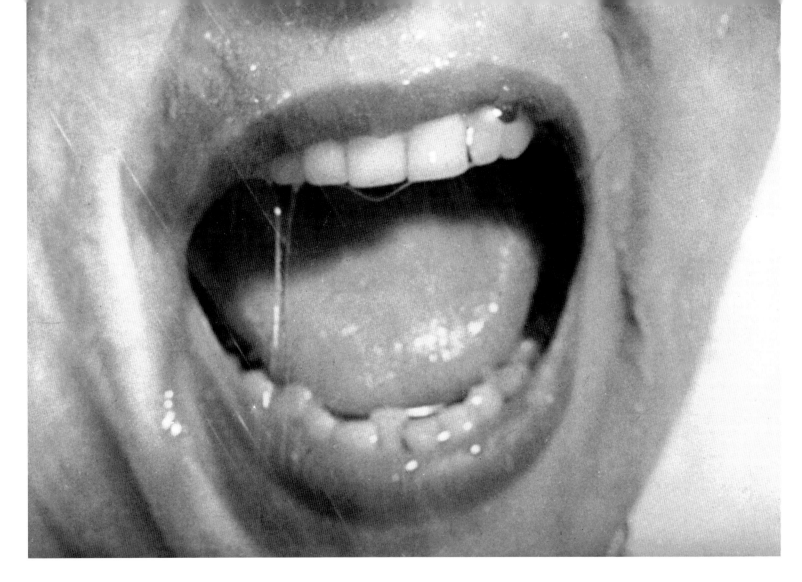

did not enjoy. He preferred the controlled conditions of the sound stage. After he returned, he was still strangely unhappy. "I began to study the scenario as we went along, and I saw that there were weaknesses in it," said Hitchcock. "I've always been afraid of improvising on the set because, although one might get a new idea, there isn't sufficient time in the studio to examine the value of such an idea." One scene that bothered him had Lydia go to her neighbor's house, knock on the door, go in, walk down the hallway, and then find him lying dead in his bedroom, his eyes gouged out by birds. "This doesn't make sense," Hitchcock said to himself. "She calls the farmer and he doesn't answer. Well, a woman in that position wouldn't push it any farther. She'd walk out of the house." What Hitchcock later described as an "emotional siege" pushed him to do what he had never done. He improvised, calling on the property man to break five teacups so that Lydia would have something to make her suspicious. On the set, meanwhile, suspicions were being aroused by Hitchcock's obsessive attention to Hedren. Her polite but firm resistance was apparently the cause of his inquietude.

Becoming Hitchcock's newest star had been at first exhilarating for Hedren, but six months of unwanted attentions from a mercurial director were taking a toll. As Hedren discovered, "There are times when you're making a film when it can become dangerous." Early in the film, Mitch refers to Melanie as a "bird in a gilded cage." She eventually finds herself trapped in a telephone booth, with birds diving at her. "It's a reversal of the age-old conflict between men and birds," Hitchcock explained. "Here the human beings are in cages and the birds are on the outside." In an ironic reflection of her real-life plight, Hedren had to huddle in a booth on a Universal sound stage while model birds swung down on wires to hit the windows of the booth. Hedren was told that the glass was shatterproof; it was not. A makeup man spent the better part of an hour removing tiny shards of glass from her face. Much worse was the climactic attic scene. Hedren had been told repeatedly that she would do the scene with mechanical birds. On the Monday morning on which the scene was to be shot, the assistant director came into her dressing room. Looking at the floor, he nervously mumbled that they were not going to use the mechanical birds; they did not work.

"Uh, well, what *are* we going to use?" she asked.

"There's a bunch of ravens and crows," he answered, and quickly departed.

"I just blanched white," she recalled. "I had seen the bird trainers with leather gauntlets up to their shoulders [and] the scratches *they* had from the birds."

When she saw that a cage had been built around the set to contain live birds, she deduced that Hitchcock had never intended to use mechanical birds. Then she saw the live birds. "There were three great big cartons of ravens and seagulls." Hedren took her place on the set and the ordeal began. "Prop men with leather gauntlets hurled birds at me for five days. It was really grisly. I literally had to fight them off. They didn't attack—birds don't do that—it was just them coming *at* me." On Wednesday, Cary Grant

Hitchcock shot seventy-eight angles for **PSYCHO**'s famous shower scene. "It wasn't a message that stirred the audiences, nor was it a great performance or their enjoyment of the novel," he said. "They were aroused by pure film." The scene also affected Janet Leigh. "I just couldn't get back in a shower after that," she said many years later.

visited the set, and after watching a few minutes of torment, walked up to Hedren, and said, "I think you're the bravest lady I've ever met."

As Tandy remembered it: "She was alone in that caged room, acting, with the birds coming at her, and with costume changes, and makeup applications, and all the stage blood, she couldn't even go to the commissary for lunch. She lived with that hour after hour." Hitchcock kept telling Hedren, "Just one more hour, just one more shot." She began to doubt the director's motives. "I had always heard that his idea was to take a woman—usually a blonde—and break her apart, to see her shyness and her reserve broken down, but I thought this was only in the plots of his films." On Friday, she was on the floor for the end of the scene, with birds tied to her costume. "They always talk about the danger to your eyes when birds are involved," said Berwick. "The seagulls would deliberately go for your eyes. I got bitten in the eye region at least three times." Hedren was holding up under the last attack until a bird that was tied to her arm managed to pull loose from his restraints and lunge for her eye.

"That's *enough!*" Hedren said, pulling all the birds off her. Filming was shut down. As she tried to collect herself, she sank into a chair in the middle of the sound stage and sobbed. "I was so exhausted," she said. "And everybody left. They just left me there. I don't remember the weekend. And I don't remember driving to the studio the following Monday. I got into my dressing room and lay down on the couch. My makeup man couldn't wake me." The studio

doctor was called, and he sent Hedren to the hospital. When Hitchcock came to visit her, the attending physician advised him that Hedren needed a week's rest.

"We have nothing else to shoot," protested Hitchcock. "She has to come back."

"Are you trying to kill her?" asked the physician. Hedren stayed in the hospital, and Hitchcock used a double to finish the scene. Hedren did return to do the scene in which the humans sneak out of the house. The last shot of the film is a panorama from the porch, showing their car slowly moving through a thicket of feathered sentries. "The final scene of the birds was done with about sixteen exposures on one piece of film," said Hitchcock. "It's by far the most difficult single shot I've ever done, but nobody will ever know."

An electronic soundtrack and an ad campaign with the slogan "*The Birds* Is Coming" helped to drum up business in March 1963, but the film was not nearly as successful as *Psycho*; it only made $11 million. Critics did not care for the romantic plot or for Hedren, and that unpredictable factor, the audience, wanted to know why the birds suddenly decided to attack people. Not until years later did Hitchcock reveal their motivation. "It's rabies," he said. "I based the film on information I got about bats in Carlsbad Caverns, New Mexico." The Master of Suspense returned to his métier and left horror to his many imitators.

"While I was shooting in Bodega Bay, there was an item in a San Francisco paper about crows attacking lambs," Hitchcock said. "I met a farmer who told me how the crows had swooped down to kill his young lambs." His research contributed to this harrowing scene from **THE BIRDS**.

William Castle, Master of Gore and Gimmicks

The most publicized imitation of *Psycho* was the 1961 Columbia release *Homicidal*. Its director, William Castle, was one of those low-end successes who had made Alfred Hitchcock envious. Director Roman Polanski described Castle as "a red-faced giant of a man with a thatch of close-cropped white hair and a cigar clamped permanently between his teeth." Screenwriter Robb White said: "Bill was a cut-and-print director. He'd say to the actors, 'Do such-and-such a thing,' and he'd never take another shot because it was too expensive." Oddly enough, Castle and Hitchcock had found a horror matrix in the same film. On a rainy night in the spring of 1956, Castle and his wife, Ellen, stood in line at the Beverly Canon Theatre in Beverly Hills to see *Les Diaboliques* (a.k.a. *Diabolique*), a French thriller directed by Henri-Georges Clouzot. Castle was surprised to see so many teenagers fidgeting under umbrellas. He asked the two in front of him why they wanted to see a foreign film with subtitles.

"My friends told me it really scares the shit out of you," replied the boy.

"That's what I heard too," his girlfriend chimed in.

Once inside, Castle found that anticipation did not exceed the fact. Clouzot had created a troubling atmosphere, sharply drawn characters, and revolting images. "A dead body coming out of a tub; glassy eyes, milky white, being taken from their sockets" surprised Castle. *Diabolique* also had a twist ending. Was the audience affected? "There was a roar of shock that rocked the theater," he recalled. "The collective emotional release of all those screaming kids was exhilarating, incredible!" In a departure from convention, the film's end titles read: "Don't be diabolical yourself. Don't spoil the ending for your friends by telling them what you've just seen!" Everything about this film felt new except, of course, the good, old-fashioned shrieks. "Leaving the theater," said Castle, "I felt a strange sensation, a reawakening of some sort." He had been directing B pictures for twelve years, making a comfortable living, but there was something missing, something he had wanted to do since childhood.

"When I was thirteen years old, in 1927," he later wrote, "I bought a balcony seat with $1.10 I had taken from my sister's purse, eager to see the play, *Dracula*, starring Bela Lugosi. Enchanted, I watched Count Dracula suck his victims' blood." As long as his sister's purse yielded $1.10, young Castle was able to return. Each night he leaned over the balcony, in thrall to a great performance. After two weeks, he was not only watching Lugosi but also analyzing audience reactions to lines and business he now knew by heart. "I knew then what I wanted to do with my life," he said. "I wanted to scare the pants off audiences."

Thirty years later, Castle decided to follow his dream by imitating Clouzot. Castle's debt to the French director was not so much in style as it was in presentation. That end title grabbed him, recalling the curtain speeches delivered by Edward Van Sloan in *Dracula* and *Frankenstein*. The device of communicating with—and engaging—an audience with a message near the beginning or end of a reel (where it could easily be replaced or removed) had been virtually untried. It may have been a gimmick, but this was show business.

Castle had gotten his start from Lugosi himself, when the actor had hired him at fifteen to be Broadway's youngest assistant stage manager. For the next fourteen years, Castle studied the theater from the footlights up. After that, associations with Orson Welles and Harry Cohn taught him about the great American movie audience. Now he wanted to capture that audience. All he needed was the right story and the right gimmick.

A wide-ranging search yielded a book written by twelve members of the San Francisco chapter of the Mystery Writers of America. *The Marble Forest* was their collaborative story of a girl buried alive in a cemetery. Her father has to find out who did it so he can save her from suffocating. Castle had to find all twelve authors and convince them to sign a contract. "What a job!" recalled Castle. "It took two lawyers seven months to find all of them." Next he had to raise $86,000. He mortgaged his house and formed a partnership with his screenwriter, Robb White. "Bill said he was gonna put up fifty percent and I was gonna put up fifty percent, but somehow he couldn't quite make it," White recalled. "So I put up the money." Next Castle had to find a better title. *The Marble Forest* became *Ghastly*, then *Gruesome*. Nothing sounded right. "What's our picture about, Robb? It's a dance of death. Let's call the picture *Macabre*."

"Who the hell can pronounce that?" White asked.

"Who the hell cares? It sounds good," answered Castle, who then produced and directed his film with the same illogical but workmanlike approach. It took him nine days. On the set, it looked to him like "a masterpiece—another *Diabolique*—only much better." In the screening room, he was less certain. "One ingredient's missing," he admitted. "But I can't put my finger on it." Castle's friend, producer Howard W. Koch, could. He took White outside and told him: "That is the worst movie I have ever seen in my whole life. I just advise you to forget the $86,000 it cost you, and take up another line of work." In Castle's opinion, the missing ingredient was a gimmick. It came to him during a bout with insomnia. "Wake up, Ellen! I've got it! An insurance policy!" His wife reminded him that they already had one and then tried to get back to sleep. "Not for *us*," he yelled. "For *everybody*! I'm going to insure the entire world against death by fright during the showing of *Macabre*."

Lloyd's of London was willing to play along with Castle, even though their actuarial tables showed no statistics for death from fright during a movie. The agents based the policy on a projected five deaths and charged Castle $1,000 for each; he arranged to pay the premium in installments. Seeking a distributor, he was turned down by Columbia and underbid by Warner Bros. but given a chance by Allied Artists. On February 27, 1958, a full-page advertisement ran in *Daily Variety*. In a box was the legend: "$1,000 in case of DEATH BY FRIGHT* during the showing of *Macabre*. *Not valid for people with known heart conditions or for suicide."

The film's West Coast premiere took place in San Francisco on April 30. In a week, the *San Francisco Chronicle* was running an ad that said: "CROWDS! CROWDS!

In William Castle's 1958
HOUSE ON HAUNTED HILL,
Vincent Price scares his
scheming wife with this contraption. It was not scary
enough for audiences, so
William Castle turned it into
a live theater gimmick.

CROWDS! 39,473 San Franciscans have crowded the RKO Golden Gate to be shocked . . . Thousands have screamed . . . Many have fainted, but none have collected the $1,000 because of death by fright! So *Macabre* stays for a second horrific week!" That made sense since the film had grossed $24,000 in its first week there. Charles Stinson of the *Los Angeles Times* took a dim view of the hysteria. "Well, you can throw away those Lloyd's of London policies. They don't cover death from boredom." *Macabre* ultimately made $4 million.

Having paid off his debts, Castle's next hurdle was getting, if not a star, at least a name. True, he had once directed Raymond Burr as Antony and Rhonda Fleming as Cleopatra in *Serpent of the Nile*, but they had been under contract to Columbia. Driving through a rainstorm, he pondered the small pool of talent available to him. He stepped into a Hollywood coffee shop, where he chanced to sit down next to Vincent Price. The actor did not remember him from a long-ago backstage introduction, but felt like chatting. "I'm depressed," Price said offhandedly. As Castle quietly drank his coffee, Price volunteered, "I just lost out on an important picture this morning. A part I wanted to play was given to another actor."

"Mr. Price, fate has brought us together this rainy night," said Castle with his patented sincerity. Price knew he was being pitched but listened politely. Castle began to relate the plot of a film he was starting in a few weeks. "A millionaire invites six people to spend the night in a haunted house. The millionaire—the part I want you to play—has plotted to kill his wife. She plots to kill you. It's a battle of wits."

"Who wins?"

"You do, of course." Castle explained that the millionaire would use a phony skeleton to make his wife think that she had succeeded in throwing him into a vat of boiling acid. Then the skeleton would attack her, causing her to lose her balance and fall into the vat. Price could not picture where he was all this time. "You're working your phony skeleton, like a puppeteer!"

"I think I'll have another piece of pie," said Price. Before he could finish the pie, Castle had cut a deal.

In November 1958, the Golden Gate Theatre was the scene of a second Castle triumph. *House on Haunted Hill*'s gimmick was called "Emergo." During the scene in which Price was working his skeleton, a tall black box next to the screen creaked open. From this box emerged a glow-in-the-dark skeleton, which then traveled on a wire above the heads of the audience. To experience this ephemeral thrill, thousands of children waited in line for hours. The suspense was too much for some of them. "They stampeded on opening night," said Price. "They knocked out the first eight rows of seats." An incredulous Castle ran to a phone booth to call Allied Artists president Steve Broidy. "Steve, we're completely sold out!" Castle shouted over the din in the lobby. "We've done the biggest gross in the theater's history!" The film made $4 million, and, in concert with *The Fly*, made Price America's new horror star. "I was suddenly really in demand," recalled Price, "but to play nasty chaps in movies calculated to frighten filmgoers out of their seats. I took to my new career with relish."

Price took advantage of his new status with Twentieth's *Return of the Fly*, then returned to Columbia in 1959 for

another round of gore and gimmicks with Castle. *The Tingler* featured a lobsterlike organism that has grown on the spine of a deaf-mute woman (Judith Evelyn) who is unable to release fear by screaming. When her husband frightens her to death, Price surgically removes the Tingler, which inevitably escapes. The rubbery creature crawls into a silent-movie theater that is reviving the 1921 Henry King film, *Tol'able David*. Castle presents this film within a film in the same derisive manner as did the television show *Fractured Flickers*. Then he cuts loose with his newest gimmick. As the Tingler crawls down the aisle and under the seats, Price turns out the lights and announces to both the onscreen audience and the real audience: "The Tingler is loose in the theater! Scream for your lives!" At this point, theater managers would activate "Percepto," a network of tiny war-surplus motors wired under seats. When it worked perfectly, it gave selected audience members a vibrating sensation and gave Castle the satisfaction he had been craving for years. It did not always work perfectly. "We opened in a theater in Boston," said Price, "and it didn't work at all." Another projectionist in that city heard of this and thought it wise to test the device before the opening. A matinee audience full of Catholic women was intently watching Audrey Hepburn pray in *The Nun's Story*. It was not the power of prayer that suddenly gave them a buzz.

In the next few years, Castle threw more films (and gimmicks) at audiences. The 1960 film *13 Ghosts* was a tepid thriller that required viewers to don glasses. "Illusion-O" made unconvincing spirits wiggle on the screen. The 1961 *Mr. Sardonicus* had a "Punishment Poll" that gave viewers the choice of two endings. In one, the bad man would die an agonizing death; in the other, he would go free. According to Castle, audiences "invariably" voted for death. Not that it mattered; there was no alternate ending. "Bill was absolutely the coldest, most ruthless con man I've ever known," said White. "All he knew was promotion. He could sell anything."

The aforementioned *Homicidal* had a gimmick too. At the film's climax, a clock was superimposed on a freeze-frame of the old, dark house in the film, and viewers were given forty-five seconds to run up the aisle for a refund. They could not have found the prominently placed "Coward" signs very encouraging. However, *Homicidal* was one Castle film that did not need an exhibition gimmick. It was possessed of an intrinsic weirdness. Conceived by Castle and White as an imitation of *Psycho*, it bested Hitchcock's film, not with cinematic skill or a clever plot, but with a perversity that no major Hollywood film had ever attempted. There had never been anything like it because no working actor would have wanted to do what its script required.

Homicidal begins with an angular blonde beauty shoving a knife into a justice of the peace at a bogus midnight wedding. She escapes. We learn that she is Emily (Jean Arless), the Danish caregiver of (yet another) disabled character, the crippled, mute Helga (Eugenie Leontovich). The film builds suspense by showing the strong-willed, short-tempered Emily mistreating Helga and bullying everyone else around her. She marries the epicene young man of the house, Warren, just as he is about to inherit $10 million. Warren's suspicious half-sister Miriam (Patricia Breslin) bravely goes into the darkened house to help Warren but finds Helga beheaded in her wheelchair. Before Miriam can

run for help, the knife-wielding Emily confronts her. To Miriam's horror, Emily pulls off a blonde wig, puts in a dental appliance, and is instantly transformed into Warren—she has been masquerading as "Warren" since childhood. Her father's will stipulated that the fortune go to a male heir, so, in collusion with a few greedy relatives, she pretended to be one.

At this point in 1961, it was hard to tell who was more shocked—Miriam or the audience. They had been watching Warren for more than an hour. He looked like a man, walked like a man, sounded like a man . . . what was he? At the end of the film, Castle got off the hook by using a split screen to show both Warren and Emily bowing to the audience. Of course, the device still begged the question that bothered even White: "Was that a girl or a guy?" Castle only said, "I've always wanted to do the Hitchcock type of picture." *Time* magazine said that *Homicidal* surpassed *Psycho* "in structure, suspense, and sheer nervous drive." Castle did it with the help of a relatively unknown actress, Joan Marshall. When she had first come to his office, he was looking for a man to play both parts.

"Mr. Castle," said Marshall, "I know I can play both parts and do a wonderful job. Please give me a chance."

Castle sent her to the Columbia makeup department. When she returned two hours later, his secretary did not recognize the "young man." Castle was sold. He submitted Marshall to a secret makeover, changed her name to the neutral-sounding Jean Arless, and, as a precaution, did not tell the film company what he was up to. "Coming on the set dressed in men's clothing and speaking in a deep voice," said Castle, "she fooled everyone, even the crew." What Castle did not anticipate was the unsettling effect that Marshall's portrayal of Warren would have on young viewers. In the same way that the face of a werewolf would return for days after a horror movie, Warren's androgynous features confused, disturbed, and haunted impressionable adolescents. Some things could not be explained away.

Castle continued to rely on gimmicks until he was stung by the critical assertion that he could not make a thriller without them. "Never having had the luxury of a big star for my films," Castle wrote, "I had been forced to build my little empire on ingenious showmanship. Hollywood was a snobbish town, and important stars refused to associate themselves with my modest-budget exploitation pictures." After *Psycho*, the stigma of appearing in a horror film was fading. If Janet Leigh could do it, why not another star looking for a challenging role? While Castle watched and waited, a star who had once worked with Lon Chaney took the plunge.

Contrary to the evidence of this photograph, Glenn Corbett is not stabbed by Jean Arless in William Castle's 1961 **HOMICIDAL**, although two other cast members are. Arless usually acted under the name of Joan Marshall, but the unusual requirements of this role necessitated a new name.

If William Castle thought it up, it got into the papers. Outdoing Alfred Hitchcock's cameos, Castle introduced most of his films in facetious prologues.

An accidental meeting with William Castle led to **HOUSE ON HAUNTED HILL**, the 1958 film that made Vincent Price a horror star. In real life, Price was a well-liked art collector, gourmand, author, and host. "At one of Vincent Price's parties in 1964," recalled USC screenwriting professor Ken Evans, "I walked in and there were Norma Shearer *and* Greta Garbo!"

Horror Queens

After the unexpected international success of Alfred Hitchcock's *Psycho*, Janet Leigh's star was shining. She was offered a few horror roles but instead she chose a political thriller, *The Manchurian Candidate*, and a musical comedy, *Bye Bye Birdie*, where her vivacity and intelligence continued to win fans. Leigh's career had begun with a curious connection to the horror film. In 1946, when she was eighteen and living a quiet life in central California, her portrait caught the attention of the recently retired Norma Shearer, who had worked with Lon Chaney and whose former husband, the late Irving Thalberg, had in great measure been responsible for the American horror film.

"What a pretty face," said Shearer, looking at the framed portrait of Leigh on the registration desk of a California ski lodge. "She should be in pictures."

The hotel clerk, who happened to be Leigh's father, proudly gave Shearer the photograph. The powerful star took it back to Hollywood and showed it to an unimpressed Lew Wasserman, who never imagined that its winsome sub-

In the 1959 **SUDDENLY, LAST SUMMER**, Katharine Hepburn plays one of several monsters who spring full-grown from the forehead of playwright Tennessee Williams. Her character, Mrs. Venable, is a wealthy Southern matriarch whose Gothic world (designed by Oliver Messel) revolves around her spectacularly charismatic (and unmarried) son, Sebastian. This was the first film to turn an aging star into a horror queen.

ject would figure in his corporate fortunes. Leigh, likewise, never dreamed that Shearer's elegant contemporaries would stray into the horror genre. A few aging stars—Myrna Loy, Paulette Goddard, Merle Oberon—had horror films in their résumés, but these exquisite products of the Hollywood star system knew how hard it was to look beautiful while screaming. "Everything in those days was aimed at glamour," said actor Robert Taylor, who had costarred with most of these legendary beauties. "I tell you, when women like Joan Crawford and Norma Shearer went out, you knew you were looking at stars."

In 1959, inside the metal cans that held Shearer's personal print of *Marie Antoinette*, time stood still. There she was a luminous thirty-seven, photographed to look twenty by cameraman William Daniels. "I don't care what lighting scheme you use," Thalberg once told a cameraman. "My stars have to look beautiful." Outside the frozen celluloid, in the dull glare of a smoggy Beverly Hills noon, Shearer was fifty-nine years old. She had not made a film in eighteen years. The reason? She knew exactly what lighting, filters, and angles could do to create the illusion of youth. She also knew that advancing age would one day render those tools useless. That day had come in 1941, when she had seen ineradicable signs of age spoiling her closeups. She was only forty-one then, but she knew that motion-picture film could not be retouched. "A great star should always leave them laughing—or crying for more," said Shearer as she quit the business. Never mind that she was at the height of her powers and on the verge of an even more distinguished career as a character actress. She had collaborated with M-G-M on an image, and the only way to maintain that image was to preserve it in nitrate. She would not sully it by playing grandmothers. Her contemporaries, except for the very rich Oberon, Goddard, and Garbo, could not afford the luxury of retirement.

In that same year, Myrna Loy was fifty-four and still working. Bette Davis was fifty-one and enduring what she would later call her "ten black years," the slow period that followed her blaze of glory in *All About Eve*. She was subsisting on character parts, TV appearances, and occasional stage work. Katharine Hepburn was fifty-two and had not made a film in two years. Joan Crawford was fifty-five and a recent widow. Her husband, Pepsi-Cola executive Alfred Steele, had just died, leaving her hundreds of thousands of dollars in debt. She was forced to sell her Brentwood home and work for Pepsi while she considered a variety of odd roles. A British producer told her that she would be a wow in 3-D. "I'd like to come out of the screen," Crawford replied, "but on the strength of my own personality." She was reduced to taking a glorified guest part in *The Best of Everything*, a melodramatic showcase for an ensemble of young actors. True to the prediction of Billy Wilder's *Sunset Blvd.*, Hollywood had no interest in former stars. A new horror cycle would change that.

The cycle began that year with, of all people, Katharine Hepburn. Producer Sam Spiegel was packaging the Tennessee Williams play *Suddenly, Last Summer* as a Columbia film for Elizabeth Taylor, and he wanted Hepburn too. Williams had written the sensational mid-length play in 1957 while undergoing psychoanalysis, and, true to form, he had used characters etched in acid to personify his private demons of fear and guilt. His great fear was that he would lose his life to drugs, alcohol, or homosexual promiscuity. His lifelong guilt came from allowing his mother to authorize a lobotomy on his sister. Twenty years later, he still regarded his mother with both reverence and resentment, and he was terrified that he might lose his mind to hereditary insanity. From his tortured introspection came *Suddenly, Last Summer*, the story of a brain specialist, Dr. Cukrowicz, who is pressured by the rich, imperious Mrs. Venable to perform a lobotomy on her niece Catherine, a young woman who is troubled but not clinically insane. If the doctor will silence Catherine's disjointed stories about the mysterious death of Mrs. Venable's son Sebastian, the hospital will be enriched.

Spiegel wanted Hepburn to play Mrs. Venable but could not offer her first billing. Liz Taylor, the world's number one box-office draw, would expect top billing for playing Catherine. For the first time since 1933, Hepburn agreed to second billing. Taylor also expected her friend Montgomery Clift to play Dr. Cukrowicz. Although Clift's star was on the wane because of drug and alcohol abuse, he was still as well known as Marlon Brando or Paul Newman. There was, however, the question of insurance. If a star could not be insured against sudden failure to work, a major studio would not hire him. Spiegel scheduled a physical examination for Clift with Columbia's insurance company. The actor missed one appointment, then showed up for the second appointment so tranquilized that the doctor, recognizing that Clift might go off the deep end at any time, declared him uninsurable. Spiegel cast him anyway. The company flew to London, except for the slippery Spiegel, who went to the PCA office to wangle a Code seal from Geoffrey Shurlock, who had called Gore Vidal's *Suddenly, Last Summer* script "revolting."

Reminding Spiegel of the Code section that said, "Sex perversion or any inference of it is forbidden," Shurlock told him that director Joseph Mankiewicz could not film the scene in which Catherine reveals that Sebastian was a magically charismatic sociopath who used her and his mother to procure teenage boys for him in exotic ports of call. The script called for a flashback to show how Sebastian, "suddenly, last summer" in Spain, realizes he is not young any more and loses his powers of manipulation. Sensing his vulnerability, his exploited playthings turn on him and punish him in some unspeakable manner. This was a horror story with multiple monsters—a domineering mother, a predatory homosexual, and a band of swinging delinquents. Shurlock refused to approve it. Spiegel defied him and told Mankiewicz to start shooting. The director was still coping with Clift.

Even when sober, "Monty" Clift was troublesome. At a formal dinner with the director, Clift ate with his fingers, threw food, and shouted gibberish. Taylor tried to calm him during rehearsals, but she had her own problems. After a year of grieving for her third husband, Mike Todd, who was killed in a plane crash, she had just married singer Eddie Fisher, whom she had snatched from his wife, Debbie Reynolds. Mercedes McCambridge was playing Taylor's mother in the film. As she recalled:

> Elizabeth was still mourning Mike Todd. Miss Hepburn was suffering through Spencer Tracy's illness.

> . . . Joe Mankiewicz had some kind of skin disease on his hands and he had to wear gloves all through the picture. You don't think of Gore Vidal or Tennessee Williams as particularly happy people. Of course, Monty was in torment. Everybody connected with the film was going through some kind of personal anguish and it showed.

The hunter becomes the prey in **SUDDENLY, LAST SUMMER**. In a Spanish seaside resort, the handsome Sebastian (played by an unbilled actor) pays the price for looking good enough to eat.

Suddenly, Last Summer went into production on May 25, 1959, at Shepperton Studios, fifteen miles southwest of London, just as a heat wave rolled in. Clift tried to cool himself by drinking fruit punch from the thermos that he always carried with him. Screenwriter Edward Anhalt once made the mistake of pouring himself a drink from it. "What the hell is this?" he asked through pursed lips.

"Bourbon, crushed Demerol, and fruit juice," Clift smiled in his gentle way.

Mankiewicz had been treating Clift coldly since the ruined dinner party. Now, as Clift constantly trembled, blew his lines, or just stared blankly, the director told the producer to replace him. Spiegel asked Taylor to talk to Clift. "I've tried to get through to him and I just can't," she answered. Hepburn then took it upon herself to nurse Clift through shakes, sweats, and agitation. Mankiewicz looked askance at her and began to favor Taylor. "Mankiewicz was anxious to court friendship with Elizabeth," said Spiegel. "He was downright disrespectful to Katie." Hepburn thought he was being cruel to Clift by making no secret that he wanted to get rid of him. The distress off camera contributed to the tenor of Taylor's scenes, especially the halting monologue that climaxes the film.

The horror-queen cycle moved into high gear with Robert Aldrich's 1962 film **WHAT EVER HAPPENED TO BABY JANE?** In it, Bette Davis plays Baby Jane Hudson, an aging has-been whose memorabilia is a shocking reminder of her own decay, except when she drinks—which is most of the time. Aldrich called Davis's performance a "bravura, all-out Gothic eye-catcher."

At the very top of the hill—a place—a ruin—broken stones—like the entrance to a ruined temple—they overtook him—there . . . I heard Sebastian scream. *He screamed just once* . . . I ran—they let me run—they didn't see me—I ran—*down*—the waiters, police, people—ran out of buildings—back up to where—to where Cousin Sebastian—he was—lying—*naked*—on the broken stones . . . and this you won't believe—nobody, nobody, nobody could believe it—it looked as if—as if they had *devoured him*—as if they had torn or cut parts of him away with their hands or with knives or the jagged tin cans they made music with—as if they'd torn bits of him away and stuffed them into those *gobbling mouths!*

At the end of this ten-minute speech, Taylor was sobbing. Her performance was so heartfelt that her coworkers moved to comfort and congratulate her. Still sobbing, she pushed them away and ran to her dressing room.

On the day that Hepburn completed her scenes, she walked up to Mankiewicz and faced him. "Are you quite sure we're finished?" she asked him, three times over. When he assured her that they did not need her for retakes or looping, she paused, reared back, and spat in his face. Hav-

ing expressed her opinion of him, she walked off the film.

Suddenly, Last Summer was released on December 22, 1959, not long after Spiegel placated the PCA by agreeing to slice one line from the soundtrack and one shot from the negative. The line was "We were procuring for him." The shot showed two shirtless youths rubbing against each other.* The token censorship fooled no one. "I assumed the youngest child in the audience would get the point," wrote Pauline Kael. They did and immediately told their friends, who made the film, along with *Psycho*, one of 1960's highest-grossing films. *Variety* called it "the most bizarre motion picture ever made by a major American company." Suddenly *that* summer, two horror films with monstrous mothers were all the rage.

Rage was the point, if writer Philip Wylie was any indication. His much-talked-about 1942 book, *Generation of Vipers*, attacked the mother-son relationship that was Williams's stock in trade. "Oh, Sebastian," Mrs. Venable says to her son. "What a lovely summer it's been. Just the two of us. Sebastian and Violet. Violet and Sebastian. Just the way it's always going to be. Oh, we *are* lucky. To have one another. And need no one else. Ever." The idea of an aging beauty dominating an effete son drove Wylie into spasms of hyperbole. "And when we agreed upon the American Ideal Woman—the Dream Girl of National Ado-

lescence, the Pin-up, the Glamour Puss—we insulted women and disenfranchised millions from love. We thus made mom [a] taloned, cackling residue of burnt-out puberty."

Generation of Vipers went into more than twenty printings, inciting as much anger as it did recognition, especially when Wylie accused the military of convincing thousands of soldiers "that they are momsick and would rather talk to her than take Betty into the shrubs." Whom *were* they taking into the shrubs? The warning that the moms of these healthy American males would turn them into adolescent-seducing Sebastians came through loud and clear in Wylie's unequivocally damning echo of Dr. Pretorius's "I give you . . . the Monster" in *Bride of Frankenstein*.

"I give you mom," wrote Wylie. "I give you the destroying mother."

Wylie no longer had to. The Hollywood Glamour Puss was about to teach the Frankenstein Monster a lesson, both onscreen and off.

The next horror movie to star an aging movie queen took a circuitous route from the printed page to the silver screen. In 1961, William Frye, producer of the NBC TV series *Thriller*, found a novel by Henry Farrell called *What Ever Happened to Baby Jane?* He submitted it to Wasserman as a package starring Bette Davis and Olivia de Havilland and directed by Ida Lupino. Wasserman turned it down because Davis had been meddlesome while working on a recent *Wagon Train* episode. Director Robert Aldrich heard about the book from a former secretary. Her new boss had just optioned it. If Aldrich wanted it, he could have it for a nominal $10,000.

Aldrich had directed Joan Crawford in the 1956 suspense film *Autumn Leaves*. In the years since, Crawford had written him numerous times, reminding him that she wanted to do a film with Davis. Perhaps Crawford was thinking of *The Great Lie*, in which supporting actress Mary Astor not only stole the show from Davis but also won an Oscar. Davis never again worked with any actress who might give her competition, and she had always maintained a cool distance from Crawford, whom she called "that mannequin from M-G-M." The rivalry was a longstanding one, according to M-G-M publicist Dore Freeman, who knew Crawford for fifty years. "Bette Davis was the Big Actress at Warners when Joan Crawford showed up there in the forties. Bette didn't take her seriously until Joan got an Oscar and started grabbing parts that Bette thought were hers. Which is what Norma Shearer was doing to Joan at Metro before. And this is what made Bette and Joan into rivals." Still Crawford kept after Aldrich. "She said she wanted to work with Bette Davis," he recalled. "I could never see them working together in anything. Then I read *Baby Jane*."

Aldrich sent the book to Crawford, who was promoting Pepsi-Cola in New York. Meanwhile, the option lapsed. Before Aldrich could act, an agent named Sid Beckerman bought the book and assigned Harry Essex, the screenwriter of *It Came from Outer Space*, to adapt it. Aldrich still wanted to do it, but Beckerman wanted $61,000. Aldrich did not have the money, but his new producer, Joseph E. Levine, was willing to advance it. Essex got $28,500 to stop in his tracks, Beckerman got the rest, and Aldrich got his book—almost. When Levine and Aldrich parted company,

Aldrich had to pay Levine $85,000 for the book and for the screenplay that Aldrich and Lukas Heller had already written from it. Aldrich finally had his property. Now all he had to do was get a broomstick with *two* wicked witches on it.

In January 1962, Bette Davis was appearing at the Royale Theatre on Broadway as the blowsy Maxine Faulk in Williams's *Night of the Iguana*. She was sitting in her dressing room after a performance one night when who should come calling but the bejeweled Joan Crawford, who beamed at her, presented her with *What Ever Happened to Baby Jane?*, and said respectfully, "I have always wanted to work with you." Davis frowned at the book, reluctantly accepted it, and spent the weekend at her home in Connecticut reading it. "Well, it could work," she recalled saying to herself. "It's all there. Phony Joan and Crazy Bette." Davis had lunch with Frye in New York the following week. "You'll never believe it," she said. "Crawford gave me a copy of the book with a note suggesting I play the younger sister. I told her *never*. The only part I'm interested in is Baby Jane." Davis soon heard from Aldrich, who sent her a script and a letter: "If this isn't the best screenplay you've ever read, don't see me." A meeting took place.

"What part will I be playing?" Davis asked.

"Jane, of course," Aldrich replied.

"Good," she said. "I just wanted to be sure." She paused. "Have you slept with Joan?"

"No," replied Aldrich, grinning slyly. "Not that I haven't had the opportunity."

"I just wanted to be sure there was no partiality involved," said Davis.

Aldrich began shopping the project around. "When Aldrich tried to interest the studios in Joan Crawford and myself," Davis recalled, "the moguls said, 'We wouldn't give you a dime for those two washed-up old broads.'" Four majors said no, but Aldrich kept asking. "Three distributors read the script and looked at the budget," he remembered. "Two of these said they might be interested if I would agree to cast younger players." Then Eliot Hyman called him—the same Eliot Hyman who had bought the Warner Bros. film library in 1956 and then made such a large profit on old Davis, Bogart, and Crawford films that he was able to start his own company, Seven Arts, only two years later. "I think it will make a fabulous movie," said Hyman, "but I'm going to make very tough terms because it's a high-risk venture." Now Aldrich had to cut costs without losing his stars. "From my rapidly narrowing slice of the pie," he said, "I offered each actress a piece of the picture plus some salary." Crawford would receive ten percent of net profit and $40,000. Thanks to a stubborn agent, Davis would get five percent and $60,000. Everyone in the industry wondered what kind of movie would need two old stars. A story about two old stars, of course!

What Ever Happened to Baby Jane?, as adapted by Heller and Aldrich, was a bubbling brew of entertainment history, sibling rivalry, momism, aging, disability, guilt, grudges, hatred, insanity, and murder. The fiftyish Hudson sisters share a "Hollywood Spanish" mansion. This home is not really in Hollywood, but neither are they. Jane Hudson is a frumpy alcoholic trying to relive her childhood stardom as the singing vaudeville moppet Baby Jane. She lives off her sister Blanche, a fading beauty who was a rich 1930s

movie star until the envious Jane, a failed actress, ran a car into her and crippled her. Now they reside on the fringes of reality, connected by a tether of hate. Blanche wants a fuller life but Jane is slipping into psychosis. When Blanche makes the first tentative efforts to sell the house and have Jane committed, Jane cuts Blanche off from the outside world, terrorizing and starving her, while using her money to pay an obese mama's boy to write a Baby Jane comeback act.

The script could have served any number of aging actresses—Myrna Loy and Rosalind Russell, Norma Shearer and Miriam Hopkins, even Greta Garbo and Marlene Dietrich—but they might have made it a psychological study, a melodrama, or a tragedy. What Crawford and Davis brought to it was a distillation of their own well-known personas, the exophthalmic viciousness Davis had displayed in *The Little Foxes* and the tear-blinking self-sacrifice Crawford had shown in *Mildred Pierce*. By squeezing their bigger-than-life characters onto the tiny stage of a shabby man-

sion, Davis and Crawford created horror. What they created on the set was a battle royal that made the ordeal of *Suddenly, Last Summer* look like a tea party.

Before Davis and Crawford squared off in front of the camera, they had turf skirmishes with the various artists at Producers' Studio on Melrose Avenue. Crawford wanted her costumes to be flattering. Designer Norma Koch had to talk her out of wearing sexy negligees or dresses that would show her legs since the character's leg muscles would have atrophied. When it was time for Crawford to make wardrobe tests, Aldrich used a moving camera to track in and show the costumes in motion. Script supervisor Bob Gary took notes. "By the time the camera got to Joan's face," recalled Gary, "she was crying. She was wearing the dress she was supposed to die in . . . and the tears began to fall. She is the only person I have ever seen who cried at her own wardrobe tests."

Koch's costumes for Davis were grotesque. "I designed grown-up versions of dresses that a little girl would wear,"

In **WHAT EVER HAPPENED TO BABY JANE?** audiences were spellbound by the birth of two horror stars. A reviewer praised the film's "rattlesnake repartee," but the public knew that the hatred displayed by Bette Davis (left) toward Joan Crawford (right) was real—the result of a twenty-year rivalry. A reviewer saw "the isolated decay of two spirits left to dry on the desert by the receding flood of fame." The film turned the actresses into sought-after horror queens.

said Koch. "They were supposed to be extensions of the child star she once was." The script called for Jane to wear a wig that apes her childhood mop of curls. Davis's hairdresser rented a Shirley Temple "Curly Top" wig from Max Factor, but Aldrich did not like the way it tested. He secretly approached Crawford's hair stylist Peggy Shannon. "Peggy, you worked on all those old musicals at M-G-M. Can you help us out?" That day after work, Shannon visited old pals at M-G-M and found a platinum blonde wig. When Davis put it on the next day and looked in the mirror, she exclaimed: "It's the *nuts*! I love it!" No one told Davis that the wig had been worn by Crawford in 1930's *Our Blushing Brides*.

When it was time for makeup, Davis found a look worthy of Jack Pierce. "She, more than I," said Aldrich, "decided on her Baby Jane makeup, that ugly, chalky mask." She was inspired by gossip. "I wanted to look outrageous, like Mary Pickford in decay," said Davis. Shannon told her about the extras in M-G-M Technicolor musicals. "They were so in love with the way they looked that they never washed their faces. You would see them days later, walking down La Brea Avenue with the original makeup still on." This was all Davis needed to hear. "Jane never washes her face," she beamed. "She just adds another layer of makeup each day." Crawford, meanwhile, refused to approve her own makeup. Monte Westmore had followed Aldrich's instructions that Blanche should look as ravaged as Jane. "I had put huge lines under her eyes," said Westmore, "and the shadows on her face made her look like she had jowls. She looked rotten, like she had been on dope." Crawford and Aldrich compromised, letting Crawford begin the film looking mature but not wrecked. She also prepared for her role by studying with a disabled war veteran who showed her how to do "transfers" from the wheelchair to the bed. "He taught me how to hoist my body into the bed first and then lift each leg, and how to fall out of the chair—straight forward, and then roll over." Rehearsals ended on July 20, 1962, and Crawford uttered the famous last words: "I have been waiting twenty years to work with Miss Davis."

The typical day on the set of *What Ever Happened to Baby Jane?* began as Crawford arrived with an entourage—her chauffeur, a junior agent from the William Morris agency, her maid, her secretary, her makeup artist, and her hairstylist. Davis arrived alone. Cinematographer Ernest Haller had photographed Davis's Academy-Award-winning performances in *Dangerous* and *Jezebel* and Crawford's in *Mildred Pierce*. On this film there were no black net scrims on their key lights and no diffusion disks on the camera lens. "If I'd lit either of them this way ten years ago," said Haller, "they'd have had my head!" At lunchtime, Davis walked to Lucey's Restaurant in full Baby Jane makeup and then wondered why traffic was stopping. To her friends, Loretta Young and Barbara Stanwyck, Crawford would say, "You should see the way Bette dresses at the studio. She walks around in bedroom slippers and an old, ragged terrycloth robe with makeup stains on the collar." At the end of the day, Crawford would head for her limousine. "This entire entourage would follow her," recalled photographer Phil Stern. "Then you'd see Davis, stepping over cables on the floor, going home alone."

A few days later, when Crawford and Davis saw the first rushes, they both burst into tears. Crawford turned to

Haller: "Why do I have to look so damn old? It's like I have a grandmother playing my part."

Wiping her nose, Davis perked up. "Joan, if you're so unhappy with this film, I'll play your part and you'll play mine."

"I can't play *her*," sniffed Crawford. "She's *twice* as ugly."

Davis stopped looking at the rushes, but not before she noticed that Crawford's closeups were becoming softer and more numerous. "There were far more closeups than the script called for," Haller admitted. Crawford began sending Davis a red rose every day. Davis responded by ignoring her or cutting her short. In response, Crawford would say "Bless you." Both stars had an autobiography published during the production. After Crawford gave *A Portrait of Joan* to Davis, she expected a copy of Davis's *The Lonely Life*. Davis hemmed and hawed, not wanting to write "Dear Joan." Finally she thought of something. "Joan," she wrote, "Thanks for wanting my autograph." Crawford was beginning to get the message, recalled Frye, that Davis "actively despised" her. Crawford was bewildered but not without her own animus. "Each one coveted what the other possessed," said director George Cukor. "Joan envied Bette's incredible talent and Bette envied Joan's seductive glamour." As the production moved into its fourth week, a rebuffed Crawford started keeping score.

Davis would watch while Crawford rehearsed, then casually ask her, "Is that how you're really going to do it?"

"Yes, Bette. Why?" Crawford would ask.

"Never mind," Davis would yawn.

Crawford also saw Davis appropriating credit for discovering the book and getting preferential treatment from Aldrich. "Bette did everything in her power to antagonize Crawford, but in a very quiet way," recalled actress Anna Lee. "She would put little notes on her dressing room door—'Of all my relations, I prefer sex the most'—and she thought Joan would be shocked by that." Crawford saw Davis treating actor Victor Buono coldly, so she spent extra time helping him with his reaction closeups. Davis caught on and told him she liked his acting style. Crawford worried that she looked flat-chested in her bedridden scenes so she began wearing larger falsies. "She's supposed to be shriveling away," observed Davis, "but her tits keep growing. I keep running into them, like the Hollywood hills." When Crawford asked Aldrich if the cast and crew could watch one of her TV appearances, Davis walked to a corner of the soundstage and began to sing her Baby Jane song with a record player, trying to drown out the TV. On another day, Davis screamed at a crew member, cursing out Crawford in full hearing of her dressing-room door, which slowly closed after a few moments of invective.

Crawford began telephoning Aldrich at night "Bob, dear, did you see what Bette did to me today?"

As soon as the director would hang up, Davis would call. "What did Crawford call you about?"

"Mother was on the phone to Aldrich at least an hour every night," recalled B. D. Hyman, Davis's daughter. "She'd rehash everything that happened on the set that day that Aldrich had to apologize for . . . and all the terrible things Joan had done to her, which he would have to prevent her from doing the following day." The calls came like clockwork. "First one, then the other," said Aldrich. "I could

rely on it every night. They were like two Sherman tanks."

Just as Davis's daughter listened in on her mother, Aldrich's son Bill overheard the nightly calls. "My dad had to spend an awful lot of time trying to keep them happy," he recalled. "But he never took sides. Luckily he had worked with some very tough guys in his time, so he played it right down the middle with the two ladies. He was just as tough as they were." Veteran columnist Sidney Skolsky analyzed their respective styles. "Joan resembles M-G-M. Bette resembles Warners. The war is between two kingdoms, two Movie Queens, each with an ego that has to be fed with driving activity." As the stars literally threw themselves into scenes of unprecedented grimness—falling down stairs, slapping, kicking, killing—the war of nerves escalated.

The ongoing stress gave Crawford a head cold. She was starting to feel poorly after numerous takes on a confrontation scene with Davis. "Could we have a break for a few minutes, please? I feel terrible."

"You'd think after all these years we'd all be troupers," said Davis. Crawford gave her a withering look and walked in the direction of the Pepsi machine that she had arranged to have on the soundstage. "She spikes her Pepsi," Davis said, not so sotto voce. "That bitch is loaded half the time." If Crawford was drinking a bit more than usual, it was because she was apprehensive about shooting the scene in which Jane kicks Blanche all over the floor of the music room. Aldrich shot some angles with a Blanche dummy. Davis kicked it so hard that she looked as if she might hurt her foot. When it was time for Crawford to do the other angles with Davis, Crawford took Aldrich aside. "I'm not doing it," she whispered to him. "I don't trust Miss Davis. She's going to kick my teeth in." Aldrich shot a few more angles with the dummy, then carefully rehearsed Crawford and Davis. When the camera rolled, Davis kicked convincingly, missing Crawford's head once, twice—and then connected. Crawford screamed and rolled over. Davis walked off. "She raised a fair-sized lump on Joan's head," reported gossip columnist Hedda Hopper the next day. There were unconfirmed reports of stitches. There were no reports of apologies.

One of the last scenes to be shot required the demented Baby Jane to lift her dying sister Blanche from the bed and carry her out of the bedroom where she has kept her a prisoner. As they rehearsed, Davis asked Crawford not to make her body a dead weight because she did not want to aggravate her back problems. "There is a way of making it easy on the actor who is doing the carrying," said Aldrich. The small set was tense as the crew readied itself for the shot. "It was one continuous take," recalled Heller. "Bette carried her from the bed, across the room, and out the door." For some reason, Crawford looked heavier now. "You could clearly see that when Bette lifted Joan off the bed she was straining herself," said Gary. "Then, as soon as she got into the hallway, out of the camera's range, she dropped Joan and let out this bloodcurdling scream," said Heller.

"My back! Oh, God! My back!"

As the crew stared in disbelief, Crawford got up and sauntered to her dressing room. She may have been wearing weights under her costume. Davis was out of commission for four days. When she returned, the company moved

to the beach for the dreamlike finale. Crawford and Davis were no longer speaking. "I think it's proper to say that they really detested each other," recalled Aldrich, "but they behaved absolutely perfectly." He had not yet realized that the film had created two monsters.

Filming ended September 12, and Aldrich's editors worked in teams around the clock for weeks to ready the film for an October 20 preview in Long Beach. Its primarily teenage audience had an unusual reaction. They liked *What Ever Happened to Baby Jane?* so much that they wanted the theater to run it again. A few days later, a *Hollywood Citizen-News* critic voiced the opinion of many. "For months, the word in the industry was that Bette and Joan had thrown what was left of their careers down the toilet by doing this B movie. No one expected it to be this good." Paul V. Beckley of the *New York Herald Tribune* wrote: "If Miss Davis's portrait of an outrageous slattern with the mind of an infant has something of the force of a hurricane, Miss Crawford's performance as the crippled sister could be described as the eye of that hurricane, abnormally quiet, perhaps, but ominous and desperate." *Variety* appreciated one of the film's many ironic moments. "In one superb bit, Miss Crawford reacting to herself on television makes her

face fairly glow with the remembrance of fame past." *What Ever Happened to Baby Jane?* recouped its $980,000 cost in eleven days and eventually grossed $3.5 million. "I must say we are gloating," Davis told Jack Paar on *The Tonight Show*. She had even more reason to gloat when she was nominated for an Academy Award—and Crawford was not. The Queen of Warners had trounced the Mannequin from Metro. Mannequin or monster?

On Academy Awards night, April 8, 1963, Davis stood in the wings of the Santa Monica Civic Auditorium stage, waiting for the announcement of the Best Actress winner. Davis had already presented the Best Original Screenplay award. Crawford was also there, having just presented the Best Director award. Crawford, according to Frye, "was a sight to behold that evening. Edith Head had crafted a breathtaking beaded silver sheath for her. Crawford topped that off with caviar pearls and diamonds on her fingers, wrists, neck, and ears." Davis did not know that Crawford had made arrangements to accept the award for any nominee who was not present. It would not have mattered if

Davis knew; she fully expected to win her third Oscar that night. She got her first shock when she heard the announcement of Anne Bancroft as the winner for *The Miracle Worker*. She got her second shock when she heard the next announcement: "Accepting for Anne Bancroft is Miss Joan Crawford." According to Associated Press columnist Bob Thomas, "Bette felt a hand on her arm. 'Excuse me,' said Joan as she strode past Bette and crossed the stage amid heavy applause. It was a moment Bette Davis would never forget."

Watching from the Hollywood sidelines was the opportunistic William Castle, who wasted no time in mounting a horror film around a malevolent mom. His first choices were unavailable. Crawford, suddenly in demand, was playing a tough mental hospital administrator in *The Caretakers*. Davis was costarring with the only actress she could trust not to upstage her. Through the miracle of movie magic, Davis was playing opposite herself as twin sisters in *Dead Ringer*. Anyone else would have been happy to play one good twin and one evil twin; in this film, both twins were wicked.

Joseph Biroc's imaginative lighting made **HUSH . . . HUSH, SWEET CHARLOTTE** a Gothic delight, as did the masterly performances of Agnes Moorehead and Olivia de Havilland.

"Stone Age, here I come," says Olivia de Havilland in the 1963 **LADY IN A CAGE**, a horror-queen vehicle in which a disabled woman becomes a prisoner in her own elevator. "I was happy in my little cage," the affable actress later said. "I didn't want to be let out between setups. I just sat there patiently in a corner on the floor and asked that somebody hand me a coffee on the end of a pole between the bars every now and then."

A lucky Castle ran into Crawford at a Hollywood party after an accident had forced him to shut down production on his latest film, *Strait-Jacket*. He could not conceal his excitement at encountering her. Putting his cigar aside and fetching her a fresh glass of one-hundred-proof Smirnoff vodka, he shamelessly lied that he had been preparing a script especially for her. The writer was the famous author of *Psycho*, Robert Bloch. The script was called *Strait-Jacket*. "I'm listening, Mr. Castle," said Crawford. He related the far-fetched story of Lucy Harbin, a fifty-year-old woman who comes to live on a farm with her daughter after spending twenty years in a mental institution. When Lucy was thirty, she found her husband and a barroom floozy in bed and chopped off both their heads with an axe. Now she just wants to live a quiet life, but axe murders begin to recur.

"Mm hm," said Crawford, biting her lip.

"She is the suspected killer," Castle continued. "She believes it herself."

"And?" asked Crawford.

"She is arrested. *But*—she's not the killer," Castle grinned. "It's her twisted daughter!"

"The little bitch," said Crawford, taking another sip. "When can I see the script?" Still busy with Pepsi promotions, Crawford took the script with her to New York, read it, and then convened a meeting with Castle, Bloch, and Leo Jaffe, executive vice-president of Columbia. "*Strait-Jacket* will have to be completely rewritten as a vehicle for me or I won't accept the role," she said quietly over the lunch she had prepared for them. Her guests gulped and finished their quiche lorraine. The film did become a Crawford vehicle, making Lucy ten years younger and giving her the requisite number of showy scenes, but Castle spent more time directing horror effects than performances.

His main concern was to simulate the sound of a head being chopped off. He first tried a wet telephone book. The flat sound evoked nothing. "The following day," he recalled, "I brought a large watermelon that I had stolen from Ellen's refrigerator. Wielding an axe, the prop man cut it in half. The squish was perfect. It sounded exactly like a head being lopped off."

When it came time to sell *Strait-Jacket* to the public, Castle deviated slightly from form. "I always have some sort of a sales gimmick or hook," he told *Variety*. "However,

I use it at the point of sale—the box office—rather than on TV as Hitchcock and Disney do." This time, instead of using a mechanical gimmick, Castle had his star pitch the film with personal appearances in twenty theaters in seven major cities. Crawford would speak, answer questions, and for a finale, she would swing a three-foot axe. The tour was a mobbed sensation but critics cluck-clucked. "It's time to get Joan Crawford out of those housedress horror B movies and back into haute couture," wrote Judith Crist. "Miss Crawford, you see, is high class. Too high class to withstand in mufti the banality of Robert Bloch's script, cheap-jack production, and direction better suited to the mist-and-cobweb idiocies of the Karloff school of suspense." Crawford's profit participation soothed the sting of such reviews. Meanwhile, horror queens multiplied.

"I've gone from gore to pure suspense and shock," Castle announced as he cast Barbara Stanwyck in another exercise in fright. *The Night Walker* was the thrown-together tale of a woman bedeviled by dreams of an attractive man in a business suit. "It is not a horror film," clarified Stanwyck, "because even I would be too scared to do a horror film!" She was correct, because the man in the suit (Lloyd Bochner) was not very scary. Nor was Robert Taylor, unmasked at the end of the film as a madman in contact lenses, but Stanwyck was as good a screamer as she was an actress. *Newsweek* writer David Slavitt interviewed Castle in his suite in the Sherry-Netherland Hotel after telling him what he thought of *The Night Walker*. Castle was unfazed.

"Do you think I'd invite you up here to sit on my couch and drink my coffee and insult my picture if I didn't enjoy it?" he asked Slavitt. "I don't need you to tell me what kind of picture I made. I know what kind of picture I made. But go ahead. This is the high spot of my day."

Castle made one more horror-queen movie with Crawford, *I Saw What You Did*. In it, two rambunctious teenage girls (Andi Garrett and Sarah Lane) play a telephone game while their parents are away. Running their bored fingers down the page of a telephone book, they choose a name at random, dial the number, and breathily say: "I saw what you did and I know who you are." As the script would have it, they call a man who has just committed a murder (John Ireland). His neighbor (Crawford), who has designs on him, mistakes one of the pranksters for a romantic rival. In her one good scene, a bewigged, bedizened Crawford chases

In 1963, when she made William Castle's **STRAIT-JACKET**, Joan Crawford was firmly linked in the public's mind with Pepsi-Cola, the soft drink that was advertised "For those who think young." *Time* magazine reviewed her film: "As for Pepsi-Cola Board Member Crawford, she plainly plays her mad scenes For Those Who Think Jung."

a properly terrified teen away from her quarry, shouting at her. "You little tramp! Throwing yourself at him! Chasing him! Get outta here!"

"It was just a game!" the girl protests.

"I know what kind of game! With a man over twice your age! Now, *get outta here!*" Crawford roars with all the authority of the M-G-M lion. Her demise a few minutes later is hard to believe, since she is the scariest thing in the movie.

Castle attempted to justify the silly film by presenting it as a cautionary tale about "the current teenage rebellion against parental control that includes . . . destruction of property, mass adoration of public figures, [and] choices of music and reading material." Crawford also stressed the film's social value. "I think this film will have a terrific audience identification with both parents and teenagers." She could not fool the veterans with whom she had made so many classic films. "She would write to me about these pictures, actually believing that they were quality scripts," said director George Cukor. "You could never tell her they were garbage."

One of the worst horror-queen movies starred one of Hollywood's most esteemed actresses, forty-eight-year-old Olivia de Havilland, who had been off the screen for several years. *Lady in a Cage* was a grimy, misogynistic little film that subjected a graceful, good-natured star to awful indignities in the name of some disingenuous social commentary. Mrs. Hilyard (de Havilland) is the doting mother of an effeminate twenty-nine-year-old son, Malcolm (William Swan). Disabled because of hip surgery, she becomes trapped in her elevator while Malcolm is away for the weekend. Her home is invaded, ransacked, and trashed by a wino (Jeff Corey), a prostitute (Ann Sothern), and a gang of hoodlums, whose leader (James Caan) devastates her by reading Malcolm's farewell letter to her. "Give me my half of what's in the living room safe," writes the ungrateful son. "Release me from your beauty. Release me from your generosity. Release me from your love." Screenwriter Luther Davis must have read *Generation of Vipers*. He has Mrs. Hilyard, laid low by this senseless cruelty, make an absurd confession. "It's all true," she says. "I'm a monster . . . a monster." *Life* magazine chided de Havilland for lowering her standards. "Add Olivia's name to the list of movie actresses who would rather be freaks than forgotten." It was also noted that the film's cinematographer was the gifted Lee Garmes, who had shot De Havilland in *Gone with the Wind*. In spite of its amateurish direction and hypocritical preachment, *Lady in a Cage* broke even. De Havilland returned to her home in Paris, but not for long. She would soon be dragged into a rematch between Crawford and Davis, and this time it was not a battle royal. It was war.

Robert Aldrich was a brave man, braver than director Edmund Goulding, who, in 1943, when faced with the prospect of directing the feuding, intransigent, cantankerous duo of Miriam Hopkins and Bette Davis a second time, faked a heart attack. Aldrich, however, had done well by *Baby Jane*. It made sense to do a sequel with the same stars before his imitators ran the cycle into the ground. Farrell, *Baby Jane*'s author, had come up with another saga of hate, *What Ever Happened to Cousin Charlotte?* Crawford agreed to costar in it with Davis, but, even though Davis

would be playing Charlotte, Crawford wanted top billing. She also expected $50,000, and twenty-five percent of net profits. Davis screamed at Aldrich when she heard this and demanded $200,000 and fifteen percent.

"That is the same amount I'm getting for producing and directing," he fumed. "That makes us partners on this picture."

"Partners," said Davis, puffing on her fifty-first cigarette of the day. "All the way down the line. I will hold you to that." Twentieth Century–Fox agreed to Aldrich's budget of $1.3 million, part of which went to paying off Farrell and hiring Heller to write the script. Davis soon threatened to quit, complaining that Aldrich had not yet changed the "cheap" title or hired a cinematographer. To placate her, Aldrich hired the painterly Joseph Biroc, raised Davis's percentage to twenty-five percent, and gave her equal billing with Crawford—in "alphabetical order." And the film would now be called *Hush . . . Hush, Sweet Charlotte*. It was the story of another aging recluse, Charlotte, who asks her cousin Miriam to help her save the old family mansion from demolition by the Louisiana Highway Commission. Charlotte fears that the building will yield evidence that her father killed her married lover, John, in 1927. Charlotte is haunted by dreams and hallucinations of the unsolved murder, in which a mystery killer surprised John and then chopped off his hand and his head.

Rehearsals and wardrobe tests began at Twentieth in mid-May 1964, postponed for a month because Crawford could not get out of her Pepsi commitments. The turf tiffs began immediately. Davis had a closed set for her wardrobe tests. Crawford wanted to see what Davis would be wearing.

"What does it matter, Joan? I am going to be a mess and you are going to be your usual gorgeous self."

"Dear Bette," said Crawford with a million-dollar smile. "Bless you."

The *Sweet Charlotte* company flew to Baton Rouge on May 31, but Crawford made the mistake of flying in a few days late. Davis was taking her status as Aldrich's partner quite seriously. She had already ingratiated herself with the crew. When Crawford landed, there was inexplicably no one at the airport to meet her. Her lodging arrangements were also confused. When she arrived at the location, the Houmas House Plantation in Burnside, Louisiana, it was apparent that Davis was relishing her role as unofficial producer. Crawford, sensing that she was at a disadvantage, decided to keep out of her way and stayed with her entourage.

"Bette lets her hair down," wrote gossip columnist Sheilah Graham, "but Joan surrounds herself with the aura of a great of yesterday. Times have changed and she doesn't seem to realize that." Crawford did realize that she had to put on a good face, so she made attempts to win Davis over. "Miss Crawford always says 'Good morning,' when she walks onto the set," wrote columnist Lily May Caldwell. "Miss Davis seldom answers her." Davis usually walked away, swigging a Coke and snickering to anyone who would listen: "Old 'Bless you' is at it again." Rebuffed, Crawford went back to her trailer and poured herself a Pepsi (with Smirnoff). "Crawford obviously wants to clear the air," wrote Len Baxter of *Motion Picture* magazine. "But

Davis is not able to kiss and make up. She doesn't know how to say 'I'm sorry,' and Crawford doesn't feel that *she* has anything to be sorry for." Davis certainly thought so, according to her secretary, Vik Greenfield. "After the business with the Oscar, this was war."

Bit by bit, hour by hour, Davis saw to it that Crawford was undermined and ostracized. "Bette was a formidable presence on the set," said Aldrich regular Gary. "She and Aldrich were very tight," recalled unit publicist Harry Mines. "She was always by his elbow." Aldrich's son, Bill, was again working with the two legends. "Bette was something else," he recalled. "She worked the company, the crew. She was a very strong lady who was still carrying on a one-way feud with Crawford." Davis began to sit in front of the camera, watching Crawford do her scenes, a highly unprofessional situation for Aldrich to allow. Just as before, when Crawford would do a line reading for a last rehearsal, Davis would turn to Aldrich. "My God! Is that the way she's going to play it?" Crawford was gracious about the unsolicited opinions, but even the most casual observer could see that her armor was cracking. She spent more and more time in her trailer.

"[*Hush . . . Hush, Sweet Charlotte*] couldn't have been more the opposite than its predecessor," recalled Aldrich. "A terribly hostile atmosphere prevailed." Davis was now making remarks about Crawford's advanced age to reporters. Crawford was sixty and looking quite presentable. Davis was fifty-six and showing the effects of years of nicotine addiction. The clincher came for Crawford when she phoned Aldrich at his hotel room one night to set things straight. She started talking about the script, then heard a familiar voice in the background. "It was Miss Davis," she recalled. Whether Davis was sleeping with Aldrich or not, she had his ear; Crawford was in trouble. "I'd looked forward to working with Bette again," Crawford

said later. "I had no idea of the extent of her hate and that she planned to destroy me."

The coup de grace was delivered on June 12, the last day of location shooting. While Crawford napped in her trailer, waiting to be called back to the set, the company pitched its tents and drove to the airport without notifying her or arranging for her transportation. She had to book her own flight on a commercial airline. For two weeks, Crawford had been going back and forth between her fifty-five-degree trailer and the hot, humid outdoor location. Isolated from the company because of Davis's machinations, she stayed in her hotel room at night and drank. The climate, the alcohol, and the stress took their toll. On Saturday, June 13, she checked into Cedars of Lebanon Hospital with an "upper respiratory virus infection." On a visit with Crawford, Hopper noted that she had her script with her in the hospital bed. She was making changes in it. When Aldrich and Davis refused her changes—longer, more glamorous scenes—her illness turned into pneumonia.

A month later, she was well enough to report to work at Twentieth Century–Fox. Davis was standing by the camera again. Crawford was shooting a scene with Joseph Cotten. Davis interrupted. "I am cutting some dialogue," she informed Crawford, who didn't fight back but soon started missing work. Aldrich tried to force Crawford's hand with an examination by a specialist. Crawford's doctor sent her back to the hospital in an ambulance. "At that stage," said Aldrich, "the insurance company offered us the alternatives of finding a replacement for Miss Crawford within two weeks or scrapping the picture."

Crawford was well aware of what had happened to Marilyn Monroe and George Cukor two years earlier on *Something's Got to Give*. "Twentieth had closed down my last movie because no actress wanted to take over for Monroe," said Cukor. "The picture was [insured] and I think Joan figured they would do the same thing for her." Aldrich took the kinder view. "There's no doubt in the world that Crawford was sick, seriously sick," he said. "If she'd been faking, either the insurance company would never have paid the claim or she would never have been insurable again. Insurance companies here are terribly tough, and there's no such thing as a made-up ailment that they pay off on." If Cukor was correct, Crawford may have taken the precaution of warning Stanwyck and Young to decline the role because, when Aldrich approached them, they both said no. Crawford no doubt knew that if the studio closed down *Hush . . . Hush, Sweet Charlotte*, Davis would lose: (1) the role of Charlotte; (2) more than $100,000 in pending salary; and (3) her percentage points of the film's profits. Whether Crawford was faking or not, the result would be the same: Crawford would defeat Davis.

While Crawford lay in the hospital and recovered—or faked, depending on what one believed—Aldrich looked at his options and decided to continue. He asked vice-president in charge of production Richard Zanuck if he would approve an additional $285,000. Zanuck said yes and Aldrich began shopping for a new Miriam. "Davis had star approval," said Aldrich. "Until then it had been academic because she had approved Crawford, but it now became vitally important." Before Davis could veto her, Hepburn said no. Aldrich suggested Vivien Leigh and

In 1964, Universal's Ray Jones photographed the formerly married veteran stars Barbara Stanwyck and Robert Taylor for William Castle's "horrible" suspense film **THE NIGHT WALKER**. "The only horrible part of [the film]" wrote a *Newsweek* reviewer, "is Castle's use of old actors of distinction. His operation is a kind of artistic milk route on which these thoroughbreds are hitched to sordid wagons of commerce."

warned that Davis had better make up her mind quickly. "I will not do Charlotte with the very British Miss Leigh," Davis wrote Aldrich. "For Twentieth to suspend me is nonsense. . . . Why go from the frying pan to the fire? This is what you would be doing. Trust my lousy female instincts. They have been known to be right every now and then." Leigh had her own ideas. "No, thank you," said Leigh to a Twentieth Century–Fox executive. "I could just about stand looking at Joan Crawford's face at six o'clock in the morning, but not at Bette Davis's."

Aldrich's next candidate was de Havilland, who was traveling. "[Davis] tried to persuade Olivia to do the part, helped me talk to her on the phone," said Aldrich. "No good. So I went off to Switzerland to try to convince de Havilland in person. It was terribly difficult. I'm not quite sure why, but I think it has to do with Miss de Havilland's opinion of what her image is vis à vis what it *may* be." Sitting on a mountain top, they went back and forth about Miriam's character.

"In the first script she was written as rude," said de Havilland. "That's what threw me and put me off frightfully. She depressed me because she was so wicked."

"You mean the ambivalence, the counterpoint, the duality don't interest you?" Aldrich asked her.

"That's just what she *doesn't* have," de Havilland replied. "She's all one color—black, solid black. If one thing were changed—her rudeness—if you take that away and give her the opposite—exquisite manners, exquisite courtesy—then she becomes really dangerous. . . . It's always the charming ones of evil intent who are the dangerous ones."

Aldrich offered de Havilland $100,000. She accepted, and Aldrich called Davis with the news. She was pleased. Then he asked her to keep it quiet for two days until he could give Crawford's lawyer formal notice. He might as well have saved his breath. Davis immediately alerted her press agent, who made surreptitious calls to the Hollywood press. Crawford was in her hospital bed when she heard the news on the radio. "Aldrich knew where to long-distance me all over the world when he needed me," she told reporters. "But he made no effort to reach me here to alert me that he had signed Olivia. He let me hear it for the first time in the radio release. And, frankly, I think it stinks."

Of course, the same question was in everyone's mind. How can nice Olivia be as mean to Bette as Joan would have been in the part of Miriam? After working with Davis in a 1942 John Huston film called *In This Our Life*, de Havilland knew what to expect. And if she had forgotten, Davis reminded her. De Havilland gave a surprising performance, especially in the scenes where she berates, threatens, and slaps Davis. The roughest scene was the one in which Davis accidentally kills Joseph Cotten. "You wretched *idiot!*" groans de Havilland. Davis begs her to help bury the body. When Davis starts to lose her nerve, de Havilland turns into a growling virago. "*Damn you*. Now will you *shut your mouth!*" Her voice lowers. "You'll do as I tell you. And if I tell you to lie, you'll do that too." Her voice becomes a snarling whisper. "*I'm never going to suffer for you again. Not ever. Do you understand?*" With De Havilland as Miriam, Aldrich had created yet another horror queen. Could Crawford have summoned up the monstrous rage

Joan Crawford was not the only one who wondered how she ended up in bed with two severed heads in **STRAIT-JACKET**. "I guess Joan couldn't handle getting old," said her favorite photographer George Hurrell years later.

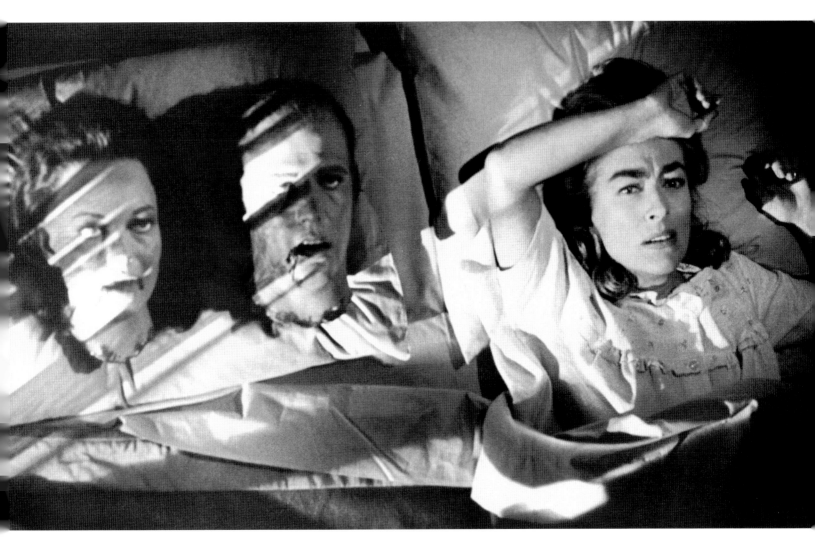

that de Havilland did? Probably. But to finish that movie might have killed her. Or Davis. Or both of them.

The film hit the theaters on Christmas Eve 1964. *Time* said:

> *Hush . . . Hush, Sweet Charlotte* is a gruesome slice of shock therapy that, pointedly, is not a sequel to *What Ever Happened to Baby Jane?* The two films are blood relatives, as producer-director Robert Aldrich well knows, but *Charlotte* has a worse play, more gore, and enough bitchery to fill several outrageous freak shows. The choicest holdover from *Jane* is Bette Davis, unabashedly securing her clawhold as Hollywood's *grande dame* ghoul.

Davis took exception to such reviews. "*Hush . . . Hush, Sweet Charlotte* was not a horror film," she claimed. "It was the study of a very sad woman who had a terrible thing happen in her life." More to her liking was the review written by British critic Kenneth Tynan: "An accomplished piece of Grand Guignol is yanked to the level of art by Miss Davis's performance as the raging, aging Southern belle. This wasted Bernhardt, with her screen-filling eyes and electrifying vocal attack, squeezes genuine pathos from a role conceived in cardboard."

In a few more years, the cardboard crumbled. "I'm not going to put old stars in a horror picture again," said Aldrich as he prepared a war film called *The Dirty Dozen*. "It's kind of sad when you think about it, isn't it?" Years later, Crawford had thought about it. "Robert Aldrich is a man who loves evil, horrendous, vile things," she told a New York audience. When asked how she handled Davis, she smiled. "I knitted. I knitted a scarf from here to Malibu." Semi-retired Myrna Loy could not understand Davis's need to stay on top. "Yes, she is a star, and a great one," said Loy. "But is it worth playing all those demented old ladies to maintain that status?" Cukor, who himself would work until the age of eighty, conceded that Crawford was temperamentally unable to quit. "She was a star, and this was 'the next picture,'" he said. "She had to keep working, as did Bette. But the two of them spawned a regrettable cycle in motion pictures." As that cycle ended, a few other veterans were keeping horror alive.

Roger Corman

"I love the beauty of rain," said Boris Karloff in 1957 to a journalist who was interviewing him about Shock! Theater. Standing on the balcony of the Chateau Marmont, watching Los Angeles bathe in monochrome cascades, Karloff answered questions about the film that was now appearing on thousands of local television schedules. After decades of sequels, reissues, and imitations, *Frankenstein* was still going strong. Its director, James Whale, had died a few months before the advent of Shock! Theater, but Karloff was benefiting from this new exposure. "I'm most grateful for it," he said, "because it has served to keep me going and introduces me to a brand new audience." He was not receiving residual checks for these round-the-clock broadcasts, but he was getting loads of fan mail and many more offers of work, all thanks to a twenty-six-year-old movie.

"It's a lovely film, a great film, and I'm devoted to the Monster," he said. "He's the best friend I ever had. He changed the course of my entire life. Can you blame me for being fond of the brute?"

As the rain poured down on Sunset Boulevard and the new Hollywood beyond, Karloff reminisced about his professional life since the Val Lewton films. After the Gothic horror cycle had ended with self-cannibalizing monster rallies, he had made a few more film appearances and then thrown himself into the new medium of television, where he soon averaged one appearance a month. He had moved from Hollywood to the stately Dakota Apartments in New York because most television was broadcast from the East—and because of Broadway. Karloff played the aging professor in J. B. Priestley's *The Linden Tree* in 1947, Captain Hook in Sir James Barrie's *Peter Pan* in 1950, and Bishop Cauchon in Jean Anouilh's *The Lark* in 1955.

When Karloff made television appearances in Los Angeles, he stayed in the Chateau Marmont penthouse, which boasted a library and Louis XV furnishings. A mile from this majestic setting, also on Sunset Boulevard, were the offices of American International Pictures, where Roger Corman was working to finish eight feature films by the end of 1957. The single-minded thirty-one-year-old had both admirers and detractors. "He was a brilliant man," recalled actress Beverly Garland. "When you went on location with Roger, you knew that if the director died and the script got lost and the cameraman broke his neck, the picture would still get made because Roger knew how to do everything. And he did it well." And he usually did it in a week, which made for some harried actors. "Roger wanted to accomplish a lot," remembered Susan Cabot. "He had the drive to do it, and he pushed through. He *punched* through! With a lot of energy—and a lot of disregard at times." Actor Richard Devon found Corman at first prepossessing. "You meet him in his office and he's absolutely charming. That boyish face of his, he digs his toes into the carpet, and all that jazz. You get him on the set, and he's Attila the Hun. With Roger, if anything costs more than what he has figured, it's a disaster for everybody."

Attack of the Crab Monsters, which he had made for Allied Artists early that year, had almost been that kind of disaster, thanks to the film's one special effect, a large crab. "When they made *Them!*," said actor Mel Welles, "I think they spent about twelve or fourteen thousand dollars for each of those giant ants. Roger spent a few hundred dollars building that crab." Corman's screenwriter Charles Griffith, doubling as underwater cameraman, took the crab to Catalina Island, where he and his crew ran into problems. "They discovered that the crab was made of Styrofoam and so it wouldn't sink," said Welles. "They tried winching it under the water, and it exploded." Corman's frugal *legerdemain* kept the film within its $70,000 budget; after millions of teenagers satisfied their curiosity about what kind of crabs these were, Corman declared the film "the most successful of all the early low-budget horror films."

Not of This Earth was another Allied Artists film that Corman made in defiance of time, money, energy—everything except gravity. In it, Paul Birch, who had been working with Corman and AIP since their first film, played a man from outer space who must have regular transfusions of blood. When a refrigerator stocked with plasma runs low, he taps unwilling donors by removing his dark glasses and staring at them with eyeballs that look like the tops of martini shakers. To achieve this hypnotic effect, Corman had Birch wear full-sized contact lenses. Special-effects designer Paul Blaisdell recalled that Birch found the lenses painful to wear. "A couple of hours passed and Birch felt like his eyes were burnt holes in a blanket," said Blaisdell. "Then he took the lenses out and his eyes hurt so bad he couldn't see straight." Birch complained but Corman pressed on with his breakneck schedule. The film was budgeted for $100,000 and nothing could deter him from finishing it on time. Locations were reserved, the crew was booked, and a release date was already set. Screenwriter Robert Towne understood Corman's motivation. "He felt that if he didn't do it quick, he did it wrong," said Towne. When Corman tried to hurry Birch, the actor had had enough. He called Corman onto the lawn in front of the house where they were shooting. "They took their glasses off and squared off," said cowriter Griffith, "and then they pushed and shoved and so on." Hostilities ceased when Birch stepped back, declared that he was quitting the film, and stomped off. After a short delay, Corman found actor Lyle Latell, who bore a superficial resemblance to Birch, put dark glasses on him, and finished the film.

Not of This Earth became part of a drive-in double bill, as did all of Corman's films; like the rest, it earned a lot of money. "There was a system that was working well," said Corman, "doing two low-budget pictures and sending them out in a combination: two science-fiction or two teen films." Corman obviously knew his audience and what they wanted. So what if the critics did not like him or his company? "There is no better medium than a cheap AIP movie in which to convey a cheap, rotten universe," wrote one critic. By 1959 Corman had become a wealthy young man, so he ignored critical snipes. Even so, he was outgrowing the AIP formula. "They had been selling their double bills a

bit too long," he said. "Although the profits were good, they weren't as big as they once were. I was also getting very restless with this format, partially because of the financial restrictions and partially because I simply wanted to make bigger pictures." Horror films had done the best for him, so he could not have failed to notice the abundance of classic horror—and horror stars—on television.

If Bela Lugosi had lived to see Shock! Theater, he would no doubt have been rediscovered and offered a TV series; but his death had left a clear field for Karloff. In 1960 the British actor, seventy-three and living in the Knightsbridge district in London, parlayed his monthly visibility into a weekly appearance as the host of NBC's *Thriller*, popularizing the catchphrase: "As sure as my name is Boris Karloff." Karloff enjoyed making the program, and guest actors competed for the thrill of working with the world's most famous monster. "I just pestered him, almost," recalled actor Ed Nelson, "sitting with him and talking about the old days and talking about his friend, Bela." The anthology series got such good Nielsen ratings that it aroused the envy of another NBC host, who pressured MCA's Lew Wasserman to cancel it. Not wanting to lose *Alfred Hitchcock Presents*, Wasserman persuaded NBC to pull the plug on *Thriller* in 1962.

Karloff was still receiving numerous film offers, including William Castle's remake of Priestley's *The Old Dark House*. "I sent back the script—wanted no part in it," said Karloff, who was aware of trends being set by Castle, Hitchcock, and Corman. "Villain by profession though I may be," he explained, "I must say that my approval of good, scary fun does not extend to shows where blood and guts are sloshed around wholesale, simply to create nightmares." Acknowledging "practically every film that I was ever in has been revived at some time or other on TV," he preferred to call them *terror* films. "I quarrel with the use of the word *horror* in describing those pictures," he said. "*Horror* connotes revulsion, disgust, recoil. The object is not to turn

Ed Nelson crouched inside this outsized crustacean for the 1957 **ATTACK OF THE CRAB MONSTERS**, the most profitable of Roger Corman's early low-budget horror films. Nelson recalled that the most important part of portraying a giant crab was not to let the camera see his own feet.

your stomach but merely to make your hair stand on end. I believe the Frankenstein-type story fills a deep-seated human need. One finds it rooted in the folk literature of every race, even in nursery rhymes and fairy tales." If Karloff was impervious to the blandishments of "horror" producers, another veteran star was not. Relishing his newfound stardom, Vincent Price was taking all comers, and that included Corman.

At a lunch meeting with Jim Nicholson and Sam Arkoff, Corman said, "Look, instead of making two ten-day black-and-white films for $100,000, why don't we make one movie in fifteen days for $300,000?" Aware of the formula's diminishing returns, his partners were interested in Corman's suggestion of Edgar Allan Poe's "The Fall of the House of Usher," which he had read as a high-school junior. He assured them he could make it quickly, leaving most of the budget for Pathecolor, CinemaScope, and casting. "Vincent Price was my first and only choice for the lead role of Roderick Usher," said Corman, but Price would cost $50,000. "That was a lot of money for AIP," recalled Arkoff, "and I wasn't really sure we could afford Vincent. We were a very young company at the time." Luckily, Price was amenable to a deferred salary and percentage points. To adapt Poe's 1839 short story, Corman hired Richard Matheson, who had followed *The Incredible Shrinking Man* with episodes for *The Twilight Zone*. The speed he had demonstrated in his TV writing made him an ideal choice for the celeritous Corman.

"I never cared for those monster movies, atomic radiation things, or giant insects," said Matheson. "I always preferred fantasy movies. When I was a teenager, I was a big fan of Val Lewton's." His favorite was *Cat People*, and it prompted him to correspond with Lewton for a time. Now he brought the same cunning restraint to AIP. The studio liked his detailed outline, so he went right into the screenplay, bearing in mind Corman's vision. "The world of Poe to a large extent was the world of the unconscious," said Corman. "I thought it could be re-created better within the

artificial confines of a stage than it could be in broad daylight. I didn't want to use location shots. I didn't want the film to be shot realistically." Matheson agreed with this approach. "I knew I would be working within a limited budget," he said, "but I tried not to let that fact affect my writing. The story was so simple anyhow. What could they spend money on? You had a bunch of people stuck in an old house." Poe's anecdotal story concerns Roderick and Madeline Usher, twin brother and sister, who are the last of an inbred family. Roderick suffers from heightened senses. Madeline suffers from catalepsy. The decaying mansion is bent on destroying the last of the Ushers. "Poe's story is very brooding and ruminating," said Matheson, "and not too much plot, movement, or dialogue, so I kind of faked the Poe touches." At the final preproduction meeting, Arkoff questioned the script. "There's no monster in the picture," he said, invoking the sine qua non of AIP box office.

"The house is the monster," interjected Corman. "Can't you see it? It's the house!"

Arkoff could not see it, but he approved the script. Corman then made sure that Matheson added dialogue to emphasize the house's menace: "The house lives. The house breathes." When Price was preparing, he asked Corman about it. "That line is there so we can make the picture," Corman answered. Price agreed to emphasize the line for Arkoff's sake.

Price's characterization began with two departures from his established image. He shaved off his trademark mustache, stripped the color from his hair, and then threw himself into the role, bringing an uncanny quality to the scenes in which Roderick speaks of his vulnerability to sensation. Corman was not known for helping actors find "the interpretation that sticks." Matheson recalled: "Corman was very good with pace and giving things an interesting look, but he didn't work with actors, and the actors in the Poe films were not usually very good." He was fortunate to have the skilled, deliberate Price. "Vincent would prepare," said

Corman. "He would not be making party conversation and then get up and jump into it. He would sit quietly and think about it and be ready."

Corman finished the film in fifteen days and renamed it *House of Usher*. The critics who previewed it in June 1960 were pleasantly surprised. "It is a film that should attract mature tastes as well as those who come to the cinema for sheer thrills," wrote *Variety*. "It's also a potent, rewarding attraction for children. All things considered, pro and con, the fall of the *House of Usher* seems to herald the rise of the House of AIP." The critic went on to praise Corman's collaborators, including production designer Daniel Haller and special-effects technician Pat Dinga. "Their cobweb-ridden, fungus-infected, mist-pervaded atmosphere of cadaverous gloom has been photographed with great skill by Floyd Crosby." The *Los Angeles Examiner* called *House of Usher* "a film that kids will love that never once insults adult intelligence." *House of Usher* grossed $2 million in seven months, startling Arkoff and Nicholson. "It made so much money that they couldn't believe their wallets," said Matheson. "That American International could make something that had some semblance of quality, and still make a lot of money, I don't think had ever occurred to them."

For his next film Corman went from a $270,000 budget to a $27,000 marathon. *The Little Shop of Horrors* was filmed in fewer than five days and one night because Corman gained access to sets at the Chaplin studio that were about to be torn down. Griffith was again doing double duty, as both writer and second-unit director. "Roger shot for two days on the stage," said Griffith. "I directed the exteriors, which took two days and four nights. I used skid-row bums for my crew [and as actors at ten cents a head]. We had them doing all kinds of things, shooting craps, stabbing each other, falling down." The bizarre little movie about a man-eating plant stumbled at the box office, then became a rebound hit after a screening at the Cannes Film Festival, quite a step up for AIP. "You can't say it was successful because of Roger's wonderful direction," said its star, Jonathan Haze. "If there's any one factor you can point to, I think it's that the picture is so sleazy. If it had been made by a big studio, I don't think it would have been the same."

In January 1961, with money still rolling in from *House of Usher*, Corman got Matheson to adapt Poe's *The Pit and the Pendulum* for Price. Its most famous passage read: "What boots it to tell of the long, long hours of horror more than mortal, during which I counted the rushing oscillations of the steel! Inch by inch—line by line—with a descent only appreciable at intervals that seemed ages—down it came!" Matheson's problem was that this was one of the few objective passages in the story. "*Pit and the Pendulum* was ridiculous," he said, "because we took a little short story about a guy lying on a table with that huge, razor-sharp blade swinging over him and had to make a whole movie out of it."

With a $200,000 budget and a sixteen-day schedule, the production had moments of unexpected humor. The rubberized pendulum blade swung too close to actor John Kerr and got stuck on his chest. It was replaced by a sharp metal blade that required Kerr to wear a protective steel band under his costume. Haller noticed that Kerr was perspiring under his restraints, "and no wonder. That pendu-

lum was carving a fifty-foot arc just above his body." The set piece was impressive, but nothing could upstage Price. "Vincent Price gives a characteristically rococo performance as the slightly mad Spanish aristocrat," wrote the *Hollywood Reporter*. "Price mugs, rolls his eyes continuously, and delivers his lines in such an unctuous tone that he comes near to burlesquing the role," wrote the *Los Angeles Times*. *Pit and the Pendulum* did well, both critically and financially, moving the *New York Times* to call it "Hollywood's most effective Poe-style horror flavoring to date."

AIP's next entry in what had become a Poe series was *Tales of Terror*, which Matheson based on three stories: "Morella," "The Black Cat," and "The Case of M. Valdemar." Embellishing the formula, AIP lured genre veterans Peter Lorre and Basil Rathbone to flank Price. The film also differed from *House of Usher* in that the central story of its trilogy is played for laughs by Price and Lorre, who turn a wine-tasting scene into a comic showstopper. "Comedy and terror are very closely allied," said Price. "We tried to make audiences enjoy themselves, even as they were being scared." The combination worked. "The executives at AIP had found out that the middle portion in *Tales of Terror*, which had been done for laughs, was very successful, so they decided to do a whole funny picture," said Matheson. "Anyway, I couldn't have done another serious one. It would have been more than I could stand. I had to do them for laughs by then." This time, Corman gave Matheson license to create a story from scratch using Poe's *The Raven* as a title. The only connection to the famed poem would be Price's reading of it in the film's opening scene. Using Poe as bait was a throwback to Universal's *Black Cat* and *Raven* movies; so was its casting, advertised as "The Great Triumvirate of Terror."

Joining Price and Lorre was none other than Boris Karloff, making his first feature film in five years. The part of a gracious but dangerous wizard fighting a duel of magic against Price's second-rate magician appealed to him. Lorre would be playing a ne'er-do-well whom Karloff turns into a

Vincent Price and Basil Rathbone, who had first worked together in the 1939 *Tower of London*, were reunited in Corman's Edgar Allan Poe series. Price reveled in these gruesome romps. Rathbone wished he were elsewhere. This publicity still is from the 1962 **TALES OF TERROR**.

loquacious raven. "Well, the original script of *The Raven* was supposed to have comedy overtones," said Price. "And Boris, Peter, and I got together and read through it and decided that it didn't make any sense at all. So then we all sort of dreamed up the broader laughs." They were joined on Haller's splendid sets by the voluptuous British actress Hazel Court, whose acting was a distinct improvement on Corman's usual supporting players, and by twenty-six-year-old Jack Nicholson, whose acting was not.

As usual the pace was rushed, but television had inured Karloff to speed. He was letter-perfect in his lines and ready to roll. Lorre was not. "He never quite got his lines right," said Court. "He'd just do *his* version, and the rest of us would just muddle along." Price had seen a bit of this behavior on *Tales of Terror*, but now Lorre was doing it all the time. "In one scene we had together," recalled Price, "I said, 'Shall I ever see Lenore again?' And Peter said, 'How the hell should I know? What am I? A fortune teller?'"

Corman liked Lorre's lines (and did not want to spend time on a retake), so they stayed. "Peter kept everyone on their toes, myself included," said Corman. "Peter loved to make jokes and ad-lib during the filming," said Price, who decided to play along with him. "He didn't always know the lines, but he had a basic idea what they were. He loved to invent. Improvisation was part of his training in Germany." Karloff had problems with Lorre's inventiveness. "Boris, who

was very methodical in terms of his craft, was a bit befuddled," said Corman. "Amused, but befuddled." Karloff finally gave up and joined in the ad-libbing. When Arkoff looked at the rushes, he asked, "What the devil are we breeding here?" Three troupers with more than a hundred combined years of experience were having fun, in spite of the breakneck pace and some physical problems. Matheson remembered watching Karloff "walk down these really precipitous steps in *The Raven* and he was in such pain." The shot was shortened later. "Peter Lorre was not well at all on that picture," recalled Court. "He perspired all the time, and his eyes were always teary. But nothing would hold him back. He was a wonderful pro."

Corman finished the film several days ahead of schedule. He had film left over and the sets were still standing. He had an idea. He approached Karloff and Jack Nicholson and asked them to spend three days shooting scenes for an entirely new movie. Karloff was willing to do it, but doubted that Corman was prepared. "You haven't got a story," Karloff said.

"That's all right," Corman replied. "I know exactly what I'm going to do." Two days later, Arkoff visited the set and saw Corman making an unscheduled and unbudgeted movie. He just shook his head and walked away. "I was in every shot, of course," said Karloff. "Sometimes I was walking through and then I would change my jacket and walk back." This was Corman's way of saving time and money. Actor Anthony Eisley described how Corman would "set up one camera angle on a setting that may appear in the picture five times. And then you would do all five scenes, changing your clothes between each scene. Then he'd set up the *other* camera angle, over your shoulder, and you'd do the five different scenes again, changing your clothes five times *again*." This time Corman truly needed to hurry; the sets were being dismantled. "As they were being pulled down around our eyes," said Karloff, "Roger was dashing around with me and a camera two steps ahead of the wreckers. It was really very funny." The last scene was not so funny. Corman subjected Karloff and Nicholson to a flood sequence. "He nearly killed me in it," said Karloff. "The last day he had me in a tank of cold water for about two hours." The exertion and cold combined to aggravate Karloff's emphysema and arthritis. To finish this three-day wonder, which he titled *The Terror*, Corman hired a series of young directors, including Francis Ford Coppola.

The Raven was released in January 1963. Bosley Crowther wrote that it was "strictly a picture for the kiddies and the bird-brained." If so, there were many of them. *The Raven* was more profitable than any of the previous Poe films, probably because the beloved Karloff's return to the big screen was trumpeted by every publication from *Look* to *Castle of Frankenstein*. *The Terror* came out six months later; a Nebraska exhibitor took Corman to task for "delivering the year's worst pile of garbage."

Before going to England to make more Poe films with Price, Corman had Matheson pitch a final all-star horror feature to AIP. "I had a good relationship with James Nicholson," said Matheson. "I gave him the idea about a couple of rascally undertakers who, when business was slow, went out and killed people, providing their own customers." *The Comedy of Terrors* united Price, Karloff, Lorre, and Rathbone. "I remember the first luncheon we all went out to," said Matheson. "They were looking forward to doing the picture." Before long, Price and Karloff were trying to decide what frightens people.

"Cobwebs," said Karloff.

"Oh, come on, Boris," said Price. "Cobwebs don't scare anybody."

"They scare *men*. Men *hate* cobwebs."

Price asked Corman to put a large cobweb in one of his scenes. "I walked right into it, and this thing went right across my face." Price was able to judge Karloff's idea at a preview. "The whole male audience went: 'Yeeech!'" It was this kind of creative cooperation that enlivened the film. Bothered by worsening arthritis, Karloff asked Rathbone if they could switch roles; Karloff played a slow-moving, grizzled old man and Rathbone played a spry, Shakespeare-reciting landlord. Price and Lorre were once again a serio-

Boris Karloff and Jack Nicholson spent three days with Roger Corman making a film that had no budget, no schedule, no script, and almost no sets. "I believe the funniest hour I ever spent in a projection room was watching the dailies for **THE TERROR**," Nicholson later recalled.

comic team, and Price was in his element. "Vincent liked horror," said Arkoff. "It did something for him, and that really wasn't true of the others. Boris didn't really mind it. Peter Lorre didn't really like it. To Vincent, it was like doing Shakespeare."

In that technique Price deferred to Rathbone, who was still working to pay for the extravagant parties he and his wife Ouida had thrown in their glory days. "He had been a great Shakespearean actor in the theater," said Price, "but most people thought of him as Sherlock Holmes or as a villain." Rathbone felt typecast but needed the work. When Matheson visited the set, he spent a memorable day listening to the great actor reminisce. "He told me how they spent three days filming his duel with Errol Flynn in *The Adventures of Robin Hood*," said Matheson. "Here we were doing a picture that had a ten-day shooting schedule, and he's telling me about taking three days *just* to shoot the dueling scene." Even Arkoff sensed Rathbone's contempt for low-budget films. "I always had the feeling about Basil that he would just as soon have been in a different type of picture," recalled the producer. The rushed schedule of the film was no doubt taxing for Rathbone, and more so for Karloff and the seriously ailing Lorre, who would collapse, panting, into a canvasback chair after each take. Karloff managed to keep up, but after three films with Corman he was starting to wonder why.

> James Whale was a brilliant technician with the camera and all the rest of it, just as Roger Corman is. That, I think, is Corman's strong point. But I think Whale had the advantage because he was an older, more experienced man. Whale had the background of the theater, and was more used to directing actors. Corman expects an actor to get on with it himself. . . . Vincent Price, Peter Lorre, and I had to find our own way because Corman had all he wanted. He said, "You're experienced actors. Get on with it. I've got the camera, the lighting, and my angles. I know how I'm going to put this together." And if you asked him about advice on a scene, he'd say, "That's *your* pigeon. Go on. I'm busy with this."

Corman's haste may not have hurt the performances, but it did the film. "With a two-week shooting schedule, you can't spend too much time on anything," said Matheson. "That's all the time AIP ever spent on any of those pictures. That's how they made their money."

Released in January 1964, *The Comedy of Terrors* was roundly panned. A *Los Angeles* Times critic wrote: "The undiscriminating may find this labored nonsense funny or 'scary' now and then, but I am inclined to echo one Rathbone comment as a summation of the whole situation: 'What jiggery and pokery is this?'" Critic Alton Cook wrote: "The story is one of the thinnest to ever find its way to a movie screen." *Kinematograph Weekly* wrote: "Boris Karloff as the doddering old man seems to be wasted among so much rich ham." The horror magazines were, of course, more kind, and they brought young fans to theaters, making the film another success for AIP. As dollars poured into its coffers, numerous articles honored its esteemed stars. For one of them, the honors came too late.

Peter Lorre died of a cerebral hemorrhage on March 23, 1964. Rathbone and Price continued to work for AIP, their careers energized by the Poe series. Karloff, still the King of Horror, pushed his aching bones and muscles to do the next job of acting, whatever and wherever it might be, invigorated by the love of his craft.

2001: A Space Odyssey

In the mid-1960s Hollywood looked on moviegoers as a mysterious entity, the "market." Their tastes and reactions, as Alfred Hitchcock had learned, were increasingly difficult to predict. In 1960 weekly movie attendance had been 30 million. Five years later it was down to 20 million. Before approving the next project for William Castle, Robert Aldrich, or Roger Corman, studios needed to know who comprised this market. How old were they? What did they want to see? How much did they have to spend? Producers could see, without resorting to polls, that the market was young. Crowding schools, playgrounds, parks, supermarkets, libraries, bookstores, record shops, and theater lobbies, baby boomers were everywhere. Teenagers accounted for only one-fifth of the population, but for three-quarters of the market. These capricious consumers were just as likely to stay home studying as they were to go out to a movie. They knew what they liked—or disliked—and why. College attendance, which had almost quadrupled since the end of World War II, made for a discerning audience, especially in urban centers and college towns. The San Francisco Bay Area had long been cultivating such an audience.

With a concentration of painters, sculptors, writers, photographers, poets, performers, immigrants, beatniks, homosexuals, communists, devil worshipers, and uncategorized eccentrics, San Francisco had tolerance for everything except people from Los Angeles. The legendary animosity between the two cities was fueled by San Francisco intellectuals who pointed out that, while studio vaults in Hollywood were treasure troves of vintage movies, there was no theater in Los Angeles showing them. In New York there was the Museum of Modern Art, which did collect and exhibit early films. "In those days, *The Cabinet of Dr. Caligari* was the cineaste's dream picture," recalled Orson Welles. "You saw it every time you went to New York. That and *Blood of a Poet* by Cocteau and Buñuel's *Un Chien Andalou*." These films also played art houses in major cities, but it was the Bay Area city of Berkeley that finally hosted America's first film repertory. In 1951, Edward Landberg took a big chance and opened the Cinema Guild Theatre in a Telegraph Avenue storefront. The Guild was unique. For less than a dollar, audiences could sit on folding chairs or hard benches and watch films that had not been shown in America for decades—titles like *Alexander Nevsky*, *Citizen Kane*, and *Nosferatu*. "I was essentially a movie fan turned into an exhibitor," recalled Landberg. "I was somebody running a business as an art." When packed houses began to overwhelm him, Landberg wrote to KPFA, America's first listener-sponsored radio station, asking for help.

Thirty-three-year-old Pauline Kael was a single mother with a philosophy degree from the nearby University of

California, Berkeley, and a movie reviewer on KPFA. She responded to Landberg's letter and agreed to write program notes for the Cinema Guild. Before long there was a sister theater, the Studio, and Kael was ordering films for both. "I did have a lot of fun programming things that had not played in Berkeley," said Kael. "It was an unusually cultivated audience, a remarkably bright audience." Producer Tom Luddy, at that time a UC student, went from programming films on campus to working at the Cinema Guild. "It was where a whole lot of people got their real education," Luddy recalled. "It was the first center of reflective film culture."

Kael's eclectic tastes expanded the theater's range of offerings and introduced young audiences to films that had not even been on TV yet, much less in revivals. "People were packing the Cinema Guild and Studio to see the Bogart films, the W. C. Fields films, Rogers and Astaire, long before they started attracting crowds at universities in other parts of the country," said Kael. "We were way ahead of Boston and Cambridge in film revivals." It was only a matter of time before the rest of the country caught up. New York proved a fertile ground for repertory, with the Bleecker Street Cinema, the Thalia, the New Yorker, and the Elgin. When San Francisco initiated a film festival, New York followed.

Besides reviving American films and premiering foreign films, these programs brought to prominence young directors of experimental or underground films. Artists such as Bruce Baillie, Stan Brakhage, James Broughton, Bruce Conner, Maya Deren, the Kuchar brothers, Jonas Mekas, and Andy Warhol made their films in 16mm, with loosely synchronized soundtracks, and running times of under an hour. Almost none of the films used what people expected from movies, a traditional dramatic format. There were no three acts, no beginning, middle, or end. Whether loosely structured, symbolic, or totally abstract, films such as the Kuchars' *Sins of the Fleshapoids*, Broughton's *Adventures of Jimmy*, and Conner's *Mothlight* gave adventurous audiences a taste for expanded cinema. Now lines formed not only for *The Raven* but also for underground film festivals. Universities, state colleges, and even some high schools began to teach film appreciation courses. As a result, 16mm rental companies such as Films Incorporated, which had been renting Hollywood films primarily to convalescent homes, convents, prisons, and grammar schools, suddenly had to add scores of old movies to their catalogues. It was not nostalgia that prompted the demand; it was intellectual curiosity. "Going to movies, thinking about movies, talking about movies became a passion among university students and other young people," wrote critic Susan Sontag. This, then, was the audience that Hollywood was trying—and failing—to reach.

Part of the problem was that the typical director, after working his way through the Byzantine studio system, was too old to know what young audiences wanted. A notable exception to this rule was Bronx-born Stanley Kubrick, who, at seventeen, had joined *Look* magazine in 1945 as a staff photographer and then detoured into filmmaking. Before he was thirty-five, he had already made *Spartacus* for Universal, *Lolita* for MGM, and *Dr. Strangelove* for Columbia. Industry veterans were awed by this wild-eyed young man

who knew as much (or more) than they did about cinematography and editing. "Cameras and the stories they tell have been my hobby, my life, and my work," explained Kubrick. Before the Hollywood hierarchy could declare him the latest boy wonder, Kubrick moved to England and made himself pointedly unavailable. "Stanley isn't antisocial," disclosed a friend. "It's just that he isn't interested in the swiftest route to Palm Springs or how to vacuum a swimming pool. He's really only interested in one thing—making movies."

In 1964, after his usual two years away from directing, Kubrick contemplated the next project. "I became convinced that the universe was full of intelligent life," he said, "and so it seemed time to make a film." Although he had been such a poor student that he could not get into college, Kubrick was now an enthusiastic reader. "He called up," recalled aide Roger Caras, "and told me to get copies of everything that had been written about space, and I mean everything. I did, and he read all of it." His reading included a 1950 short story, "The Sentinel," by science-fiction writer Arthur C. Clarke. Kubrick liked the first-person narrative of an American space traveler who discovers a mysterious artifact on the moon, "a glittering, roughly pyramidal structure, twice as high as a man, that was set in

the rock like a gigantic, many-faceted jewel." The narrator decides that the structure was left millions of years earlier by visitors from somewhere else in the universe. Its purpose is to alert them when earth men grow sophisticated enough for space travel, at which time they will return. The narrator ends his tale with the words: "I do not think we will have to wait for long."

In real life, outer space was on the minds of many Americans. The Soviet Union had maintained its lead since Sputnik I, putting the first man into space in 1959. The United States had caught up in 1962, when it sent astronaut John Glenn on a short trip; but by 1964, the National Aeronautics and Space Administration (NASA) had not launched a manned mission in eleven months and was spending $10 million a day to reach the moon before Russia. As might be expected, televised images of real men in space took the wind out of science fiction's sails. There had been no space film other than Byron Haskin's 1960 *Robinson Crusoe on Mars*. In April 1964, Kubrick sent word to Clarke that he would like to make the "proverbial good science-fiction movie." Kubrick maintained an apartment in New York, and, although he had a pilot's license, he refused to fly on commercial flights, so Clarke had to travel from his home in Ceylon.

"Our first meeting took place at Trader Vic's in the Plaza Hotel," recalled Clarke. "We talked for eight solid hours about science fiction, *Dr. Strangelove*, flying saucers, politics, the space program, Senator Goldwater—and, of course, the projected next movie." The professorial writer and the reclusive director hit it off, and Kubrick opened up. "He wanted to make a movie about man's relation to the universe," recalled Clarke. "He was determined to create a work of art which would arouse the emotions of wonder, awe, even, if appropriate, terror." Kubrick's previous films had been intimate epics, films of massive scope that still kept the audience in touch with the characters. He had never tried horror or science fiction. He now took a crash course from Clarke, consulting with the writer five hours a day in unlikely settings such as art galleries, restaurants, and automats. "Besides talking endlessly," said Clarke, "we had a look at the competition: *Destination Moon*, *The War of the Worlds*, *The Day the Earth Stood Still*, *The Thing*, and *Forbidden Planet*." Kubrick was not terribly impressed with any of them.

In May, Kubrick signed Clarke to cowrite a screenplay titled *Journey Beyond the Stars*, a.k.a. *How the Solar System Was Won*. Kubrick's next move was a peculiar one. He proposed that he and Clarke, instead of writing a

screenplay, cowrite the film as a novel, and then submit that outline to MGM. In late June, Kubrick set Clarke up with an electric typewriter in his Central Park West office. "After one day [there]," remembered Clarke, "I retreated to my natural environment in the Hotel Chelsea, where I could draw inspiration from the company of Arthur Miller, Allen Ginsberg, Andy Warhol, and William Burroughs." Kubrick cheered Clarke on. "What we want is a smashing theme of mythic grandeur," the director explained.

In August, NASA sent Ranger VII, an unmanned reconnaissance craft, to the moon. It crash-landed but was able to send back pictures. This upset Kubrick, who then tried to insure his production against ruination by the inevitable moon-walk pictures; Lloyd's of London turned him down. Meanwhile, Clarke was typing away in Suite 1008 of the Chelsea. On September 29, he wrote in his diary: "Dreamed that shooting had started. Lots of actors standing around, but I still didn't know the story line." On November 21, he wrote: "Getting slightly desperate now, but after six hours' discussion, Stan had a rather amusing idea. Our E. T.'s arrive on earth and teach commando tactics to our pacifistic ancestors so that they can survive and flourish." On Christmas Eve, Clarke had the satisfaction of delivering the first draft of the novel to Kubrick, who, after requesting extensive rewrites, began the screenplay.

"Science-fiction films have always meant monsters and sex," said Clarke to an interviewer, "so we have tried to find another term for our film." Kubrick explained: "For the Greeks the vast stretches of the sea must have had the same sort of mystery and remoteness that space has for our generation. About the best we've been able to come up with is a space Odyssey—comparable in some ways to the Homeric Odyssey." Their title became *2001: A Space Odyssey*. Once MGM approved the project, preparing it took seventeen months, in large part due to Kubrick's lofty standards. "I felt it was necessary to make this film in such a way that every special-effects shot in it would be completely convincing," he said, asserting that this was "something that had never been accomplished in a motion picture." MGM president Robert O'Brien would only say, "It won't be a Buck Rogers type of space epic." The executive then approved a special-effects budget of $6.5 million, allowing Kubrick to "conceive, design, and engineer completely new techniques."

To do this, Kubrick consulted experts at IBM, Kodak, DuPont, Bausch and Lomb, General Mills, and NASA, determining how the twenty-first-century world would look. NASA scientists Frederick Ordway and Harry Lange advised Kubrick on the spacecraft in the film. Kubrick's new techniques were accomplished by a special-effects team that included Wally Veevers, Douglas Trumbull, Con Pederson, and Tom Howard. Among their innovations were a forty-by-ninety-foot reflective screen used for front projection and scores of spacecraft models in different sizes. According to Trumbull: "Basic construction of models was of wood, fiberglass, Plexiglas, steel, brass, and aluminum. Fine detailing was made up of special heat-forming, plastic cladding, flexible metal foils of different textures and thicknesses, and of wire, tubing, and thousands of tiny parts carefully selected from hundreds of plastic model kits, ranging from boxcars and battleships to aircraft and Gemini spacecraft."

All this ingenuity was being marshaled by Kubrick to tell a still-unfinished story. For the purpose of launching the project, he had expounded it to MGM, but to no one else. In Part One, "The Dawn of Man," a prehistoric ape is transformed from a fearful forager into a weapon-wielding force by contact with a tall, smooth, rectangular black slab that materializes from nowhere. Four million years later, an American scientist, Dr. Heywood Floyd (William Sylvester), travels to the semicolonized moon to investigate the appearance in the crater Clavius of a monolithic black slab dubbed TMA 1 (Tycho-Magnetic Anomaly One). When he and his colleagues approach it, it emits a high-pitched signal (that may or may not kill them).

In Part Two, "Jupiter Mission, Eighteen Months Later," the spaceship Discovery heads to Jupiter on an undisclosed mission, carrying Dr. Dave Bowman (Keir Dullea), Dr. Frank Poole (Gary Lockwood), three crew members who are sleeping in hibernacula, and an omniscient, infallible computer, the HAL 9000 ("Heuristically programmed ALgorithmic computer"). Their monotonous routine is shaken up when HAL warns of the impending failure of a communication unit. When Bowman and Poole bring it into the ship and test it, all evidence points to the impossible: they are being lied to by the computer (which may or may not be acting under its own will). They conspire to disable HAL,

The space station in Kubrick's **2001** was like the rest of his new world: cold, sterile, and unwelcoming. "The most terrifying fact about the universe," said Kubrick, "is not that it is hostile but that it is indifferent; but if we can come to terms with this indifference and accept the challenges of life within the boundaries of death—however mutable man may be able to make them—our existence as a species can have genuine meaning and fulfillment. However vast the darkness, we must supply our own light."

not realizing that it is reading their lips. In short order, HAL kills Poole, kills the hibernating astronauts, and then tries to kill Bowman. The last astronaut outwits HAL and disconnects its memory. As the computer dies, Bowman finds a recording in which Dr. Floyd reveals the purpose of the mission—to find the origin of the signal received by TMA 1.

In Part Three, "Jupiter and Beyond the Infinite," Bowman pilots the Discovery toward Jupiter but, upon encountering an orbiting monolith, enters an alternate consciousness in which he sees abstract and symbolic scenes that (may or may not) represent his death and rebirth.

In December 1965, the same month that American spacecraft met and docked in space for the first time, Kubrick began shooting his unconventional film on the second-largest soundstage in Europe, Stage H at Shepperton Studios, six miles south of London. Clarke visited the set and saw his monolith realized. "TMA 1 is quite impressive," he wrote, "though someone had smeared the black finish. Stanley went on a rampage when I pointed it out to him. . . . The scene would certainly have been wrecked if naked fingerprints had appeared on the ebon surface before it had been touched by the gloved hands of the astronauts." Another imposing set was a $750,000 rotating centrifuge with a diameter of thirty-eight feet, built at the MGM-British Studios at Elstree, Borehamwood. Journalist Jeremy Bern-

stein watched Kubrick crawl around the gravity-defying set, Polaroid camera in hand, shooting photos of lighting setups. "I asked Kubrick if it was customary for movie directors to participate so actively in the photographing of a movie," wrote Bernstein. "He said succinctly that he had never watched any other movie director work."

The scene being filmed showed Lockwood jogging around the interior of the Discovery, a track that encompassed a full 360 degrees. Bernstein noted that this appeared to "defy logic as well as physics, since when he was at the top he would have needed suction cups on his feet to stay glued to the floor. I asked Kubrick how he achieved this effect and he said that he was definitely, absolutely not going to tell me." The actor was happy to be in the film. "Working with Kubrick is like working with a great military commander," Lockwood said. "He has this huge labor force working with him and he's always in control of every detail." When a Soviet air attaché visited the set, he noted details such as the realistic instruction panels (including "Zero Gravity Toilet"), then said, "You realize, of course, that all these should be in Russian."

For seventeen months of preparation, eighteen months of shooting, and a year of editing, Kubrick pushed his colleagues and himself. "Emotionally I am optimistic," he said. "Intellectually, I'm not. I do things in spite of all the things

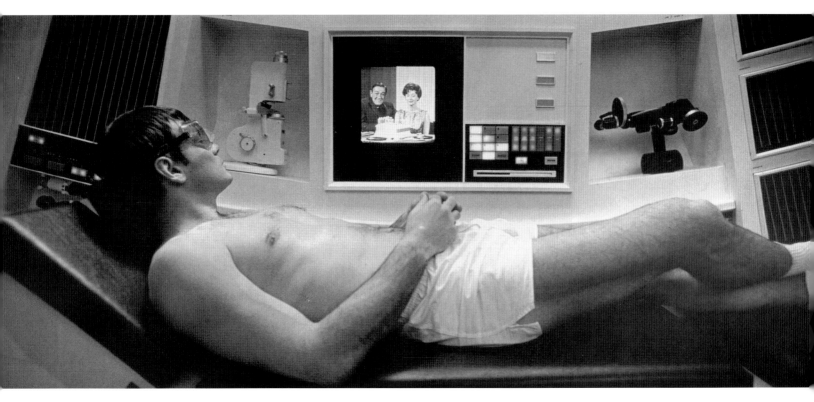

I'm intellectually aware of, such as the burden of my own mortality." Such statements provoked as much curiosity as the mammoth scale of his production and caused interviewers to vie for his almost nonexistent free time. "I don't like to talk about 2001 because it's essentially a nonverbal experience," he told *The New Yorker*. "It attempts to communicate more to the subconscious and to the feelings than it does to the intellect. I think clearly that there's a basic problem with people who are not paying attention with their eyes. They're listening. And they won't get much from listening to this film."

Kubrick's most daring innovation was to depict Bowman's very subjective "trip beyond the infinite." For this sequence, Kubrick decided to work in the tradition of experimental film, using abstract shapes and colors to convey the astronaut's progress through a corridor of light. To make these abstractions, artist Hal Naisbitt assembled a group of architectural renderings, circuit-board diagrams, moiré patterns, op-art paintings, and electron micrographs. These were then photographed on a 65mm slit-scan camera to produce the effect of pure energy roaring past the viewer.

There was one upset during postproduction. Alex North, the composer of musical scores for *A Streetcar Named Desire* and *Cleopatra*, had worked day and night for two weeks to complete forty minutes of music for the first recording session. "With the stress and strain, I came down with muscle spasms and back trouble," said North. "I had to go to the recording in an ambulance." Kubrick heard the music and made suggestions. North rewrote and then waited for eleven days for the next section to be scored. Then he received a terse message from Kubrick: no more scoring was needed. When North went to a preview screening, he saw that Kubrick had replaced his score with themes from Richard Strauss, Johann Strauss, Jr., and Aram Khatchaturian. Kubrick later claimed that North's score "was completely inadequate for the film," adding that "it's hard to find anything much better than 'The Blue Danube' for depicting grace and beauty in turning. It also gets about as

far away as you can from the cliché of space music."

The final tab for *2001: A Space Odyssey* came to $10.5 million. Before the film's press preview on April 1, 1968, Clarke made an unfortunate statement. "If you understand 2001 on the first viewing," he said, "we will have failed." According to the middle-aged audience in MGM's New York screening room, they had not failed. "Nobody slept at the New York press preview of 2001, but only because the raucous and silly noise from the soundtrack screamed painfully into our ears," wrote science-fiction author Lester del Rey. "Almost half the audience had left by intermission, and most of us who stayed did so from curiosity and to complete our reviews." Standing in the lobby during the intermission, Kubrick heard people trying to figure out what was going on. "A number of people thought Floyd went to the 'planet' Clavius," he said impatiently. "Why they think there's a planet Clavius, I'll never know. . . . They don't see he's going to the moon?" One MGM executive grabbed his hat and coat, saying over his shoulder, "I have never seen such a piece of junk in my life."

That del Rey, a respected sci-fi writer, did not understand the film was a bad sign. Granting that the "pictorial part was superb . . . and the special effects and technical tricks were the best ever done," he logged a catalogue of complaints.

> The whole affair dragged. Every trick had to be stretched interminably and then repeated over and over again. Nothing was explained or given coherent flow. . . . First we get the theme of man's humanoid ancestors being given intelligence by an alien slab only to become murderers. Next we go to the moon to find future men have dug up the same slab—excellent background but no drama—and no reason for it being there. Then we take a trip to Jupiter because—men think the slab came from there. This episode has a conflict between men and an articulate computer. It might have been good,

As he takes an ultraviolet treatment in space, astronaut Frank Poole (Gary Lockwood) pays token attention to a prerecorded birthday message from his parents. Critic Stanley Kauffmann wrote that **2001** "is so dull, it even dulls our interest in the technical ingenuity for the sake of which Kubrick has allowed it to become dull. He is so infatuated with technology—of film and of the future—that it has numbed his formerly keen feeling for attention span."

except for the lack of rationality. No motivation is provided for the computer's going mad, and the hero acts like a fool. . . . Finally, we get an endless run of obvious and empty symbols on the screen, followed by our hero in a strange room. Apparently he's undergone intergalactic transfer and now grows old and dies in the room, followed by a metaphysical symbol at the end. The alien contact we've been promised is no more than a brief shot of the slab again.

New York's most eminent critics were equally ill at ease. "The uncompromising slowness of the movie makes it hard to sit through," wrote Renata Adler in the *New York Times*. "People on all sides when I saw it were talking almost throughout the film. Very annoying. With all its attention to detail—a kind of reveling in its own I.Q.—the movie acknowledged no obligation to validate its conclusion for those (me, for example) who are not science fiction buffs." She too thought the film lost clarity by straddling both dramatic and experimental forms. "Three unreconciled plot lines—the slabs, Dullea's aging, the period bedroom—are simply left there like a Rorschach, with murky implications of theology." Writing for the *Los Angeles Times*, Charles Champlin was impressed but confused. "One can read anything or nothing into the wordless last half hour of *Space Odyssey*," he wrote. "A mirror civilization, a periodicity of the whole human experience? I don't know, and I confess to finding this evasion of a statement, this deliberate obscurantism, just that."

The New Republic's Stanley Kauffmann didn't think Kubrick's outer space was even a nice place to visit. "Space, as he shows us, is thrillingly immense," wrote Kauffmann, "but, as he also shows us, men out there are imprisoned, have less space than on earth. The largest expanse where men can look and live like men is the spaceport, which is rather like spending many billions and many years so that we can travel many miles to a celestial

Kennedy airport." Another science fiction writer felt the film's coldness. "The test of the film," wrote Ray Bradbury, "is whether or not we care when one of the astronauts dies. We do not."

Not surprisingly, journalists asked Kubrick for clarification. The unaccommodating director reluctantly agreed to an eight-hour interview with *Books* magazine and then edited it to four sentences. The only intelligible one said: "I'd rather not discuss the film." In an interview with *Action* magazine he blamed negative reviews on the advanced age of the screening audience. "I attribute the poor reaction to [this] audience and to the originality of the film," he said. "The film departs about as much as possible from the convention of the theater and the three-act play as is possible. Not many films have departed farther than that, certainly not the big films." He made it clear that he felt no obligation to explain anything. "How could we possibly appreciate the *Mona Lisa* if Leonardo had written at the bottom of the canvas: 'The lady is smiling because she is hiding a secret from her lover.' This would shackle the viewer to reality and I don't want this to happen to *2001*." Before departing for a local editing room, he fired a parting shot.

"No reviewer has ever illuminated any aspect of my work for me," said Kubrick. "A lot of critics misunderstand my films—probably everybody's films. Very few of them spend enough time thinking about them. They look at the film once, they don't really remember what they saw, and they go away and write the review in an hour." This opinion did not allow that critics were trained to analyze a film on one viewing. Even NASA's Ordway felt that the uninitiated might want to understand what they were watching. "The Dawn of Man scene should be shortened, and above all, narrated," he wrote Kubrick. "No one with whom I talked understood the meaning of this visually beautiful and deeply significant sequence." Clarke's novel, which partially explained the film's symbolism, would not be published for several months. Something had to be done. Kubrick

In **2001**, astronaut Dave Bowman (Keir Dullea) is at the controls—or is he? "To play a twenty-first-century astronaut," said Dullea, "I tried to show him as a man without emotional highs and lows—an intelligent, highly trained man, lonely and alienated, not too imaginative." An interviewer praised Kubrick's depiction of flight, then asked him why he chose not to fly. "I suppose it comes down to a rather awesome awareness of mortality," answered the forty-year-old artist, who died in his sleep thirty-three years later.

worked around the clock for several days and cut twenty minutes from the film's 161-minute running time. *2001* officially opened on April 3, advertised as "The Ultimate Trip." Splicing cement was not the only chemical that helped it find an audience.

In the nine years since the scene in *The Tingler* when Vincent Price takes lysergic acid diethylamide 25 (LSD), American youth had gone from laughing at drugs on the screen to laughing with them at home. LSD was outlawed in 1966, an index of its increasing use, but a statute could do little to slow a trend. The same cities that had been a haven for poets, beatniks, and film-loving intellectuals now hosted a counterculture of hippies. By 1967, San Francisco's Haight-Ashbury neighborhood and Berkeley's Telegraph Avenue had become the scenes of happenings and love-ins, offbeat behavior admittedly inspired by liberal helpings of mescaline, hashish, marijuana, and, of course, LSD.

While only a tiny minority of young people actually espoused the hippie lifestyle, its cultural influence was considerable. A Gallup poll reported that only twelve percent of urban adults between the ages of 21 and 29 had tried marijuana; nevertheless, a large portion of that group showed up for *2001*. The smells of patchouli oil and marijuana mingled with the aroma of buttered popcorn as long-haired fans clustered in front rows to get the maximum impact from Dave Bowman's aptly named "trip." In a Los Angeles theater, a young man walked up to the screen, crying out that he was seeing God. An interviewer asked Kubrick if he had ever taken LSD. "No," answered Kubrick. "I believe that drugs are basically of more use to the audience than to the artist."

Pauline Kael, now reviewing movies for *Harper's*, wrote: "The ponderous blurry appeal of the picture may be that it takes its stoned audience out of this world to a consoling vision of a graceful world of space, controlled by superior godlike minds, where the hero is reborn as an angelic baby. It has the dreamy somewhere-over-the-rainbow appeal of a new vision of heaven. *2001* is a celebration of cop-out." Del Rey also saw *2001* as a "head" film. "This isn't a normal science-fiction movie at all, you see. It's the first of the New Wave-Thing movies, with the usual empty symbolism. The New Thing advocates were exulting over it as a mind-blowing experience. It takes very little to blow some minds." Not every young person who saw the film was high on pot. Most of them were educated, had seen experimental films, and had read science fiction. All of them, unlike the preview audience, had been raised not on words, but on moving images, and it was to this group, the first totally film-reared generation, that Kubrick spoke. And they answered him, making the film a sudden success.

"I thought it was great!" wrote one teenager. "It's about time somebody made a film about the true science fiction of today. After a while, you get sick of seeing nothing but giant monsters from outer space." Later in the year, a graduate student wrote: "When one can sit in front of a television screen for two hours waiting for Robert Kennedy's funeral train to pass, just sit before a view of a railroad track, then one can easily give up the laws of drama which demand a beginning, middle, end, which demand concentrated conflict and action within a two-hour span, which demand that every minute be as exciting as the next." A

deeply moved fan wrote: "How can man be content to consider the trivial and mundane when you have shown him a world full of stars, a world beyond the infinite?"

After repeat viewings, some critics began to come around. "At first I thought Kubrick had flipped his lid," wrote Sam Lesner in the *Chicago Daily News*. "Now I believe he is a genius who sees with incredible clarity a vision of earth-man turning himself into a total nonentity as he pushes on and on." *The New Yorker*'s Penelope Gilliatt raved. "I think Stanley Kubrick's *2001: A Space Odyssey* is some sort of great film, and an unforgettable endeavor," she wrote. "The film is not only hideously funny—like *Dr. Strangelove*—about human speech and response at a point where they have begun to seem computerized, and where more and more people sound like recordings left on while the soul is out. It is also a uniquely poetic piece of sci-fi, made by a man who truly possesses the drives of both science and fiction." The reticent director responded: "If *2001* has stirred your emotions, your subconscious, your mythological yearnings, then it has succeeded." Arthur C. Clarke was more to the point: "As for the dwindling minority who still don't like it, that's their problem, not ours. Stanley Kubrick and I are laughing all the way to the bank." *2001: A Space Odyssey* went on to make $56,715,371.

The End of Two Eras

The revolution in motion-picture art exemplified by *2001: A Space Odyssey* was only one panel in the tumultuous tableau of the late 1960s. Across the United States, numerous confrontations between old and new were playing themselves out. President Lyndon B. Johnson had set out to correct the country's ills with his Great Society programs, but, despite the apparent gains of the Civil Rights Act, a routine traffic stop in the Watts district of Los Angeles in the hot August of 1965 ignited a riot that left thirty-four dead and four thousand arrested.

In 1966, energized by the inclusion of the word *sex* in the Civil Rights Act, a group of disenfranchised New York women founded the National Organization of Women, which was soon followed by the Chicago Women's Liberation Group. The emergence of the women's movement came on the heels of the sexual revolution, which in turn had been started in 1960 by the birth-control pill. By 1966, more than 11 million women all over the world were enjoying worry-free sex.

The sexual revolution soon reached Hollywood, where aging censors tried to control sex in films with a thirty-year-old Production Code. Predictably, their polite letters had little effect on the stream of licentiousness pouring through the office mail slot. *The Pawnbroker*, *Zorba the Greek*, and *The Knack* all flouted the Code. In May 1966, MCA head Lew Wasserman recruited White House aide Jack Valenti to head the leaderless Motion Picture Association of America (MPAA). "I did not take the job of president of the Motion Picture Association in order to preside over a feckless Code," Valenti warned Hollywood.

Within months, two intelligent, adult-themed films—*Who's Afraid of Virginia Woolf?* and *Alfie*—were proved unredeemable by the Code. *Woolf*'s director Mike Nichols spoke out against the absurdity of trying to rewrite a swinging sixties picture to fit Joe Breen's creed. "People do certain things in bed that we all know they do, and people say things to each other that we all have heard. The whole point of the sexual revolution that's happening today is to let those things take their place and then go back into proportion." Valenti wanted to both maintain the integrity of these films and serve his constituency, so in September 1966 he instituted a less stringent Production Code. It was immediately tested by a film called *Blow-Up*, which contained scenes of full-frontal nudity. The controversy that followed was only one of many in the late sixties, a time of change, dissent, and turmoil.

The counterculture had taken firm root in Los Angeles, turning Hollywood's playground, the glamorous Sunset Strip, into a hippie hangout. Replacing the Mocambo, the Trocadero, and Ciro's were rock-and-roll clubs such as Pandora's Box, Gazzari's, and the Whiskey-a-Go-Go, where miniskirted girls danced in elevated cages to live music by groups such as the Doors. In November 1966, curfew enforcement and the closing of Pandora's caused the Sunset Strip riots, which were celebrated in the 1967 Buffalo Springfield song "For What It's Worth": "Young people speaking their minds/Getting so much resistance from behind." Another 1967 hit, "San Francisco (Be Sure to Wear Some Flowers in Your Hair)," promised tourists something more stimulating than cable cars: "If you come to San Francisco/Summertime will be a love-in there." As might be expected, San Francisco saw a huge influx of young people in 1967, as 100,000 pilgrims flew, drove, and hitchhiked from all over the country to participate in the "Summer of Love."

During that same summer, 400,000 Americans were visiting Vietnam—but not as tourists. One hundred young soldiers were dying there each week in an undeclared war that was costing $25 billion a year. Leaders such as Dr. Martin Luther King Jr. and Senator Robert Kennedy criticized Johnson's policy, but the futile anticommunist war went on. Young people watching adults trying to fix a not-so-great society decided to do it themselves, and the growing antiwar movement got a sudden infusion of youth. Television stations aimed 16mm Auricon cameras at them, capturing color film of long-haired postadolescents who chanted "Hell, no! We won't go!" while being beaten by police.

In 1967, twenty percent of American households owned a color television. For the first time in history, families could eat dinner while watching fellow citizens being killed overseas and brutalized at home—all "in living color." Not even the alleged generation gap could prevent the spiritual indigestion that followed. To Hollywood, Vietnam and Watts were equally far away, but parents in the film capital had to take notice when the battle between political pragmatism and youthful idealism stopped traffic and added tear gas to summer smog. "It was like the ground was in flames and tulips were coming up at the same time," recalled producer Peter Guber. Inevitably, the studios regained their wits and responded. First came exploitation fare like American-International's *Riot on Sunset Strip* and *The Trip.* Then came three films that, with their politicized horror and their defiance of the Code, signaled the fall of censorship and the end of the traditional horror film.

The first of these films was Twentieth Century–Fox's *Planet of the Apes*, the "pet" project of a tenacious young producer who loved *King Kong.* Arthur P. Jacobs was a graduate of the University of Southern California Cinema School who became, instead of a director, a high-powered publicist for 1950s stars such as Marlene Dietrich, James Stewart, and Marilyn Monroe. After Monroe's death in 1962, Jacobs founded Apjac Productions so he could package movies for the big studios, attracting star clients to literary properties. His first was a project originally planned for Monroe, the all-star *What a Way to Go!* Like actors Rock Hudson and Roddy McDowall, Jacobs was a film collector who had regular screenings at his Beverly Hills home. Anyone who knew him was aware that his favorite film was *King Kong.* Jacobs was in a Paris literary agency in 1963 when the topic came up.

"Speaking of *King Kong,*" said an agent, after failing to sell him Françoise Sagan's latest novel, "I've got a thing here, and it's so far out I don't think you can make it." Having gotten Jacobs's attention, the agent synopsized the 1963 Pierre Boulle novel *La Planète des Singes.* In it, a space explorer leaves a war-torn Earth, hoping to find something better, and flies to the planet Betelgeuse, 300 light years away. After he lands, he is captured by the planet's denizens, intelligent apes who wear clothes and speak. The only humans on the planet live miserable lives as slaves to chimpanzees and orangutans. The explorer is at first treated as a celebrity by the apes, but, when he tries to plan his own destiny, he is sentenced to a lobotomy.

"I'll buy it," said Jacobs, without waiting to read it. He then returned to Hollywood and collaborated with J. Lee Thompson, director of *What a Way to Go!* and *Cape Fear*, on a proposal for "a rip-roaring horror story, a classic thriller utilizing the best aspects of *King Kong*, *Frankenstein*, *Dr. Jekyll and Mr. Hyde*, and other film classics." Paramount, Twentieth, and UA turned down the proposal. "It was very different from the kind of films the studios were making," recalled Thompson. "The kind of message we were getting

Mia Farrow, Sidney Blackmer, and Maurice Evans were part of the splendid ensemble gathered by William Castle and Roman Polanski for the Paramount film **ROSEMARY'S BABY**. Evans, who had shared James Whale's first stage success in the 1929 West End production of *Journey's End*, distinguished two 1968 horror hits, *Planet of the Apes* and this film.

was: 'Are you crazy? A lot of talking apes? What is this?'" Thompson gave up, but Jacobs was not easily discouraged. After the novel was published in the United States in 1964 as *Planet of the Apes*, he hired Rod Serling, writer-producer of TV's *Twilight Zone*, to adapt it. Serling had suffered anti-Semitic prejudice in college. His writing for the Golden Age of live television, in teleplays such as *Patterns* and *Requiem for a Heavyweight*, explored the theme of man's hostility to anyone who looks different, a trait incidentally observed by scientists in the great apes. Jacobs asked Serling to use *King Kong*'s structure—a long, suspenseful buildup and an hour-long chase—and paid him a handsome $125,000 for his work. It was early 1965 when Jacobs pitched Serling's *Planet of the Apes* script to Warner Bros. with the help of director Blake Edwards, only to have the studio decline what looked like a $10 million project.

At this point, Jacobs hired Mort Abrahams, producer of the TV series *The Man from U.N.C.L.E.*, to help him sell another project about animals, *Doctor Dolittle*, to Twentieth. Their frequent visits to the office of production head Richard Zanuck took on a pattern. Working as a team, they would set up Zanuck with a discussion of *Dolittle* and then switch to an *Apes* pitch. After several times, Zanuck had only to hear "*Planet of the Apes*?" to answer "No." He could not visualize Mr. and Mrs. Kong debating human rights. "There was a chance that it could be comical," he said, "that apes talking in perfect English back and forth to one another could bring the house down." After a certain point, Zanuck would not even let Jacobs start his pitch.

Jacobs was so persistent that Zanuck called Abrahams. "Mort, I have to tell you, I want to do business with you guys, but if either of you ever mentions *Planet of the Apes* to me again, that will be the end of our relationship." Jacobs was prevented from talking but not from thinking. He had sold *What a Way to Go!* and *Doctor Dolittle* by including at least one star in the package. He would use his publicist's connections to do the same for the *Apes*. After flirtations with Marlon Brando and Paul Newman, Jacobs approached Charlton Heston, the star of Cecil B. DeMille's *The Ten Commandments* and a conspicuous presence (with fellow actors Lena Horne, Sidney Poitier, and Harry Belafonte) at the historic 1963 march for civil rights in Washington, D.C. He read the script and agreed to join the project. "I smelled a hit," he later said. Joining Heston was his friend Franklin J. Schaffner, who had directed Serling's *Patterns* live on NBC in the golden days. His recent features included the powerful adaptation of Gore Vidal's *The Best Man* and Heston's hit *The War Lord*.

Another vote of confidence came from Edward G. Robinson, the formerly blacklisted star of classics such as *Little Caesar* and *Double Indemnity*, who agreed to make a screen test with Heston in March 1966. Defying Zanuck's gag rule, Jacobs told the executive about the test. Zanuck relented. He not only wanted to see it but also wanted his father, chairman of the board Darryl F. Zanuck, to see it. The doughty mogul was in New York, so Jacobs flew there with his precious test reel. "There were nine guys in that screening room," recalled Jacobs. "If any one of them laughed, we'd be dead." When Robinson, wearing orangutan whiskers and orange hair, conversed with Heston, there were no laughs. The subsequent breakthrough of another science-fiction film, *Fantastic Voyage*, sealed the deal.

In September 1966, three years after he had bought the book, Jacobs got a $5 million budget from the younger Zanuck for *Planet of the Apes*. Jacobs and Abrahams then hired formerly blacklisted screenwriter Michael Wilson to write the screenplay and John T. Kelley to polish dialogue. Both writers brought a political sensibility to the piece, making it reflect the turbulent sixties. In the final script, the Earth man is not lionized by the apes; he is hunted, trapped, studied, and declared a dangerous relic of the human species. True to Wilson's experience, the trial scenes have the bitter flavor of the HUAC hearings. Underlying the narrative is a mystery, a question that this man must answer: how and why did apes gain supremacy over humans? Jacobs and Abrahams made a pact not to speak to anyone about undertones that might not sit so well in conservative Hollywood. "We never discussed the political aspects with the studio or the actors because that would have raised an issue," said Abrahams. "If they picked it up, we would handle it, but unless they did, we weren't about to."

The challenge of designing and applying a believable makeup for an entire ape society fell to John Chambers, who had spent years making facial prosthetics for World War II veterans before designing Dr. Spock's ears for TV's *Star Trek*. Twentieth gave him a healthy $1 million budget, which meant that costs had to be cut elsewhere. Robinson, whose faith in the project had helped sell it, was the first

Charlton Heston starred in the 1968 **PLANET OF THE APES,** the "pet" project of producer Arthur Jacobs, whose favorite film was *King Kong*. Standing outside a theater where *Planet of the Apes* had played, ape actor Lou Wagner heard a five-year-old child tell his father that he was going to treat his pets better.

cost to be cut. He was asking $150,000 for his services. Apjac paid him $50,000 severance and signed Maurice Evans for $25,000. Julie Harris was hired to play the sympathetic chimpanzee Dr. Zira, but, when she saw the amount of makeup she would have to tolerate, she bolted. Jacobs replaced her with former client Kim Hunter. "He was my publicity agent when I won my Oscar [for the 1951 *A Streetcar Named Desire*]," Hunter recalled. She asked her agent how the studio planned to make actors look like apes. "Twentieth Century–Fox is a reputable firm," he said. "They'll find some way—put little bits of fur here and there."

When Hunter went to the studio for a "fitting," she was told that it was not for costumes; it was for a makeup appliance. First she had to submit to the application of a life mask. Instead of putting straws in her nostrils so she could breathe through the gooey impression, the staff put a block of wood between her teeth. The chimpanzee makeup would not have usable nasal passages, so she would have to breathe through her mouth the entire time she wore it. She began to have an inkling of why Harris had fled. A few days later, when the four-part appliance was ready, Chambers spent four and a half hours attaching it to her face. "We're either gonna be real or it's gonna be Mickey Mouse," he told her. "And we won't know until it gets on the screen."

Hunter's private preparation began with a visit to her doctor, to whom she described the claustrophobic makeup procedure. "This is going to be terrible," she told him. "I need some kind of tranquilizer for the makeup period and then I have to be as sharp as a tack once we start working." Her doctor prescribed Valium. Hunter researched her role at the Bronx Zoo, where there was one chimp in residence. "He saw me watching him and it got him very angry," she said. "I kept trying to hide. I'd get behind groups of people that came into the ape building, but he'd spot me and turn his back." Fellow ape actors Roddy McDowall and Lou Wagner had similar experiences in Los Angeles and San Diego.

Planet of the Apes started shooting in May 1967 at Lake Powell on the Arizona-Utah border in 100-degree heat. Actors in heavy costumes and crew members without shirts both began fainting, but Heston jogged two miles a day. Evans had a makeup artist remove his wig and pour water on his head. Actors were dismayed to learn at the end of a sweaty day that the makeup took one and a half hours and strong chemicals to remove. One day McDowall grew impatient, and, not wanting to wait for the artist, ripped off his makeup. An eyebrow came with it. Hunter wisely worked out an end-of-day routine with her makeup artist, Leo Lotito. "He had his Scotch," she recalled, "and I had my gin." Evans had another reaction to the makeup removal. "It takes so long to get it off that one finds oneself inhaling the fumes," he said. "You get quite a buzz." In June, the *Apes* company moved to the ape village, a futuristic set built in Malibu Canyon by art director William Creber. Now ape actors had to contend with coastal cold instead of desert heat. Meanwhile, forty-five-year-old producer Jacobs suffered a major heart attack. Fortunately for the production, he recovered quickly.

Filming took three months. It was an exercise in endurance for even the spartan Heston, who wrote in his diary: "There's hardly been a scene in this bloody film in which I've not been dragged, choked, netted, chased, doused, whipped, poked, shot, gagged, stoned, leaped on, or generally mistreated." He had survived strenuous scenes in *Ben-Hur*, but nothing had prepared him for the work allowed by the revised Code. "It's the first time I've ever done a nude scene," wrote the embarrassed actor, "even photographed from the rear." No visitors were allowed on the set, but a female crew member remarked to Heston: "Mmmm. Nice buns." When visitors were allowed on the set, Hunter found them disconcerting and rude. "They'd come up and poke our faces with their fingers," she said.

"Oh, that isn't real!" they would exclaim, pulling at the appliance. "That isn't *your* ear, is it?"

"We finally got Fox to stop bringing around visitors," she recalled. "We felt like we were in a zoo." Jacobs could not tell one ape actor from another. "Who the hell was that?" he asked Abrahams when Hunter waved at him. "You see someone in ape drag, and you don't know who the hell it is." Looking like an ape day in and day out had an unexpected effect on Hunter. While she was resting between scenes one afternoon, she fell asleep. "I had the nightmare of my life," she recalled. "I couldn't see down below, but I was sure that my legs and everything had become like an ape's! 'It's happened,' I said to myself. 'I have *become* one!'"

Heston was pleased with what he saw in the rushes. "I think we've got something more than mere entertainment here," he told the producers.

"Jesus," said Jacobs, perhaps thinking of his pact. "as long as it's not a message picture."

"We've got entertainment *and* a message in this picture," said Heston proudly, although he never did tell Jacobs what type of message he thought it was.

In January 1968, *Planet of the Apes* was ready for a sneak preview. Studio policy at that time was to preview a film at a theater that was showing a similar type of film, but not to tell the preview audience anything about the new film. Zanuck turned to Jacobs at a theater in Phoenix and said, "Arthur, I know the first fifteen minutes of the film will be fine, because it's just Heston and the crash and all of that, but let's just pray we survive the first ape exchange." The lights dimmed and the Hollywood contingent prayed. "Not until the apes started talking and the audience sat riveted and enjoyed every minute of it did we realize that it was working," recalled Zanuck. The film was released a month later. The reviews recognized what Jacobs and Abrahams had slipped past their colleagues, what was causing audiences to gasp at the film's climax. In a purely cinematic moment conceived by production artist Don Peters and refined by Edwards, Jacobs, Abrahams, et al., Heston sees the sickening evidence of what has dropped man to a level below the apes: an apocalyptic war. *Variety* wrote:

> Rather precise parallels exist in the allegorical writing to real world events over, say, the past twenty years. Suppression of dissent by means fair or foul; peremptory rejection of scientific data by maintainers of the status quo; double-standard evaluation of people and events. It's all here. Screenplay probably

could not have been filmed ten years ago, and the disturbing thought lingers that it might not be possible in another ten years, when engineered public and political opinion swings into another distorted extreme.

Most critics conceded that the film, with its startling role reversal, was exciting and convincing; many saw its deeper significance. "The film catches us in a particularly wretched moment in the course of human events," wrote Joseph Morgenstern in *Newsweek*, "when we are perfectly willing to believe that man is despicable and a great deal lower than the lower animals." Pauline Kael was full of left-winged compliments. "*Planet of the Apes* is an enormous, many-layered black joke on the hero and the audience," she wrote. "Part of the joke is the use of Charlton Heston as the hero. I don't think the movie could have been so forceful or so funny with anyone else." Zanuck later said, "We weren't trying to send a message or preach any social statement," but Schaffner admitted, "More or less it was a political film with a certain amount of Swiftian satire and perhaps science fiction last." Whatever it was, it was also one of the biggest non-roadshow successes in the history of Twentieth Century–Fox, grossing a Kong-sized $32.6 million. The film that Jacobs almost could not get made spoke the language of its time.

The second film to adapt horror to the sixties was *Rosemary's Baby*. In 1967, fifty-three-year-old William Castle's career was in a slump. He had forsaken gimmicks after *Homicidal*, thinking that his directorial skills would suffice, but after three consecutive flops—*The Night Walker*, *The Spirit Is Willing*, and *The Busy Body*—he was persona non grata at Paramount. After returning to his office at the end of a frustrating day, he saw that literary agent Marvin Birdt had left galleys of a Random House novel on his desk. Birdt soon called to push Ira Levin's *Rosemary's Baby*. "You know the bottom has fallen out of horror films," Castle groaned, pushing the novel aside. Birdt insisted that Castle read it that night. After much coaxing, Castle took it home and read it in three hours flat. His nervous system convinced him to buy it. "My face was bathed in sweat," he later wrote, "and I was shaking."

Both Castle and Birdt believed that every major studio would want this cinematically constructed thriller. *Rosemary's Baby* was the story of a young New Yorker who begins to fear that her actor husband has conspired with a coven of witches to sell her unborn child to the devil. At first glance, Castle was an unlikely target for the property. Less creative than Roger Corman but equally hasty, his directorial repertoire consisted of "wide shot-medium shot-close shot." An exercise in style was beyond him. His vulgar showmanship, however, had made him a wealthy producer, a status that even Alfred Hitchcock grudgingly acknowledged. When Birdt asked $250,000, he knew Castle was desperate to reinstate himself—and good for $200,000. Castle dickered. Birdt yawned. Castle's final offer was $150,000 in cash, plus $50,000 more if the book became a best-seller, and five percent of net profits. Birdt submitted the offer. Levin accepted. Castle had beaten all of Hollywood to the most desirable title of the year. His phone began to ring the next day.

The first person to call was Paramount's head of production, Robert Evans, for whom Castle had been losing money. Evans had, of course, heard about *Rosemary's Baby*. "I hope we'll be able to make it together," said the honey-tongued Evans. "Don't forget. You're one of the family." The next to call (three days later) was another "family member," studio manager Bernard Donnenfeld, who nervously asked if Castle could come to a meeting at four that very afternoon with the new owner of the studio, Charles Bluhdorn—the Austrian entrepreneur who had built a Michigan auto-parts business into the $2 billion Gulf & Western empire. No sooner said than done, answered Castle, and sure enough, at four o'clock sharp he was sitting across a desk from the ruthless Mr. Bluhdorn. "How much would you want for *Rosemary's Baby*, Mr. Castle?" he asked from behind his famous steel-rimmed spectacles.

"For my services as producer-director," answered Castle from behind his famous cigar, "$400,000 and sixty percent of the profits."

"You are a clown," Bluhdorn laughed without smiling. "A big, ridiculous clown. Come down, Pinocchio. I'll offer you $150,000 and thirty percent of the profits."

"No deal," said Castle, rolling the cigar from one side of his mouth to the other.

"I have another appointment," said Bluhdorn, rising. "Let's close for $200,000 and forty percent."

Castle sat tight, his teeth clenched on the cigar.

"Well, Castle? Yes or no?" Bluhdorn asked, coming around his desk. "If I walk through that door, *Rosemary's Baby* is finished at Paramount. No one—and I mean no one—will renegotiate."

"Make it . . . $250,000 and fifty percent of the profits," said Castle.

"It's a deal," said Bluhdorn, who had no intention of letting Castle direct the film. Evans had already given the galleys to Roman Polanski, the acclaimed Polish director. He, too, wanted to direct it. Evans had described Castle to Polanski as "a producer of cheap horror movies" who was not qualified to direct such an important film. Bluhdorn and Evans could apply pressure to Castle, but they thought it better to let Polanski present his own case. He met with Castle.

"I took an instant dislike to him," wrote Castle. "Dressed in the Carnaby Street fashion of the time, he seemed cocky and vain, continually glancing into the mirror in my office." Polanski proved as skillful a diplomat as he was a director. He convinced Castle that he was modest enough to work for a great showman and brilliant enough to create a hit. Enjoying the flattery but smart enough to know that he was beaten at his own game, Castle decided to take all the money for doing half the work; he agreed to let Polanski direct.

The thirty-three-year-old filmmaker had come a long way to reach the gates of Hollywood. At nine, he saw his father marched off to a concentration camp. Polanski eluded it but his mother did not; she died there. He later credited the escapism of the movies for saving his sanity. He enrolled in the Lodz film school, eventually earning critical plaudits for *Knife in the Water*, *Repulsion*, and *Cul-de-Sac*. Polanski approached *Rosemary's Baby*'s monotheistic parable as an agnostic. "I no more believed in Satan as evil incarnate than I believed in a personal god," he wrote. "The whole idea conflicted with my rational view of the world. For credibility's sake, I decided that there would have to be a loophole: the possibility that Rosemary's supernatural experiences were figments of her imagination." Figments or real, these experiences were frightening, especially the one in which Rosemary is raped by Satan. To Castle's relief, the narrative ambiguity was the only change that Polanski made in the story. Working with the single-minded young director as he wrote the script, cast the film, and collaborated with Richard Sylbert on its design, Castle grew increasingly impressed with Polanski. By the end of the first week of shooting, however, Castle was having second thoughts.

He first sensed trouble when the company began working on the sidewalk in front of the Dakota Apartments in New York. On a humid night, Rosemary (Mia Farrow) and Guy (John Cassavetes) return from a walk to find that their next-door neighbor, Terry (Angela Dorian), has jumped out the window. Castle watched Polanski spend more than an hour trying to get the consistency of blood he wanted on Dorian's inert form. "Blood is phony," he said. "Make new blood." When he got that right, he found something else wrong and fussed with that for another hour. Director Elia Kazan, who lived nearby, walked up to Castle in the wee hours of the morning. "Thought I'd watch Polanski at work," Kazan said. "He's slow, isn't he?"

"Roman will pick up speed once he gets going," said Castle while thinking to himself, I could have finished this scene in several hours. More long nights passed. Polanski fell farther behind schedule. Donnenfeld began to phone for progress reports. Entering the Dakota, actress Lauren Bacall recognized Castle and invited him in for a drink. She mentioned that Boris Karloff had lived on the top floor of the building. "You seem uptight, Bill," Bacall observed. "Relax. You'll last longer."

"We should have been out of here days ago."

"Do you know *Rosemary's Baby* is number two on the best-seller list?" asked Bacall, which only reminded Castle that he now had to pay Levin $50,000 more.

Shooting on a Paramount sound stage, Polanski still moved slowly. "Roman preferred to film long scenes in one shot, moving actors and the camera with precision," wrote Farrow. "Because of the inherent technical demands [of this method] and Roman's perfectionism, he frequently shot as many as thirty or forty takes." This technique suited veteran stage actors Ruth Gordon and Sidney Blackmer, who were playing Rosemary's nosy neighbors, but it annoyed Cassavetes, who, besides being an in-demand actor, was a more famous director than Polanski. Cassavetes was known for an entirely different approach. In 1959, Cassavetes had made the groundbreaking *Shadows*, which introduced American audiences to the French New Wave style of improvised filmmaking. The idea of doing forty takes of a scripted scene was anathema to him. "John felt that this killed all the life in a scene," said Farrow. Cassavetes also disliked Polanski's cavalier attitude toward women. Talking about his wife, actress Sharon Tate, Polanski said that long-term monogamy was impossible because sexual attraction was a short-lived thing. As Farrow recalled, Cassavetes

told Polanski that he "knew nothing about women or relationships and that he, John, was more attracted than ever to his wife, Gena Rowlands." Polanski stared blankly and said nothing.

When Polanski fell weeks behind, Evans and Donnenfeld called him on the carpet.

"Look," replied Polanski. "I've had it up to here. You want me to shoot fast? No problem. I'll shoot twenty pages of script a day from now on and bring the picture in by the end of the week. I hope you'll like it."

Evans made a tart remark to Donnenfeld and then turned to Polanski. "Roman, just go back on the set and do it your way," Evans said. "I'll take responsibility." Evans liked the rushes so far, but not only for the direction. The exec with an eye for beauty could see that Polanski was getting a great performance from Farrow, the twenty-two-year-old star of TV's nighttime soap opera *Peyton Place*. This was her first starring role in a feature film and she was in almost every scene. If her work continued to be this good, she might well become a Paramount star. She had become a household name a year earlier with a marriage to fifty-one-year-old Frank Sinatra. At the time, Sinatra's "Rat Pack" buddy Dean Martin had teased the waiflike girl. "Hey," he said. "I've got a bottle of Scotch that's older than you."

The daughter of director John Farrow and actress Maureen O'Sullivan, Farrow was an iron butterfly whose resolve had been forged by a childhood case of polio and the sudden deaths of her brother and father only a few years earlier. Week after week, Polanski watched her bounce between the make-believe world of Rosemary and the equally unreal world of a superstar known for his addictions to cards, booze, and broads. "Sinatra never disguised that his was a man's world," said Polanski. "What he liked best was man talk at the bar of his Beverly Hills home. Mia, on the other hand, was a sensitive flower child, a sucker for every conceivable cause from ecology to the rights of American Indians, and a committed opponent of the Vietnam War, which Sinatra supported." A studio crew was filming a documentary about the making of *Rosemary's Baby*. One day they shot footage of Mia Farrow painting her mobile dressing room. "Roman was humming, 'If you're going to San Francisco, be sure to wear some flowers in your hair,'" recalled Farrow, "as I painted the walls of my dressing room with rainbows, flowers, and butterflies." On its exterior, she painted "Peace" and "Love" and danced around the set to her own private music, trying to cope with an increasingly stressful life.

"One day I found myself," wrote Farrow, "tied to the four corners of a bed, ringed by chanting elderly witches . . . [A] perfect stranger with bad skin and vertical pupils was grinding away on top of me. I didn't dare think. After finishing that scene, the actor climbed off me and said politely, in all seriousness, 'Miss Farrow, I just want to say it's a real pleasure to have worked with you.'" Sinatra was also looking forward to working with Farrow. He had cast her in his new film, *The Detective*, which was already shooting in New York. "Frank was baffled and outraged by the pace of our filming," remembered Farrow. Her director appeared to be the problem. "[Sinatra] knew we were shooting slowly, with numerous takes," said Polanski, "a

process he scorned because he never did more than one or at most two." The powerful Sinatra, who was unaccus- tomed to waiting for anyone, called Castle from his loca- tion. "When is Polanski finishing with my wife? I can't get a straight answer from anybody."

"We're behind schedule, Frank, but I guess you already know that," said Castle, apologetically.

"Mia's supposed to start in my picture on Monday. Will she be finished by then?"

"No, Frank. I'm afraid that's impossible," said Castle. "Even working Saturdays, she'll be at least three weeks."

"Then I'm pulling her off your picture tomorrow."

"That'll mean shutting us down, Frank."

"Sorry to have to do that to you, Bill, but there's no other choice."

"Then Paramount will shut your picture down, too. And nothing will be gained."

"I'll have my wife with me," Sinatra said; he hung up.

Farrow confided in no one, but she appeared con- flicted. There was no word from Sinatra and she continued to report to work. One day, while setting up a party scene in which Rosemary nearly faints from pain, Polanski noticed an unfamiliar face at the edge of the kitchen set. A man carrying a brown envelope identified himself as Mickey Rudin, Sinatra's lawyer, and said he had important papers for Farrow. Polanski called a break as Farrow and Rudin repaired to her dressing room. Inside, Rudin presented the unsuspecting Farrow with divorce papers. Outside, Polanski was so busy with a rehearsal that he did not see the lawyer leave. When it was time to shoot, the assistant director reported that Farrow did not answer. Polanski hurried to her dressing room, knocked on the door, and heard nothing. "When there was no answer to my second knock, I just went in. There she was, sobbing her heart out like a two- year-old." When she could finally speak clearly enough to be understood, Farrow told him of Sinatra's "act of cruelty." Polanski reported the situation to Evans, then came back to Farrow. "Would you like to go home?" he asked her.

"No, I'll be all right," said Farrow. "Just give me another minute or two." When she returned to the set, her face registered the pain required by the scene.

The climax of the film was the scene in which Rosemary sees her baby for the first time and learns from the witches that she has given birth to the antichrist. "Satan is his father, not Guy," intones the head of the coven. "He came up from hell and begat a son of mortal woman! Hail, Satan!" By any standards, the scene was a shocking one. Having respectable-looking middle-aged people salute the devil would never have been countenanced by the Catholic- staffed Production Code Administration in the recent past. Polanski was rehearsing it with his usual thoroughness, and Cassavetes was fed up. "While mapping out the final sequence of the movie," Farrow recalled, "John became openly critical of Roman, who yelled, 'John! Shut up!' and they moved toward each other . . . It was Ruth Gordon, with consummate professionalism, who said, 'Now, come on. Let's get back to work,' and saved the day." Filming ended shortly thereafter, and Polanski hired his countryman, Christopher Komeda, to compose music for the film, including "The Lullaby of Rosemary's Baby," which was hummed by Farrow herself and released as a 45 rpm single.

Writing in the New York Times, Renata Adler, who had disliked the unresolved plot elements in 2001, warmed to the mystery of Rosemary's Baby. "It is the fantasy of the What could have happened to me while I was asleep," she wrote. "What did I do when I was drunk, How do I know I'm awake now, What if everyone is lying to me, What if I am really pregnant with—? . . . One begins to think it is the kind of thing that might really have happened to her, that a rough beast did slouch toward West 72nd Street to be born." The film had cost Paramount $3.8 million to make. The booming sales of Levin's novel were no guarantee that the film would be accepted, especially as Castle began receiving crank mail—an average of thirty letters a day. All of them had the same hateful message: "You have unleashed evil on the world. You will not live long enough to reap your rewards"; "Rosemary's Baby is filth and YOU will die as a result"; "Worshiper at the shrine of satanism. My prediction is you will slowly rot during a long and painful illness."

Rosemary's Baby was released June 12, 1968, and zoomed to number one, grossing $30 million and further inflaming fanatics. Castle tried to make light of the curses being hurled at him, but he and a number of people involved with the film were visited with freakish mishaps over the next two years.*

The nationwide turmoil in 1968 was impossible to ignore. In January, the antiwar movement reached a new pitch as North Vietnam's Tet offensive smashed hopes of a United States victory. Five hundred Americans were now dying weekly in Vietnam. In April, after calling for total with- drawal from the war, Martin Luther King Jr. was assassi- nated. Rioting broke out in numerous cities, followed by student takeovers of administration buildings at Columbia University. As college seniors all over the country donned caps and gowns, the number one hit was Simon and Gar- funkel's "Mrs. Robinson," the theme song of The Graduate, a Nichols film about an alienated college grad who sleeps with his girlfriend's mother. On June 4, peace candidate Robert Kennedy won the California Democratic primary. He was assassinated the same day. In August, as "The Lullaby of Rosemary's Baby" reached number eleven on the charts, Frank Sinatra divorced Mia Farrow, who decamped to an ashram in India to study meditation. In Chicago the same month, the Democratic Convention was marred by bloody clashes between war protesters and police.

Sitting in the quiet San Fernando Valley backyard of Peter Bogdanovich and his wife, Polly Platt, veteran director Howard Hawks commented on the student activists in Chicago. "If I was in charge," he said, "I'd arrest them all, cut their hair off. Shoot 'em!"

"You know, Howard," said Platt, "they have a point." "We have no business in Vietnam." She turned to her hus- band, expecting him to support her.

Bogdanovich, perhaps afraid of alienating the conserva- tive director, said nothing. The rationalization he later gave his wife disappointed her. "It has nothing to do with us," he said. "We're artists." This was an odd statement for a young filmmaker who that very month had an antiviolence film in theaters. Targets was significant for several reasons: (1) it was the first feature film directed by this thirty-year-old film scholar from New York; (2) it was the last major film to star Boris Karloff; and (3) it was the last film of the forty-five-year-old Hollywood horror cycle.

Like Jacobs and Polanski, Bogdanovich was a film autodidact. Starting at the age of eleven, he set out to watch and critique every movie possible. Nineteen years later, he had reviewed 5,300. The excellence of his program notes for the New Yorker Theater led to a dream assignment in Hollywood interviewing, among others, Billy Wilder, Cary Grant, and Jerry Lewis. He widened his scope, writing articles and books, all the while waiting for a chance to emulate his idols. "I watched Hawks do *El Dorado*, Hitchcock do *The Birds*," said Bogdanovich. "There weren't any film schools at that point. I learned how to direct by watching these guys." His chance came in the fall of 1967 when Corman, whom he had been assisting on *The Wild Angels*, remembered a debt. Corman checked his records and confirmed that Karloff still owed him two days of work. The eighty-year-old actor was increasingly hobbled by arthritis but was still managing to work on films with titles like *Mad Monster Party?* and *The Sorcerers*. Corman called Bogdanovich to his office and asked him: "Do you want to direct your own picture?"

"Are you kidding?"

Corman was not kidding; he was adding. "We have two days of Karloff's time and that's all. That's twenty minutes on the screen. We shot about twenty minutes of film we didn't use in *The Terror*. We can use that. That's forty minutes of Karloff. All you have to do is take a couple other actors, write a story around them, fill up the rest of the time, and we've got a picture."

Bogdanovich was thrilled. Boris Karloff!

"You know how Hawks shoots, don't you?" asked Corman, not waiting for a reply. "Doesn't plan anything. Rewrites on the set. You know how Hitchcock shoots, don't you? Plans every shot. Totally prepared."

"Right."

"Well, on this picture," said Corman, "I want you to be Hitchcock."

Boris Karloff! And all Bogdanovich had to do was come up with a story. Sitting in their home on Saticoy Street in Van Nuys, brainstorming, he and Platt thought of an August 1966 incident in Austin, Texas. Charles Whitman, a twenty-five-year-old architectural engineering student, had coldly shot his wife and mother and then climbed to the top of the University of Texas tower and fired on dozens of unsuspecting people below. Fourteen people died as a result of his ninety-six-minute spree, which ended when two policemen and one civilian stormed the observation deck and killed him. Bogdanovich and Platt considered balancing the topicality of modern horror with the dignity of traditional horror. "We started thinking about how real horror is the kind of random violence that the Whitman incident symbolized," recalled Bogdanovich. "The kind of Victorian horror that Boris represented really wasn't so horrible any more, and, in fact, it was cozy compared to the mindlessness of the Whitman incident." Their script, *Targets*, juxtaposed the stories of Bobby Thompson, a clean-cut young man who is turning into a sniper, and Byron Orlok, an aged horror star who is making his last public appearance. Their stories converge when Thompson chooses Orlok for his ultimate target. Bogdanovich showed the script to directors Orson

Welles and Samuel Fuller. Fuller could not see why Orlok should die so early in the story. Ten more minutes of Karloff on the screen was worth a dozen plot points.

"I've only got him for two days," explained Bogdanovich.

"Never worry about that!" said Fuller. "Write it the way you want it and worry how you're going to do it later."

Bogdanovich called Karloff in London. Yes, Karloff had read the script, but he had a question. "Since this character is very much like me, do I have to say such terrible things about myself?" The script had Orlok saying, "I know how people think of me these days. Old-fashioned. Outmoded . . . Oh, it's not that the films have got bad. *I've* got bad. I couldn't even play a straight part decently any more. I've been into the other thing too long." This was hardly how Karloff thought of himself. "I've never really *wanted* to break out of the roles I play in the cinema," he clarified.

"My feeling, Boris," Bogdanovich said earnestly into the receiver, "is that the more terrible things you say about yourself, the more the audience will say, 'No, it's not true. We don't agree.'"

"Well, I hope so," came the genial reply. "They might just agree!"

Karloff flew into town in December and met Bogdanovich and Platt for dinner. The young director, having hobnobbed with Hawks's car-and-bar crowd, was a little taken aback by the stooped octogenarian who had to use a cane to stand up and introduce himself. "He didn't look like an actor," recalled Bogdanovich. "He looked more like an aging professor of something esoteric, like coins or archeology." Karloff immediately put Bogdanovich at ease.

"You have written the truest line I've ever read in a script," he said, smiling.

"That's quite a compliment," said Bogdanovich. "What was that?"

"Where old Orlok says, 'God, what an ugly town this has become.'" Everyone laughed, but Karloff sobered them with another observation. "I believe in this picture, but you can't do it in two days."

"Nobody else is going to come up with more salary for you," said Bogdanovich, referring to the parsimonious Corman. "I'll find it myself."

Karloff told him to spend his time directing, not looking for angels. "Take as long as you like," he told him. This was a brave declaration from a person in failing health. Even at his most sanguine, Karloff admitted his limitations, which included worsening emphysema. "I suffer from shortness of breath, thanks to sunny, smoggy California," said Karloff. "I can't breathe and I can't walk. I've got this arthritic knee. Must have been the result of carrying too many bodies up stairs." As filming began, Bogdanovich and Platt could see that Karloff was not just slowed; he was crippled. "It was extremely difficult for him to move about or speak," recalled Bogdanovich, "but he never complained, was always prepared, and never held up shooting." Karloff was more than financially secure. Why was he subjecting himself to this? "I'm one of that small, lucky band of people who does what he loves," Karloff told an interviewer. "And so long as people put up with me, I'll work. I used to garden, but because of my leg, I can't bend any more. I used to play games, but *they've* given me up. So, you see, if I didn't work, I'd just sit here and grunt."

The greatest star of Hollywood's Golden Age of horror found a fitting swan song in Peter Bogdanovich's 1968 film **TARGETS**. In this scene, improvised by Boris Karloff, an elderly horror star is momentarily spooked by his own reflection. Within months of the film's August release, both Hollywood's Production Code and Karloff would be gone, ending the eras of rigid censorship and classic horror.

Karloff's generosity was tested not only by additional days of shooting but also by longer, later hours. Bogdanovich had the use of the Reseda Drive-In as a location for only one night and he had to get all the shots that included his ailing star that night. One o'clock arrived and he had not yet finished. The winter air was chilly, and Karloff's one functioning lung was complaining. Bogdanovich appealed to him. "This is our only chance," he said. "We can't afford to come back with you."

"All right," said Karloff. "We'll do it. But it's only for you. It's not for Roger Corman."

Karloff's commitment to the project was in part due to his dismay at the current epidemic of shootings. "It's a very timely movie," he told an interviewer. "The violence in this country is just appalling." Statistics showed that battle deaths in Vietnam (14,592) were exceeded by the inordinately high number of domestic homicides that year

(14,686). The interviewer noted: "The paper that very day reported sniping on the freeway."

One of the most effective scenes in the film was captured on another late night. In the scene, set in a hotel room designed by Platt, Orlok tries to come up with a suitable speech for his farewell appearance at the suburban drive-in, then settles for the fable about death from John O'Hara's *Appointment in Samarra*. By the time cinematographer Laszlo Kovacs had lit the scene, it was past midnight. Because Karloff looked tired, Bogdanovich assumed that he would want to use cue cards to film the two-page speech. "You mean *idiot* cards," said Karloff. "No. I want to do this without a script." Seated at the end of a long table, Karloff sailed through the rehearsal without missing a word; indeed, he made the one word *Samarra* sound like three. After seeing this, Bogdanovich decided to change his setup. "Stay on him," he told Kovacs. "Start with a long

shot. We'll sneak the table away as you dolly in." As the camera crept respectfully toward him, Karloff did the speech in one take, investing each phrase, each word, each syllable with the color, texture, and meaning that only a seasoned artist could know. "Spontaneous applause broke out," recalled Bogdanovich, "which you could see moved him."

What was perhaps the film's most memorable shot of the legendary actor was made at his own suggestion. The script called for the young director, Sammy (played by the young director, Peter), to wake up with a hangover on the hotel bed next to the equally hungover Orlok, then look at the famed bogeyman and let out a yelp. Karloff thought it needed another comic bit to balance it. He got up unsteadily from the bed and passed a large mirror. "Well, I could see myself in the mirror and do a little 'take,'" Karloff suggested. Bogdanovich filmed Karloff giving himself a start when he encounters his disheveled reflection in the blue morning light. Is it because he looks scary? Because he is hungover? Because he is old and running out of time? Karloff's many-layered performance touched on all these questions, answering them with the humanness found in most of his work. The gently self-mocking moment was a master's touch. Karloff completed his scenes in five days and returned to his beloved London.

Targets was finished in early 1968, but the political climate made it difficult for Bogdanovich to sell it to a distributor. Someone at Paramount came up with the idea of advertising it as gun-control propaganda. With this idea in mind, the studio bought the negative from Corman, but, due to the rash of assassinations in the spring, made only eight prints. Karloff's last film to be released by a major studio was not widely seen when it opened that August, but reviewers found it praiseworthy, both for Bogdanovich's direction and for Karloff's performance. Within weeks of its release, the Motion Picture Association of America (MPAA) began dismantling the Production Code. Karloff's swan song had come just in time.

"You know, I don't think horror films are as good as they used to be," he said in one of his last interviews. "There's a tendency to go in for shock for shock's sake and that really doesn't work. Anybody can show you a pail full of innards but you've got to have a reason. . . . But I suppose films in general are more violent. Even so, I don't really think they have that much effect on what people do. They're a reflection, not a cause, of the horror we're surrounded with. What film could match the headlines we read every day?"

Karloff, now eighty-one, confined to a wheelchair and dependent on an oxygen tank, made token appearances in a few grade-Z horror films. These exertions put him in a hospital. Trying to honor one last commitment, he recorded narration for a *Reader's Digest* album from his hospital bed, at one point remarking to his wife, "God, I'm lucky—doing what I want—even now." Karloff died on February 2, 1969.

In a 1926 film called *The Bells*, Karloff had essayed a supporting role copied from *The Cabinet of Dr. Caligari*. Playing a carnival mesmerist, he wore a cape, hat, and spectacles like those Werner Krauss had worn seven years earlier, at the dawn of the horror era. With Karloff's death, Hollywood lost its most visible link with the beginnings of the horror film, a performer whose career spanned all the permutations the genre had undergone since the days of Irving Thalberg, Lon Chaney, and Bela Lugosi.

Epilogue: Rated "Ick!"

Hollywood, with its frantic need to ballyhoo the newest thing, has never shown much respect for the past. Old stars, old movies, and old buildings are routinely pushed out of the way to make room for what is new, *new*, NEW! Occasionally old things are sacked for the sake of survival, as in the case of Twentieth Century–Fox. In the early 1960s, diminished revenues could no longer support two lush but languishing back lots, the legacy of the long-extinct Fox Film Corporation; and Darryl Zanuck decided to sell them. Their purchaser, Alcoa, was still bulldozing more than 150 acres of picturesque landscape and historic sets when Zanuck upended the main lot and shook two thousand studio employees onto the street. Billy Wilder sent him a cable chastising him for his "brutal and callous dismissal" of veterans such as Charles Brackett, Wilder's former writing partner. "No self-respecting picture maker would ever want to work for Twentieth," the director wrote Zanuck. "The sooner the bulldozers raze the studio, the better it will be for the industry." Brutality, novelty, and survival were all issues in the fall of 1968, when Hollywood decided to raze another landmark.

Since Jack Valenti's revision of the Production Code in 1966, films had grown more violent, more sexual, and less formulaic. The Code, even in its relaxed version, could not delineate between a story that used sex to enlighten its viewers and one that used sex to titillate them, and the industry, afraid that rating films would scare away audiences, continued to bow to this archaic, inflexible document. The purpose of the original Code had been to protect impressionable young minds. According to a 1958 article in *Cue* magazine, it had saved youth from Brigitte Bardot's breasts only to abandon them to a teenage Frankenstein's pectorals. "One person in every ten, according to statisticians, is emotionally disturbed. The percentage of children so affected is increasing, and it is not unlikely that these film horrors—growing week by week and battening on the pennies of thrill-hungry kids—are doing their fair share to promote this unhappy condition." Pauline Kael did not think that young filmgoers were disturbed—just disturbing. "Have the reviewers looked at the schoolgirls of America lately?" she asked. "The classmates of my fourteen-year-old daughter are not merely nubile. Some of them look badly used." Writing in the *Saturday Review*, critic Arthur Knight decried the abundance of trashy monster movies. His solution would be the same as that proposed by Jack L. Warner in the panicked spring of 1934, when everyone was casting about for alternatives to censorship. "In England," wrote Knight, "where films are not censored but *rated* as to their suitability for various age groups, these pictures invariably receive an X—suitable for adults only. Such a scheme, rigidly enforced over here, would soon see the disappearance of blobs, monsters, and ghouls from Hollywood's production schedules."

Ten years later, after political and social upheaval and numerous funerals, Hollywood censor Jack Vizzard asked:

"Are we really that corrupt, that we should leave our houses and go down to a theater and be entertained by all that flowing of blood?" The box-office receipts of *Point Blank*, *The Dirty Dozen*, and a few lesser efforts gave an unnerving affirmative. Unlike violence, though, increased sexual content was not limited to several conspicuous films. Sex, as the saying goes, was here to stay. "Last year we gave you the dirty words," said Bob Hope at the 1968 Academy Awards. "This year we give you the pictures to go with them." Warner agreed: "The studios now have clean toilets and dirty pictures." Valenti saw that it was too late to turn the tide. Perhaps there was time to post tide warnings.

Warner's idea of a ratings system had been to classify films A for adults and F for family. The 1958 horror boom had led some politicians to call for age classification, but the studios had successfully lobbied against it, and again in 1962 and 1963. By early 1968, such a system appeared to be the only solution. Valenti announced that, as of November 1, a "ratings system" would take effect. The system would function with four classifications. G meant that the film's content was suitable for general audiences. M meant the film contained mature material for which parental discretion was advised. R meant that no one under sixteen would be admitted unless accompanied by an adult. X meant that no one under sixteen would be admitted. Last but not least, the new office of Code and Rating Administration (CARA) meant that the Production Code Administration was no more. After thirty-four years and four months, Joseph I. Breen's Production Code was going to the big file cabinet in the sky.

How would this affect horror films? The answer was simple. Horror films in the tradition of the Gothic castle, the exotic jungle, the Art Deco laboratory, the old dark house, and the flying saucer were no more. They had all frightened audiences by transporting them to an alien world and then revealing a monster that shared some of their own problems. Their effectiveness came not from what they showed, but from what they did not show. Robert Wise, whose 1963 *The Haunting* was a terrifying film that never revealed its monster, had learned his trade from Val Lewton. "Val always said that the greatest fear that people have is of the unknown," Wise recalled. By the 1970s, the horror of mystery and restraint was as long gone as the Fox Film lot at Sunset and Western. The frightening, unseen Thing that used to lurk behind a shadowy, cobwebbed black-and-white door was now sitting in your lap, naked and in bloody color.

A month after the ratings system went into effect, a Chicago film critic was so alarmed by a new horror film that he wrote an editorial about it. Roger Ebert's article "Just Another Horror Movie—Or Is It?" ran in the *Chicago Sun-Times* on January 6, 1969. No less a cultural arbiter than *Reader's Digest* chose to reprint it a few months later. Ebert began:

> It was a typical Saturday matinee in a typical neighborhood theater. There were a few parents, but mostly just the kids—dumped in front of the theater for a movie titled *Night of the Living Dead*. There was a cheer when the lights went down. The open-

ing scene was in a cemetery (lots of delighted shrieks from the kids), where a teenage couple are placing a wreath on a grave. Suddenly a ghoul—looking suitably decayed and walking in the official ghoul shuffle—attacks. The boy is killed, and the girl flees to a nearby farmhouse. (More screams from the kids. Screaming is part of the fun, you'll remember.)

The film was in black and white, an oddity for 1968. For the past three years, only a handful of Hollywood producers could get financing for a black-and-white feature. With the exception of *Morituri*, *Who's Afraid of Virginia Woolf?*, and *In Cold Blood*, every major studio release since 1965 had been in color. Kids usually groaned if the studio logo was not in color: "Black and white! Boo!" The lack of color made *Night of the Living Dead* look like the documentaries for which students tried to stay awake in darkened classrooms after lunch. However, they had no trouble staying awake after an onscreen TV announcer said: "It has been established that persons who have recently died have been returning to life and committing acts of murder. A wide investigation of reports from funeral homes, morgues and hospitals has concluded that the unburied dead are coming back to life and seeking human victims."

Night of the Living Dead, observed Ebert, even as it introduced a staggering, silent army of dead folks intent on eating the flesh of seven people holed up in an old house, was just another horror movie. It was a little scary, a little corny, and, except for a black hero named Ben (Duane Jones), referred to by Ebert as "the Negro," it was fairly predictable. It even had comic relief. A local TV reporter (Bill Cardille) asks a sheriff (George Kosana) how the search-and-destroy effort is going. It turns out that the living dead can be stopped by a bullet in the head.

"Are they slow-moving, Chief?" asks the reporter.

"Yeah," replies the deadpan sheriff, who then says with impeccable comic timing, "They're dead . . . they're . . . all messed up."

After this lighthearted interlude, the film takes a sudden, gut-twisting turn. Two high school sweethearts go for help in a pickup truck as Ben holds off the living dead with a gasoline-fueled torch. At the moment when any other film would have the teens roar off into the night, the torch accidentally sets the truck on fire. It explodes with the couple inside. The living dead back off. "Now the mood of the audience changed," wrote Ebert. "There wasn't a lot of screaming any more. The place was pretty quiet."

It was not bad enough that the would-be heroes had to die. The audience now got another unprecedented shock. "The fire dies down and the ghouls rip apart the bodies," Ebert continued. "One eats with relish a nice mess of intestines. Others devour flesh, dripping blood, off bones." Before the film ends, other revolting images include Ben killing an intractable compatriot; the compatriot's young daughter coming back from the dead, eating her father, and stabbing her mother in the chest repeatedly with a trowel; and the abduction of the girl who has survived since the film's opening by her living-dead brother. Nothing, however, prepared the audience for the moment in which the resourceful, heroic Ben is mistaken for one of the living

dead and shot through the forehead by the sheriff's best marksman.

"The kids in the audience were stunned," wrote Ebert. "There was almost complete silence. A little girl across the aisle from me, maybe nine years old, was sitting very still in her seat and crying . . . I don't think the younger kids really knew what hit them. They'd seen horror movies before, but this was something else. This was ghouls eating people—you could actually see what they were eating." Ebert explained that the film had no R rating to alert parents. The new system was of no use if a distributor, in this case the Walter Reade Organization, was not an MPAA signatory and did not submit its films to CARA for rating. He concluded the article by asking: "But what are parents thinking when they dump their kids off to see a film titled *Night of the Living Dead*?"

Parents who had to get out of bed to comfort a child in the throes of a nightmare may have wondered just who made this mean-spirited, offensive little movie. *Night of the Living Dead* was shot on weekends for seven months in 1967 by a group of industrial filmmakers in Evans City, Pennsylvania. Working with a budget of $114,000, a cast and crew of volunteers, and lots of Bosco chocolate syrup and mortician's wax, twenty-seven-year-old director George A. Romero enjoyed a freedom that no Hollywood horror director had ever known, thanks to the new system.

"There was no MPAA censor's office or local censor board any more," recalled Romero, "so you didn't have that panel of experts that were issuing dictates and reviewing films, saying, You can leave this in, but you have to take that out. But there *was* this unwritten law which said you had to be polite and just show the shadow and not show the knife entering flesh." Romero was not interested in becoming a test case but he saw no reason to observe the conventions of a moribund studio system. *Night of the Living Dead* broke all the unwritten laws. "I think it just came from the anger of the times," he said. "This was 1967 and nobody was in a very gleeful mood about the way the world was going." Beyond acknowledging the societal malaise, he got a perverse payoff from doing something bad. "I just wanted to make it as gross as I could," admitted Romero.

Once the film was finished, he had an understandably hard time finding a distributor. Companies strongly suggested that Romero delete graphic violence and shoot a happy ending. Romero refused, and he finally found a company that would release the film uncensored. Thanks to Ebert and the *Reader's Digest*, the film became a $12 million success, intestines and all. The new era of horror had begun.

Seven years earlier, Boris Karloff had run into Robert Bloch at a party given by producer William Frye. Bloch was

People from all walks of life came to Evans City, Pennsylvania, to be made up with mortician's wax and play hungry ghouls in George Romero's decidedly independent film **NIGHT OF THE LIVING DEAD**.

writing scripts for Karloff's show *Thriller*. The subject turned to Bloch's *Psycho* and then to increasingly bloody imitations such as *Homicidal*. Karloff grew thoughtful and leaned toward Bloch.

> Think about it for a moment. There's nothing pleasant, nothing appealing about the word *horror*. It doesn't promise entertainment. You and I, each in his own way, have devoted a career to providing chills, shocks, shudders. But we've done so only to amuse, to fulfill the same function as the time-honored teller of ghost stories who offers a few cold shivers to his audience in front of a warm fireplace on a winter's evening. No harm in that surely. But I'll be blasted if either of us ever deliberately set out to horrify anyone. All this violence and brutality today, shown against a "realistic" background—now *that's* downright horrible!

For forty-five years, the horror film was the escape valve of the American psyche. No matter what was happening in the world outside the picture palace, the moviegoer could snuggle into a theater seat and travel to a place where screaming felt good. After the film, there was the reward of returning to reality without having had one's values threatened or stomach turned. Highbrow critics called it catharsis. In 1968, with no Code as a filter, the psychological escape

valve got clogged with blood. From then on, the horror film, oozing gore from every sprocket hole, was something different. It was, of course, born of a different world than the classic horror film, and every other genre had changed too. But horror itself was not the same. It could not be. Improved technology and artistic freedom mandated something new. Thus the new generation of horror directors created a new type of film. As in the past, there were hits, flops, junk, and masterpieces: *Dawn of the Dead*, *Magic*, *Carrie*, *The Exorcist*, *The Stepford Wives*, *Jaws*, *Alien*, *Friday the 13th*, and *Halloween*. Yet many viewers looked backward, longing for cobwebs, bats, and saucers. The cozy quality noted by Peter Bogdanovich was missing. The mystery, the elegance, the otherworldliness were gone, perhaps forever. Or were they?

Happily, the classic horror films have proven to be as undead as some of their characters. At a robust eighty years of age, the genre has survived the passage of time and vagaries of taste, just as cellulose nitrate film stock has endured changes in humidity, temperature, and studio politics. The legendary stage performances of Bela Lugosi as Dracula flitted into the ether when the last person who could remember them died, but the impressions Lugosi made in nitrate have outlived most of the people who first saw them. Alfred Hitchcock once predicted that his work would not outlast him. "A hundred years from now," he said, "it'll all have turned to cornflakes in the can." Fortunately

Bill Heinzman, Russell Streiner, and a blurred Judith O'Dea usher in the new age of screen horror in the 1968 film **NIGHT OF THE LIVING DEAD**.

for future audiences, he may have been wrong. *King Kong*, about which I was writing on March 24, 2003, the seventieth anniversary of its Hollywood premiere, is being transferred to yet another electronic medium. There is cause for optimism. The Eighth Wonder of the World will continue to thrill as long as there exists one DVD, one videotape, or one 1956 TV print of *King Kong*. A creature that was never really born may prove to be immortal, thanks to the Hollywood horror film.

Notes to the Text

Preface
7   (caption) *As in every other . . .* Price, *Vincent Price*, 179.
9   *Don't step on . . .* Blake, *Lon Chaney*, 85.
10   *It's murderous, hideous . . .* Ibid., 119.

Chapter 1: Silent Prototypes

The Monster Born and Bred
13   *soft-eyed, skimpy . . .* Hecht, *Charlie*, 171.
    He lived two-thirds . . . Gabler, *An Empire of Their Own*, 218.
    When Thalberg saw . . . Amory and Bradlee, *Cavalcade of the 1920s and 1930s*, 129.
    (caption) *In The Phantom . . .* MacQueen, "*Phantom of the Opera* – Part II," 35.
    (caption) *some of the . . .* Unsourced clipping, *The Sorrows of Satan* file, Margaret Herrick Library, Center for Motion Picture Study, Academy of Motion Picture Arts and Sciences, Beverly Hills (hereinafter CMPS).
14   *When a make-up . . .* Blake, *Lon Chaney*, 110.
    The mystery angle . . . MacQueen, "The 1926 *Phantom of the Opera*," 35.
    The romance needs . . . Ibid.
    a perfect role . . . Blake, *Lon Chaney*, 135.
    If we do . . . Ibid.
    He was extremely . . . MacQueen, "The 1926 *Phantom of the Opera*," 36.
15   *His nose is . . .* Ibid., 133.
    It's an art . . . MacQueen, "*Phantom of the Opera* – Part II," 35.
    He suffered . . . Ibid., 35.
    I remember seeing . . . Blake, *A Thousand Faces*, 158.
16   *The entire audience . . .* Blake, *Lon Chaney*, 140.
    The kick of . . . Ibid., 138.
    There's too much . . . MacQueen, "*Phantom of the Opera* – Part II," 39.
    Lon Chaney stands . . . Kinnard, *Horror in Silent Films*, 181.

The German Influence
16   *We say no . . .* Spoto, *Lenya*, 39.
    There was a . . . Ibid., 37.
    (caption) *The scenes in the . . .* Battle, "Journey's End?," 52.
17   *dynamic synthesis . . .* Clarens, *An Illustrated History of Horror and Science Fiction Films*, 14.
    The film image must . . . Kracauer, *From Caligari to Hitler*, 35.
    a revelation of . . . Ibid., 17.
18   *horror tale of the . . .* Clarens, *An Illustrated History of Horror and Science Fiction Films*, 31.
    Nothing of the sort . . . Kinnard, *Horror in Silent Films*, 192.
    But it's Griffith . . . Unsourced clipping, *The Sorrows of Satan* file, CMPS.
19   *Few pictures have . . .* Thompson, *Between Action and Cut*, 124.
    If one can . . . Fragmentary clipping, *Los Angeles Examiner*, October 23, 1927, *The Cat and the Canary* file, CMPS.
    Mr. Leni has . . . Kinnard, *Horror in Silent Films*, 200.
    May McAvoy's voice. . . *The Shattered Silents*, 87.
    (caption) *Given the quiet . . .* "Filming at Night."
20   *interminable twaddle . . .* Agate, *Around Cinemas*, 30.
    *Unless otherwise noted, quotations from intertitles or dialogue have been transcribed from VHS tapes provided by the respective copyright holders of the films cited.
22   (caption) *I have tried to . . .* Unsourced clipping, *The Man Who Laughs* file, CMPS.

Lon Chaney and Tod Browning
22   *I like to . . .* "Tod Browning, Chaney Director, Discusses Career."
    Never having been . . . Ibid.
    about fifty . . . Maas, *The Shocking Miss Pilgrim*, 62.
    sordid and morbid . . . Skal and Savada, *Dark Carnival*, 294.

23   *He was armless . . .* Crawford, *A Portrait of Joan*, 30.
    Lon, don't you . . . Skal and Savada, *Dark Carnival*, 112.
    He kept . . . Ibid.
    Every time Browning . . . Kinnard, *Horror in Silent Films*, 211.
    The case of . . . Skal, *The Monster Show*, 72.
    One can imagine . . . "The Unknown."
    Lon Chaney's concentration . . . Crawford, *A Portrait of Joan*, 30.
    a commotion on . . . "The Lon Chaney I Knew," 60.
    (caption) *When we're getting . . .* Dickey, "A Maker of Mystery."
24   *If you let . . .* Paris, *Garbo*, 93.
    I have never . . . "Discoveries About Myself," 106.
    He's six feet two . . . "The True Life Story of Lon Chaney."
    From his slobbering . . . Riley, *London After Midnight*, 34.
    Chaney wanted to . . . Skal and Savada, *Dark Carnival*, 117.
    (caption) *This time his deformity . . .* Blake, *Lon Chaney*, 153.
25   *I don't feel . . .* Stine, *The Hurrell Style*, 15.
    Great not only . . . Thomas, "A Gallery of Grotesques."
    (caption) *An Outpouring . . .* "An Outpouring of the Cesspools of Hollywood," 1.
26   (caption) *I don't want to . . .* Nelson, "Chaney Comes Back," 33.
    (caption) *I'd worked with . . .* MacQueen, "The 1926 *Phantom of the Opera*," 36.

Chapter 2: The Horror Film

Tod Browning's *Dracula*
29   *Beautiful women with . . .* Riley, *Dracula*, 30.
    When I was . . . Hall, "The Feminine Love of Horror."
30   *I think sound . . .* Tazelaar, "Director of Chaney Prefers Lighter Side of Murder."
    I used to love . . . Bowman, "The Strange Odyssey of Helen Chandler," 70.
    The director does . . . Ibid.
    It's one of . . . Skal and Savada, *Dark Carnival*, 139.
    (caption) *Some day this . . .* Mank, *Dwight Frye's Last Laugh*, 58.
31   *At your request . . .* Schatz, *The Genius of the System*, 89.
    in [the] face of . . . Skal, *Hollywood Gothic*, 107.
    De Bram Stoker . . . Cremer, *The Man Behind the Cape*, 115.
32   *As he told me . . .* Ibid., 118.
    I didn't even . . . "Carla Laemmle," 82.
33   *He was mysterious . . .* Skal, *Hollywood Gothic*, 132.
    After I had been . . . *Dracula* press book.
    (caption) *The cat has . . .* Mank, *Dwight Frye's Last Laugh*, 99.
35   *this man was . . .* Skal, *The Monster Show*, 120.
    Tod Browning has . . . "At Last a Screen Actor . . ."
    The studios were . . . Ibid., 131.
    Tod Browning was . . . Skal, *Hollywood Gothic*, 130.
    I hope never . . . Ibid., 132.
    Ninety per cent of . . . *Dracula* press book.
    Lugosi outdoes any . . . Weight, "Dracula."
    Had the rest of . . . Ibid.
    I always dreamed . . . Riley, *Dracula*, 7.
    With Dracula making . . . "U Has Horror Cycle All to Self."
    As a result of . . . Turner, *The Cinema of Adventure, Romance, and Horror* [hereinafter *The Cinema of Adventure*], 87.
    (caption) *An evil expression . . .* Gifford, *A Pictorial History of Horror Movies*, 82.

James Whale's *Frankenstein*
36   *One day after work . . .* Underwood, *Karloff*, 42.
    I saw—with shut . . . Ibid., 59.
    I don't believe in . . . Curtis, *James Whale*, 127.
    Junior listened impatiently . . . Riley, *Frankenstein*, 22.

    (caption) *At forty-two . . .* Karloff, "Memoirs of a Monster," 78.
37   *His head was . . .* Gatiss, *James Whale*, 70.
    was not going to . . . Ibid.
    These trials were . . . Ibid.
    At first I thought . . . Curtis, *James Whale*, 127.
    I was offered . . . Taves, "Universal's Horror Tradition," 42.
    to get some ideas . . . "Inside Stuff-Pictures," 43.
    sorry for the . . . Curtis, *James Whale*, 133.
    I want the picture . . . "'Frankenstein' Finished."
    Frankenstein's nerves . . . Ibid.
    Jimmy was absolutely . . . Curtis, *James Whale*, 77.
    I was having lunch . . . Brosnan, *The Horror People*, 44.
38   *Your face has . . .* Lindsay, *Dear Boris*, 54.
    What for . . . Brosnan, *The Horror People*, 44.
    I made drawings . . . "James Whale and Frankenstein."
    This is going . . . Karloff, "My Life as a Monster," 34.
    Of course I . . . Lindsay, 54.
    yellow skin barely . . . Underwood, *Karloff*, 59.
    I studied every . . . Turner, *The Cinema of Adventure*, 92.
    was in a position . . . Lindsay, *Dear Boris*, 54.
    We had to . . . Curtis, *James Whale*, 138.
    There are six . . . "Oh, You Beautiful Monster."
    We had the . . . Edwards, "Interview with Boris Karloff."
    The Egyptians . . . "Oh, You Beautiful Monster."
    inlets for electricity . . . Ibid.
    overjoyed . . . Karloff, "My Life as a Monster," 34.
    The scene where . . . Karloff, "Memoirs of a Monster," 78.
    Each day he'd . . . Turner, *The Cinema of Adventure*, 91.
    After an hour's . . . Karloff, "Memoirs of a Monster," 78.
    I got into the . . . Edwards, "Interview with Boris Karloff."
    (caption) *I used to receive . . .* Morhaim, "Love That Monster."
41   *When he saw . . .* Jensen, *Boris Karloff and His Films*, 24.
    He and Boris . . . Curtis, *James Whale*, 81.
    Whale and I . . . Gifford, *Karloff*, 45.
    (caption) *I have been asked . . .* Karloff, "My Life as a Monster," 34.

A Cycle Spawned
41   *U Has Horror . . .* "U Has Horror Cycle All to Self."
    Is this the . . . Joy, letter to Hays, December 5, 1931, *Dracula* file, in the Production Code Administration papers, MPAA Collection, Margaret Herrick Library, Center for Motion Picture Study, Academy of Motion Picture Arts and Sciences, Beverly Hills (hereinafter PCA).
    All human beings . . . Turner, "Two-Faced Treachery," 193.
    You're crazy . . . Higham, *The Celluloid Muse*, 152.
    I wanted . . . Turner, "Two-Faced Treachery," 193.
    My God, if . . . Westmore, *The Westmores of Hollywood*, 9.
    I wanted to put . . . Mank, *Hollywood Cauldron*, 14.
43   *I had the camera . . .* Higham, *The Celluloid Muse*, 153.
    I felt that the sound . . . Turner, "Two-Faced Treachery," 194.
    The Hyde makeup . . . Ibid., 193.
    Wally [Westmore] . . . Senn, *Golden Horrors*, 43.
44   *Irving's right so . . .* Marx, *A Gaudy Spree*, 132.
    There was a certain . . . Schulberg, *Moving Pictures*, 314.
    I think he got . . . Skal, *Dark Carnival*, 171.
    It was very, very . . . Kobal, *People Will Talk*, 53.
    And I make him . . . Ibid., 52.
    Not even the most . . . *The American Film Institute Catalog, 1931–1940*, 700.
    The film opened . . . Ibid., 175.
47   *Chandu carries the . . .* Rhodes, *Lugosi*, 241.
    (caption) *This young animal . . .* Mank, *Hollywood Cauldron*, 14.
48   *just took a cardboard . . .* Turner, *The Cinema of Adventure*, 152.

*John Dudgeon was a name assumed by actress Elspeth Dudgeon at the urging of director Whale, who felt that the superannuated Roderick would be better portrayed by her than by a man.

Somehow she felt . . . Priestley, *Benighted*, 53.
With James . . . Mank, *Women in Horror Films, 1930s*, 135.

Chapter 3: Pre-Code Horrors

Madness Reigns

51 *This is absolute* . . . Edwards, "Interview with Boris Karloff."
been formed into . . . Mank, "The Mask of Fu Manchu," 49.
Oriental super . . . Turner, "Behind *The Mask of Fu Manchu*," 71.
Say, this is obscene . . . Jensen, *Boris Karloff and His Films*, 55.
Boris and I . . . Kotsilibas-Davis, *Being and Becoming*, 76.
I could not use . . . Roman, "Boris Karloff," 396.
snake-like lisp . . . Gifford, *Karloff*, 51.
(caption) *King Kong was never* . . . Haver, *David O. Selznick's Hollywood*, 116.

52 *makes the doctor* . . . Mank, *Hollywood Cauldron*, 83.
a bird of . . . Senn, *Golden Horrors*, 95.
makes Frankenstein . . . MacQueen, "Doctor X—a Technicolor Landmark," 38.
nauseating and . . . . Senn, *Golden Horrors*, 165.
I used to sit . . . MacQueen, "The Mystery of the Wax Museum," 48.
(caption) *I want to do* . . . Curtis, *James Whale*, 214.

53 *I knew there* . . . MacQueen, "The Mystery of the Wax Museum," 48.
After witnessing . . . Mank, *Hollywood's Maddest Doctors*, 39.
(caption) *This guy ought* . . . Senn, *Golden Horrors*, 203.

54 *go screwy playing* . . . Ibid., 159.
Who do you have . . . Ibid., 203.
The strange thing . . . Curtis, *James Whale*, 198.
(caption) *About a week* . . . Mank, *Hollywood Cauldron*, 64.

55 *[Wells] agreed with* . . . Curtis, *James Whale*, 200.
This is one . . . James Wingate, letter to Hays, June 19, 1933, *Invisible Man* file, PCA.
I don't give . . . Gatiss, *James Whale*, 99.
become the . . . Curtis, *James Whale*, 214.

Karl Freund's *The Mummy*

55 *I have been* . . . Carroll, "Boris Karloff Is Bespoken for Chaney Mantle."

56 *He worked for the* . . . *Mummy Dearest*.
For the heroine . . . Riley, *The Mummy*, 59.

58 *Miss Johann* . . . Mank, *Women in Horror Films, 1930s*, 181.
It's more money . . . Senn, *Golden Horrors*, 142.
Boris was . . . Riley, *The Mummy*, 19.
Well, you've done . . . *Mummy Dearest*.
Physical exhaustion . . . Riley, *The Mummy*, 25.
The most trying . . . Senn, *Golden Horrors*, 143.
for purposes of . . . Ibid., 142.
Surely the mantle . . . Riley, *The Mummy*, 31.
There will only . . . Jensen, *Boris Karloff and His Films*, 172.

Jungle Horrors

58 *continually mobbed* . . . "Charlie Chan at the Opera."
Billy, save every . . . Lindsay, *Dear Boris*, 69.

59 *who had a* . . . Lanchester, *Charles and I*, 106.
Charles felt very . . . Ibid.
[Kenton] had been . . . Higham, *Hollywood Cameraman*, 129.

60 *Although the attempt* . . . Ibid.
deliberate and . . . "Island of Lost Souls."
at times driven to . . . Mank, *Women in Horror Films, 1930s*, 208.
See, one side . . . Ibid., 46.
(caption) *It must be said* . . . Ibid., 204.
(caption) *The best thing that* . . . Ibid., 211.

61 *RKO was never* . . . Haver, *David O. Selznick's Hollywood*, 87.
(caption) *I remember each* . . . Senn, *Golden Horrors*, 151.

62 *combine the sweep* . . . Haver, *David O. Selznick's Hollywood*, 68.
All of Schoedsack's . . . Ibid., 76.
The only way . . . Ibid., 81.
It was a helluva . . . Ibid., 86.
Hey, Kong is . . . Goldner, *The Making of King Kong*, 131.
(caption) *against nature* . . . Lanchester, *Charles Laughton and I*, 108.

63 *using just the kind* . . . Goldner, *The Making of King Kong*, 80.
innocent and brave . . . Haver, *David O. Selznick's Hollywood*, 87.
You're going to . . . Wray, *On the Other Hand*, 124.
It was not too . . . Haver, *David O. Selznick's Hollywood*, 101.
Excuse me . . . Goldner, *The Making of King Kong*, 71.
It was made . . . Behlmer, *King Kong*, 24.
(caption) *I was uncomfortable* . . . Wray, *On the Other Hand*, 142.

64 (caption) *I had two Kongs* . . . "Interview With Marcel Delgado."
(caption) *Full of weird* . . . Goldner, 191.
(caption) *I think I had some* . . . Unsourced clipping, author's collection.

66 *There was a* . . . Wray, *On the Other Hand*, 126.
constant exclamations . . . Senn, 177.
Never saw greater . . . Haver, *David O. Selznick's Hollywood*, 116.
So great is its . . . Goldner, *The Making of King Kong*, 195.

Edgar Ulmer's *The Black Cat*

68 *Junior gave me* . . . Mank, *Karloff and Lugosi*, 49.
Meyrink at that time . . . Ibid., 50.
where he immortalizes . . . Ibid., 63.
Sequence E-6: This scene . . . Breen, letter to Harry Zehner, February 26, 1934, *The Black Cat* file, PCA.
Ulmer had made . . . Mank, *Women in Horror Films, 1930s*, 252.
He got into bed . . . Nollen, *Boris Karloff*, 77.
more foolish . . . Senn, *Golden Horrors*, 239.
Lots of screams . . . Ibid.
A truly horrible . . . Mank, *Karloff and Lugosi*, 81.
(caption) *It was very, very* . . . Ibid., 59.

69 (caption) *They had a big* . . . Mank, *Women in Horror Films, 1930s*, 252.

70 (caption) *Throughout this* . . . Breen, letter to Harry Zehner, February 26, 1934, *The Black Cat* file, PCA.
(caption) *My biggest job* . . . Nollen, *Boris Karloff*, 77.

Chapter 4: Gothic Moderne

Variations on a Gothic Theme

73 *The screen is* . . . Skal, *The Monster Show*, 205.
After seeing . . . Forman, *Our Movie Made Children*, 109.
Sometimes I go . . . Ibid., 106.
I was so frightened . . . Ibid., 110.
Mr. Boris Karloff . . . Senn, *Golden Horrors*, 319.
Where is the . . . "Interview With Ian Wolfe."
(caption) *was treated* . . . Senn, *Golden Horrors*, 319.

74 *He never took* . . . Roman, "Boris Karloff," 397.
stuffed with . . . Mank, *Karloff and Lugosi*, 117.
Pete Lorre's . . . Harmetz, *Round Up the Usual Suspects*, 158.
one of the most . . . Mank, *Hollywood Cauldron*, 148.
The producers must . . . Ibid., 149.
(caption) *suggesting the most* . . . Ibid., 148.

75 (caption) *He liked to go* . . . Ibid., 126.

76 *We had cobwebs* . . . Higham, *Hollywood Cameramen*, 87.
We worked in mud . . . Skal, *Dark Carnival*, 197.
Bela Lugosi was . . . Higham, *Hollywood Cameramen*, 87.

(caption) *Here is a handsome* . . . Mank, *Hollywood's Hissables*, 22.

77 (caption) *a strange, wispy* . . . Skal, *Dark Carnival*, 194.

WereWolf of London

79 *He was, of course* . . . Mank, *Women in Horror Films, 1930s*, 327.
I knew Mr. Hull . . . Senn, *Golden Horrors*, 294.
It was a pretty . . . Ibid., 295.
The studio . . . Ibid.
(caption) *We understand* . . . Skal, *The Monster Show*, 194.

Bride of Frankenstein

80 *I squeezed the idea* . . . Henderson and Turner, "Bride of Frankenstein," 103.
The producers realized . . . Gifford, *Karloff*, 55.
I demand a . . . Mank, *The Bride of Frankenstein*, 25.
He knew it was . . . Jensen, *The Men Who Made the Monsters*, 52.
I think he had . . . Curtis, *James Whale*, 238.
At conferences . . . *Bride of Frankenstein* press book, 1.
(caption) *Boris had a pet* . . . Mank, *Women in Horror Films, 1930s*, 40.
(caption) *The shots in which* . . . Breen, letter to Universal, December 5, 1934, *Bride of Frankenstein* file, PCA.
(caption) *Mary Shelley's dress* . . . Lanchester, *Elsa Lanchester, Herself*, 134.

82 *They made a great* . . . Gifford, *Karloff*, 55.
Time and time again . . . Senn, *Golden Horrors*, 285.
Throughout the script . . . Breen, letter to Universal, July 23, 1934, *Bride of Frankenstein* file, PCA.
something to make . . . Riley, *Bride of Frankenstein*, B-12.
prissy and bitter . . . Jensen, *The Men Who Made the Monsters*, 55.
He was one of . . . Mank, *Women in Horror Films, 1930s*, 324.
the stitchin' bitch . . . Curtis, *James Whale*, 240.
He was inclined . . . Ibid.
He had complete . . . Ibid., 237.
James's feeling . . . Mank, *Women in Horror Films, 1930s*, 305.
(caption) *Certainly, with* . . . Ibid., 325.
(caption) *Henry's wife came* . . . Henderson and Turner, "Bride of Frankenstein," 108.

85 *I know the Bride's* . . . Ibid., 243.
He and Jack Pierce . . . Lanchester, *Elsa Lanchester, Herself*, 135.
Jack Pierce really . . . Mank, *Women in Horror Films, 1930s*, 306.
I had been warned . . . Mank, *Women in Horror Films, 1930s*, 322.
The watery opening . . . Gifford, *Karloff*, 55.
I admired Whale's . . . *Elsa Lanchester, Herself*, 135.
He was very . . . Mank, *Women in Horror Films, 1930s*, 306.
You don't know how . . . Jensen, *The Men Who Made the Monsters*, 55.
I've often been . . . Lanchester, *Elsa Lanchester, Herself*, 135.
(caption) *[Pierce] had his* . . . Ibid., 135.
(caption) *I didn't particularly* . . . Ibid.

86 *I've always been* . . . Ibid., 137.
I did get a . . . Mank, *Women in Horror Films, 1930s*, 308.
I had a nice time . . . Higham, *Charles Laughton*, 61.
Nothing will be . . . Cook, "Franz Waxman," 417.
It was a 'super horror' . . . Waxman, *Sunset Boulevard*, 8.
This picture seems . . . Breen, letter to Universal, December 5, 1934, *Bride of Frankenstein* file, PCA.
(caption) *Ernest Thesiger was* . . . Mank, *Women in Horror Films, 1930s*, 307.
(caption) *Colin Clive was* . . . Ibid., 323.
(caption) *Most monsters* . . . Ibid., 322.
(caption) *It's sometimes pleasant* . . . Lanchester, *Elsa Lanchester, Herself*, 135.

88   *This tops all . . .* Ibid., 136.

Dracula's Daughter
88   *We want love . . .* Skal, *The Monster Show*, 197.
      The use of a . . . Ibid.
      Why should Cecil . . . Mank, *Women in Horror Films, 1930s*, 352.
      This story, which . . . Ibid., 353.
      There still remains . . . Ibid.
      (caption) *The English censor . . .* "Horror!" 70.
89   *rather moody . . .* Mank, *Women in Horror Films, 1930s*, 359.
91   *Universal is . . .* Rhodes, "Horror!" 70.

Son of Frankenstein
92   *One day I drive . . .* Rhodes, "Horror!" 72.
      Grosses from the . . . Skal, *The Monster Show*, 204.
      They cut . . . Mank, *It's Alive!*, 78.
      Those God-damned . . . Ibid., 79.
      The interpretation . . . Ibid., 85.
      It would be pretty . . . Mank, *Hollywood's Maddest Doctors*, 79.
      The director . . . Mank, *Women in Horror Films, 1930s*, 379.
      (caption) *penny dreadful . . .* Senn, *Golden Horrors*, 393.
93   *"[Frank] would . . .* Mank, *It's Alive!*, 83.
      Forceful narration . . . Ibid., 84.
      a star-spangled . . . Ibid., 83.
      a masterpiece . . . Ibid.
      Bela Lugosi is . . . Ibid.
      I could see the . . . Bean, "Boris Is Back," 52.
      Movie producers . . . "The Son of Frankenstein Starts a New Horror Cycle," *Look*, February 28, 1939, 39.
      (caption) *God, he was . . .* Mank, *It's Alive!*, 85.
94   (caption) *Michelangelo had . . .* Mank, *Karloff and Lugosi*, 197.
      (caption) *In the third . . .* Gifford, *Karloff*, 55.
      (caption) *The sets were . . . Son of Frankenstein* Press Book, 5.
      (caption) *And there I am . . .* Beck, *Heroes of the Horrors*, 116.

Chapter 5: Universal, the Horror Factory

House of Horrors
97   (caption) *I am not afraid . . .* Brunas, Brunas, and Weaver, *Universal Horrors*, 296.
      (caption) *It took five to . . .* Riley, *The Wolf Man*, 60.
98   *I was told . . .* Brunas, Brunas, and Weaver, *Universal Horrors*, 267.
      I targeted the . . . Daniels, *Famous Monsters Chronicles*, 145.
      I studied many . . . Riley, *The Wolf Man*, 14.
      What gets me . . . Brunas, Brunas, and Weaver, *Universal Horrors*, 269.
      They must be once . . . Banzak, *Fearing the Dark*, 143.
      These things are . . . Gifford, *Karloff*, 57.
      Opening night . . . Weaver, *Return of the B*, 77.
      (caption) *I was standing . . .* Riley, *The Wolf Man*, 11.
99   *George, why don't . . .* Brunas, Brunas, and Weaver, *Universal Horrors*, 336.
      He finally did it . . . Riley, *Frankenstein Meets the Wolf Man*, 17.
      If Dr. Frankenstein . . . Ibid., 64.
100   *It sounded so . . .* Ibid., 23.
      (caption) *Roosevelt meets . . .* Ibid., 25.
      (caption) *It was great fun . . .* Seymour, "Louise Allbritton," 78.
101   *He didn't want to . . .* Brunas, Brunas, and Weaver, *Universal Horrors*, 363.
      We had been in . . . Ibid.
      It was the picture . . . Ibid., 447.
102   (caption) *It was usually . . .* Ibid., 434.
103   *He was sick . . .* Jensen, *Boris Karloff and His Films*, 135.
      the great cleansing . . . Senn, *Golden Horrors*, 159.
      There is no . . . Rhodes, *Lugosi*, 298.
      As long as I . . . Mank, *Karloff and Lugosi*, 283.
      (caption) *The real monsters . . .* Thompson, *Between Action and Cut*, 210.

(caption) *We never had . . .* Brunas, Brunas, and Weaver, *Universal Horrors*, 450.

In the Gothic Tradition
103   *Naturally, I won't . . .* Higham, *Charles Laughton*, 96.
      suffering under . . . Westmore, *The Westmores of Hollywood*, 68.
104   *You're going about . . .* Ibid.
      While everyone . . . Ibid., 69.
      Give me a . . . Ibid., 70.
      Charles, listen . . . Higham, *Charles Laughton*, 99.
      When England . . . Ibid., 98.
      It naturally will . . . "Fantastic Dr. Cyclops," 17.
      (caption) *I bet he's a . . .* Mank, *Hollywood's Maddest Doctors*, 234.
      (caption) *All characters . . .* Mank, *Hollywood Hissables*, 360.
105   *somewhat akin . . .* "Among the Living."
      Never once losing . . . "Whelan, Rathbone Take the Honors."
      usually the hero . . . Mank, *Hollywood Hissables*, 343.
      makes scientists . . . The American Film Institute Catalog, 1941–1950, 1598.
      Hollywood's unhappiest . . . Mank, *Hollywood's Maddest Doctors*, 227.
      I didn't know . . . Sierchio, "Interview With a Wolf Man," 34.
      When they first . . . Hepburn, *Me*, 274.
      went on such a . . . Westmore, *The Westmores of Hollywood*, 173.
      It's like constructing . . . Hepburn, *Me*, 274.
      Tracy wisely . . . Thompson, *Between Action and Cut*, 51.

Chapter 6: Big-Budget Chills

Glossy Hauntings
109   *Humor is to horror . . .* "Charlie Chan at the Opera."
      The Cat and the . . . Hope and Thomas, *The Road to Hollywood*, 31.
      You know Charles . . . Ibid., 32.
      Streamlined . . . Marx, *The Secret Life of Bob Hope*, 136.
      a great director . . . Gilbert, *Opposite Attraction*, 161.
      (caption) *Every film I ever . . .* Ibid.
110   *unacceptable . . .* Letter, Joseph I. Breen to Charles Brackett, *The Uninvited*, PCA.
      I had just got . . . "Ruth Hussey Remembers *The Uninvited*," 28.
      I was suspended . . . "Elizabeth Russell Remembers *The Uninvited*," 31.

Music and Madness
111   *report for work . . . The American Film Institute Catalog, 1941–1950*, 2661.
      I am, after all . . . Mank, "Laird Cregar," 33.
      Sammy had a . . . Mank, *Hollywood Cauldron*, 255.
      I had been very . . . Ibid., 35.
      You're so silly . . . Ibid.
      In all the . . . Mank, *Hollywood Cauldron*, 250.
112   *gave him a . . .* Mank, "Laird Cregar," 45.
      The Lodger is . . . Mank, *Hollywood Hissables*, 226.
      Interesting reaction . . . Mank, "Laird Cregar," 48.
      Without the aid . . . Mank, *Hollywood Hissables*, 228.
      The theater was . . . Mank, *Hollywood Cauldron*, 260.
      Now I don't . . . Mank, *Hollywood Hissables*, 229.
      I read about . . . Mank, *Hollywood Cauldron*, 327.
      The story is . . . Ibid., 328.
      (caption) *He was fundamentally . . .* Mank, *Hollywood Hissables*, 235.
      (caption) *I have been . . .* Mank, "Laird Cregar," 34.
113   *They tell me . . .* Mank, *Hollywood Cauldron*, 332.
      A tragic resolve . . . Sanders, *Memoirs of a Professional Cad*, 116.
      It was not . . . Mank, *Hollywood Hissables*, 233.
      Miss Darnell wanted . . . Mank, *Hollywood Cauldron*, 335.

I hated to . . . Mank, *Hollywood Hissables*, 237.
      The thermometer . . . Mank, *Hollywood Cauldron*, 333.
      Shooting was . . . Ibid.
      How dare you . . . Mank, *Hollywood Hissables*, 423.
      Laird wanted . . . Mank, *Hollywood Cauldron*, 339.
      Well, I think . . . Ibid., 343.
      Cregar saw himself . . . Ibid., 255.
      I defy anyone . . . Mank, "Laird Cregar," 33.
      Laird Cregar . . . Mank, *Hollywood Cauldron*, 324.
      For all his . . . Ibid., 344.
      (caption) *It started . . .* Terenzio, "John Howard," 59.

The Terror of Evil
114   *Walter Huston . . .* Weld, *September Song*, 181.
      That's all, Brother . . . Harmetz, *Round Up the Usual Suspects*, 159.
115   *mechanical hand . . .* Taves, "Whose Hand?" 211.
      the only movie . . . Nolan, "Robert Siodmak," 229.
      They hate me . . . Marx, *A Gaudy Spree*, 127.
      used Sanders . . . Mank, *Hollywood Cauldron*, 301.
      not the type of . . . Felleman, *Botticelli in Hollywood*, 45.
      Albert Lewin cast . . . Mank, *Hollywood Cauldron*, 300.
116   *abnormal sex theme . . .* Ibid., 297.
      There will be no . . . Breen, letter to Pandro S. Berman, September 13, 1943, *The Picture of Dorian Gray* file, PCA.
      I'm delighted . . . Mank, *Hollywood Cauldron*, 311.
      Lewin was intellectual . . . Ibid.
      Masters at . . . "Albright Twins."
      Al, I don't see . . . Arkadin, "Film Clips," 47.
117   (caption) *The film didn't . . .* Mank, *Hollywood Cauldron*, 321.
118   *His is a passive . . .* Tyler, "Dorian Gray," 21.
      Albert Lewin's . . . Agee, *Agee on Film*, 147.
      laughed at the right . . . Felleman, *Botticelli in Hollywood*, 61.
      A very young fellow . . . Ibid.
      (caption) *There was a strike . . .* Nolan, "Robert Siodmak," 229.

Chapter 7: Val Lewton and the Psychology of Fear

Poetry and Danger
121   *the greatest electric . . .* Leaming, *Orson Welles*, 174.
      In case of an . . . Niven, *Bring on the Empty Horses*, 28.
      had managed a lot . . . Mank, *Hollywood Cauldron*, 211.
      They may think . . . Bodeen, "Val Lewton," 210.
      Mr. Koerner, who . . . Ibid., 211.
      Let's see what . . . Ibid.
      There's no helping . . . Ibid., 212.
      When I first . . . Ibid., 213.
      He would move . . . Ibid. 215.
      My wife and I . . . Higham, *The Celluloid Muse*, 246.
      He had a folk . . . Siegel, *The Reality of Terror*, 28.
      (caption) *The actors we used . . .* Siegel, "Tourneur Remembers," 25.
122   *We tossed away . . .* Siegel, *The Reality of Terror*, 31.
      The stories he . . . Bodeen, "Val Lewton," 215.
      Take a sweet . . . Siegel, *The Reality of Terror*, 31.
      In the darkness . . . Fujiwara, *Tourneur*, 78.
      Val was the . . . Siegel, "Tourneur Remembers," 25.
      If you make the . . . Siegel, *The Reality of Terror*, 32.
      We believed in . . . Higham, *The Celluloid Muse*, 248.
      The shadow . . . Ibid.
      From the other side . . . Ibid., 237.
      I have a friend . . . Mank, *Women in Horror Films, 1940s*, 105
      a strange . . . Ibid.
      The preview was . . . Bodeen, "Val Lewton," 218.
      It was with . . . Mank, *Hollywood Cauldron*, 234.
      although the café . . . Mank, *Women in Horror Films, 1940s*, 104.

(caption) *I think that came* . . . Mank, *Hollywood Cauldron*, 209.

123 *Cat People saved* . . . Siegel, *The Reality of Terror*, 40.

We were all . . . Ibid., 41.

We'd work late . . . Ibid., 42.

I Walked . . . Ibid., 51.

After a horror . . . Peary, "Mark Robson Remembers," 36.

A love story . . . Ibid., 31.

made during the war . . . Higham, *The Celluloid Muse*, 248.

We were making . . . Higham, *The Celluloid Muse*, 246.

See if it's . . . Brosnan, *The Horror People*, 79.

It was during the . . . Ibid., 80.

Life has betrayed . . . Mank, *Women in Horror Films, 1940s*, 258.

Horror spots must . . . Siegel, *The Reality of Terror*, 32.

The Seventh . . . Higham, *The Celluloid Muse*, 237.

124 *We were interested* . . . Peary, "Mark Robson Remembers," 35.

We thought everything . . . Ibid.

The Curse of the . . . Brosnan, *The Horror People*, 81.

125 *was constantly* . . . Mank, *Women in Horror Films, 1940s*, 105.

Val had been . . . Peary, "Mark Robson Remembers," 34.

We would ask the . . .Ibid., 35.

Send out a . . . Siegel, *The Reality of Terror*, 58.

I remember after . . . Brosnan, *The Horror People*, 84.

And when the picture . . . Banzak, *Fearing the Dark*, 237.

I esteem them . . . Siegel, *The Reality of Terror*, 59.

Horror Meets Terror

125 *I now find* . . . Siegel, *The Reality of Terror*, 66.

126 *In a way, I think he* . . . Ibid., 36.

Jack Gross called . . . Ibid., 71.

I dislike the word . . . Bean, "Boris Is Back," 52.

When it started to . . . Ibid.

It was strange . . . Lindsay, *Dear Boris*, 111.

Between shots . . . Ibid.

(caption) *He was quite a* . . . Nollen, *Boris Karloff*, 154.

127 *because of the repellent* . . . Breen, letter to Pandro S. Berman, September 27, 1944, *The Body Snatcher* file, PCA.

It breaks my heart . . . Siegel, *The Reality of Terror*, 77.

Boris was very . . . Banzak, *Fearing the Dark*, 299.

Henry Daniell was . . . Mank, *Karloff and Lugosi*, 254.

a pro, a real . . . Roman, "Boris Karloff," 401.

He had back . . . Banzak, *Fearing the Dark*, 299.

Lugosi was quite ill . . . Mank, *Karloff and Lugosi*, 264.

He was a little . . . Nollen, *Boris Karloff*, 154.

I always appreciated . . . Ibid.

God damn it . . . Mank, *Karloff and Lugosi*, 258.

an unqualified lulu . . . Banzak, *Fearing the Dark*, 299.

After the pallbearers . . . Siegel, *The Reality of Terror*, 75.

(caption) *as brutally frightening* . . . Ibid., 74.

128 *The first part of* . . . Jensen, *Boris Karloff and His Films*, 143.

I came home . . . Nollen, *Boris Karloff* , 162.

Don't ask me . . . Berg, "Farewell to Monsters."

We make horror . . . Siegel, "Letter to the Editors."

The stories of his . . . Siegel, *The Reality of Terror*, 36.

Boris used to . . . Banzak, *Fearing the Dark*, 299.

Horror too often . . . Roman, "Boris Karloff," 401.

129 *I think that few* . . . Siegel, *The Reality of Terror*, 82.

Mr. Karloff has . . . Berg, "Farewell to Monsters."

Pressure was placed . . . Siegel, *The Reality of Terror*, 83.

Fighting for what . . . Mank, *Karloff and Lugosi*, 276.

The whole aspect . . . Siegel, *The Reality of Terror*, 93.

I never knew . . . Mank, *Karloff and Lugosi*, 278.

(caption) *Karloff was not* . . . Nollen, *Boris Karloff*, 154.

(caption) *the personification* . . . Mank, *Hollywood Cauldron*, 376

130 (caption) *If you're going* . . . Fujiwara, *Tourneur*, 71.

(caption) *I'd like to have* . . . Turner, *The Cinema of Adventure*, 237.

(caption) *He was very* . . . Mank, *Hollywood Cauldron*, 212.

Chapter 8: Poisoned Air

Kiss Me Deadly

133 *Victor Saville, who* . . . Higham, *The Celluloid Muse*, 30.

He was quiet . . . Spillane, *Kiss Me, Deadly*, 150.

The gun pressed . . . Ibid., 152.

We just took the . . . Higham, *The Celluloid Muse*, 30.

We have discovered . . .Ferrell, *Off the Record*, 55.

134 *It did have a* . . . Higham, *The Celluloid Muse*, 30.

The scriptwriter . . . Ibid.

We worked a long . . . Ibid.

(caption) *Hollywood's idea of* . . . Riordan, "Atomic Blonde," 84.

135 *It was really Aldrich's* . . . Ibid., 85.

no purpose except to . . . *Variety*, June 8, 1955, 1.

(caption) *She was always* . . . Pace, "Man of Steel," 55.

Lab Work

136 *It seems that in* . . . Weaver, *Return of the B*, 312.

We're leaning over . . . Pace, "Man of Steel," 55.

For years I'd imagined . . . Haver, *The 5,000 Fingers of Dr. T.*

from a man who . . . "The New Pictures," 84.

They have built . . . Williams, "Roaming the Sound Stages," 82.

decorated with the . . . "The New Pictures," 84.

The teacher . . . Berg, "Dr. Seuss's 5,000 Fingers."

Chapter 9: Poisoned Waters

Modern Inconveniences

139 *I came out of* . . . Newsom, "The Ray Harryhausen Story: Part One," 26.

My mother's fur . . . Harryhausen, *Film Fantasy Scrapbook*, 25.

Every joint . . . Ibid.

I had my favorite . . . Ibid., 19.

One outline was . . . Weaver, *They Fought in the Creature Features* [hereinafter *They Fought*], 202.

I doubt that . . . Ibid.

We did a lot . . . "Watch Out for Herman."

140 *I found it an* . . . Harryhausen, *Film Fantasy Scrapbook*, 33.

The scene of the . . . Weaver, *They Fought*, 205.

Oh, am I . . . Ibid.

The picture is built . . . Jensen, *The Men Who Made the Monsters*, 108.

something new and . . . Brosnan, *Movie Magic*, 167.

The assistant . . . Weaver, *Attack of the Monster Movie Makers*, 348.

If the budget . . . Harryhausen, *Film Fantasy Scrapbook*, 37.

At that period . . . Ibid., 50.

It was very hot . . . Parla, "Sandy Descher," 106.

I didn't ruin . . . Ibid.

The whole idea . . . Weaver, *Interviews With B Science Fiction and Horror Movie Makers* [hereinafter *Interviews With B*], 148.

I'd report . . . Weaver, *Attack of the Monster Movie Makers*, 33.

142 *It fit perfect* . . . Ibid.

I would heat . . . Ibid.

We were shooting . . . Weaver, *They Fought*, 101.

I made sure . . . Reemes, *Directed by Jack Arnold*, 50.

I wanted to create . . . Ibid.

(caption) *We're in the* . . . Rubin, "The 'She' in 'Them!'," 48.

143 *I want him to* . . . Weaver, *Attack of the Monster Movie Makers*, 35.

The eyes of the . . . Ibid.

The day we shot . . . Weaver, *They Fought*, 7.

I was wearing . . . Weaver, *Attack of the Monster Movie Makers*, 39.

He scraped . . . Weaver, *They Fought*, 7.

And she let . . . Weaver, *Attack of the Monster Movie Makers*, 39.

I wanted to make . . . Reemes, *Directed by Jack Arnold*, 50.

When a picture . . . Weaver, *They Fought*, 5.

(caption) *You are bad* . . . Ibid., 205.

144 (caption) *Jack Arnold and* . . . Parla, "Revenge of the Creatures," 93.

(caption) *Every graceful* . . . Westmore, *The Westmores of Hollywood*, 183.

(caption) *wanted some kind* . . . Scrivani, "The Gertzenstein Monsters," 96.

(caption) *The Creature scared* . . . Weaver, *They Fought*, 10.

Cheap Thrills

144 *The only natural* . . . Reemes, *Directed by Jack Arnold*, 51.

Any time a science . . . Pace, "John Agar," 70.

It was a place . . . Brosnan, *The Horror People*, 92.

When Mara . . . Pace, "John Agar," 70.

What we did . . . Brosnan, *The Horror People*, 92.

When we were . . . Pace, "John Agar," 70.

Bill Alland . . . Weaver, *Interviews with B*, 7.

This won't work . . . Pace, "John Agar," 70.

they did not tell . . . Parla, *Screen Sirens Scream*, 192.

There were two . . . Ibid., 194.

146 *I'm not going down* . . . Weaver, *Science Fiction Stars and Horror Heroes* [hereinafter *Science Fiction Stars*], 404.

falling through . . . Parla, *Screen Sirens Scream*, 193.

She screamed . . . Weaver, *Science Fiction Stars*, 404.

There were all these . . . Pace, "John Agar," 70.

Science fiction . . . Medved, *The Golden Turkey Awards*, 76.

Like the story . . . Ibid., 77.

I told him I wanted . . . Pace, "John Agar," 70.

Herb, is my . . . Weaver, *Interviews with B*, 318.

She was a sweet . . . Ibid.

147 *The twin robots* . . . Ibid., 316.

If he was sitting . . . Weaver, *Interviews with B*, 259.

He enjoyed playing . . . Medved, *The Golden Turkey Awards*, 257.

Ed used to drive . . . Ibid., 260.

One night we . . . Weaver, *Interviews with B*, 252.

(caption) *The Mole man mask* . . . Parla, *Screen Sirens Scream*, 194.

148 *Oh, take those* . . . Weaver, *Interviews with B*, 251.

I cannot describe . . . Mank, *Karloff and Lugosi*, 296.

This re-hashed . . . Rhodes, *Lugosi*, 264.

Herr Director . . . Mank, *Karloff and Lugosi*, 301.

I am now more . . . Rhodes, *Lugosi*, 265.

149 *Perhaps some day* . . . Ibid., 299.

We were all sitting . . . Weaver, *Interviews with B*, 255.

I made myself up . . . "Interview With the Vampira," 63.

(caption) *He was a gentleman* . . . Ibid.

Chapter 10: The Science-Fiction Film

Unearthly Subversion

153 *In some sort of* . . . *Race for the Superbomb*.

a total of twenty . . . "Symposium on Unidentified Flying Objects," 47.

The secret of science . . . *It Came from Outer Space* press book.

an age of A-Bombs . . . Weiler, "Red Planet Mars," 15.

It was hot . . . Johnson, *Cheap Tricks and Class Acts*, 257.

He was the best . . . Weaver, *Interviews with B*, 289.

He was always lost . . . Weaver, *Attack of the,* 256.

I warn you . . . McCarthy, *They're Here,* 42.

(caption) *He almost took a nosedive . . .* Weaver, *They Fought,* 164.

(caption) *Every time I . . .* Rubin, "Retrospect," 21.

155 (caption) *Liquid latex . . .* Turner, "A Case for Insomnia," 79.

156 He needed a job . . . Weaver, *Interviews with B,* 55.

They'd gathered . . . McCarthy, *They're Here,* 66.

Wanger and I . . . Durgnat, "Invasion of the Body Snatchers," 50.

(caption) *I nearly broke . . .* McCarthy, *They're Here,* 66.

157 Nobody gave . . . McCarthy, *They're Here,* 241.

Broidy insisted . . . Ibid., 250.

Don hated the . . . Ibid., 236.

How can I admit . . . Ibid., 85.

I suppose it will . . . Ibid.

The Good Neighbor Policy

157 Oh, television . . . Davis, *The Glamour Factory,* 370.

Weekly movie attendance . . . Finler, *The Hollywood Story,* 15.

158 documentary of the . . . Hagerty, "The Making of George Pal's *Destination Moon,*" 52.

High latitude . . . Ibid., 54.

(caption) *That's it . . .* Rubin, "Retrospect," 22.

(caption) *the tall, thin . . .* Taylor, "Director Robert Wise Remembers," 73.

159 No one wanted . . . Weaver, *Science Fiction Stars,* 100.

(caption) *It would get into . . .* Parla, "The Woman from Planet X," 72.

160 The door opens . . . Skotak, "*The Man from Planet X Files,*" 83.

Ulmer showed . . . Ibid.

science fiction 'terror' . . . Ibid., 82.

He complained . . . Weaver, *Interviews with B,* 79.

We worked from . . . Ibid.

The idea of tackling . . . Rubin, "Retrospect," 10.

Our theme is . . . Ibid.

161 The thing that grabbed . . . Ibid.

To hell with . . . Ibid., 9.

When you open . . . Custen, *Twentieth Century's Fox,* 330.

radiated kindness . . . .Rubin, "Retrospect," 6.

I was picked . . . Rennie, "The Role I Liked Best."

We were starting . . . Rubin, "Retrospect," 18.

It was a picture . . . Taylor, "Director Robert Wise Remembers," 70.

I had originally . . . Rubin, "Retrospect," 18.

nasty confrontation . . . Ibid.

The Breen Office . . . Ibid.

We must have an . . . Behlmer, *Memo from Darryl F. Zanuck,* 193.

It's more than . . . Rubin, "Retrospect," 22.

This was the height . . . Reemes, *Directed by Jack Arnold,* 24.

We have stepped . . . Galbraith, "Where It Really Came From," 54.

Control of the . . . Weaver, *They Fought,* 27.

162 There was no total . . . Rubin, "Making *Forbidden Planet,*" 8.

You can't . . . Ibid., 7.

Metro was . . . Weaver, *They Fought,* 27.

It was a science . . . Ibid., 165.

I got that part . . . Ibid., 162.

At the time it . . . Ibid.

Up to that . . . Rubin, "Making *Forbidden Planet,*" 22.

The total concept . . . Ibid., 23.

We wanted . . . Ibid., 16.

We decided we'd go . . . Ibid., 20.

This gave us . . . Ibid.

I was fascinated . . . Ibid., 29.

Green Meanies

163 What are people . . . McCarthy, *Howard Hawks,* 472.

Forgetting that almost . . . Turner, "*The Thing from Another World,*" 35.

I thought it would be . . . McCarthy, *Howard Hawks,* 472.

It is important that . . . Turner, "*The Thing from Another World,*" 35.

Make him look . . . McCarthy, *Howard Hawks,* 476.

We all thought . . . Ibid.

On a Hawks picture . . . Weaver, *They Fought,* 117.

When you are being . . . McCarthy, *Howard Hawks,* 481.

We'd come in . . . Ibid., 480.

I was getting . . . Weaver, *They Fought,* 121.

I thought to myself . . . Ibid., 118.

164 I can't improve . . . Zubatkin, "A Mant for All Seasons," 78.

I almost fell . . . Weaver, *Attack of the,* 345.

The audience just . . . Weaver, *They Fought,* 122.

165 The War of the . . . Rubin, "The War of the Worlds," 6.

166 George, this script . . . Ibid., 16.

You're crazy . . . Weaver, *Attack of the,* 294.

Go ahead and . . . Ibid.

We wanted the machines . . . Ibid.

It came from . . . Ibid.

167 Byron taught me . . . Weaver, *Attack of the,* 294.

When you're trying . . . Rovin, *From the Land beyond Beyond,* 101.

Universal had . . . Riley, *This Island Earth,* 22.

I'd never been . . . Ibid., 19.

(caption) *A bit of the . . .* Weaver, *They Fought,* 115.

168 It was not a . . . Skotak, *This Island Earth,* 61.

You had no idea . . . Weaver, *They Fought,* 212.

I'm so glad . . . Ibid., 213.

This was a totally . . . Riley, *This Island Earth,* 22.

We didn't have . . . Ibid., 26.

It stained the . . . Johnson, *Cheap Tricks and Class Acts,* 196.

Science fiction done . . . Skotak, *This Island Earth,* 96.

(caption) *There was a sense . . .* Weaver, *They Fought,* 219.

Chapter 11: Drive-in Terror

The Last of the Epics

171 It needed a . . . Davis, *The Glamour Factory,* 363.

It became almost . . . Davis, *The Glamour Factory,* 364.

When a family . . . Ibid., 374.

172 Drive-ins were . . . Weaver, *Interviews With B,* 18.

The girls yell . . . Alpert, "The Horror of It All," 86.

(caption) *Trying to act . . .* Johnson, *Cheap Tricks and Class Acts,* 124.

173 The day of the . . . "Vital Statistics on *The Fly,*" 3.

It has the celebrated . . . Ibid.

(caption) *That's the head . . .* Schoell, "The Making of *A Journey to the Center of the Earth,*" 56.

174 We were playing . . . Svehla, *Vincent Price,* 115.

The last scene . . . "Monstrous for Money," 84.

I sing songs . . . Schoell, "The Making of *A Journey to the Center of the Earth,*" 53.

She began to scream . . . Ibid., 55.

(caption) *It is left to . . .* Weaver, *Keep Watching the Skies,* 438.

175 I hated the style . . . Linaweaver, "First Man-to-Fly," 50.

This foul-smelling . . . Shinnick, "Retrospect: *The Time Machine,*" 32.

176 George Pal went . . . Ibid., 30.

The Time Machine . . . "The Time Machine," *Time,* August 22, 1960.

177 The movie business . . . Alpert, "The Horror of It All," 76.

Those Monsters Next Door

177 With justifiable lack . . . Alpert, "The Horror of It All," 86.

They find it easier . . . Ibid.

178 Young adults were . . . Weaver, *Interviews With B,* 18.

The majors have been . . . McGee, *The Fast and the Furious,* 26.

As this hodgepodge . . . McGee, *Faster and Furiouser,* 47.

In my advertising . . . Ibid., 89.

We do our planning . . . McGee, *The Fast and the Furious,* 18.

The worst thing . . . "Monstrous for Money," 84.

I don't care . . . McGee, *The Fast and the Furious,* 20.

Sitting in his . . . McGee, *Faster and Furiouser,* 51.

You don't need . . . Brosnan, *The Horror People,* 125.

Herm, can you . . . McGee, *Fast and Furious,* 53.

I thought of doing . . . Ibid.

It's got the worst . . . Weaver, *Science Fiction Stars,* 70.

I can't do this . . . Ibid.

I was trying to . . . Ibid.

You're kidding . . . Ibid., 75.

179 We thought he had . . . Weaver, *Attack of the,* 54.

Then all of a sudden . . . Ibid., 56.

Then people from Time . . . McGee, *Faster and Furiouser,* 88.

It has a haunting . . . Ibid., 85.

180 She was a very pretty . . . Ibid., 93.

Horror movies are . . . Alpert, "The Horror of It All," 86.

I think he'd film . . . McGee, *Faster and Furiouser,* 93.

We had two . . . Weaver, *Science Fiction Stars,* 77.

I gave them a . . . Ibid.

They took one look . . . Johnson, *Cheap Tricks and Class Acts,* 242.

For the dissolving . . . Ibid., 199.

(caption) *Fellows, it was . . .* Brosnan, *The Horror People,* 98.

181 typical of the . . . Weaver, *Science Fiction Stars,* 290.

I'm gonna give ya . . . Ibid., 291.

the commonplace becomes . . . Brosnan, *The Horror People,* 95.

The shot where the . . . Reemes, *Directed by Jack Arnold,* 66.

I wanted to make . . . Brosnan, *The Horror People,* 95.

That guy looked . . . Weaver, *Science Fiction Stars,* 293.

In that situation . . . Reemes, *Directed by Jack Arnold.*

To the studio . . . Ibid. , 61.

The science-fiction . . . Ibid., 102.

Its premise is . . . Ibid., 105.

Thank God for . . . Alpert, "The Horror of It All," 86.

Don't Step on It!

182 To me it was very . . . Weaver, *They Fought in,* 240.

I had to get my . . . McGee, *Faster and Furiouser,* 106.

They began to cannibalize . . . Parla, "Talking Eye to Eye," 104.

If AB-PT and its . . . Weaver, *Keep Watching the Skies,* 438.

Many in the audience . . . Ibid.

The movie audience . . . Alpert, "The Horror of It All," 86.

183 Listen, what I want . . . Weaver, *Interviews With B,* 198.

We discovered . . . Ibid., 200.

I'll say one thing . . . "Monstrous for Money," 84.

184 When I first met . . .Parla, "Beauty and the Beasts," 110.

We poor benighted . . . Weaver, *They Fought in,* 218.

Well, Katzman was . . . Parla, "Beauty and the Beasts," 110.

I went to a sneak . . . Weaver, *They Fought in,* 218.

You want me to . . . Weaver, *Science Fiction Stars,* 329.

(caption) *This picture has as . . .* Brunas, "Inside the Alligator People," 59.

185 The producers needed . . . Parla, "Wooden Performance," 62.

They would unintentionally . . . Ibid., 63.

I was disappointed . . . Ibid.

Filming The Alligator . . . Brunas, "Inside the Alligator People," 59.

I walk in and here . . . Weaver, *Interviews With B,* 165.

I just played her . . . Brunas, "Inside the Alligator People," 59.

I had to be a bit . . . Weaver, *Interviews With B,* 164.

186 What were they going . . . Ibid.

I was supposed to bite . . . Ibid., 72.

The real horror . . . Alpert, "The Horror of It All," 76.

He didn't want people . . . Weaver, *Attack of*, 203.

When the fifty-foot . . . Weaver, *Science Fiction Stars*, 373.

187 *The fact that he . . .* Cohen, "The Legend of Rubirosa," 254.

This is our chance . . . Weaver, *Interviews With B*, 57.

Ben went to the . . . Ibid.

(caption) *Here on this planet . . .* Ibid., 57.

188 *Trying to paste . . .* Ibid.

I'm little, but . . . Weaver, *Interviews With B*, 340.

But, by God . . . Ibid., 341.

189 (caption) *My role in* It . . . *It Came from Outer Space* press book.

Chapter 12: Last Hurrahs

Alfred Hitchcock

191 *Sex in films . . . Psycho* press book.

From my sun-drenched . . . Niven, *Bring On the Empty Horses*, 326.

Mr. Hitchcock was . . . Rebello, *Alfred Hitchcock and the Making of* Psycho [hereinafter *Alfred Hitchcock and*], 28.

(caption) *overall sound . . .* Auiler, *Hitchcock's Notebooks*, 519.

192 *The plot was inspired . . .* Historian Tom Weaver contends that Robert Bloch based his physical description of Norman and the offscreen arguments with Norman's mother on Calvin Thomas Beck, the publisher of *Castle of Frankenstein* magazine.

I made Norman . . . Ibid., 13.

Mary started to . . . Ibid., 10.

The thing that . . . Truffaut, *Hitchcock*, 269.

Well, you're not . . . Rebello, *Alfred Hitchcock and*, 23.

a middle-aged . . . The Making of Psycho.

I wish Norman . . . Rebello, *Alfred Hitchcock and*, 39.

I cannot make . . . The Making of Psycho.

193 *When I asked him . . .* Rebello, *Alfred Hitchcock and*, 40.

I would like to see . . . The Making of Psycho.

Tsk-tsk . . . Rebello, *Alfred Hitchcock and*, 145.

You had an entire . . . Ibid., 72.

It's rather unusual . . . Truffaut, *Hitchcock*, 269.

I used my TV . . . Higham, *The Celluloid Muse*, 111.

We did between . . . Rebello, *Alfred Hitchcock and*, 84.

I will take out the . . . Leigh, *Psycho*, 112.

(caption) *He wanted someone . . .* Rebello, *Alfred Hitchcock and*, 61.

194 *Hitch was nervously . . .* Ibid., 138.

The prologue opens . . . Cook, "Bernard Herrmann," 408.

When Mother's knife . . . Rebello, *Alfred Hitchcock and*, 143.

When that knife . . . Ibid.

a blot on an . . . Leigh, *Psycho*, 112.

Director Hitchcock . . . Ibid.

We got these stories . . . Rebello, *Alfred Hitchcock and*, 161.

I saw people . . . Ibid., 162.

I've always been . . . Ibid., 163.

What will you do . . . Ibid., 169.

I have to . . . Ibid., 172.

Sea Bird . . . Spoto, *The Dark Side of Genius*, 448.

If the story . . . Truffaut, *Hitchcock*, 285.

(caption) *It was my idea . . .* Spoto, *The Dark Side of Genius*, 418.

195 *We did not want this . . .* Counts, "The Birds," 26.

I was interested in . . . Ibid., 18.

We would offer . . . Ibid., 26.

There are no stars . . . Ibid., 20.

Hitchcock loved to . . . Rebello, *Alfred Hitchcock and*, 184.

The sort of education . . . Ibid., 63.

Hitchcock was the real . . . Counts, "The Birds," 26.

the gruesome details . . . Gardner, *The Censorship Papers*, 96.

The Birds posed . . . Higham, *The Celluloid Muse*, 111.

(caption) *I don't care about . . .* Truffaut, *Hitchcock*, 282.

196 *I began to study . . .* Ibid., 290.

This doesn't make . . . Ibid.

There are times . . . All About The Birds.

It's a reversal . . . Truffaut, *Hitchcock*, 288.

Uh, well . . . Counts, "The Birds," 33.

I just blanched . . . All About The Birds.

There were three . . . Ibid.

(caption) *It wasn't a message . . .* Truffaut, *Hitchcock*, 282.

(caption) *I just couldn't get . . .* Lammers, "Psycho Memories Never Wash Away," 85.

197 *I think you're . . . All About* The Birds.

She was alone in . . . Spoto, *The Dark Side of Genius*, 459.

Just one more . . . Ibid.

I had always heard . . . Ibid., 457.

They always talk . . . Counts, "The Birds," 21.

That's enough . . . All About The Birds.

We have nothing else . . . Lammers, "Tippi Hedren Takes* The Birds *Under Her Wing," 83

The final scene . . . Higham, *The Celluloid Muse*, 112.

It's rabies . . . Counts, "The Birds," 3.

(caption) *While I was shooting . . .* Truffaut, *Hitchcock*, 287.

William Castle, Master of Gore and Gimmicks

198 *a red-faced giant . . .* Polanski, *Roman*, 264.

Bill was a cut-and-print . . . Weaver, *Science Fiction Stars*, 416.

My friends told me . . . Castle, *Step Right Up!*, 133.

A dead body . . . Ibid., 134.

There was a roar . . . Ibid.

Leaving the theater . . . Ibid.

When I was thirteen . . . Law, *Scare Tactic*, 7.

I knew then . . . Ibid.

What a job . . . Schaefer, "Macabre," 45.

Bill said he was . . . Weaver, *Science Fiction Stars*, 416.

What's our picture . . . Castle, *Step Right Up!*, 135.

a masterpiece . . . Law, *Scare Tactic*, 55.

That is the worst . . . Weaver, *Science Fiction Stars*, 419.

Wake up . . . Law, *Scare Tactic*, 55.

$1,000 in case . . . Schaefer, "Macabre," 47.

CROWDS! CROWDS . . . Ibid., 48.

199 *Well, you can . . .* Ibid., 49.

I'm depressed . . . Castle, *Step Right Up!*, 145.

They stampeded . . . Svehla, *Vincent Price*, 121.

Steve, we're completely . . . Castle, *Step Right Up!*, 149.

I was suddenly . . . Law, *Scare Tactic*, 55.

We opened in . . . Svehla, *Vincent Price*, 121.

200 *Bill was absolutely . . .* Weaver, *Science Fiction Stars*, 415.

Was that a girl . . . Ibid., 430

I've always wanted . . . Thomas, "Castle, the Gimmick Maestro," 13.

in structure, suspense . . . Law, *Scare Tactic*, 94.

Mr. Castle . . . Castle, *Step Right Up!*, 154.

Never having . . . Ibid., 165.

201 (caption) *At one of Vincent . . .* Ken Evans to author, November 4, 1981.

Horror Queens

202 *What a pretty . . .* Leigh, *Psycho*, 17.

Everything in those . . . Leyda, *The Voices of Film Experience*, 455.

I don't care . . . Kobal, *The Art of the Great Hollywood Portrait Photographers*, 89.

A great star . . . Dore Freeman to author, December 1, 1975.

ten black years . . . Stine, *Mother Goddam*, 241.

I'd like to come out . . . Dore Freeman to author, December 1, 1975.

203 *revolting . . .* Miller, *Censored Hollywood*, 187.

Elizabeth was . . . LaGuardia, *Monty*, 205.

What the hell . . . Ibid., 174.

I've tried to get . . . Ibid., 207.

Mankiewicz was . . . Ibid., 210.

204 *Are you quite sure . . .* Ibid.

*Spiegel must have cut the material only from release prints. Most prints now have the scenes.

I assumed the . . . Kael, *I Lost It at the Movies*, 140.

the most bizarre . . . Miller, *Censored Hollywood*, 188.

And when we agreed . . . Wylie, *Generation of Vipers*, 194.

(caption) *bravura, all-out . . .* Higham, *The Celluloid Muse*, 40.

205 *that they are momsick . . .* Wylie, *Generation of Vipers*, 189.

I give you . . . Ibid., 215.

Bette Davis was . . . Dore Freeman to author, December 1, 1975.

She said she wanted . . . Considine, *Bette and Joan*, 294.

I have always wanted . . . Ibid., 295.

You'll never . . . Frye, "The Devil in Miss Davis," 230.

If this isn't . . . Miller, *The Films and Career of Robert Aldrich*, 141.

What part will . . . Davis, *This 'N That*, 135.

When Aldrich . . . Thomas, *Joan Crawford*, 222.

Three distributors . . . Stine, *Mother Goddam*, 289.

I think it will . . . Silver, *What Ever Happened to Robert Aldrich?* 23.

From my rapidly . . . Aldrich, "The Care and Feeding of Baby Jane."

206 *By the time . . .* Considine, *Bette and Joan*, 301.

I designed . . . Ibid., 299.

(caption) *the isolated decay . . .* Stine, *Mother Goddam*, 293.

207 *Peggy, you . . .* Considine, *Bette and Joan*, 300.

She, more than . . . Higham, *The Celluloid Muse*, 40.

I wanted to look . . . Considine, *Bette and Joan*, 306.

They were so in . . . Ibid., 307.

Jane never . . . Davis, *This 'N That*, 137.

I had put huge . . . Considine, *Bette and Joan*, 307.

He taught me . . . Ibid., 299.

I have been waiting . . . Stine, *Mother Goddam*, 289.

If I'd lit either . . . Considine, *Bette and Joan*, 307.

You should see . . . Thomas, *Joan Crawford*, 221.

This entire . . . Considine, *Bette and Joan*, 303.

Why do I have . . . Ibid., 308.

There were far more . . . Ibid.

Dear Joan . . . Frye, "The Devil in Miss Davis," 230.

Each one coveted . . . Considine, *Bette and Joan*, 108.

Bette did everything . . . Weaver, *Science Fiction Stars*, 268.

She's supposed to be . . . Considine, *Bette and Joan*, 310.

Bob, dear, did . . . Ibid., 306.

209 *My dad had to . . .* Ibid., 305.

Joan resembles . . . Ibid., 67.

I'm not doing it . . . Ibid., 316.

There is a way . . . Ibid., 317.

I think it's proper . . . Higham, *The Celluloid Muse*, 39.

For months, the . . . "What Ever Happened to Baby Jane?"

If Miss Davis's . . . Stine, *Mother Goddam*, 289.

In one superb bit . . . Quirk, *The Films of Joan Crawford*, 211.

210 *I must say . . .* Thomas, *Joan Crawford*, 222.

was a sight to . . . Frye, "The Devil in Miss Davis," 234.

Bette felt a . . . Thomas, *Joan Crawford*, 223.

211 *I'm listening . . .* Considine, *Bette and Joan*, 334.

Strait-Jacket will . . . Castle, *Step Right Up!*, 167.

The following . . . Ibid., 171.

I always have some . . . "Castle's Balleyhooey."

(caption) *I was happy . . .* De Havilland, "Come Out Fighting," 21.

212 *It's time to get . . .* Quirk, *The Films of Joan Crawford*, 215.

I've gone from gore . . . "Castle's Balleyhooey."

It is not a . . . Smith, *Starring Miss Barbara Stanwyck*, 288.
Do you think . . . "Whistling in the Dark."
(caption) *As for Pepsi-Cola* . . . Quirk, *The Films of
Joan Crawford*, 215.

213 *the current teenage* . . . "Castle's Balleyhooey."
I think this film . . . "Dial Terror."
She would write . . . Considine, *Bette and Joan*,
365.
Add Olivia's . . . Ibid., 360.
That is the same . . . Ibid., 337.
What does it . . . Ibid., 339.
Bette lets . . . Ibid., 343.
Miss Crawford always . . . Ibid., 345.
Crawford obviously . . . Ibid., 346.

214 *Bette was* . . . Ibid., 348.
Bette was something . . . Ibid., 349.
My God . . . Thomas, *Joan Crawford*, 224.
[*Hush* . . . *Hush, Sweet* . . . Higham, *The Celluloid
Muse*, 40.
It was Miss Davis . . . Considine, *Bette and Joan*,
360.
upper respiratory . . . Thomas, *Joan Crawford*,
225.
At that stage . . . Higham, *The Celluloid Muse*, 41.
Twentieth had . . . Considine, *Bette and Joan*,
358.
Davis had star . . . Higham, *The Celluloid Muse*,
41.
(caption) *The only horrible* . . . "Whistling in the
Dark."

215 *I will not do* . . . Considine, *Bette and Joan*, 359.
No, thank you . . . Ibid., 360.
"[Davis] tried to . . . Higham, *The Celluloid Muse*,
41.
In the first script . . . De Havilland, "Come Out
Fighting," 21.
Aldrich knew . . . Stine, *Mother Goddam*, 310.
(caption) *I guess Joan couldn't* . . . George Hurrell
to author, November 1, 1975.

216 *Hush* . . . *Hush* . . . Ringgold, *The Films of Bette
Davis*, 186.
Charlotte was not . . . Considine, *Bette and Joan*,
366.
An accomplished . . . Stine, *Mother Goddam*, 310.
I'm not going to . . . "Whistling in the Dark."
Yes, she is a . . . Considine, *Bette and Joan*, 365.
She was a star . . . Ibid., 365.

Roger Corman

216 *I love the beauty* . . . Morhaim, "Love That Mon-
ster," 15.
I'm most grateful . . . Nollen, *Boris Karloff*, 238.
He was a brilliant . . . McGee, *Faster and
Furiouser*, 38.
Roger wanted to . . . Weaver, *Interviews With B*,
69.
When you meet him in . . . Weaver, *Science Fic-
tion Stars*, 54.
When they made Them! . . . Weaver, *Interviews
with B*, 385.
They discovered that . . . Ibid.
the most successful . . . Naha, *Brilliance on a Bud-
get*, 112.

217 *A couple of hours* . . . McGee, *Roger Corman*,
135.
He felt that if . . . Di Franco, *The Movie World of
Roger Corman*, 29.
They took their glasses . . . McGee, *Roger Cor-
man*, 135.
There was a system . . . Price, *Vincent Price*, 211.
There is no better . . . Will, *Roger Corman: The
Millennic Vision*, 27.
They had been selling . . . Naha, *Brilliance on a
Budget*, 28.
I just pestered . . . Weaver, *Attack of the*, 245.
I sent back . . . Nollen, *Boris Karloff*, 229.
Villain by . . . Karloff, "Memoirs of a Monster," 78.
practically every film . . . Nollen, *Boris Karloff*, 238.
I quarrel with . . . Morhaim, "Love That Monster,"
16.

218 *Look, instead of* . . . McGee, *Faster and Furiouser*,
179.
Vincent Price was . . . Price, *Vincent Price*, 211.
I never cared . . . Weaver, *Science Fiction Stars*,
295.

The world of Poe . . . Naha, *Brilliance on a
Budget*, 31.
I knew I would be . . . Ibid., 30.
Poe's story is . . . Price, *Vincent Price*, 212.
There's no monster . . . McGee, *Faster and Furi-
ouser*, 179.
The house is the . . . Price, *Vincent Price*, 212.
That line is there . . . McGee, *Faster and
Furiouser*, 179.
Corman was very good . . . Brosnan, *The Horror
People*, 133.
Vincent would prepare . . . Williams, *The Com-
plete Films of Vincent Price*, 164.

219 *It is a film that* . . . McGee, *Fast and Furious*, 115.
Their cobweb-ridden . . . Svehla, *Vincent Price*,
144.
a film that kids . . . McGee, *Roger Corman*, 115.
It made so much . . . Naha, *Brilliance on a Budget*,
32.
That American . . . Weaver, *Science Fiction Stars*,
294.
Roger shot for . . . McGee, *Roger Corman*, 126.
You can't say it . . . Ibid., 31.
Pit and the . . . Price, *Vincent Price*, 213.
and no wonder . . . McGee, *Roger Corman*, 140.
Vincent Price gives . . . Price, *Vincent Price*, 214.
Price mugs . . . McGee, *Faster and Furiouser*, 191.
Hollywood's most . . . Ibid., 193.
Comedy and terror . . . Price, *Vincent Price*, 214.
The executives . . . Brosnan, *The Horror People*,
128.

220 *Well, the original* . . . Jensen, *Boris Karloff and His
Films*, 163.
He never quite got . . . Weaver, *Science Fiction
Stars*, 49.
In one scene we . . . Catsos, "Priceless," 49.
Peter loved to . . . Price, *Vincent Price*, 214.
Boris, who was . . . Nollen, *Boris Karloff*, 229.
What the devil . . . Price, *Vincent Price*, 215.
walk down these . . . Weaver, *Science Fiction
Stars*, 309.
Peter Lorre was . . . Ibid., 49.
You haven't got . . . Bean, "Boris Is Back," 52.
I was in every shot . . . Ibid.
(caption) *Off the set* . . . Catsos, "Priceless," 48.

221 *set up one camera* . . . Weaver, *Interviews With B*,
130.
As they were being . . . Gifford, *Karloff*, 63.
He nearly killed . . . Jensen, *Boris Karloff and His
Films*, 164.
strictly a picture . . . McGee, *Fast and Furious*, 119.
delivering the year's . . . McGee, *Faster and Furiouser*, 210.
I had a good . . . Bradley, "And In the Beginning
Was the Word," 43.
I remember the first . . . Brosnan, *The Horror People*, 129.
Cobwebs . . . Price, *Vincent Price*, 219.
(caption) *I believe the funniest* . . . McGee, *Faster
and Furiouser*, 211.

223 *Vincent liked horror* . . . Price, *Vincent Price*, 218.
He had been a great . . . Catsos, "Priceless," 48.
He told me how . . . Bradley, "And In the Begin-
ning Was the Word," 43.
I always had the . . . Weaver, *Interviews with B*, 33.
James Whale was . . . Bean, "Boris Is Back," 52.
With a two-week . . . Brosnan, *The Horror People*,
129.
The undiscriminating . . . McGee, *Faster and Furi-
ouser*, 205.
The story is one . . . Nollen, *Boris Karloff*, 236.
Boris Karloff as . . . Gifford, *Karloff*, 323.
(caption) *My job as* . . . Price, *Vincent Price*, 214.

2001: A Space Odyssey

223 *In those days* . . . Posner, *Unseen Cinema*, 141.
I was essentially . . . Kahn, "The Birth of a
Notion," 10.

224 *I did have a lot* . . . Ibid., 11.
It was where a . . . Ibid.
People were packing . . . Kahn, "The Birth of a
Notion," 11.
Going to movies . . . Sontag, "The Decay of Cin-
ema," 61.
Cameras and the . . . Howard, *Stanley Kubrick
Companion*, 15.

Stanley isn't antisocial . . . Ibid.
I became convinced . . . Agel, *The Making of
Kubrick's 2001*, 111.
He called up . . . Ibid.
a glittering . . . Clarke, *The Lost Worlds of 2001*, 24.
(caption) *2001 has things* . . . Agel, *The Making of
Kubrick's 2001*, 306.

225 *I do not think* . . . Clarke, *The Lost Worlds of 2001*,
28.
proverbial good . . . Ibid., 17.
Our first meeting . . . Clarke, *Report on Planet
Three*, 216.
He wanted to make . . . Clarke, *The Lost Worlds of
2001*, 29.
Besides talking . . . Clarke, *Report on Planet
Three*, 217.

226 *After one day* . . . Ibid., 219.
What we want . . . Clarke, *The Lost Worlds of
2001*, 33.
Dreamed that . . . Howard, *Stanley Kubrick Com-
panion*, 104.
Getting slightly . . . Clarke, *The Lost Worlds of
2001*, 24.
Science fiction films . . . Agel, *The Making of
Kubrick's 2001*, 25.
For the Greeks . . . Ibid.
I felt it was . . . Ibid., 351.
It won't be a . . . Howard, *Stanley Kubrick Com-
panion*, 111.
conceive, design . . . Agel, *The Making of
Kubrick's 2001*, 351.
Basic construction . . . Ibid., 89.
(caption) *The most terrifying* . . . "Stanley
Kubrick." 150.

227 *TMA 1 is quite* . . . Clarke, *The Lost Worlds of
2001*, 43.
I asked Kubrick . . . Agel, *The Making of Kubrick's
2001*, 68.
defy logic as well . . . Ibid., 70.
Working with Kubrick . . . Ibid., 306.
You realize . . . Clarke, *The Lost Worlds of 2001*,
46.
Emotionally I am . . . Howard, *Stanley Kubrick
Companion*, 109.

228 *I don't like* . . . Agel, *The Making of Kubrick's
2001*, 7.
With the stress . . . Ibid., 199.
was completely . . . Howard, *Stanley Kubrick Companion*, 111.
it's hard to . . . Agel, *The Making of Kubrick's 2001*,
88.
If you understand . . . Clarke, *Report on Planet
Three*, 224.
Nobody slept at . . . Aldiss, *The Year's Best Science Fiction No. 2*, 51.
A number of . . . Agel, *The Making of Kubrick's
2001*, 102.
I have never seen . . . Ibid., 284.
pictorial part was . . . Aldiss, *The Year's Best Science Fiction No. 2*, 51.
(caption) *is so dull, it even* . . . Agel, *The Making
of Kubrick's 2001*, 225.

229 *The uncompromising* . . . Ibid., 208.
One can read . . . Ibid., 213.
Space, as he . . . Kaufmann, "Lost in the Stars,"
41.
The test of the . . . Hall, "A Conversation with Ray
Bradbury and Chuck Jones," 70.
I'd rather not . . . Agel, *The Making of Kubrick's
2001*, 285.
I attribute the . . . Ibid., 169.
No reviewer . . . Howard, *Stanley Kubrick Com-
panion*, 22.
No one with . . . Agel, *The Making of Kubrick's
2001*, 195.
(caption) *To play a twenty* . . . Ibid., 313.
(caption) *I suppose it comes* . . . "Stanley
Kubrick," 195.

230 *twelve percent of urban* . . . Gallup, *Gallup Poll*,
2221.
I believe that drugs . . . Agel, *The Making of
Kubrick's 2001*, 353.
This isn't a normal . . . Aldiss, *The Year's Best Sci-
ence Fiction No. 2*, 51.
I thought it was . . . Agel, *The Making of Kubrick's
2001*, 187.

When one can . . . Ibid., 306.
How can man . . . Ibid., 192.
At first I thought . . . Howard, *Stanley Kubrick Companion*, 113.
I think Stanley . . . Agel, *The Making of Kubrick's 2001*, 209.
If 2001 has . . . Ibid., 161.
As for the dwindling . . . Clarke, *Report on Planet Three*, 224.

The End of Two Eras

230 *I did not take* . . . Miller, *Censored Hollywood*, 200.

231 *People do certain* . . . Ibid., 202.
It was like the . . . Biskind, *Easy Riders, Raging Bulls*, 14.
Speaking of King . . . Winogura, "Dialogues on Apes, Apes, and More Apes," 4.
a rip-roaring horror . . . Pendreigh, *The Legend of the Planet of the Apes*, [hereinafter *The Legend of*], 28.
It was very different . . . Ibid., 34.

232 *There was a chance* . . . Ibid., 54.
Mort, I have to . . . Pendreigh, *The Legend of*, 54.
I smelled a hit . . . Heston, *In the Arena*, 397.
There were nine . . . Dunne, *The Studio*, 96.
We never discussed . . . Pendreigh, *The Legend of*, 11.

233 *He was my* . . . Weaver, *Science Fiction Stars*, 217.
Twentieth Century . . . Ibid., 213.
We're either gonna . . . Ibid., 217.
This is going to . . . Ibid., 215.
He saw me watching . . . Ibid.
He had his . . . Ibid., 213.
It takes so long . . . Pendreigh, *The Legend of*, 93.
There's hardly been . . . Heston, *The Actor's Life*, 374.
It's the first time . . . Ibid., 372.
Mmmm, nice . . . Heston, *In the Arena*, 395.
They'd come up . . . Weaver, *Science Fiction Stars*, 217.
Oh, that isn't . . . Pendreigh, *The Legend of*, 77.
We finally got . . . Weaver, *Science Fiction Stars*, 217.
Who the hell . . . Dunne, *The Studio*, 95.
I had the nightmare . . . Ibid., 217.
Arthur, I know the . . . Ibid., 101.
Not until the . . . Ibid., 110.
Rather precise parallels . . . "Planet of the Apes."

234 *The film catches* . . . Pendreigh, *The Legend of*, 114.
Planet of the . . . Ibid.
We weren't trying . . . Ibid., 6.
More or less . . . Ibid., 11.
You know the bottom . . . Castle, *Step Right Up!*, 186.
Don't forget . . . Ibid., 189.
How much would . . . Ibid., 191.
a producer of cheap . . . Polanski, *Roman*, 264.
I took an . . . Castle, *Step Right Up!*, 193.

235 *I no more believed* . . . Polanski, *Roman*, 265.
Blood is . . . Castle, *Step Right Up!*, 203.
Thought I'd watch . . . Ibid.
You seem uptight . . . Ibid., 205.
Roman preferred . . . Farrow, *What Falls Away*, 109.
John felt that . . . Ibid.
knew nothing about . . . Ibid.
Look, I've had . . . Polanski, *Roman*, 273.
Hey, I've got a . . . Farrow, *What Falls Away*, 90.
Sinatra never . . . Polanski, *Roman*, 271.
Roman was humming . . . Farrow, *What Falls Away*, 111.
One day I found . . . Ibid.
Frank was baffled . . . Ibid.
[Sinatra] knew we were . . . Polanski, *Roman*, 271.

237 *When is Polanski* . . . Castle, *Step Right Up!*, 213.
When there was no . . . Polanski, *Roman*, 275.
While mapping . . . Farrow, *What Falls Away*, 113.
It is the fantasy . . . Adler, "Rosemary's Baby."
You have unleashed . . . Castle, *Step Right Up!*, 218.

*Mia Farrow was not the only person connected with *Rosemary's Baby* who suffered sudden distress. In early 1969, William Castle fell ill with undiagnosed abdominal pain and under-went a long series of debilitating treatments. In late spring, Christopher Komeda was admitted to the same hospital. He had suffered a head injury while partying with another Polish émigré. He fell into a coma, then died. In August, Roman Polanski's pregnant wife, Sharon Tate, and three friends were murdered in his home by members of a cult. For a full account of the events connected with *Rosemary's Baby*, see Vincent Bugliosi's *Helter Skelter*, William Castle's autobiography, *Step Right Up!*, and Roman Polanski's autobiography, *Roman*.

If I was in . . . Biskind, *Easy Riders, Raging Bulls*, 116.
(caption) *Its success* . . . Farrow, *What Falls Away*, 134.

238 *I watched Hawks* . . . Biskind, *Easy Riders, Raging Bulls*, 114.
Do you want to . . . Ibid., 115.
We have two . . . Lindsay, *Dear Boris*, 168.
You know how . . . Biskind, *Easy Riders, Raging Bulls*, 115.
We started thinking . . . Nollen, *Boris Karloff*, 245.
Since this character . . . Ibid., 246.
He didn't look like . . . Ibid., 247.
I believe in this . . . Lindsay, *Dear Boris*, 168.
I suffer from . . . Prelutsky, "The Monstrous Mr. Karloff," 7.
It was extremely difficult . . . Jensen, *Boris Karloff and His Films*, 24.
I'm one of that . . . Prelutsky, "The Monstrous Mr. Karloff," 7.

239 *This is our only* . . . Nollen, *Boris Karloff*, 248.
It's a very timely . . . Prelutsky, "The Monstrous Mr. Karloff," 7.
Statistics showed . . . *Statistical Abstract of the United States, 1971*, 58, 253.
You mean idiot . . . Lindsay, *Dear Boris*, 172.

240 *Stay on him* . . . Ibid.
Spontaneous . . . Jensen, *Boris Karloff and His Films*, 169.
Well, I could see . . . Nollen, *Boris Karloff*, 252.
You know, I don't . . . Shivas, "Karloff Still Eager to Scare Us Witless."
God, I'm lucky . . . Lindsay, *Dear Boris*, 175.

Epilogue: Rated "Ick!"

240 *brutal and callous* . . . Gussow, *Don't Say Yes Until I Finish Talking*, 46.
One person in . . . Warren, *Keep Watching the Skies*, 26.
Have the reviewers . . . Kael, *I Lost It at the Movies*, 208.
In England . . . Alpert, "The Horror of It All," 76.

241 *Are we really* . . . Vizzard, *See No Evil*, 346.
Last year we gave . . . Ibid.
The studios now have . . . Ibid., 347.
Val always said . . . Leeman, *Robert Wise on His Films*, 44.
It was a typical . . . "Just Another Horror Movie—Or Is It?", 127.

242 *There was no MPAA* . . . "George Romero."
Think about it . . . Nollen, *Boris Karloff*, 227.
A hundred years . . . Counts, "The Birds," 20.

Bibliography

Books

Agate, James. *Around Cinemas*. London: Home and Van Thal, 1946

Agee, James. *Agee on Film*. Boston, Mass: Beacon Press, 1958.

Agel, Jerome. *The Making of Kubrick's 2001*. New York: Signet Books, 1970.

Aldiss, Brian W., and Harry Harrison. *The Year's Best Science Fiction No. 2*. London: Delta Books, 1968.

American Film Institute Catalog of Motion Pictures Produced in the United States, 1931–1940. Berkeley: University of California Press, 1993.

American Film Institute Catalog of Motion Pictures Produced in the United States, 1941–1950. Berkeley: University of California Press, 1999.

Amory, Cleveland, and Frederick Bradlee. *Cavalcade of the 1920s and 1930s*. New York: Viking Press, 1960.

Auiler, Dan. *Hitchcock's Notebooks: An Authorized and Illustrated Look Inside the Creative Mind of Alfred Hitchcock*. New York: Spike Books, 1999.

Banzak, Edmund G. *Fearing the Dark: The Val Lewton Career*. Jefferson, N.C.: McFarland & Company, 1990.

Beck, Calvin Thomas. *Heroes of the Horrors*. New York: MacMillan, 1975.

_____. *Scream Queens*. New York: Collier Books, 1978.

Behlmer, Rudy. *Memo from Darryl F. Zanuck: The Golden Years at Twentieth Century–Fox*. New York: Grove Press, 1993.

Biskind, Peter. *Easy Riders, Raging Bulls: How the Sex-Drugs-and-Rock'n'Roll Generation Saved Hollywood*. New York: Simon and Schuster, 1998.

Blake, Michael. *Lon Chaney: The Man behind the Thousand Faces*. Lanham, Md.: Vestal Press, 1990.

_____. *A Thousand Faces: Lon Chaney's Unique Artistry in Motion Pictures*. Lanham, Md.: Vestal Press, 1995.

Brownlow, Kevin. *The Parade's Gone By*. New York: Ballantine Books, 1969.

Brosnan, John. *The Horror People*. New York: St. Martin's Press, 1976.

_____. *Movie Magic: The Story of Special Effects in the Cinema*. New York: St. Martin's Press, 1974.

Brunas, Michael, John Brunas, and Tom Weaver. *Universal Horrors: The Studio's Classic Films, 1931–1946*. Jefferson, N.C.: McFarland & Company, 1990.

Bull, Clarence Sinclair, with Raymond Lee. *The Faces of Hollywood*. New York: A. S. Barnes and Company, 1968.

Castle, William. *Step Right Up!: I'm Gonna Scare the Pants Off America*. New York: Pharos Books, 1992.

Clarens, Carlos. *An Illustrated History of Horror and Science Fiction Films*. New York: Da Capo Press, 1997.

Clarke, Arthur C. *The Lost Worlds of 2001*. New York: Signet Books, 1972.

_____. *Report on Planet Three and Other Speculations*. New York: Signet Books, 1973.

Considine, Shaun. *Bette and Joan: The Divine Feud*. New York: E. P. Dutton, 1989.

Crawford, Joan, with Jane Kesner Ardmore. *A Portrait of Joan*. Garden City, N.Y.: Doubleday, 1962.

Cremer, Robert. *Lugosi: The Man Behind the Cape*. Chicago: Henry Regnery Company, 1976.

Curtis, James. *James Whale: A New World of Gods and Monsters*. Boston: Faber and Faber, 1998.

Custen, George. *Twentieth Century's Fox: Darryl F. Zanuck and the Culture of Hollywood*. New York: BasicBooks, 1997.

Daniels, Dennis. *Famous Monsters Chronicles*. Los Angeles: FantaCo Enterprises, 1991.

Davidson, Muriel, and Frank Westmore. *The Westmores of Hollywood*. New York: Berkley, 1977.

Davis, Bette, and Michael Herskowitz. *This 'n That*. New York: G. P. Putnam's Sons, 1987.

Davis, Ronald L. *The Glamour Factory: Inside Hollywood's Big Studio System*. Dallas: Southern Methodist University Press, 1993.

Di Franco, J. Philip. *The Movie World of Roger Corman*. New York: Chelsea House, 1979.

Douglas, Helen Gahagan. *A Full Life*. Garden City, N.Y.: Doubleday, 1982.

Dunne, John Gregory. *The Studio*. New York: Limelight Editions, 1985.

Farrow, Mia. *What Falls Away*. New York: Bantam Books, 1998.

Felleman, Susan. *Botticelli in Hollywood: The Films of Albert Lewin*. New York: Twayne Publishers, 1997.

Ferrell, Robert H. *Off the Record: The Private Papers of Harry S. Truman*. New York: Harper and Row, 1980.

Finler, Joel. *The Hollywood Story*. New York: Crown, 1988.

Fischer, Dennis. *Horror Film Directors, 1931–1990*. Jefferson, N.C.: McFarland & Company, 1991.

Forman, Henry James. *Our Movie-Made Children*. New York: MacMillan, 1933.

Friedman, Favius. *Great Horror Movies*. New York: Scholastic Book Services, 1974.

Fujiwara, Chris. *Jacques Tourneur: The Cinema of Nightfall*. Jefferson, N.C.: McFarland & Company, 1998.

Gabler, Neal. *An Empire of Their Own: How the Jews Invented Hollywood*. New York: Anchor Books, 1989.

Gallup, George. *The Gallup Poll, Public Opinion 1935–1971, Volume 3: 1959–1971*. New York: Random House, 1972.

Gardner, Gerald. *The Censorship Papers*. New York: Dodd, Mead & Company, 1987.

Gatiss, Mark. *James Whale*. London: Cassell, 1995.

Gifford, Denis. *Karloff: The Man, the Monster, the Movies*. Teaneck, N.J.: Curtis Film Books, 1973.

_____. *A Pictorial History of Horror Movies*. London: Hamlyn Publishing Group, 1973.

Gilbert, Julie. *Opposite Attraction: The Lives of Erich Maria Remarque and Paulette Goddard*. New York: Pantheon Books, 1995.

Goldner, Orville, and George E. Turner. *The Making of King Kong*. Cranbury, N.J.: A. S. Barnes and Company, 1975.

Greenberg, Joel, and Charles Higham. *The Celluloid Muse*. New York: Signet Books, 1972.

Gussow, Mel. *Don't Say Yes Until I Finish Talking*. New York: Doubleday, 1971.

Harmetz, Aljean. *Round Up the Usual Suspects: The Making of* Casablanca: *Bogart, Bergman, and World War II*. New York: Hyperion, 1992.

Harryhausen, Ray. *Film Fantasy Scrapbook*. Cranbury, N.J.: A. S. Barnes and Company, 1972.

Haver, Ronald. *David O. Selznick's Hollywood*. New York: Alfred A. Knopf, 1980.

Hecht, Ben. *Charlie: The Improbable Life and Times of Charles MacArthur*. New York: Harper & Brothers, 1957.

Hepburn, Katharine. *Me: Stories of My Life*. New York: Alfred A. Knopf, 1992.

Heston, Charlton. *The Actor's Life: Journals, 1956 to 1976*. New York: Pocket Books, 1979.

_____. *In the Arena: The Autobiography*. New York: Boulevard, 1997.

Higham, Charles. *Charles Laughton: An Intimate Biography*. Garden City, N.Y.: Doubleday, 1976.

_____. *Hollywood Cameramen*. Bloomington, Ind.: Indiana University Press, 1970.

Hope, Bob, and Bob Thomas. *The Road to Hollywood: My Forty-Year Love Affair With the Movies*. Garden City, N.Y.: Doubleday, 1977.

Howard, James. *Stanley Kubrick Companion*. London: B. T. Batsford, 1999.

Jensen, Paul. *Boris Karloff and His Films*. New York: A. S. Barnes and Company, 1974.

_____. *The Men Who Made the Monsters*. New York: Twayne Publishers, 1996.

Johnson, John "J. J." *Cheap Tricks and Class Acts: Special Effects, Makeup and Stunts from the Films of the Fantastic Fifties*. Jefferson, N.C.: McFarland & Company, 1996.

Kael, Pauline. *I Lost It at the Movies*. Boston: Little, Brown and Company, 1965.

King, Stephen. *Danse Macabre*. New York: Berkley Books, 1981.

Kinnard, Roy. *Horror in Silent Films: A Filmography, 1896–1929*. Jefferson, N.C.: McFarland & Company, 1995.

Kobal, John. *The Art of the Great Hollywood Portrait Photographers*. New York: Alfred A. Knopf, 1980.

_____. *People Will Talk*. New York: Alfred A. Knopf, 1985.

Kotsilibas-Davis, James, and Myrna Loy. *Being and Becoming*. New York: Alfred A. Knopf, 1987.

Kracauer, Siegfried. *From Caligari to Hitler: A Psychological History of the German Film*. Princeton, N.J.: Princeton University Press, 1947.

LaGuardia, Robert. *Monty: A Biography of Montgomery Clift*. New York: Avon Books, 1978.

Lambert, Gavin. *Norma Shearer: A Life*. New York: Alfred A. Knopf, 1990.

Lanchester, Elsa. *Elsa Lanchester, Herself*. New York: St. Martin's Press, 1983.

Law, John W. *Scare Tactic: The Life and Films of William Castle*. New York: Writers Club Press, 2000.

Leaming, Barbara. *Orson Welles: A Biography*. New York: Limelight Editions, 1995.

Lebo, Harlan. *Citizen Kane*. New York: Doubleday, 1990.

Leeman, Sergio. *Robert Wise on His Films: From Editing Room to Director's Chair*. Los Angeles: Silman-James Press, 1995.

Leigh, Janet, and Christopher Nickens. *Psycho: Behind the Scenes of the Classic Thriller*. New York: Harmony Books, 1995.

Lennig, Arthur. *The Count: The Life and Times of Bela "Dracula" Lugosi*. New York: G. P. Putnam's Sons, 1974.

Leyda, Jay. *The Voices of Film Experience*. New York: MacMillan, 1977.

Lindsay, Cynthia. *Dear Boris*. New York: Alfred A. Knopf, 1975.

Maas, Frederica Sagor. *The Shocking Miss Pilgrim: A Writer in Early Hollywood*. Lexington, Ky.: University Press of Kentucky, 1999.

Mank, Gregory William. *The Bride of Frankenstein*. Absecon, N.J.: MagicImage Filmbooks, 1989.

_____. *Dwight Frye's Last Laugh*. Baltimore, Md.: Midnight Marquee Press, 1997.

_____. *Hollywood Cauldron*. Jefferson, N.C.: McFarland & Company, 1994.

_____. *Hollywood Hissables*. Metuchen, N.J.: Scarecrow Press, 1989.

_____. *Hollywood's Maddest Doctors*. Baltimore, Md.: Midnight Marquee Press, 1998.

_____. *It's Alive!* San Diego, Calif.: A. S. Barnes and Company, 1981.

_____. *Karloff and Lugosi: The Story of a Haunting Collaboration*. Jefferson, N.C.: McFarland & Company, 1990.

_____. *Women in Horror Films, 1930s*. Jefferson, N.C.: McFarland & Company, 1999.

_____. *Women in Horror Films, 1940s*. Jefferson, N.C.: McFarland & Company, 1999.

Marx, Arthur. *The Secret Life of Bob Hope*. New York: Barricade Books, 1993.

Marx, Samuel. *A Gaudy Spree*. New York: Franklin Watts, 1987.

McCandless, Barbara. *New York to Hollywood: The Photography of Karl Struss*. Albuquerque, N.M.: University of New Mexico Press, 1995.

McCarthy, Kevin, and Ed Gorman. *"They're Here . . .": Invasion of the Body Snatchers: A Tribute*. New York: Berkley Boulevard Books, 1999.

McCarthy, Todd. *Howard Hawks*. New York: Grove Press, 1997.

McGee, Mark Thomas. *Fast and Furious: The Story of American International Pictures*. Jefferson, N.C.: McFarland & Company, 1996.

_____. *Faster and Furiouser: The Revised and Fattened Fable of American International Pictures*. Jefferson, N.C.: McFarland & Company, 1996.

_____. *Roger Corman: The Best of the Cheap Acts*. Jefferson, N.C.: McFarland & Company, 1988.

Medved, Harry, and Michael Medved. *The Golden Turkey Awards*. New York: Berkley Books, 1981.

Miller, Arnold. *The Films and Career of Robert Aldrich*. Knoxville, Tenn.: University of Tennessee Press, 1986.

Miller, Frank. *Censored Hollywood: Sex, Sin and Violence on Screen*. Atlanta: Turner, 1994.

Milne, Tom. *Mamoulian*. London: Thames and Hudson, 1969.

Naha, Ed. *Brilliance on a Budget: The Films of Roger Corman*. New York: Simon and Schuster, 1984.

Niven, David. *Bring on the Empty Horses*. New York: Dell, 1976.

Nollen, Scott Allen. *Boris Karloff: A Gentleman's Life.* Baltimore, Md.: Midnight Marquee Press, 1999.

Paris, Barry. *Garbo: A Biography.* New York: Alfred A. Knopf, 1995.

Parla, Paul, and Charles P. Mitchell. *Screen Sirens Scream.* Jefferson, N.C.: McFarland & Company, 2000.

Pendreigh, Brian. *The Legend of the Planet of the Apes (Or How Hollywood Turned Darwin Upside Down).* London: Boxtree, 2001.

Polanski, Roman. *Roman.* New York: William Morrow, 1984.

Posner, Bruce. *Unseen Cinema: Early American Avant-Garde Film 1893–1941.* New York: Black Thistle Press, 2001.

Price, Victoria. *Vincent Price: A Daughter's Biography.* New York: St. Martin's Press, 1999.

Priestley, J. B. *Benighted.* London: Ballantyne Press, 1927.

Quirk, Lawrence. *The Films of Joan Crawford.* Secaucus, N.J.: Citadel Press, 1988.

Rebello, Stephen. *Alfred Hitchcock and the Making of Psycho.* New York: St. Martin's Griffin, 1998.

Reemes, Dana M. *Directed by Jack Arnold.* Jefferson, N.C.: McFarland & Company, 1988.

Rhodes, Gary Don. *Lugosi: His Life in Films, on Stage, and in the Hearts of Horror Lovers.* Jefferson, N.C.: McFarland and Company, 1997.

Riley, Philip J. *Dracula.* Absecon, N.J.: MagicImage Filmbooks, 1990.

_____. *Frankenstein.* Absecon, N.J.: MagicImage Filmbooks, 1989.

_____. *London After Midnight.* New York: Cornwall Books, 1985.

_____. *The Mummy.* Absecon, N.J.: MagicImage Filmbooks, 1989.

_____. *This Island Earth.* Absecon, N.J.: MagicImage Filmbooks, 1990.

_____. *The Wolf Man.* Absecon, N.J.: MagicImage Filmbooks, 1993.

Ringgold, Gene. *The Films of Bette Davis.* Secaucus, N.J.: Citadel Press, 1973.

Rovin, Jeff. *From the Land beyond Beyond: The Films of Willis O'Brien and Ray Harryhausen.* New York: Berkley Windhover, 1977.

Sanders, George. *Memoirs of a Professional Cad.* New York: G. P. Putnam's Sons, 1960.

Schatz, Thomas. *The Genius of the System.* New York: Pantheon Books, 1988.

Schulberg, Budd. *Moving Pictures: Memories of a Hollywood Prince.* New York: Stein and Day, 1981.

Senn, Bryan. *Golden Horrors: An Illustrated Critical Filmography of Terror Cinema, 1931–1939.* Jefferson, N.C.: MacFarland and Company, 1996.

Siegel, Joel. *Val Lewton: The Reality of Terror.* Viking Press, 1973.

Silver, Alain, and James Ursini. *What Ever Happened to Robert Aldrich?* New York: Limelight Editions, 1995.

Skal, David J. *The Monster Show: A Cultural History of Horror.* New York: W. W. Norton, 1993.

_____, and Elias Savada. *Dark Carnival: The Secret World of Tod Browning.* New York: Anchor Books, 1995.

Smith, Ella. *Starring Miss Barbara Stanwyck.* New York: Crown, 1974.

Spillane, Mickey. *Kiss Me, Deadly.* New York: Signet Books, 1952.

Spoto, Donald. *The Dark Side of Genius: The Life of Alfred Hitchcock.* New York: Da Capo Press, 1999.

_____. *Lenya: A Life.* New York: Ballantine Books, 1989.

Statistical Abstract of the United States, 1971. Washington: Government Printing Office, 1971.

Stine, Whitney. *The Hurrell Style.* New York: John Day Company, 1976.

_____. *Mother Goddam.* New York: Hawthorn Books, 1974.

Svehla, Gary J., and Susan Svehla. *Vincent Price.* Baltimore, Md.: Midnight Marquee Press, 1998.

Thomas, Bob. *Joan Crawford.* New York: Bantam Books, 1979.

Thompson, Frank. *Between Action and Cut: Five American Directors.* Metuchen, N.J.: Scarecrow Press, 1985.

Truffaut, François. *Hitchcock: Dialogue between Truffaut and Hitchcock.* New York: Simon and Schuster, 1983.

Turner, George. *The Cinema of Adventure, Romance, and Terror.* Hollywood, Calif.: ASC Press, 1989.

Underwood, Peter. *Karloff: The Life of Boris Karloff.* New York: Drake Publishers, 1972.

Vizzard, Jack. *See No Evil: Life Inside A Hollywood Censor.* New York: Simon and Schuster, 1970.

Walker, Alexander. *The Shattered Silents.* New York: William Morrow, 1979.

Warren, Bill. *Keep Watching the Skies.* Jefferson, N.C.: MacFarland and Company, 1997.

Weaver, Tom. *Attack of the Monster Movie Makers.* Jefferson, N.C.: MacFarland and Company, 1994.

_____. *Interviews with B Science Fiction and Horror Movie Makers: Writers, Producers, Directors, Actors, Moguls and Makeup.* Jefferson, N.C.: McFarland & Company, 1988.

_____. *Science Fiction Stars and Horror Heroes: Interviews with Actors, Directors, Producers and Writers of the 1940s through 1960s.* Jefferson, N.C.: McFarland & Company, 1991.

_____. *They Fought in the Creature Features.* Jefferson, N.C.: MacFarland and Company, 1995.

Weld, John. *September Song.* Lanham, Md.: Scarecrow Press, 1998.

Westmore, Frank, and Murial Davidson. *The Westmores of Hollywood.* New York: Berkley Medallion Books, 1976.

Will, David, and Paul Willemen. *Roger Corman: The Millennic Vision.* Edinburgh, Scotland: Edinburgh Film Festival, 1970.

Williams, Lucy Chase. *The Complete Films of Vincent Price.* Secaucus, N.J.: Citadel Press, 1995.

Wylie, Philip. *Generation of Vipers.* New York: Pocket Books, 1955.

Signed Articles

Adler, Renata. "Screen: *Rosemary's Baby*, a Story of Fantasy and Horror." *New York Times.* June 13, 1968, fragmentary clipping, CMPS.

Aldrich, Robert. "The Care and Feeding of Baby Jane." *New York Times.* Nov. 4, 1962, fragmentary clipping, CMPS.

Alpert, Hollis, and Charles Beaumont. "The Horror of It All." *Playboy* (Mar. 1959): 69–88.

Arkadin [John Russell Taylor]. "Film Clips." *Sight and Sound* 37, no. 1 (winter 1967–68): 47.

Battle, Pat Wilks. "Journey's End?" *Filmfax* 74 (Aug.–Sept. 1999): 50–56.

Bean, Robin. "Boris Is Back." *Films and Filming* 11, no. 9 (May 1965): 52–53.

Berg, Louis. "Dr. Seuss' 5,000 Fingers." *This Week Magazine, Los Angeles Times.* Aug. 20, 1952.

_____. "Farewell to Monsters." *Los Angeles Times.* May 12, 1946, fragmentary clipping, CMPS.

Bodeen, DeWitt. "Val Lewton." *Film in Review* XIV, no. 4 (Apr. 1963): 210–25.

Bowman, David. "The Strange Odyssey of Helen Chandler." *Filmfax* 35 (Oct.–Nov. 1992): 67–72.

Bradley, Matthew R. "And in the Beginning Was the Word." *Filmfax* 42 (Dec. 1993–Jan. 1994): 40–44, 78–82, 98.

Brunas, John. "Inside the Alligator People." *Filmfax* 1, no. 4 (Oct.–Nov. 1986): 56–61.

Carroll, Harrison. "Dial Terror." *Los Angeles Herald Examiner.* Nov. 15, 1964, fragmentary clipping, CMPS.

Catsos, Gregory J. M. "Carla Laemmle." *Filmfax* 80 (Aug.–Sept. 2000): 68–71, 82.

_____. "Priceless." *Filmfax* 42 (Dec. 1993–Jan. 1994): 45–49.

Cohen, Gary. "The Legend of Rubirosa." *Vanity Fair* no. 508 (Dec. 2002): 242–64.

Cook, Page. "Bernard Herrmann." *Films in Review* XVIII, no. 7 (Aug.–Sept. 1967): 398–412.

_____. "Franz Waxman." *Films in Review* XIX, no. 7 (Aug.–Sept. 1968): 415–30.

Counts, Kyle B. "The Birds." *Cinefantastique* 10, no. 2 (fall 1980): 3, 15–35.

De Havilland, Olivia. "Come Out Fighting." *Films and Filming* (Mar. 1966): 19–21.

Dickey, Joan. "A Maker of Mystery." *Motion Picture Classic* (Apr. 1928): 33, 80.

Durgnat, Raymond. "Invasion of the Body Snatchers." *Films and Filming* (Feb. 1969): 49–50.

Ebert, Roger. "Just Another Horror Movie—Or Is It?" *Reader's Digest* (June 1969): 127–28.

Frye, William. "The Devil in Miss Davis." *Vanity Fair* no. 488 (Apr. 2001): 222–57.

Galbraith, Stuart IV. "Where *It* Really Came From." *Filmfax* 50 (May–June 1995): 51–57, 94–95.

Hagerty, Jack. "The Making of George Pal's *Destination Moon.*" *Filmfax* 80 (Aug.–Sept. 2000): 50–59.

Hall, Gladys. "Discoveries About Myself." *Motion Picture* (July 1930): 59, 106.

_____. "The Feminine Love of Horror." *Motion Picture Classic* (Jan. 1931): 21–22, 67.

Hall, Mary Herrington. "A Conversation with Ray Bradbury and Chuck Jones: The Fantasy Makers." *Psychology Today* 1, no. 11 (Apr. 1968): 28–37, 70.

Haver, Ron. "*The 5000 Fingers of Dr. T.*" Los Angeles County Museum of Art Program, CMPS.

Henderson, Jan A., and George E. Turner. "*Bride of Frankenstein*: A Gothic Masterpiece." *American Cinematographer* 79, no. 1 (Jan. 1998): 102–9.

Kahn, Brady. "The Birth of a Notion." *The Express* 7, no. 17 (Dec. 28, 1984): 1, 10–14.

Karloff, Boris (as told to Arlene and Howard Eisenberg). "Memoirs of a Monster." *Saturday Evening Post* 235, no. 39 (Nov. 3, 1962): 77–80.

_____. "My Life as a Monster." *Films and Filming* (Nov. 1957): 11, 34.

Kaufmann, Stanley. "Lost in the Stars." *New Republic* 158, no. 118 (May 4, 1968): 22, 41.

Lammers, Tim. "Psycho Memories Never Wash Away." *The Big Reel* 318 (Nov. 2000): 85–86.

_____. "Tippi Hedren Takes *The Birds* Under Her Wing." *The Big Reel* 318 (Nov. 2000): 83–84.

Linaweaver, Brad. "First Man-to-Fly: An Interview with David 'Al' Hedison." *Filmfax* 68 (Aug.–Sept. 1998): 48–51, 122–23.

Locan, Clarence A. "The Lon Chaney I Knew." *Photoplay* (Nov. 1930): 58–60, 106, 108.

MacQueen, Scott. "Doctor X—a Technicolor Landmark." *American Cinematographer* 67, no. 6 (June 1986): 34–42.

_____. "*The Mystery of the Wax Museum.*" *American Cinematographer* 71, no. 4 (Apr. 1990): 42–50.

_____. "The 1926 *Phantom of the Opera.*" *American Cinematographer* 70, no. 9 (Sept. 1989): 34–40.

_____. "*The Phantom of the Opera* – Part II." *American Cinematographer* 70, no. 10 (Oct. 1989): 34–40.

Mank, Gregory William. "Laird Cregar: Hollywood's Reluctant Ripper." *Video Watchdog* no. 15 (Jan./Feb. 1993): 30–48.

Morhaim, Joe. "Being a Monster Is Really a Game." *TV Guide* (Oct. 15, 1960): 17–19.

_____. "Love That Monster." *TV Guide* (Jan. 11, 1958): 14–15.

Murf. "Planet of the Apes." *Variety* (Feb. 1, 1968): fragmentary clipping, CMPS.

Nelson, Bradford. "Chaney Comes Back." *Screenland* (May 1930): 32–33, 116–17.

Newsom, Ted. "The Ray Harryhausen Story: Part One, The Early Years, 1920–1958." *Cinefantastique* (Dec. 1981): 14–28.

Nolan, Jack Edmund. "Robert Siodmak." *Films in Review* XX, no. 4 (Apr. 1969): 218–31.

Pace, Terry. "Man of Steel." *Scarlet Street* no. 39 (summer 2000): 52–57, 78.

Parla, Donna, and Paul Parla. "Revenge of the Creatures." *Filmfax* 59 (Oct. 1996–Jan. 1997): 91–94.

Parla, Paul. "Beauty and the Beasts." *Filmfax* 59 (Oct. 1996–Jan. 1997): 108–11.

_____. "The Woman from Planet X" *Filmfax* 59 (Oct. 1996–Jan. 1997): 71–77.

_____, and Charles P. Mitchell. "Sandy Descher: The Space Child Who Cried 'Them!'" *Filmfax* 59 (Oct. 1996–Jan. 1997): 105–7.

_____, and Donna Parla. "Talking Eye to Eye: An Interview with Duncan 'Dean' Parkin." *Filmfax* 59 (Oct. 1996–Jan. 1997): 102–4.

_____, and Donna Parla. "Wooden Performance: Tree Monster Chester Hayes Speaks." *Filmfax* 55 (Mar.–Apr. 1996): 61–63.

Peary, Dannis. "Mark Robson Remembers RKO, Welles, and Val Lewton." *Velvet Light Trap* no. 10 (fall 1993): 32–37.

Prelutsky, Burt. "The Monstrous Mr. Karloff." *Los Angeles Times West Magazine* (June 9, 1968): 7.

Rankin, Ruth. "A Child of the Theater." *The New Movie Magazine* (Jan. 1932): 109.

Rennie, Michael. "The Role I Liked Best." *The Saturday Evening Post* (Apr. 17, 1954): fragmentary clipping, CMPS.

Rhodes, Gary Don. "Horror! The 1939 Revival of a Genre." *Scarlet Street* no. 26 (fall 1998): 68–74, 80–81.

Riordan, Paul M. "Atomic Blonde." *Filmfax* 63–64 (Oct. 1997–Jan. 1998): 82–85.

Roman, Robert C. "Boris Karloff." *Films in Review* 15, no. 7 (Aug.–Sept. 1964): 389–412.

Rubin, Steve. "Retrospect: *The Day the Earth Stood Still*." *Cinefantastique* 4, no. 4 (winter 1976): 5–22.

_____. "*The War of the Worlds*." *Cinefantastique* 5, no. 4 (spring 1977): 5–23.

_____, and Frederick S. Clarke. "Making *Forbidden Planet*." *Cinefantastique* 8, no. 2 (spring 1979): 4–87.

Rubin, Steven Jay. "The 'She' in 'Them!': An Interview with Joan Weldon." *Filmfax* 50 (May–June 1995): 45–49.

Schaefer, Christopher. "*Macabre*: William Castle's First Horror Film." *Cult Movies* no. 37 (spring 2003): 45–49.

Schoell, William. "The Making of *A Journey to the Center of the Earth*." *Filmfax* 55 (Mar.–Apr. 1996): 51–57, 74.

Scrivani, Richard. "The Gertzenstein Monsters: Irving Getz and Herman Stein." *Scarlet Street* no. 22 (fall 1996): 37–41, 96–97.

Seymour, Blackie. "Louise Allbritton, Vivacious Blonde." *Classic Images* 295 (Jan. 2000): 78–80.

Shinnick, Kevin G., and Harriet Harvey. "Retrospect: *The Time Machine*." *SPFX: Special Effects* no. 3 (spring 1995): 29–35.

Shivas, Mark. "Karloff Still Eager to Scare Us Witless." *New York Times*. Apr. 4, 1968, fragmentary clipping, CMPS.

Siegel, Joel. "Letter to the Editor." *Velvet Light Trap* no. 11 (winter 1974).

_____. "Tourneur Remembers. " *Cinefantastique* 2, no. 4 (summer 1973): 24–25.

Sierchio, Pat: "Interview With a Wolf Man." *Written By* 4, issue 1 (Jan. 2000): 28–35.

Skotak, Robert. "Creating the Special Effects for *This Island Earth*." *Filmfax* 33 (June–July 1992): 78–82, 94–97.

_____. "*The Man from Planet X* Files." *Filmfax* 68 (Aug.–Sept. 1998): 74–83.

_____. "*This Island Earth*." *Filmfax* 33 (June–July 1992): 50–59.

Slavitt, David. "Whistling in the Dark" *Newsweek* (Feb. 1, 1965): 76.

Sontag, Susan. "The Decay of Cinema." *New York Times Magazine* (Feb. 25, 1996): 59–62, 84.

Taves, Brian. "Whose Hand?: Correcting a Buñuel Myth." *Sight and Sound* 56, no. 3 (summer 1987): 210–11.

_____. "Universal's Horror Tradition." *American Cinematographer* 68, no. 4 (Apr. 1987): 36–48.

Taylor, Al. "The Forgotten Frankenstein." *Fangoria* 2 (fall 1979): 40.

_____, and Doug Finch. "Director Robert Wise Remembers *The Day the Earth Stood Still*." *Filmfax* 17 (Oct.–Nov. 1989): 70–75.

Tazelaar, Marguerite. "Director of Chaney Prefers Lighter Side of Murder." *New York Herald Tribune*, fragmentary clipping, author's collection.

Thirer, Irene. "Tod Browning, Chaney Director, Discusses Career." *New York Daily News*, Jan. 14, 1928, p. 22.

Thomas, Bob. "Castle, the Gimmick Maestro." *Los Angeles Mirror*, Nov. 23, 1960, p. 13.

Thomas, Kevin. "A Gallery of Grotesques." *Los Angeles Times*, June 26, 1983.

Turner, George. "A Case for Insomnia." *American Cinematographer* 78, no. 3 (Mar. 1997): 77–81.

_____."*The Thing from Another World*." *American Cinematographer* 72, no. 1 (Jan. 1991): 35–42.

_____. "Two-Faced Treachery." *American Cinematographer* 80, no. 3 (Mar. 1999): 188–96.

_____, and Michael Price. "Behind *The Mask of Fu Manchu*." *American Cinematographer* 76, no. 1 (Jan. 1995): 68–74.

Tyler, Parker. "Dorian Gray: Last of the Movie Draculas." *View* 7, no. 1 (Oct. 1946): 21.

Waterbury, Ruth. "The True Life Story of Lon Chaney (Part I). *Photoplay* (Dec. 1927): 32–33, 110–14.

Weaver, Tom, and Michael Brunas. "Rose Hobart." *Filmfax* 27 (Oct.–Nov. 1991): 56–63.

Weight, Harold. "Dracula." *Hollywood Filmograph* (Apr. 4, 1931): 20.

Weiler, A. H. "Red Planet Mars." *New York Times*, June 16, 1952, p. 15.

Williams, Dick. "Roaming the Sound Stages." *Los Angeles Mirror*, Mar. 7, 1952, fragmentary clipping, CMPS.

Winogura, Dale. "Dialogues on Apes, Apes, and More Apes." *Cinefantastique* 1, no. 2 (summer 1972): 4–19.

Wood, Bret. "*The Unknown*." *Filmfax* 31 (Feb.–Mar. 1992): 73–79.

Zubatkin, Marc. "A Mant for All Seasons." *Filmfax* 62 (Aug.–Sept. 1997): 74–81.

Anonymous Articles

"Albright Twins." *Life* (Mar. 27, 1944): fragmentary clipping, CMPS.

"Aldrich Hits Back at CBS Censorship of 'Deadly.'" *Variety* (June 8, 1955): 1.

"Among the Living," *Variety*, fragmentary clipping, CMPS.

"An Outpouring of the Cesspools of Hollywood." *Harrison's Reports* 11, no.1 (Jan. 5, 1929): 1, 4.

"At Last a Screen Actor Who Gives the Director All the Credit." *Hollywood Filmograph* 10, no. 40 (Oct.18, 1930): 12.

Bride of Frankenstein press book copy, author's collection.

"Castle's Balleyhooey." *Variety* (Sept. 16, 1964): fragmentary clipping, CMPS.

"Charlie Chan at the Opera." Press release, Karloff file, CMPS.

"Clive of 'Frankenstein.'" *New York Times*, Nov. 15, 1931, sect. 8, p. 4.

"Fantastic Dr. Cyclops." *International Photographer* (Mar. 1940): 17.

"Filming at Night." *The Photoplayer* (Oct. 9, 1926): fragmentary clipping, CMPS.

"'Frankenstein' Finished" *New York Times*, Oct. 11, 1931, sect. 8, p. 5.

"Frankenstein Remembered." *Long Beach Times*, Dec. 5, 1971, pp. 19, 23–27.

"George Romero." Unsourced interview, author's collection.

"Inside Stuff—Pictures," *Variety* (July 14, 1931): 43.

"Interview With the Vampira." *Filmfax/Outré* 1, no. 1 (1994): 59–64, 82.

"Island of Lost Souls," *Daily Variety*, Dec. 2, 1932, fragmentary clipping, CMPS.

It Came from Outer Space press book copy, author's collection.

"James Whale and 'Frankenstein.'" *New York Times*, Dec. 20, 1931, sect. 8, p. 4.

"The Man Who Sees." *The New York Telegraph*, Jan. 27, 1924, fragmentary clipping, CMPS.

"Master of Horror Films Reveals His Technique." *Los Angeles Times*, Aug. 10, 1945, fragmentary clipping, CMPS.

"Monstrous for Money." *Newsweek* (July 14, 1958): 84.

"The New Pictures: *The 5,000 Fingers of Dr. T*." *Time* (May 24, 1952): 84.

"Oh, You Beautiful Monster" *New York Times*, Jan. 29, 1939, sect. 8, p. 4.

Psycho press book copy, author's collection.

Son of Frankenstein press book copy, author's collection.

"'Son of Frankenstein' Starts a New Horror Cycle." *Look* (Feb. 28, 1939): 39.

"Stanley Kubrick." *Playboy* 15, no. 9 (Sept. 1968): 85–96, 150, 180–86, 190–95.

"The Time Machine." *Time* (Aug. 22, 1960): fragmentary clipping, CMPS.

"U Has Horror Cycle All to Self." *Variety* (Apr. 8, 1931): 2.

"The Unknown." *Harrison's Reports* 9, no. 26 (June 25, 1927): 103.

Untitled item, *Hollywood Spectator* 12, no. 7 (Sept. 12, 1931): 14.

"Vital Statistics on *The Fly*." Twentieth Century–Fox press release, CMPS.

"Watch Out for Herman, He's Prehistoric." *Los Angeles Daily News*, May 5, 1953.

"What Ever Happened to Baby Jane?" *Hollywood Citizen-News*, Oct. 24, 1962, fragmentary clipping, CMPS.

"Whelan, Rathbone Take the Honors." *Hollywood Reporter*, Feb. 7, 1941, fragmentary clipping, CMPS.

Government Documents

"Symposium on Unidentified Flying Objects," Science and Astronautics Committee Hearings, House of Representatives (Ninetieth Congress, Second Session, July 29, 1968).

Audio Tape

Dockter, Phil. "Interview with Ian Wolfe." Glendale, California, Dec. 30, 1985. Unpublished audio tape in the author's collection.

Edwards, Colin. "Interview With Boris Karloff." Carmel, California, 1964. Unpublished audio tape in the author's collection.

Lane, Jim. "Interview with Marcel Delgado." Hollywood, California, Aug. 16, 1970. Unpublished audio tape in the author's collection.

Compact Disc Liner Notes

Behlmer, Rudy. *King Kong*. Rhino R2 75597.

Waxman, John W. *Sunset Boulevard: The Classic Film Scores of Franz Waxman*. BMG 0708-2-RG.

Documentary Film

PBS documentary, *Race for the Superbomb*.

Universal Studios Home Video DVD *The Mummy* documentary, *Mummy Dearest*.

Universal Studios Home Video DVD *The Birds* documentary, *All About* The Birds.

Acknowledgments

Hollywood Horror: From Gothic to Cosmic owes a debt to some unusual contributors. There are, of course, the institutions and individuals who help every scholar; I acknowledge them below. First, however, I wish to thank a different group of people. Without them this book would not exist, because without them this author would not exist.

In March 2000, shortly after completing my initial research, I was involved in a near-fatal auto vs. pedestrian accident. Quick intervention by a Good Samaritan brought the paramedics in time to restart my heart, but surgeons were only able to save one of my legs. During those first traumatic days, I called my editor and my agent to tell them that I did not want to lose this book project. They assured me that I would not. In less than a week, I had a laptop computer on my hospital bed and was working on the book. I was in the hospital for a month, recovering, reading, and taking notes. Once at home, I began writing.

Between sessions of physical therapy and darkroom work, I was able to complete five chapters and select all the photographs by November 2000. Then I found myself unable to concentrate. By November 2001, two more false starts had gotten me only as far as Chapter Ten. I left the manuscript there and fought post-traumatic stress disorder for a year. It was during that time that my physical therapist at USC transcribed for me the words of Abraham Lincoln: "If I had eight hours to chop down a tree, I would spend six hours sharpening my axe."

On Halloween 2002, I asked my editor what we should do about the book; I was still feeling poorly. She and the editor-in-chief suggested that I rethink the original concept and try to complete the book as a pictorial history with expanded captions and reduced text. God bless them. Once I started writing, I was unable to contain my fervor—or my word count. The text became even more detailed than I had originally planned. Five months later, I have a manuscript that I am very proud to submit. The project that was supposed to take six months in 2000 has taken three years and gained an unexpected dimension. Without dwelling on details, I can say that I am now qualified to write about horror. I have lived it.

The good people who helped me survive this experience deserve thanks and praise. Some of them I cannot remember or name, due to drugs and indisposition, but I want to express my indebtedness to all. Ted Atkins was the quick-thinking gentleman with the telephone and the tourniquet. The paramedics were miraculous and reassuring. The doctors in the emergency room at the University of California, Los Angeles, Medical Center were considerate and skillful, as were the staff members of the intensive-care unit and the medical center itself. I wish to thank Dr. Andrew Da Lio, who saved my remaining leg with a series of surgeries. I spent three weeks at Daniel Freeman Hospital in Marina Del Rey; I thank the kind staff there, including Rosemary Tiedemann; I owe special thanks to physical therapist Jean Demeo.

Upon returning home, I began rehabilitation with numerous health care professionals: Christy Stewart and her coworkers at Sun Plus; Julie Kasperson and Danielle Robertshaw of Queens Care; Renee Steele of Action Health Care; and Sister Anne Marie of St. Vincent's Hospital. I thank Todd Greenwald and Fred Fleming. I thank the Beer Medical Group. I thank Father John McDaniels and Father Bob Gavotto for referrals and prayers. I wish to thank the caring people at my parish, Precious Blood Church: Patricia Ibarra, Leo Tamayo, and Cande Bak. I thank the anonymous donor who helped me get to physical therapy. I also thank the dedicated caregivers who helped me get through that first year: Iris Almaraz, Carolyn Mixon, Ramon Ramirez, Ruben Lazo, Lesther Way, Cynthia Lazar, Horalia Way, and Leonel Way.

When it was time to put my only foot forward, these people tended to my nervous system, repaired my knee, and taught me to walk: Jann Hoffman, Pauli Moss; Charles T. Daily; Robert David Hall of the MAAF; David Patterson and Jane Duffy; Dawn Lucia of Hyperion Health Care; Jesse Henriquez and Ruth Ann Markusen of the Didi Hirsch Community Mental Health Center; Dr. John Itamura and Dr. Kelly Vince at the USC University Hospital; Dr. Stephen Richeimer and Dr. Lisa Victor at USC Pain Management; and my prosthetist, Colin Richardson of L.A. Orthotics and Prosthetics. I owe special thanks to Alice Baltimore at Blue Cross of California, whose friendly calls helped as much as her efficient case management. For an amazing combination of professionalism and compassion, I offer sincere thanks to Dr. Yogi Matharu and the staff of USC Physical Therapy Associates.

For helping me achieve a return to teaching, I thank Michael Daruty, Vice President of Post Production at Universal Studios; archivist Bob O'Neil; Don Lewis and the staff of Film Shipping; and at Film Services, Paul Koszak and Merrilee Griffin. I also thank Jackie Wells and Nancy Pearce for special assistance. I thank Starlight Studio staff members Louisa Gauerke, Manuel Chay, Lois Tryk, and Kurt Bier.

I offer gratitude to only some of the many friends who helped me go from sedation to production. Thanks go to Kirk Terry and P. R. Tooke for bringing me a Walkman; to Andy Montealegre, John Giriat, Rob McKay, Matias Bombal, and John Cavallo for sending me the tapes to play on it; to Bradley and Edel Vera for bringing me that wonderful laptop; to Hal Masonberg for getting me on line when I was not even on my feet; to Anita Bennett; Everen T. Brown; Lisa Burks; Martin Camarillo and Carlos Rodriguez; Eric Chafkin; Chummie Chico; John Connolly; Bernice Dransfield; Beverly Ferreira; Jessie Glasser; David Hagan; Maggie Hamilton; Jan Harrelson; Robert L. Hillmann; Ray Hooper; Geoffrey Inglis; Donna Kent; Maresa Leeder; Dom and Saachiko Magwili; Gilda Medeiros; Marian Mogel; Paul Newman; Phil Ochoa; Naomi Roberts; Sherrie Sanet; Jennifer Sims; Michael Schwieger; Deborah Thalberg; and Roberto Valdivia.

I thank Ben Carbonetto for helping me continue to interpret the glory that was Hollywood. I thank Andy Montealegre for doing what he promised my father the day after the accident—seeing me through to complete recovery. I thank Howard Mandelbaum for twenty-five years of a friendship that produces projects like this one. I offer a special thank you to Bronni Stein, who became an extraordinary blend of researcher, promoter, and Florence Nightingale.